Economics of Ecological Resources

NEW HORIZONS IN ENVIRONMENTAL ECONOMICS

General Editor: Wallace E. Oates, *Professor of Economics, University of Maryland*

This important series is designed to make a significant contribution to the development of the principles and practices of environmental economics. It includes both theoretical and empirical work. International in scope, it addresses issues of current and future concern in both East and West and in developed and developing countries.

The main purpose of the series is to create a forum for the publication of high quality work and to show how economic analysis can make a contribution to understanding and resolving the environmental problems confronting the world in the late twentieth century.

Recent titles in the series include:

Estimating Economic Values for Nature
Methods for Non-Market Valuation
V. Kerry Smith

Models of Sustainable Development
Edited by Sylvie Faucheux, David Pearce and John Proops

Contingent Valuation and Endangered Species
Methodological Issues and Applications
Kristin M. Jakobsson and Andrew K. Dragun

Acid Rain and Environmental Degradation
The Economics of Emission Trading
Ger Klaassen

The Economics of Pollution Control in the Asia Pacific
Robert Mendelsohn and Daigee Shaw

Economic Policy for the Environment and Natural Resources
Techniques for the Management and Control of Pollution
Edited by Anastasios Xepapadeas

Welfare Measurement, Sustainability and Green National Accounting
A Growth Theoretical Approach
Thomas Aronsson, Per-Olov Johansson and Karl-Gustaf Löfgren

The Economics of Environmental Protection
Theory and Demand Revelation
Peter Bohm

The International Yearbook of Environmental and Resource Economics 1997/1998
A Survey of Current Issues
Edited by Henk Folmer and Tom Tietenberg

The Economic Theory of Environmental Policy in a Federal System
Edited by John B. Braden and Stef Proost

Economics of Ecological Resources
Selected Essays
Charles Perrings

Economics of Ecological Resources

Selected Essays

Charles Perrings

Professor of Environmental Economics and Environmental Management, University of York, UK

NEW HORIZONS IN ENVIRONMENTAL ECONOMICS

Edward Elgar

Cheltenham, UK • Lyme, US

Published by
Edward Elgar Publishing Limited
8 Lansdown Place
Cheltenham
Glos GL50 2HU
UK

Edward Elgar Publishing Company
1 Pinnacle Hill Road
Lyme
NH 03768
US

A catalogue record for this book
is available from the British Library

Library of Congress Cataloguing in Publication Data
Perrings, Charles.
    Economics of ecological resources: selected essays/Charles
Perrings.
    — (New horizons in environmental economics)
    Includes bibliographical references.
    1. Environmental economics. 2. Sustainable development.
3. Natural resources—Management.   I. Title. II. Series.
HC79.E5P448   1997
333.7—dc21   96–52255
                                                                 CIP

Printed and bound in Great Britain by Bookcraft (Bath) Ltd

ISBN 1 85898 473 4

Contents

Figures

Tables

Acknowledgements

The publishers wish to thank the following who have kindly given permission for the use of copyright material.

Ambio for article: 'Ecology, Economics and Ecological Economics', *Ambio*, **24** (1), 1995, pp. 60–64.

Columbia University Press for article: 'Reserved Rationality and the Precautionary Principle: Technological Change, Time and Uncertainty in Environmental Decision-making', in R. Costanza (ed.), *Ecological Economics: The Science and Management of Sustainability*, 1991, pp. 153–67.

Elsevier Science for articles: 'Towards an Ecological Economics of Sustainability', *Ecological Economics*, **6**, 1992, pp. 7–34; 'Environmental Bonds and Environmental Research in Innovative Activities', **1** (1), 1989, pp. 95–115.

Island Press for the article: 'Biotic Diversity, Sustainable Development and Natural Capital', in A. Jansson, M. Hammer, C. Folke and R. Costanza (eds), *Investing in Natural Capital*, 1994, pp. 92–112.

Kluwer Academic Publishers for article: 'Conservation of Mass and Time Behaviour of Ecological–Economic Systems', in P. Burley and J. Foster (eds), *Economics and Thermodynamics: New Perspectives on Economic Analysis*, 1994, pp. 99–118.

North-Holland Press for article: 'An Optimal Path to Extinction? Poverty and Resource Degradation in the Open Agrarian Economy', *Journal of Development Economics*, **30**, 1989, pp. 1–24.

Oxford University Press for article: 'Ecological Sustainability and Environmental Control', *Structural Change and Economic Dynamics*, **2**, 1991, pp. 275–95.

Presses Universitaires de Grenoble for article: 'Ecological Resilience in the Sustainability of Economic Development', *Economie Appliquée*, **48** (2), 1995, pp. 121–42.

Springer-Verlag for article: 'Stress, Shock and the Sustainability of Resource Use in Semi-Arid Environments', *Annals of Regional Science*, **28**, 1994, pp. 31–53.

Every effort has been made to trace all the copyright holders but if any have been inadvertently overlooked the publishers will be pleased to make the necessary arrangements at the first opportunity.

Introduction: the nature of economics and the economics of nature

1 THE BOUNDS OF SCIENCE

All science depends on simplification. Complex problems are made tractable by bounding the set of variables and the set of effects to be analysed. This is generally accomplished by appropriately structuring the experiments or models on which analysis is based. In this respect, economic science does not differ from any of the natural sciences. Analysis of some things is facilitated by treating others as given or as irrelevant to the problem at hand. The effect is to ignore any links between the endogenous and exogenous variables of a problem. All partial equilibrium analysis, for example, ignores feedbacks between the variables whose behaviour is analysed and the rest of the economic system. All short-run analysis ignores feedbacks that occur with a lag greater than that allowed by the structure of the problem.

This is not necessarily bad science. If the feedbacks between endogenous and exogenous variables in a problem are very weak, little may be lost by ignoring them while much may be gained in terms of tractability and focus. Indeed, this sort of simplification is the basis of scientific discipline. It is what allows the specialization that has enabled science to progress. It is bad science only if effects that are excluded from the analysis of a problem are important to its solution.

There is, however, a tendency for the solution to a problem to be defined by reference to the discipline within which it is framed in a way that blurs the distinction between good and bad science. For example, analysis of the epidemiology of malaria that excludes the population dynamics of the *anopheles* mosquito would generally be recognized as bad science. But analysis of the population dynamics of the *anopheles* mosquito that excludes public expenditures on drainage and sewage treatment would not. In both cases something important is being omitted, but whether its importance is recognized depends on the discipline within which the problem has been formulated. Since different disciplines formulate problems in different ways it is common to find science that is 'good' by the standards of a particular discipline, but that nevertheless ignores critically important feedbacks.

The development of ecological economics as a field of inquiry stems from the perception that much 'good' ecological and economic science of the environment does exactly this. Ecologists analysing the behaviour of heavily impacted ecological systems and economists analysing the behaviour of the economic activities they support both assume that ecosystem dynamics are independent of economic behaviour. They leave important effects out of account. Simplification in both sciences has led each to make fundamental errors about the importance of feedbacks between the ecological and economic components of the system. Ecological economics has developed as a field to address this problem.

Not all of the chapters in this book would be characterized as ecological economics. Indeed, a number were written before the term was coined. But all explore the allocation of ecological resources in jointly-determined ecological–economic systems. All assume the interdependence of the economic and ecological components of those systems, and seek to endogenize aspects of the allocation process that have historically been treated as exogenous. The chapters in Part I are concerned with the dynamics of joint systems, and with the implications of this fact for the control and conservation of ecological resources. In this sense they develop ideas first explored in the context of a general equilibrium system in Perrings (1987). Those in Part II focus on the conditioning effect of the economic environment on private decisions in low-income resource-dependent economies. In one sense this is more familiar ground for environmental economists. However, the questions raised – concerning the impact of the income effects of price changes on the rate of time preference, rural underemployment and the sustainability of resource use – will not be familiar to most. The chapters in Part III focus on the way that decision-makers handle the uncertainty that is an integral feature of the evolution of the ecological–economic system. More particularly, they are concerned with perceptions of uncertainty and changes in the set of opportunities in evolving ecological–economic systems.

The postscript considers how ecological and economic analysis can jointly be brought to bear on many of the problems addressed in the book. In so doing it picks up a number of the themes introduced below: the evolutionary nature of the joint system, the significance of scale and threshold effects, the uncontrollability and unobservability of ecological systems, and the pervasiveness of uncertainty. But it also illustrates these themes in the context of a particular problem – the problem of biodiversity loss. This is among the most complex of environmental problems. It involves spatially and temporally distant effects that are highly uncertain. Some effects have the properties of local public goods. Others have the properties of a global public good. In many cases the costs of biodiversity loss are contingent on what other anthropogenic environmental change occurs. For example, among the most significant potential costs of biodiversity loss today is the inability of ecological systems to function under altered future climatic conditions. This is due to the elimination of species today, that may be capable of mediating key ecological functions and processes under future conditions. The uncertainty attaching to such costs is clearly very large, but so too, is their potential magnitude.

2 EVOLUTION AND CONTROL OF DYNAMICAL ECOLOGICAL–ECONOMIC SYSTEMS

While there are common themes running through all the chapters in the book, the three parts are stimulated by different literatures. The first has several strands, the most important of which concern the physical properties of ecological–economic systems (stimulated by, *inter alia*, Boulding, 1966; Georgescu-Roegen, 1971; Daly, 1973; Ayres, 1978), and the potential for optimal economic control of such systems (stimulated by Clark, 1976; Clark et al., 1979). The literature on the physical properties of ecological–economic systems drew economists' attention to the necessity for physical production and consumption to respect the basic laws of physics. The first mass-balance economic models to explore the link between growth in material output and environmental stress made the point that increasing levels of economic output implied increasing levels of waste to be assimilated by the environment (Ayres and Kneese, 1969; Mäler 1974). The dynamic implications of these models are explored in Chapters 1 and 2. They are that higher rates of economic growth imply higher rates of change in the processes of the environment. Change in one component implies change in the other, and the more highly 'connected' are the two, the more pronounced are the feedback effects between them (Boulding, 1978).

The structure of the joint system – its 'connectedness' in ecological terms – turns out to be critically important not just for the dynamics of the system, but for the existence and management of external environmental effects. The structure of the joint system may be such, for example, that processes which are apparently unrelated over one time horizon may be highly related over another. Similarly, a relation that is insignificant at one scale of activity may be highly significant at another (Perrings, 1987). For example, lags in the transmission of toxic substances through the food chain may be such that pollution which poses no health threat over one time horizon is extremely serious over another. Similarly, a pollution event of given size may be insignificant if the stock of pollutants is low relative to the assimilative capacity of the environment, but may be catastrophic if the stock of pollutants is high relative to the assimilative capacity of the environment.

The spatial and temporal structure of the joint system, and the relation between the scale of economic activity and the nature of change in ecological systems, are the main foci of ecological economics. Ecological–economic systems are 'co-evolutionary' systems in Norgaard's (1984) terms, and the evolution of any one subsystem depends on both the way it is linked with other systems and its scale relative to other systems. The linkages between the components of complex ecological systems have been on the ecology research agenda for some time. Ecological systems have been characterized as nested hierarchies in which small fast-moving systems are embedded in and constrained by large slow-moving systems (Wiens, 1989; Holling, 1992; Levin, 1992). The dynamics of each level of the structure are predictable so long as the biotic potential of the level is consistent with bounds imposed by the remaining levels in the hierarchy (Allen and Starr, 1982). Change in either the structure of environmental constraints or the biotic potential of the level may induce threshold effects that lead to complete alteration in the state of the system. The spatial and temporal structures of such systems affect the evolutionary response of system components to changes in environmental conditions. Adaptive moves by one organism tend to deform the 'fitness landscape' of those organisms with which it interacts, and small adaptive moves may trigger 'avalanches' of evolutionary response (Kauffman and Johnsen, 1991). In dryland systems, for example, it has been shown that grazing pressure beyond some critical threshold can induce a non-reversionary switch in vegetation type (Walker and Noy-Meir, 1982; Walker, 1988; Westoby et al., 1989).

Economists have been slower to address the same problem (Anderson et al., 1988). Such work as has been undertaken has been driven by an interest in the dynamic behaviour of financial markets (Scheinkman and LeBaron, 1989; Hommes, 1991; Granger and Terasvirta, 1992) – although rationalized by reference to the work on complex non-linear systems in epidemiology, biology and ecology (Brock, 1992). So far economists have paid no attention to spatial scale and its significance at or near system thresholds (though see Puu, 1989), but there is now a growing body of literature with roots in geography which seeks to inject a spatial dimension into non-linear economic models (see, for example, White, 1990; Hannon, 1994).

There is also an economic analogue to the biologist's interest in evolution, albeit a weak one. It has often been observed that economic development is not a stationary process, that human understanding, preferences and technology all change with development and that such change is generally non-linear and discontinuous (Wilkinson, 1973; Common, 1988). This has prompted economists to seek to endogenize technological change. The work of Romer (1990a, 1990b) and Barro (1990) has begun to generate a flow of papers on endogenous growth and its application to environmental resources and environmental technology (for example, Huang and Cai, 1994).

Against this background, Chapters 1 and 2 address the most elementary drivers of change in systems away from equilibrium, and consider the implications that this has for the controllability of those systems. The first of the two chapters shows the increasing necessity for both technological and ecological change as the scale of the economic system increases relative to its environment. The second explores a corollary of this: that the system itself becomes less and less controllable. Since the controllability of the relevant system is critical to the application of most of the tools of renewable resource economics, the uncontrollability of stressed ecological systems is by no means a trivial problem. Indeed it changes the nature of the management task. It may not be realistic to think in terms of the optimal control of ecological resources. Ecological systems may, at best, be 'stabilizable'. That is, demands on uncontrolled ecological systems may be constrained to levels at which they are 'stable' in the sense that their responses to economic shocks are bounded. More generally, demands on uncontrollable ecological systems may be limited to protect their resilience.

My starting point, then, is that the economy and its environment are jointly-determined systems, and that the scale of economic activity is such that this matters both for the rate of change or evolution and for the controllability of the joint system. The dynamics of the joint system are characterized by discontinuous change around critical threshold values both for economic and for ecological resources, and its stability depends on the resilience of the uncontrolled parts of that system.

3   SUSTAINABILITY, SCALE AND RESILIENCE

It is hard to overstate the importance of scale. The popular perception is that the ecological impacts of individual activities would be less significant in a world with a smaller human population and lower levels of consumption. This perception is not misplaced. Ecosystem responses to stress are a non-linear function of the level of stress. Indeed, this is what lies behind such basic ecological concepts as carrying and assimilative capacity. Some biologists argue that current consumption levels are already beyond the long-run carrying capacity of the biosphere. The resultant degradation of the resource base will, they argue, inevitably call for some sort of Malthusian population crash (Ehrlich and Ehrlich, 1990; Daily and Ehrlich, 1992; Ehrlich et al., 1993; Kendall and Pimentel, 1994). There are various reasons to be cautious about such a conclusion, the most important of which is that the carrying capacity of the biosphere is not fixed, but depends on the way in which environmental resources are used. That is, it depends on both technology and preferences as well as the properties of the ecosystem (Arrow et al., 1995). The important point, however, is that if ecosystems are stressed beyond their assimilative or carrying capacity, the resultant change in both ecological structure and function may substantially reduce their value to human users.

To elaborate, ecological–economic systems are characterized by multiple locally stable states, the properties of which are different. States that are less productive of economically valuable ecological goods and services are said to be degraded relative to states that are more productive of those goods and services. The boundaries of each local stability domain mark points of discontinuity or thresholds between such states. They are typically defined in terms of the level or density of system components. Thresholds in predator–prey systems, for example, are defined in terms of the relative density of the predator and prey species. If these thresholds are crossed, the system will frequently experience discontinuous and unpredictable change as it flips from one state to another. The discontinuous change in vegetation in semi-arid rangelands observed by Walker and his colleagues is, for instance, a function of herd densities being forced above some critical threshold. In this case a gradual increase in grazing pressure as a result of the independent decisions of many individual pastoralists causes a sudden and irreversible (or only slowly reversible) switch in vegetation types that permanently (or for a very long period) reduces the economic value of the resource.

There exist numerous other examples of sudden ecological failure as a result of a gradual build-up of economic pressure due either to population growth, or to a price- or income-induced increase in demand for natural resources. Where people have not been able to respond to ecological failure by adapting technology or preferences, the result has historically been a Malthusian population crash, massive out-migration or both. Where people have been able to respond by adapting technology or preferences, on the other hand, the result has often been a dramatic change in patterns of production or consumption. This has often substantially reduced or changed the nature of the pressure on the resource base (Boserup 1965, 1981; Heath and Binswanger, 1996). Indeed, this is the basis for the technological optimism that supports widespread indifference towards the degradation of ecological systems. But a lot is being asked of technology. In today's crowded world, migration is no longer a serious option. Hence, if we cannot avoid the failure of ecological systems by exercising restraint, ever more rapid technological adaptation to the limitations of degraded ecological systems may be the only alternative to Malthusian crash.

The linkages between locally stable equilibria, threshold effects and the sustainability of development are addressed in Chapter 3 using the ecological notion of resilience. Resilience is used in different ways in the ecological literature, but it is taken here to mean the propensity of a system to retain its organizational structure following perturbation (that is, *sensu* Holling, 1973, 1986). It is an index of the 'integrity' or 'health' of the system (Kay, 1991; Costanza et al., 1992), and may be measured by the severity of the shock that can be absorbed before the system flips from one stability domain to another (Holling et al. (eds), 1995).

The connection between the resilience and the sustainability of any state is immediate. Under any of the multiplicity of definitions in the literature, sustainability requires maintenance of the productive potential of the system concerned. If maintenance of the productive potential of a system depends on its being in a particular state, the resilience of the system in that state is a necessary condition for its sustainability. A system will be resilient in some state if it is able to continue to function as the environmental conditions change, where environmental conditions include both natural conditions (temperature, precipitation and so on) and economic conditions (resource prices, market structures, institutional conditions and the like).

It turns out that the most important factor in the resilience of ecological systems is the diversity of organisms that mediate essential ecosystem functions and processes. It is the diversity of organisms that underpins the ability of the system to continue to function as environmental conditions (including the stresses imposed by economic activity) change. Consider an example. The effect of activities already undertaken on the concentration of greenhouse gases will involve very significant change in the biogeosphere irrespective of whether or not corrective measures are taken now. That is, it will change the environmental conditions within which ecological systems are exploited. In many cases this will alter the set of species required to assure the functioning of ecosystems. It follows that the loss of currently redundant species in many ecosystems will compromise the resilience of those systems before future shocks (Holling et al. (eds), 1995).

Protecting the resilience of critical ecosystems is therefore an important element in any strategy of sustainable development, and it can be thought of primarily as a strategy for managing risk and uncertainty. It has been observed – with respect to the climate change problem – that the environmental 'risks' associated with economic activity have become endogenous (the 'risks' are affected by that activity), and correlative (they are not statistically independent) (Chichilnisky and Heal, 1993). Indeed this follows from the path dependence of the system. However, in an evolutionary system, it is not generally possible to identify the set of outcomes associated with any given action, let alone the probability distribution attaching to those outcomes. That is, such 'risks' involve fundamental uncertainty.

There are, in general, two sources of uncertainty that have to be addressed in designing a sustainable management strategy. First, in any feedback control problem, optimization of the problem requires the continuous measurement of state variables. The available measures may be subject to error. Second, the system dynamics may themselves be known imperfectly, implying that feedback control will necessarily be misdirected. The main source of uncertainty of the first kind, at least in so far as the economic system is concerned, is identical to the source of market failure. Measurement error in the ecological–economic system is synonymous with the failure of prices to act as accurate system observers. Indeed, this is the basis of the problem explored in Chapter 2.

The main source of uncertainty of the second kind, again in so far as the economic system is concerned, appears to be the evolutionary nature of the system. Not all evolution creates the same amount of difficulty. Phenotypic evolution is in principle predictable, but genotypic evolution is not (Faber and Proops, 1992). Failure to predict phenotypic evolutionary trends may be due to the product of ignorance about the functional structure of ecosystems, but failure to predict genotypic evolutionary trends is inherent in the nature of the changes involved. Genotypic evolution is accordingly the least tractable source of system uncertainty. This is not to say that knowledge of the system, or at least of parts of the system, cannot be improved over time. Estimates of the distribution of possible environmental outcomes of economic activity may well be improved through, for example, a passive Bayesian learning process. But it does imply that there is likely to remain a very large measure of fundamental ignorance about the future effects of current actions.

The problem for decision-making lies in the fact that the ecological–economic system is neither observable (through the set of prices) nor controllable (through any set of incentives based on those prices). If the system is not observable, the available information set does not include a sufficient profile of the statistical properties of the unavailable information set to predict its conditioning effect on the future behaviour of the system. This may be because of the existence of novel developments whose implications for the time-behaviour of the system are unclear. That is, the distribution of outcomes associated with such developments cannot be inferred from the history of the system both because of the paucity of relevant observations, and because of the effect of novelty on the system parameters.

The point was made earlier, however, that uncontrollable ecological–economic systems may still be 'stabilizable' and that this is related to the sustainability of the joint system. That is, even if some ecological systems are not controllable, sustainability of the joint ecological–economic system may be assured providing it is not stressed beyond the point where it is resilient. Policies that safeguard the range of future options by protecting thresholds of resilience are generally conceptualized as sustainability constraints (Conway, 1987; Pearce, 1987; Perrings et al., 1992; Perrings and Opschoor 1994). Their aim is to restrict stress on ecological systems to the point where they can adapt to changing conditions.

Finally, it is worth underlining the fact that sustainability in this sense is conceptually quite distinct from sustainability as non-declining utility (or non-declining asset values) as used in the economic literature (Pezzey, 1989). The distinction is explored in Chapter 4, which argues that an ecological concept of sustainability addresses a different phenomenon – the capacity of the system to function over a range of environmental conditions. Nevertheless, ecological and economic sustainability are related. The resilience of supporting ecosystems is necessary but not sufficient for utility to be non-declining in a technologically stationary, resource-dependent economy. Moreover, sustainability must figure in the goals of individuals and society if it is to influence either individual behaviour or social policy. Recent work on the ethical basis of sustainability by Howarth (1995) provides one way of thinking about the problem. Howarth appeals to the Kantian distinction between duty and desire to argue that rules which restrain current activity in the interests of assuring the wellbeing of future generations are in the nature of duties based on moral principle. Duties, and the maxims which guide their performance, are constraints on behaviour. They are not the objectives of behaviour. Sustainability constraints, in this view, are no more than the rules guiding the performance of a duty to future generations.

4   INCOME EFFECTS AND RESOURCE USE

The second part of the book explores the effects of changes in the economic environment on the way in which resource users behave towards the natural environment. In one sense this is the familiar stuff of environmental economics – the role of prices in private resource use decisions. But my concern in these chapters is with more than just price distortions induced by the usual sources of externality, market and policy failure. Changes in the economic environment may well reflect the introduction or correction of some distortionary policy. I am concerned less with the existence of externality than with the behavioural implications of such changes on the incomes of resource users. The Brundtland Report asserted that one of the main driving forces behind the degradation of the environment is the poverty of present generations. These chapters consider why this may be so.

Chapter 5 begins by looking at the rate at which information about the future effects of current activities is screened out of current decisions. Specifically, it looks at the determination of the rate of discount in resource-dependent economies. Discounting has the effect of weighting the future consequences of current actions, and since uncertainty about these consequences is an increasing function of time, it also has the effect of weighting certain as opposed to uncertain effects. It turns out that something very similar applies to the wider (geographically distant) consequences of local actions (Perrings and Hannon, 1996). There is mounting evidence that people's perspective on both uncertainty and time is related to their income and endowments. It is reflected in the rate at which the future and wider external effects of current activity are discounted.

Recent empirical research on the relationship between per capita income and expenditure in some types of environmental improvement has shown that local environmental quality has some of the characteristics of a luxury good. There exists an empirical relationship between per capita income and some measures of environmental quality that is similar to the 'inverted U-shaped' Kuznets' relation between income and income inequality. As per capita incomes rise, environmental quality first deteriorates and then, after some point, improves (Grossman and Krueger, 1993). The implication is that rising per capita incomes eventually induce people to take greater account of the future consequences of present activities. What is interesting about the evidence, however, is that the relation differs between different types of environmental externality. Pollution of drinking water, for example, is a monotonically decreasing function of income. On the other hand, carbon emission is a monotonically increasing function of income. The evidence to date indicates that people do not act to reduce external effects that are distant in either space or time at current income levels (Arrow et al., 1995). People are still more concerned about the short-term environmental impacts of economic activity in their own neighbourhood than they are about long-term impacts falling elsewhere.

The particular problem considered in Chapter 5 is the link between an endogenously-determined discount rate, income and the degradation of ecological resources in an agrarian economy. More particularly, it is concerned with the role of an endogenous discount rate in the widely observed vicious cycle of poverty and environmental degradation. Where resource users are close to the subjective poverty level – the level below which they will dissave to maintain consumption – then the effect of an adverse income shock may be to drive up the discount rate, and hence the optimal rate at which the resource is used. If the resource is degraded in the process, the resource user can be launched into a spiral of rising discount rates, increasing environmental degradation and decreasing income.

The effect of rising discount rates in this case is to screen out information about the future consequences of present actions. People in subjective poverty are myopic because they have to be, since what matters is survival today. In screening out information on the future consequences of current actions, however, they simultaneously screen out uncertainty. The implication of path dependence in complex dynamical systems is that the predictability of the future effects of current actions decreases very sharply over time.

The remaining chapters in Part II consider the impact of changes in the price regime on the use of agricultural resources using both static (Chapter 6) and dynamic (Chapter 7) models. Chapter 6 considers the link between 'surplus' labour in dual economies and land degradation. It argues that employment of redundant labour (*sensu* Fei and Ranis, 1964) is a direct cause of land degradation. Since the optimal level of employment is a function of the private cost of land access and use, policies which affect the cost of land access and use may also affect the degradation of agricultural land. The private cost of land is defined as the sum of an 'institutional' access price and a user charge. The 'institutional' access price of land (the purchase price) is positive for private property regimes, but zero for common property or open access regimes. The user charge defines the private cost of use. It includes, for example, grazing or water fees/subsidies. Since the access price use under common property or open access regimes is zero, the sustainability of resource use under such regimes turns on the user charge. Policies that subsidize use of land in conditions where the access price is zero induce overutilization of land by stimulating employment beyond the point where the marginal product of labour is zero or positive. This increases the probability of the degradation of those resources.

Chapter 7 also looks at the effect of the economic environment on the use made of agricultural resources, but this time takes a dynamic perspective. It considers what sort of economic environment is consistent with the sustainable use of those resources. As Chapter 4 makes clear, there is no reason to believe that a set of prices which is intertemporally efficient will induce a more ecologically sustainable use of resources than one which is not. Chapter 7 draws the further conclusion that the use of border prices as proxies for the social opportunity cost of tradable resources in the small open economy offers no guarantee against the degradation of the domestic resource base. However, its main goal is to determine which sets of relative prices, and which initial endowments are sustainable in semi-arid rangelands. Simulations illustrate the implications of different sorts of changes in the economic environment.

What is interesting about the results reported in Chapter 7 is that the environmental consequences of changing costs of access and use are highly non-linear. For example, sensitivity tests of the effect on grazing pressure of changes in the net benefits of livestock holdings show that very low and very high net benefits both cause grazing pressure to fall to zero (that is, cause the system to collapse). This provides confirmation, in the context of a single simple example, of the perception that extremes of affluence and poverty may both have adverse implications for the environment.

5   THE PROBLEM OF INCOMPLETE INFORMATION

The third part of the book explores the perception and management of information in imperfectly observed and controlled systems. More particularly, it considers the way in which we handle the uncertainty associated with evolutionary systems. In an ecological–economic approach the evolution of the system is conceptualized as a product of the interactions between its component parts. It is therefore endogenous to the system. Within economics there is a growing body of literature that seeks to 'endogenize' uncertainty by calling on the properties of dynamical non-linear systems to explain fluctuations within the system. The recent work in the area of finance cited above has used the probability structure of IPS (interacting particle systems) theory to build non-linear models of asset pricing. In these models, fluctuations are 'endogenized' in the specification of the interactions between the components of the system (traders), and the adjustment dynamics of each component. What they show is that unlike the traditional linear asset-pricing models, a very small input noise can produce a very large noise in the system equilibria. However, the source of input noise is still some disturbance in the environment in which the dynamical system operates. That is, what is being modelled is the potential for noise magnification within the economic system.

The more interesting question is how the dynamics of jointly-determined ecological–economic systems affect the predictability of each component. In this, the potential for noise magnification within any one subsystem is relevant, but it is not at the core of the problem. What matters is the interaction between economic and ecological components of a general non-linear system. The evolution of a system involving a change in its equilibrium state will generally imply a change in the self-organization of the underlying ecological systems. This may involve a change in primary productivity, the composition of species and communities as well as the ecological structure of the system. For an economic system, it may imply a reallocation of resources between sectors involving a change in economic productivity, the composition of the workforce and the capital stock, and the supporting institutions. What is important is that the evolution of ecological and economic components alike are linked through multiple feedback effects, and that the joint effects are not predictable except over a very short time horizon.

In these circumstances the principal observers of the system, resource prices, are very poor indicators of the future opportunity cost of committing particular classes of resource to some economic use. In particular, they are poor indicators of the services forgone by committing ecological resources to economic use. Reasons why prices are inadequate observers of ecological resources include the structure of property rights, the effects of government policy, the public good nature of some ecological resources and so on. But they also include the unpredictability of the system dynamics. That is, if there exist many possible equilibria, most of which have not been observed, then market prices are poor observers just because the future path of the system is fundamentally uncertain.

As we have already seen, the problem for decision-makers is that information on the behaviour of the system in the basin of one attractor does not include sufficient information on its behaviour in the basin of other attractors to predict the conditioning effect of that information on the future behaviour of the system. It is not possible to calculate the actuarial value of the environmental 'risks' involved wherever these 'risks' include a loss of system resilience. It follows that any activity which causes a loss of system resilience both increases the likelihood of uncertain as opposed to risky outcomes, and reduces the value of available information. Information that has been built up on the behaviour of the system under the influence of one attractor may have little value when it is under the influence of another attractor.

This is what lies behind the problem addressed in Chapter 8. While technological change may provide a potential solution to ecological failure, novel use of environmental resources may have effects that are highly uncertain in both their spread and duration. The greater the uncertainty as to the effects of technologically innovative use of environmental resources, the greater is the difficulty in evaluating associated environmental damage or estimating the marginal social costs of resource use. The wider and more long-lasting are the environmental effects of economic activities, the less useful will market prices be as system observers. Chapter 8 argues that decision-makers in these circumstances tend to take an iterative approach, in which they reserve their position on certain data by taking an initially cautious approach that may be relaxed as the data set is enriched by experience. This is argued to be at the core of the so-called precautionary principle, and applies especially to the case where the probability of distant but potentially catastrophic environmental damage is admitted, even though it is thought to be very low.

There are numerous potential policy instruments to deal with uncertain environmental externalities. Such externalities tend to be privately uninsurable wherever the 'risk' cannot be estimated or responsibility ascribed. 'Risks' that are a consequence of loss of resilience fall into this category. Social 'insurance' against such 'risks' tends to be open-ended, but the size of the 'risk' is limited by the imposition of restrictions on the private use of ecological resources. The implicit social insurance premium is the sum of the benefits forgone by the restriction. In fisheries based on transferable quota, for example, the implicit social insurance premium is the sum of the benefits forgone by restricting catches to the quota.

Restrictions on private behaviour of this kind are analogous to the safe minimum standards of engineering design. Aside from transferable or non-transferable quotas in fisheries, examples include game licences, open and closed seasons on the predation of 'game' species, emissions permits and so on. They are a very old and historically effective way of handling fundamental uncertainty. Indeed, they work precisely by bounding activities within levels at which the system retains a degree of predictability. The rationale for safe minimum standards (or other precautionary instruments) in ecological-economic systems is clear. The existence of threshold effects involving irreversible loss of potential productivity, and the failure of markets to signal the nearness of such thresholds, both imply the need for instruments that maintain economic activity within appropriate bounds (Turner, 1988; Costanza et al., 1992). This is because the component of value least likely to be picked up in market transactions involving threshold effects is user cost – an unsystematic source of error in market indicators.[1] The tendency for specific ecosystems to experience catastrophic and irreversible change when stressed beyond some threshold level is a problem which becomes more acute the more distant the effects, which is why forward markets for environmental resource-based products are so poorly developed. What makes safe minimum standards appropriate in ecological economics is not that they involve quantitative restrictions, but that they involve discontinuous private cost functions that more closely mirror the discontinuities in social costs associated with ecological threshold effects (Perrings and Pearce, 1994).

The instrument discussed in Chapter 9 is slightly different, and focuses on the very specific problem of technological innovation. It is a variant of the long-established deposit-refund systems: environmental assurance bonds. The application of deposit-refund systems to environmental protection was initially suggested by Mill (1972) and Solow (1974). The development of environmental assurance bonds in ecological economics has focused on the private incentives they can offer to research the environmental effects of economic activity in a way that both bounds the potential harm inflicted on society and insures society against such harm (Costanza and Perrings, 1990; Farber, 1991). Agents undertaking activities for which there exist no precedents post a bond with the environmental authority equal to the 'expected' worst-case losses. This indicates the value placed by the environmental authority on allowing the activity to proceed given the current state of knowledge about its wider and longer-term effects. To accommodate the results of research, the bond may be revised in line with experimental or historical data available on the user or external costs of the activity.

Wherever the range and probability distribution of the future environmental effects of present activity is known, it is sufficient to require resource users to take out commercial insurance against environmental costs. In other words, bonds should be required of resource users only where the future environmental costs of present activities are commercially uninsurable because the actuarial risks cannot be calculated from historical data. However, since innovative use of environmental resources in a dynamic and evolving system means that fundamental uncertainty is endemic, one would expect that the class of activities for which bonds might be required in a growing economy would be very large.

It is argued that environmental assurance bonds with these characteristics both indemnify society against the potential environmental costs of unprecedented activities, and provide an incentive to the resource user to commit additional resources to research activity in proportion to the authority's best estimate of the worst-case losses arising out of the use of the resource. The bond is a precautionary instrument in the sense that it imposes the cost of anticipated environmental damage on the resource user in advance. Doubts have been raised about the effectiveness of environmental assurance bonds in guaranteeing good behaviour based on the experience of performance bonds in the labour market (Shogren et al., 1993). But this misses the point. Environmental assurance bonds are not a guarantee of good behaviour. Indeed, they provisionally assume that the probability that individuals will ignore the external costs of their actions is unity. What they do is to provide society with the resources to meet the cost of socially irresponsible behaviour. In other words they have a similar motivation and a similar incentive effect to the bonds currently levied on tenants in housing rental markets.

Chapter 10 addresses another dimension of the problem of uncertainty about the future costs of activities with external environmental effects, and that is uncertainty about the value that future generations will place on those costs. This is particularly problematic where the effects are both highly uncertain and long delayed, such as is the case with climate change or biodiversity loss. This is similar to a problem that has attracted some attention in the social choice literature. The latter is concerned with the role of freedom of choice in the ranking of opportunity sets where there is incomplete information about preferences (Sen, 1991; Pattanaik and Xu, 1992). In this case the current generation has incomplete information about the preferences of future generations, and so cannot determine which of a number of possible future states will be preferred by future generations.

Conventionally, environmental economists working with such problems have assumed perfect information about future preferences either by asserting that preferences are constant over time, or by allowing each generation to know the preferences of the next – as in the overlapping generations models. In the face of real uncertainty about future preferences, however, we need a different criterion for evaluating future states. Chapter 10 focuses on the range of options open to future generations. As in the social choice problem, it argues that any expansion in the set of future opportunities is welfare improving providing that the future opportunity set is no worse than the present opportunity set under the preference ordering of the present generation.

This establishes two conditions for safeguarding the interests of future generations. The first is that the future opportunity set should be not inferior to the present opportunity set in terms of the preferences of the present generation. The second is that the range of options open to future generations should be no worse than the range of options open to present generations. This follows the argument of Bossert et al. (1992) that an individual cannot lose by adding an alternative to some existing opportunity set, even if that alternative is strictly worse than existing alternatives. Adding to or conserving the set of alternatives open to future generations may leave them better off and cannot leave the present generation worse off. That is, the present generation cannot be made worse off by retaining an alternative (some species of plant or animal, say) that is strictly worse than all other alternatives under the current preference ordering.

6 A RESEARCH AGENDA

The concluding chapter of Perrings et al. (eds) (1995) identified two challenges for an ecological economics of biodiversity loss: the methodological challenge of developing a genuinely transdisciplinary approach to the modelling and analysis of ecological–economic systems, and the substantive challenge posed by the complex time-behaviour and in-built uncertainty of such ecological–economic systems. This book does not report the results of interdisciplinary work (for which see Perrings et al., 1992; Perrings and Walker, 1995; Folke et al., 1996). Moreover, while several chapters in this book approach the second of these, the challenge remains. Neither joint-system dynamics nor the uncertainty of future evolution are adequately addressed. These chapters raise a number of questions that have not been previously considered in the literature, and have canvassed a limited set of answers to those questions. But the project of understanding the interactions between the ecological and economic components of an increasingly stressed complex evolving system has barely begun.

Aside from the difficulty of understanding system dynamics in the neighbourhood of system thresholds, there has yet to be developed an adequate theory of decision-making under incomplete information of the sort described here. This is partly because the relation between economic and ecological systems raises normative questions that require a better understanding of the moral or ethical framework of decision-making under uncertainty than has yet been developed (at least within economics). Adequate treatment of the problems of intragenerational and intergenerational equity under real uncertainty involves much more than the specification of the appropriate social welfare function. It requires an understanding of the way that intertemporal preferences are constrained by the environment. Mäler (1995) argues, for example, that if the growth rate of environmental resources is zero, then the decentralized equilibrium interest rate should also be zero. However, little is yet known about the rate at which the current and future effects of many economic activities are either 'filtered out' or 'compensated' by the processes of the natural environment.

Similarly, Starret (1991) argues that the more 'essential' environmental resources are, the greater will be the divergence between private and social rates of discount, and the more that private decisions will underrepresent future generations. But little is in fact known about the degree to which environmental resources are essential. Indeed, the debate continues to be a sequence of crude thrusts and counterthrusts by technological optimists and pessimists, between those who believe that produced substitutes exist for almost all ecological functions and those who take the view that a very substantial proportion of ecological functions are irreplaceable.

Nor is there any agreement about the way to deal with uncertainty over these things. For much of 1996, Britain was convulsed with the problem of 'mad cow disease'. The elements of this problem are an epidemic of bovine spongiform encephalopathy (BSE) as an external effect of the indiscriminate use of sheep carcases in cattle feed; the worrying perception that BSE may be linked via the food chain to the fatal human equivalent, Creutzfeldt-Jacob disease (CJD); and the precautionary decision of the European Union to ban the export of British beef. The problem is typical of one in which standard decision models fail. While the probability that eating a BSE-infected cow may lead to CJD is thought to be very low, the costs of a CJD epidemic if a link exists are extremely high. Five years ago, in introducing the paper included here as Chapter 8 at a conference, I cited the problem of 'mad cow disease' as a classic case for a precautionary approach, precisely because it is not possible to have confidence in data about an effect that is potentially catastrophic. The paucity of observations is such that science still cannot provide reliable estimates of the cost of BSE in terms of human health. Then, as now, the decision has been to resist precautionary action that imposes significant costs on the industry but, at the same time, to take sufficient action to maintain consumer confidence in the product. Comparatively little has been done to reduce uncertainty about links between the two diseases. The public good nature of information in an era when the dominant policy trends are liberalization and privatization does not help. But the main problem remains that of understanding the dynamics of a jointly-determined evolutionary ecological–economic system.

It remains the case that environmental decision-making is compartmentalized. The contributions of the social and natural sciences are made in isolation. Natural scientists advise policy-makers on the basis of an agenda that frequently ignores the value of ecological resources in satisfying human wants. Thus the 'conservation value' of ecological systems is argued on the basis of levels of endemism, species rarity and so on without any reference to human preferences.[2] On the other hand, economists advise policy-makers on the basis of an agenda which all too often is limited to a narrow set of financial criteria, completely ignoring key ecological feedbacks that happen to be external to the market. A precondition for the integration of policy advice is the integration of the underlying models of economic and ecological behaviour.

The problem is made more difficult because there is as yet no agreement among economists on the right way to handle problems involving irreversible future effects, fundamental uncertainty, the responsibility borne by those living now for the wellbeing of the members of future generations and so on. It is also made more difficult because of disagreements in ecology about the most important characteristics of terrestrial and marine systems. None the less, it is hard to see where real progress at the systems level is going to come if not from interdisciplinary collaboration. This said, the logic of specialization continues to drive the monodisciplinary research towards smaller and more tightly focused agenda (molecular biology has its counterparts in the social sciences), while the success of that agenda continues to frustrate efforts to integrate the work of different disciplines. The more rapid the development of the techniques, concepts and methods of each discipline in isolation, the greater is the distance between it and all other disciplines. In this, the rather inbred development of economics – doubtless reflected in these pages – is itself a major cause of the difficulty economists now have in working with others. Collaboration remains, however, the first step in the development of a meaningful research agenda.

NOTES

1. User costs in this context include losses due to the depletion of biomass and inorganic matter from ecosystems or the disposal of wastes in ecosystems; the loss of ecological services deriving from biogeochemical cycles; and loss of evolutionary potential.
2. Or more precisely, without any reference to human wants other than the wants of the scientists themselves. This is a way of privileging the wants of science with respect to the wants of other economic agents.

REFERENCES

Allen, T.F.H. and Starr, T.B. (1982), *Hierarchy: Perspectives for Ecological Complexity*, University of Chicago Press, Chicago.

Anderson, P., Arrow, K. and Pines, D. (1988), *The Economy as an Evolving Complex System*, Santa Fe Institute Studies in the Sciences of Complexity, Addison Wesley, Redwood City, CA.

Arrow, K., Bolin, B., Costanza, R., Dasgupta, P., Folke, C., Holling, C.S., Jansson, B.-O., Levin, S., Maler, K.-G., Perrings, C. and Pimentel, D. (1995), 'Economic growth, carrying capacity, and the environment', *Science* **268**, 28 April: 520–21.

Ayres, R.U. (1978), *Resources, Environment and Economics: Applications of the Materials Balance Principle*, John Wiley, New York.

Ayres, R.U. and Kneese, A.V. (1969), 'Production, consumption and externalities', *American Economic Review* **59**: 282–97.

Barro, R.J. (1990), 'Government spending in a simple model of endogenous growth', *Journal of Political Economy* **98** (5): S103–25.

Boserup, E. (1965), *The Conditions of Agricultural Growth: The Economics of Agrarian Change Under Population Pressure*, George Allen & Unwin, London.

Boserup, E. (1981), *Population and Technology*, Basil Blackwell, Oxford.

Bossert, W., Pattanaik, P.K. and Xu, Y. (1992), 'Ranking opportunity sets: an axiomatic approach', unpublished paper.

Boulding, K.E. (1966), 'The economics of the coming spaceship earth', in H. Jarrett (ed.), *Environmental Quality in a Growing Economy*, Johns Hopkins University Press, Baltimore: 3–14.

Boulding, K.E. (1978), *Ecodynamics: A New Theory of Societal Evolution*, Sage, Beverly Hills.

Brock, W.A. (1992), 'Pathways to randomness in the economy: emergent nonlinearity and chaos in economics and finance', SSRI Working Paper, University of Wisconsin–Madison.

Chichilnisky, G. and Heal, G. (1993), 'Global environmental risks', *Journal of Economic Perspectives* **7** (4): 65–86.

Clark, C.W. (1976), *Mathematical Bioeconomics*, Wiley, New York.

Clark, C.W., Clarke, F.H. and Munro, G.R. (1979), 'The optimal exploitation of renewable resource stocks: problems of irreversible investment', *Econometrica* **47**: 25–49.

Common, M.S. (1988), '"Poverty and Progress" revisited', in D. Collard, D. Pearce and D. Ulph (eds), *Economics, Growth and Sustainable Environments*, Macmillan, London: 15–39.

Conway, G. (1987), 'The Properties of Agroecosystems', *Agricultural Systems* **24**: 95–117.

Costanza, R., Norton, B. and Haskell, B.D. (1992), *Ecosystem Health: New Goals for Environmental Management*, Island Press, Washington, DC.

Costanza, R. and Perrings, C. (1990), 'A flexible assurance bonding system for improved environmental management', *Ecological Economics* **2** (1): 57–76.

Daily, G.C. and Ehrlich, P.R. (1992), 'Population, sustainability, and earth's carrying capacity', *BioScience* **42**: 761–71.

Daly, H.E. (1973), 'The steady state economy: toward a political economy of biophysical equilibrium and moral growth', in H.E. Daly (ed.), *Toward a Steady State Economy*, W.H. Freeman, San Francisco: 149–74.

Ehrlich, P.R. and Ehrlich, A.H. (1990), *The Population Explosion*, Simon & Schuster, New York, NY.

Ehrlich, P.R., Ehrlich A.H. and Daily, G. (1993), 'Food security, population and the environment', *Population and Development Review* **19** (1): 1–32.

Faber, M. and Proops, J. (1992), *Evolution, Time, Production and the Environment*, Springer-Verlag, Berlin.

Farber, S.J. (1991), 'Regulatory schemes and self-protective environmental risk control: a comparison of insurance, liability, and deposit/refund systems', *Ecological Economics* **3** (3): 231–46.

Fei, J.C.H. and Ranis, G. (1964), *Development of the Labour Surplus Economy: Theory and Policy*, Yale University Press, New Haven.

Folke, C., Holling, C.S. and Perrings, C. (in press), 'Biological diversity, ecosystems and the human scale', *Ecological Applications*.

Georgescu-Roegen, N. (1971), *The Entropy Law and the Economic Process*, Harvard University Press, Cambridge, MA.

Granger, C. and Terasvirta, T. (1992), *Modelling Dynamic Nonlinear Relationships*, Oxford University Press, Oxford.

Grossman, G. and Krueger, A. (1993), *Environmental Impacts of a North American Free Trade Agreement*, MIT Press, Cambridge, MA.

Hannon, B. (1994), 'Sense of place: geographic discounting by people, animals and plants', *Ecological Economics* **10** (2): 157–74.

Heath, J. and Binswanger, H. (1996), 'Natural resource degradation effects of poverty and population growth are largely policy-induced: the case of Colombia', *Environment and Development Economics* **1** (1): 65–83.

Holling, C.S. (1973), 'Resilience and stability of ecological systems', *Annual Review of Ecology and Systematics* **4**: 1–23.

Holling, C.S. (1986), 'The resilience of terrestrial ecosystems: local surprise and global change', in W.C. Clark and R.E. Munn (eds), *Sustainable Development of the Biosphere*, Cambridge University Press, Cambridge: 292–317.

Holling, C.S. (1992), 'Cross-scale morphology, geometry and dynamics of ecosystems', *Ecological Monographs* **62**: 447–502.

Hommes, C. (1991), *Chaotic Dynamics in Economic Models: Some Simple Case Studies*, Wolters-Noordhoff, Groningen.

Howarth, R. (1995), 'Sustainability under uncertainty: a deontological approach', *Land Economics* **71** (4): 417–27.

Huang, C.-H. and Cai, D. (1994), 'Constant-returns endogenous growth with pollution control', *Environmental and Resource Economics* **4** (4): 383–400.

Kauffman, S.A. and Johnsen, S. (1991), 'Coevolution to the edge of chaos: coupled fitness landscapes, poised states, and coevolutionary avalanches', *Journal of Theoretical Biology* **149**: 467–505.

Kay, J.J. (1991), 'A nonequilibrium thermodynamic framework for discussing ecosystem integrity', *Environmental Management* **15**: 483–95.

Kendall, H.W. and Pimentel, D. (1994), 'Constraints on the expansion of the global food supply', *Ambio* **23**: 198–205.

Levin, S.A. (1992), 'The problem of pattern and scale in ecology', *Ecology* **73** (6): 1943–67.

Mäler, K.-G. (1974), *Environmental Economics: A Theoretical Enquiry*, Blackwell, Oxford.

Mäler, K.-G. (1995), in Perrings et al. (eds): 213–24.

Mill, E.S. (1972), *Urban Economics*, Scott Forseman, Glenview, Ill.

Norgaard, R.B. (1984), 'Coevolutionary agricultural development', *Economic Development and Cultural Change* **32** (3): 525–46.

Pattanaik, P.K. and Xu, Y. (1992), 'On ranking opportunity sets in terms of freedom of choice', *Recherches economiques de Louvain* **56**: 383–90.

Pearce, D.W. (1987), 'Foundations of an ecological economics', *Ecological Modelling* **38**: 9–18.

Perrings, C. (1987), *Economy and Environment: A Theoretical Essay on the Interdependence of Economic and Environmental Systems*, Cambridge University Press, Cambridge.

Perrings, C., Folke, C. and Mäler, K.-G. (1992), 'The ecology and economics of biodiversity loss: the research agenda', *Ambio* **30**: 201–11.

Perrings, C. and Hannon, B. (1996), 'A sense of time and place: an introduction to spatial discounting', Working Paper, Department of Environmental Economics and Environmental Management, University of York.

Perrings, C., Mäler, K.-G., Folke, C., Holling, C.S. and Jansson B.-O. (eds) (1995), *Biodiversity Loss: Economic and Ecological Issues*, Cambridge University Press, Cambridge.

Perrings, C. and Opschoor, J.B. (1994), 'The loss of biological diversity: some policy implications', *Environmental and Resource Economics* **4**: 1–12.

Perrings, C. and Pearce, D.W. (1994), 'Threshold effects and incentives for the conservation of biodiversity', *Environmental and Resource Economics* **4**: 13–28.

Perrings, C. and Walker, B.H. (1995), 'Biodiversity and the economics of discontinuous change in semi-arid rangelands', in C. Perrings, K.-G. Mäler, C. Folke, C.S. Holling and B.-O. Jansson (eds), *Biological Diversity: Economic and Ecological Issues*, Cambridge University Press, New York: 190–210.

Pezzey, J. (1989), 'Economic analysis of sustainable growth and sustainable development', Environment Department Working Paper No. 15, World Bank, Washington, DC.

Puu, T. (1989), *Non-Linear Economic Dynamics*, Springer-Verlag, Berlin.

Romer, P. (1990a), 'Endogenous technical change', *Journal of Political Economy* **98** (5): S71–S103.

Romer, P. (1990b), 'Are nonconvexities important for understanding growth?', *American Economic Review* **80** (2): 97–104.

Scheinkman, J. and LeBaron, B. (1989), 'Nonlinear dynamics and stock returns', *Journal of Business* **62**: 311–37.

Sen, A.K. (1991), 'Welfare, preference and freedom', *Journal of Econometrics* **50**: 15–19.

Shogren, J.F., Herriges, J.A. and Govindasamy, R. (1993), 'Limits to environmental bonds', *Ecological Economics* **8** (2): 109–34.

Solow, R.M. (1974), 'Intergenerational equity and exhaustible resources', *Review of Economic Studies*, Symposium: 29–46.

Starrett, D. (1991), 'The population externality', Stanford University, mimeo.

Turner, R.K. (1988), 'Wetland conservation: economics and ethics', in D. Collard et al. (eds), *Economics, Growth and Sustainable Environments*, Macmillan, London:

Walker, B.H. (1988), 'Autecology, synecology, climate and livestock as agents of rangelands dynamics', *Australian Range Journal* **10**: 69–75.

Walker, B.H. and Noy-Meir, I. (1982), 'Aspects of the stability and resilience of savanna ecosystems', in B.J. Huntley and B.H. Walker (eds), *Ecology of Tropical Savannas*, Springer-Verlag, Berlin: 577–90.

Westoby, M., Walker, B. and Noy-Meir, I. (1989), 'Opportunistic management for rangelands not at equilibrium', *Journal of Range Management* **42** (4): 266–74.

White, R.W. (1990), 'Transient chaotic behaviour in a hierarchical economics system', *Environment and Planning* **A 22**: 1309-21.

Wiens, J.A. (1989), 'Spatial scaling in ecology', *Functional Ecology* **3**: 385–97.

Wilkinson, R.G. (1973), *Poverty and Progress: An Ecological Model of Economic Development*, Methuen, London.

PART I

The Control and Sustainability of
Ecological–Economic Systems

1. Conservation of mass and the time behaviour of ecological–economic systems

1 INTRODUCTION

Recent analyses of the dynamics of jointly-determined economic and ecological systems have been strongly influenced by developments in the theory of complex systems. As the influence of the pioneering work of Prigogine on the behaviour of dissipative, non-equilibrium, thermodynamic systems has percolated through other disciplines concerned with the time-behaviour of the natural environment, more and more attention has been paid to the origins and implications of system complexity.[1] Within both economics and ecology, most attention has been fixed on the behaviour of systems in the neighbourhood of thresholds (unstable manifolds). That is, attention has been fixed on discontinuities in system dynamics.[2] There are, of course, very good reasons why this should be so. Crossing an ecological threshold implies a potentially fundamental change in the self-organization of the system, and so a potentially fundamental change in the availability of ecological services (including life-support services) of value to humanity. Indeed, what makes the field of ecological economics distinct from the more traditional economic approach to the management of the natural environment is precisely its focus on instruments designed to protect ecological thresholds (Perrings et al., 1992).

Rather less attention has been paid to the driving forces behind change in the organization and structure of the economic system. In a sense this is surprising. Georgescu-Roegen (1971) had earlier drawn attention to several implications of the fact that economic processes were entropic. He had argued that once economic processes were understood in thermodynamic terms, many of the explicit and implicit assumptions underpinning traditional growth theory were no longer tenable. These included assumptions about the degree of substitutability between different types of capital and the reversibility of economic processes. But they also included the notion that the organization and structure of the economic system – including consumer preferences and production technology – were exogenous to the economic growth process. Perhaps because their implications for economics were so far-reaching, however, Georgescu-Roegen's arguments were largely ignored in the subsequent development of the theory of economic dynamics. And although he has had a massive influence on the thinking of writers in ecological economics, his intellectual impact on the mainstream of economics has been slight (compare Daly, 1987; Daly and Cobb, 1989).

Some growth theorists have independently become increasingly uncomfortable with the idea that technological change is independent of the growth process (Romer, 1990a, 1990b), but the rationale for endogenizing technological change owes little to either thermodynamics or the theory of complex systems. In part this is because the economic system has continued to be treated in isolation from the environment it draws on for materials, energy and the capacity to assimilate wastes. And even where it has not, the jointly-determined system has continued to be treated as if exempt from the laws of thermodynamics.[3] In two earlier contributions (Perrings, 1986, 1987) I considered the origins of change in technology and preferences in jointly-determined economy–environment systems. This chapter revisits a central argument of these contributions to show the necessity for technological change in dynamical systems away from equilibrium. More particularly, it shows that for a system away from equilibrium and respecting the law of conservation of mass, any combination of outputs will necessitate change in the combinations of inputs in both economic and ecological processes. While both contributions adopted the form of the classical general equilibrium models of von Neumann (1946), the results hold for any specification that respects the conservation of mass condition.

These contributions were not the first to consider the implications of the conservation of mass. Boulding (1966), Daly (1968), Ayres and Kneese (1969) and Georgescu-Roegen (1979) had all explored some of the implications of the condition. However, all had missed a crucial implication of the conservation of mass condition for the time-behaviour of the system: that away from equilibrium it is inconsistent with the existence of constant technologies. Given conservation of mass, expansion of the economy or any other subsystem of the global system implies continuous change in the material transformations of both economic and ecological processes. This is sufficient to preclude its convergence to an expansion path at which the structure of production and prices of economic goods is stable over time. Moreover, since market prices in an interdependent economy–environment system are inadequate observers of the effects of economic activity on the relative scarcity of environmental resources, this change will be unanticipated. The management or control of economic processes in response to price signals will be insufficient to determine the structure of economic output, since environmental feedbacks will be present even where the economy is technically controllable and observable via the price system.

The chapter is in five sections. Section 2 describes the axiomatic structure of the model. Section 3 discusses the dynamic implications of the conservation of mass condition. Section 4 considers the place of the economy in the global system and indicates the limits of system controllability through the uses of price signals. A final section offers some concluding remarks.

2   ELEMENTS OF THE SYSTEM

The following general assumptions underpin the model described below:

i.   It is possible to identify discrete physical activities or processes that collectively describe the material transformations of the global system. The global system is materially (and thermodynamically) closed.[4] No matter passes into or out of the system. The economy represents a subset of the processes of the global system, and is assumed to be materially open with respect to the environment. Matter passes between the processes of the economy and the processes of the environment. From this it follows that we cannot meaningfully represent the economy as a closed system unless we believe that all processes in the global system are 'owned' and 'controlled' by economic agents. If this is not the case then the complement of the processes of the economy will be the processes of the environment, and the time-behaviour of each will depend on the links between them.[5]

ii. The physical relationship between the economy and the environment is assumed to reflect, on the one hand, the heterotrophic nature of economic agents (as organisms that obtain their nutritional needs by feeding on other organisms), and on the other, the status of the environment as a receptacle for the waste products generated in the economy. In other words the ecosystems of the natural environment are both a source and a sink.

iii. At any given period and any given state of nature there are fixed coefficients of production in both economic and ecological processes. That is, each process depends on a set of resources made available at the start of the period which cannot be varied in that period. The set of resources may have been selected from the menu of options available under some technique of production which allows for substitution between inputs, but once the resources are secured the coefficients are fixed.

iv. It is possible to identify the same number of linearly independent processes as there are products.[6]

v.   Consistent with the existence of high and low entropy states of matter, not all resources depreciate/degenerate at the same rate.

Assumptions peculiar to the processes of the economy are discussed below. At this point we may formalize assumptions (i) to (v).

The technology of the material transformations in an economy–environment system applied in the k-th period of its history are described by the pair of non-negative matrices $\mathbf{A}(k)\mathbf{B}(k)$, related by the equation

$$\mathbf{B}(k) = \mathbf{A}(k) + \mathbf{G}(k). \tag{1.1}$$

From assumption (iv) all three matrices are n-square. $\underline{\mathbf{a}}_i(k)$, the i-th row of $\mathbf{A}(k)$, is the vector of gross input coefficients for the n products of the system in the i-th process in the k-th period. $\mathbf{a}_j(k)$, the j-th column of $\mathbf{A}(k)$, is the vector of gross input coefficients for the j-th product in the n processes of the system in the k-th period. $\underline{\mathbf{b}}_i(k)$, the i-th row of $\mathbf{B}(k)$, is the vector of net output coefficients for the n products of the system in the i-th process in the k-th period. $\mathbf{b}_j(k)$, the j-th column of $\mathbf{B}(k)$, is the vector of net output coefficients for the j-th product in the n processes of the system. $\mathbf{G}(k)$ is an n-square matrix describing the physical change in the mass of the inputs of the system during the k-th period of production. $g_{ij}(k)$ is unrestricted as to sign. $g_{ij}(k)$ is positive, zero or negative as the j-th input is augmented, unchanged or diminished in the i-th process in the k-th period.

The period of production, indexed k, is of uniform duration. Since, from assumption (iii), there are constant returns to scale in each period, it is entirely arbitrary. From assumption (iv) the rank of $\mathbf{A}(k)$, $\mathbf{B}(k)$ is n. From assumption (v) the system is one of joint production, implying that $\mathbf{B}(k)$ is not diagonal except as a special case.

The elements of $\mathbf{A}(k)$, $\mathbf{B}(k)$ are coefficients on the resources (products of past periods) available to the system at the commencement of the reference period. To see their construction, let us first define an n-dimensional, time-indexed, row vector $\mathbf{q}(k)$, in which $q_i(k)$ denotes the quantity (mass) of the i-th product available to the system at the commencement of the k-th period. Let us further define a non-negative n-square gross input matrix $\mathbf{X}(k)$, in which $x_{ij}(k)$ denotes the quantity of the j-th resource employed in the i-th process in the k-th period. We then have $a_{ij}(k) = q_i(k)^{-1}x_{ij}(k)$. $a_{ij}(k)$ denotes the gross input of the j-th resource in the i-th process per unit of the i-th resource available to the system at the commencement of the k-th period. $b_{ij}(k)$ is similarly obtained and denotes the net output of the j-th resource from the i-th process per unit of the i-th resource available to the system in the k-th period. The time path for the physical system is thus given by the very simple first-order difference equation

$$\mathbf{q}(k) = \mathbf{q}(k-1)\mathbf{B}(k-1). \tag{1.2}$$

The outputs of the $k-1$-th period comprise the stock of resources available to the system at the commencement of the k-th period. Notice that if there is no technical change, $\mathbf{B}(k) = \mathbf{B}(0)$ for all $k \geq 0$, and the physical system has the equally simple general solution

$$\mathbf{q}(k) = \mathbf{q}(0)\mathbf{B}(0)^k. \tag{1.3}$$

3   THE CONSERVATION OF MASS

Consider now the dynamic effects of the conservation of mass condition. Notice, first, that the condition implies that for all $k \geq 0$:

$$\mathbf{q}(k)\mathbf{e} = \mathbf{q}(k)\mathbf{B}(k)\mathbf{e}; \tag{1.4a}$$
$$q_i(k)\underline{\mathbf{a}}_i(k)\mathbf{e} = q_i(k)\underline{\mathbf{b}}_i(k)\mathbf{e} \text{ for all } i \text{ in } \{1,2, \dots, n\}; \tag{1.4b}$$
$$\mathbf{q}(k) = \mathbf{q}(k)\mathbf{A}(k); \tag{1.4c}$$

where $\mathbf{e}$ is the unit vector. (1.4a) means that a closed physical system has a zero growth rate. Although any subsystem within a closed physical system may be able to expand, that is, $q_i(k) < \mathbf{q}(k)\mathbf{b}_i(k)$ for some i and some k, it will not be able to expand without limit. Sooner or later it will be bound by the conservation of mass condition. (1.4b) means that the mass of inputs in every process will be exactly equal to the mass of outputs. This is the precise meaning of the von Neumann dictum that nothing can be produced out of nothing.[7] (1.4c) means that the gross input matrix, $\mathbf{A}(k)$, will fully account for all resources in the system in the k-th period. This follows from the fact that in a closed system there is no free disposal of resources. Waste material cannot be ejected from the system. Every residual must go somewhere. This leads to the following proposition.

Proposition: Given the conservation of mass, any system generating non-zero residuals will be time varying in its coefficients of production.

The quantity of resources available to the system at the beginning of the k-th period is given by $\mathbf{q}(k)$. The quantity of resources which are required by the system in terms of the technology inherited from the previous period is given by $\mathbf{q}(k)\mathbf{A}(k-1)$, and the vector of residuals associated with $\mathbf{A}(k-1)$ is $\mathbf{q}(k)[\mathbf{I} - \mathbf{A}(k-1)]$. If there is full employment of all resources under this technology, that is if $\mathbf{q}(k) = \mathbf{q}(k)\mathbf{A}(k-1)$ and $\mathbf{q}(k)[\mathbf{I} - \mathbf{A}(k-1)] = 0$, then the inherited technology will satisfy the conservation of mass condition. But if there is less than full employment of all resources or if there is unfulfilled excess demand for any resource, that is if $\mathbf{q}(k) \neq \mathbf{q}(k)\mathbf{A}(k-1)$ and $\mathbf{q}(k)[\mathbf{I} - \mathbf{A}(k-1)] \neq 0$, $\mathbf{q}(k) \neq \mathbf{q}(k-1)$ and the inherited technology will not satisfy the conservation of mass condition.

Since, by the conservation of mass condition, $q(k) = q(k)A(k)$ for all $k \geq 0$, if $q(k) \neq q(k)A(k-1)$, it follows that $A(k) \neq A(k-1)$. Hence $A(k) = A(k-1)$ only if the vector of residuals $q(k)[I - A(k-1)]$ is equal to zero. Moreover, from (1.4b), $A(k) \neq A(k-1) \Leftrightarrow B(k) \neq B(k-1)$.

The first-order difference equation, which defines the time path of the physical system (1.2), may accordingly be written in the form:

$$q(k) = q(k-1)[B(k-2) + B_\Delta(k-2)] \tag{1.5}$$

where $B(k-2)$ represents the technology inherited from the previous period, and $B_\Delta(k-2)$ represents the changes brought about in the elements of $B(k-2)$. Wherever $q(0) \neq q(0)B(0)$ the conservation of mass condition implies that the general solution of the physical system will be defined by the expression:

$$q(k) = q(0)\prod_{i=0}^{k-1}B(i). \tag{1.6}$$

The following corollary is, again, immediate.

Corollary: A subsystem within the global economy–environment system may be technologically stationary at equilibrium in the presence of non-zero residuals, if and only if disposal of those residuals is 'free'.

A system may be technologically stationary at equilibrium only if

$$q_{i(}(k)/q_i(k-1) = b^*, \; q(k)B(0) = b^*q(k) \tag{1.7}$$

for all i in $\{1,2, \ldots, n\}$ and for all $k \geq 0$. The stability of this equilibrium implies that

$$\lim_{k\to\infty}q_i(k)/q_i(k-1) = b^*, \; \lim_{k\to\infty}q(k)B(0) = \lim_{k\to\infty}b^*q(k) \tag{1.8}$$

for all i in $\{1,2, \ldots, n\}$. Hence a system operating a technology given by $B(0)$ is defined to be stable if, in the limit, the vector $q(k)$ converges to a left eigenvector corresponding to the dominant eigenvalue of $B(0)$, b^*, for any initial vector $q(0)$. At equilibrium the structure of production will be constant over time, and all products in the system will be expanding at the rate given by b^*.

Free disposal is defined to mean that the spectrum of the net output matrix will be constant in the face of the existence of a non-negative vector of residuals. More precisely, free disposal is defined to mean that $q(k)[I - A(k)] > 0$ implies that $b(k) = b(0)$ for all $k \geq 0$, where $b(0)$ and $b(k)$ denote the set of eigenvalues of $\mathbf{B}(0)$ and $\mathbf{B}(k)$, respectively. In other words, free disposal means that the existence of residuals in the system has no effect on the technology applied.

It can be appreciated that this definition carries over very easily to cover the case of technological externalities in the economy–environment system. If the global system is partitioned to distinguish the economy from its environment, so that

$$\mathbf{B}(0) = \frac{\mathbf{B}_1}{\mathbf{B}_2}(0)$$

where $\mathbf{B}_1(0)$, describing the output coefficients of the economy, is $m \times n$, and $\mathbf{B}_2(0)$, describing the output coefficients of the environment, is $n - m \times n$, and if $\mathbf{q}(k)$ and $\mathbf{A}(k)$ are partitioned conformably, then free disposal of economic goods implies that $\mathbf{B}_1(k) = \mathbf{B}_1(0)$ for all $\mathbf{q}_1(k)[\mathbf{I} - \mathbf{A}(k)] > 0$.

A proof of the corollary is offered in the appendix. What it implies is that a system operating a given technology may be convergent if and only if residuals generated in the process of convergence generate no feedback effects. Since the conservation of mass in an indecomposable system ensures that any change in the structure of production will be associated with feedback effects, the existence of residuals and technological change under the conservation of mass condition are synonymous. The conservation of mass condition implies that there will be such change as is necessary to dispose of all residuals in all periods. But notice that it implies nothing about the nature of this change. It is of interest, therefore, to consider whether the result holds in the presence of controlled technical change in a dynamic economic system.

4   ECONOMY AND ENVIRONMENT

In order to distinguish between the processes of the economy and those of the environment, I now identify a price system involving the construction of two additional vectors. The first of these, $\mathbf{p}(k)$, is a semi-positive time-indexed n-dimensional column vector of prices, in which $p_i(k)$ is the price of the i-th resource in the k-th period, and $p_i(k) > 0$ for i in $\{1,2, \ldots, m\}$ and $p_j(k) = 0$ for j in $\{m + 1, m + 2, \ldots, n\}$. The first m components of $\mathbf{p}(k)$ are positive, indicating that the first m resources 'produced' in the general system are positively valued. The last $n - m$ components are all zero, indicating that the last $n - m$ resources 'produced' in the system are zero valued. The first m resources are thus scarce economic resources, the last $n - m$ resources are non-scarce resources: either the waste products of economic processes or unvalued environmental products. Since $\mathbf{p}(k - 1)$ is positive in its first m components only it follows that if

$a_{ij}(k) > 0$, i in $\{1,2, ..., m\}$, j in $\{m + 1, m + 2, ..., n\}$ then the agents operating the i-th process are able to obtain quantities of the j-th resource without advancing positively valued resources in order to do so. The non-scarcity of resources means that they can be obtained without surrendering positively valued products in the process. Conversely, the scarcity of resources means that their utilization by economic agents implies the commitment of positively priced products to gain their possession.

The second vector, $\mathbf{v}(k)$, is a semi-positive time-indexed n-dimensional row vector of resource values, in which $v_i(k)$ indicates the value of the i-th resource produced in the system in the k-th period. The two vectors are related by the equation:

$$\mathbf{v}(k) = \mathbf{q}(k - 1)\mathbf{B}(k - 1)D\mathbf{p}(k) \tag{1.9}$$

where $D\mathbf{p}(k) = \text{diagonal } [p_1, p_2, ..., p_n]$. $\mathbf{v}(k)$ is related to the costs of production as follows

$$\mathbf{v}(k) = \mathbf{q}(k - 1)[\mathbf{I} + Dr(k - 1)]\mathbf{A}(k - 1)D\mathbf{p}(k - 1), \tag{1.10}$$

where $Dr(k) = \text{diagonal } [r_1, r_2, ..., r_n]$ denotes the rates of profit earned in all processes. As with the price vector $Dr(k)$ is positive in the first m elements on the principal diagonal only, $r_i(k)$, i in $\{1, 2, ..., m\}$. It is an increasing function of the level of excess demand for the outputs of the i-th process, where the level of excess demand for the i-th product in the k-th period is given by $\mathbf{q}(k)\mathbf{a}_i(k - 1) - q_i(k)$.

The time path of the price vector may be described by

$$\mathbf{B}(k - 1)\mathbf{p}(k) = [\mathbf{I} + Dr(k - 1)]\mathbf{A}(k - 1)\mathbf{p}(k - 1). \tag{1.11}$$

The only property of this system that we need to note here is that prices may be stable over time only if there is zero excess demand for all resources, and if there is no technical change. Our problem is to determine the role of prices as observers and instruments of control in a time-varying system.

To see the capacity of the price system to regulate change in a time-varying system let us redefine the model discussed in Sections 2 and 3 as a control system.[8] We have already seen that wherever a system generates a set of residuals there exists a set of resources, the disposal of which has the effect of changing the technology of the system. When residuals are disposed of with a particular impact on output in view (as a purposeful act of investment) we have a controlled feedback process; the application of a linear combination of the state variables (the available resources) in order to transform the system from one state to another. The time path for the physical system may be described in terms of the state–space representation:

$$\mathbf{q}(k) = \mathbf{q}(k-1)\mathbf{B}(k-2) + \mathbf{j}(k-1)\mathbf{M}(k-1) \qquad (1.12a)$$
$$\mathbf{v}(k-1) = \mathbf{q}(k-1)D\mathbf{p}(k-1). \qquad (1.12b)$$

$\mathbf{j}(k-1)$ in (1.12a) denotes an n-dimensional row vector of control variables applied in the $k-1$-th period. It is a linear combination of the state variables, $\mathbf{q}(k-1)$. $\mathbf{M}(k-1)$ is an n-square feedback matrix describing the changes brought about in the elements of $\mathbf{B}(k-1)$ as a result of the controlled application of the residuals to the system. More particularly, the vector of control variables is a linear combination of the vector of residual resources generated by the system in the $k-1$-th period under the technology of the $k-2$-th period:

$$\mathbf{j}(k-1) = \mathbf{q}(k-1)[\mathbf{I} - \mathbf{A}(k-2)]\mathbf{K}(k). \qquad (1.13)$$

$\mathbf{v}(k)$ in (1.12b) denotes the control system 'outputs'.

A non-stationary system of this type is said to be controllable if it is possible to transform it into a system in which none of the state variables, the $q_i(k)$, are independent of the control vector. More particularly, the controllability of such a system implies that the $kn \times n$ controllability matrix constructed for an n-dimensional system controlled over k periods, $\mathbf{J}(k)$, is of rank n. The controllability matrix is formed from the sequence of state and feedback matrices as follows:

$$\mathbf{J}(k) = \begin{bmatrix} \mathbf{M}(0) \\ \mathbf{B}(1)\mathbf{M}(1) \\ \mathbf{B}(2)\mathbf{B}(1)\mathbf{M}(1) \\ \vdots \\ \prod_{t-1}^{k-1}\mathbf{B}(t)\mathbf{M}(k-1) \end{bmatrix}. \qquad (1.14)$$

This matrix describes the effects of the controls applied to the system over the k periods of the control sequence. Its importance in the determination of the final state may be seen from the equation giving the general solution of the controlled non-stationary system – the system transition equation:

$$\mathbf{q}(k) = \mathbf{q}(0)\prod_{t=0}^{k-1}\mathbf{B}(t) + \sum_{t=0}^{k-1}\mathbf{j}(t)\left(\prod_{j=1}^{k-1}\mathbf{B}(j)\right)\mathbf{M}(t). \qquad (1.15)$$

Notice first that this differs from (1.6) in the second term describing the contribution of the controls over the interval $[0, k-1]$. This term is the product of the $kn \times n$ controllability matrix $\mathbf{J}(k)$ and the $1 \times kn$ vector $\mathbf{j}(k,0)$ formed by combining the control vectors $\mathbf{j}(t)$ over the same interval. It follows that if the vector

$$\mathbf{q}(k) - \mathbf{q}(0)\prod_{t=0}^{k-1} \mathbf{B}(t) = \mathbf{j}(k,0)\mathbf{J}(k) \tag{1.16}$$

has any zero-valued components, that is if $\mathbf{J}(k)$ has any columns comprising only zeros, or is less than full rank, the general system will not be controllable.

The rank of the controllability matrix is limited by the rank of each matrix in the pair $\mathbf{B}(k)$, $\mathbf{M}(k)$. $\mathbf{B}(k)$ is of full rank by assumption. Hence, if the feedback matrices describing the technological changes associated with the controls are of less than full rank, the controls will not reach all the processes in the system. The system will not be controllable.

What is interesting here is that the controls in an economic system are triggered by changes in the control system outputs, the price signals. In other words, the system is one of linear output feedback control. $\mathbf{K}(k-1)$ in (1.13) depends on $D\mathbf{p}(k-1)$ in (1.11). More particularly, $\mathbf{K}(k-1) = \mathbf{U}(k-1)D\mathbf{p}(k-1)$ where the columns of $\mathbf{U}(k-1)$ indicate the effect of a particular resource price on the demand for the resource in each of the m processes of the economy. A necessary condition for the complete controllability of the system is therefore that it be completely observable, where the conditions for the observability of the system parallel those for its controllability. That is, the complete observability of the system requires that the rank of an observability matrix of similar construction to (1.14) be n.

In all economic systems the control instruments are the residuals or available resources in the system, but the observers differ between economic systems. The most basic form of control is that in which the physical system is observed directly through the level of residuals it generates. This type of control has been called by Kornai and Martos (1981) 'vegetative control', and its chief characteristic is that each agent has access to a very limited set of observations: 'It is a characteristic of vegetative control that it always takes place at the lowest level between producers and consumers, without the intervention of higher administrative organizations. It is autonomous, that is not directly connected to any social process ... the firm or household only watch their own stock levels' (1981: 60–61). The rank of the observability matrix confronting each agent in the system is not much greater than zero.

In the market economies the price system provides each agent with a more complete, though less direct measure of the residuals of the system. Consequently the rank of the observability matrix confronting each agent is much greater, implying that the controllability of the system is similarly greater. However, since

$p_i(k) = 0$ for i in $\{m + 1, m + 2, ..., n\}$, the control vector $\mathbf{j}(k,0)\mathbf{J}(k)$ may be positive in its first m components only, implying that the observability and hence the controllability matrices are of rank m at the most. The last $n - m$ resources in the system are not touched by the controls.

It follows that for technical change described by feedback control informed by the signals of the economy, the price system will not have determinate effects in respect of the environment. More importantly, wherever the economy and its environment are mutually dependent and are bound by the conservation of mass condition, such technical change will not have determinate effects even in respect of the economy. If the controlled allocation of resources does not satisfy the conservation of mass condition (1.4c), then there will be uncontrolled disposal of residuals, and there will exist unanticipated feedback effects.

It is these unanticipated feedback effects that are the basis of all of the so-called external effects.[9] It is, indeed, only if the economy and the environment are completely disjoint, and if there are no uncontrolled residuals, that technical change will produce no unanticipated effects. Moreover, while it is more realistic to postulate a process of 'parameter adaptive control' in which economic agents gradually uncover the parameters of the system, it is misleading to substitute the perfect information assumption normally made in control processes by the assumption of stochastic variation of the system parameters. These variations are not random, merely unobserved and unobservable given the structure of property rights prevailing in the system.

5   CONCLUDING REMARKS

To return to the problem of endogenous technological change in economic growth, the investment which drives economic growth comprises resources that are residual to the requirements of historical production and consumption patterns. In general, investment is modelled as a choice variable – the product of the consumption propensities or preferences of economic agents – and is taken to be the only residual that has an impact on the time-behaviour of the system. In terms of the general economy–environment model discussed in this chapter, however, investment is merely one form of residual. Other forms of residuals include waste products that are surplus to the historical requirements of the economic and ecological processes in which they are disposed. Free disposal of residuals, a standard assumption in most economic models, implies the absence of feedback effects. So the standard assumption is that the disposal of all residuals other than investment generates no feedback effects, while investment generates feedback effects that are positive in their net effects.

Provided that the global system is indecomposable, however, the disposal of residuals in any sector will have feedback effects on that sector, and these will involve change in the coefficients of production and consumption. This follows from the conservation of mass condition. In a materially closed system the conservation of mass condition ensures that any equilibrium path is one in which the absolute values of the components of the quantity vector will be constant over time. The only rate of growth compatible with the conservation of mass condition is the zero rate, implying that the dominant eigenvalue of the net output matrix, $\mathbf{B}(k)$, will have an absolute value of unity. It follows immediately that any arbitrary set of physical processes to which corresponds a (notional) equilibrium growth rate greater than zero, is not a materially closed system. If it is not a materially closed system then there will be material flows into and out of the system, and it will be jointly determined with its environment. Whether or not residuals generated in the system are allocated in a controlled or purposeful manner, the system will be subject to change resulting from the disposal of residuals in its environment.

There is no reason why a particular subset of processes within a materially closed system should not have a positive growth rate over some finite period, but it will necessarily be at the expense of some other set of processes in its environment. An expansion in the mass of resources at the command of a particular group of agents implies a contraction in the mass of resources at the disposal of some other group of agents. It also implies an expansion in the mass of wastes generated by the former. High rates of growth in one subset of processes imply high rates of depletion of resources generated by other processes, and high rates of residuals disposals in both sets of processes. Consequently, high rates of growth in one subset of processes imply high rates of change in the system as a whole. Not only is the growth-oriented economy itself an unstable system, it is directly responsible for destabilizing the global system of which it is a constituent part.

NOTES

1. See Prigogine and Stengers (1977, 1984), Nicolis and Prigogine (1989).
2. See, for example, O'Neil et al. (1989), Kay (1991), Rosser (1991).
3. See, for example, Hartwick (1977, 1978a, 1978b), Solow (1986, 1988).
4. A thermodynamically closed system is one that exchanges energy (such as gravity or radiant heat) with its environment, but that is entirely self-contained with respect to matter.
5. The environment is accordingly defined in terms of the referent set of processes. The definition is, however, entirely symmetrical. If the universal set of processes in the global system is denoted U, and if the set of processes of the economy, the referent set, is denoted V, then V', the complement of V in U, is the environment. The terms 'environment' and 'the complement of the referent set' are synonymous.
6. I make the very strong assumption that the number of products remains constant over time. The system is n-dimensional in all periods. This implies that only the input and output mix of different processes changes. In reality, the number of distinct products produced by the system will change

over time. If we define the dimensions of the system to be time variant, however, the results of the chapter are only strengthened.

7. The Neumann version requires only that $a_{ij}(k) > 0$ for at least one j, and that $b_{ij}(k) > 0$ for at least one i.

8. Although it is uncommon to find technological change conceptualized as a control process in economics it is well established in other disciplines. The process of evolution by natural selection, for example, has been convincingly conceptualized by biologists as a control process, initially only implicitly, as by Lotka (1956), but later explicitly, as by Rendel (1968).

9. The notion that 'technological externalities' underlie all of the external effects reported in the literature, including those associated with the common property problem, is well established. See Bator (1958), Fisher and Peterson (1976), Dasgupta and Heal (1979) and Fisher (1981).

REFERENCES

Ayres, R.U. and Kneese, A.V. (1969), 'Production, consumption and externalities', *American Economic Review* **59**: 282–97.

Bator, F.M. (1958), 'The anatomy of market failure', *Quarterly Journal of Economics* **72**: 351–79.

Boulding, K.E. (1966), 'The economics of the coming spaceship earth', in H. Jarrett (ed.), *Environmental Quality in a Growing Economy*, Johns Hopkins University Press, Baltimore:

Daly H. (1968), 'On economics as a life science', *Journal of Political Economy* **76**: 392–406.

Daly, H.E. (1987), 'The economic growth debate: what some economists have learned but many have not', *Journal of Environmental Economics and Management* **14**: 323–36.

Daly, H.E. and Cobb, J.B. (1989), *For the Common Good*, Beacon Press, Boston.

Dasgupta, P.S. and Heal, G.M. (1979), *Economic Theory and Exhaustible Resources*, Cambridge University Press, Cambridge.

Fisher, A.C. (1981), *Resource and Environmental Economics*, Cambridge University Press, Cambridge.

Fisher, A.C. and Peterson, F.M. (1976), 'The environment in economics: a survey', *Journal of Economic Literature* **14**: 1–33.

Georgescu-Roegen, N. (1971), *The Entropy Law and Economic Process*, Harvard University Press, Cambridge, MA.

Georgescu-Roegen, N. (1979), 'Energy analysis and economic valuation', *Southern Economic Journal* **45**: 1023–58.

Hartwick, J.M. (1977), 'Intergenerational equity and the investing of rents from exhaustible resources', *American Economic Review* **66**: 972–4.

Hartwick, J.M. (1978a), 'Investing returns from depleting renewable resource stocks and intergenerational equity', *Economics Letters* **1**: 85–8.

Hartwick, J.M. (1978b), 'Substitution among exhaustible resources and intergenerational equity', *Review of Economic Studies* **45** (2): 347–54.

Kay, J.J. (1991), 'A nonequilibrium thermodynamic framework for discussing ecosystem integrity', *Environmental Management* **15**: 483–95.

Kneese, A.V., Ayres, R.U. and d'Arge, R.C. (1974), 'Economics and the environment: a materials balance approach', in Wolozin (ed.), *The Economics of Pollution*, General Learning Press, Morristown, NJ:

Kornai, J. and Martos, B. (1981), 'Vegetative control', in J. Kornai and B. Martos (eds), *Non-Price Control*, North-Holland, Amsterdam:

Lotka, A.J. (1956), *Elements of Mathematical Biology*, Dover, New York.

Nicolis, G. and Prigogine, I. (1989), *Exploring Complexity*, W.H. Freeman, New York.

O'Neil, R.V., Johnson, A.R. and King, A.W. (1989), 'A hierarchical framework for the analysis of scale', *Landscape Ecology* **3**: 193–205.

Perrings, C. (1986), 'Conservation of mass and instability in a dynamic economy–environment system', *Journal of Environmental Economics and Management* **13**: 199–211.

Perrings, C. (1987), *Economy and Environment: A Theoretical Essay on the Interdependence of Economic and Environmental Systems*, Cambridge University Press, Cambridge.

Perrings C. (1991), 'Ecological sustainability and environmental control', Structural Change and Economic Dynamics' **2**: 275–95.

Perrings, C., Folke, C. and Mäler, K.G. (1992), 'The ecology and economics of biodiversity loss: the research agenda', *Ambio* **30**: 201–11.

Prigogine, I. and Stengers, I. (1977), 'The new alliance', *Scientia* **112**: 319–32 and 643–53.

Prigogine, I. and Stengers, I. (1984), *Order out of Chaos*, Heinemann, London.

Rendel, J.M. (1968), 'The control of development processes', in Drake (ed.), *Evolution and Environment*, Yale University Press, New Haven.

Romer, P. (1990a), 'Endogenous technical change', *Journal of Political Economy* **98** (5): S71–S103.

Romer, P. (1990b), 'Are nonconvexities important for understanding growth?', *American Economic Review* **80** (2): 97–104.

Rosser, J.B. (1991), *From Catastrophe to Chaos*, Kluwer, Dordrecht.

Smith, V.L. (1977), 'Control theory applied to natural and environmental resources', *Journal of Environmental Economics and Management* **4**: 1–24.

Solow, R.M. (1986), 'On the intertemporal allocation of natural resources', *Scandinavian Journal of Economics* **88** (1): 141–9.

Solow, R.M. (1988), *Growth Theory: An Exposition*, Oxford University Press, New York.

Victor, P. (1972), *Pollution, Economy and Environment*, Allen & Unwin, London.

von Neumann, J. (1946), 'A model of general equilibrium', *Review of Economic Studies* **13**: 1–7.

APPENDIX

The proposition that a time-invariant system will converge to an equilibrium growth path if and only if there is free disposal of residuals implies that in a physical system satisfying assumptions (i) to (v), if max $b(k) = $ max $q_i(k)/q_i(k-1)$, min $b(k) = $ min $q_i(k)/q_i(k-1)$, for i in $\{1, 2, ..., n\}$, then the $\lim_{k\to\infty}$ max $b(k)$ and $\lim_{k\to\infty}$ min $b(k) = b^*$ for any initial vector $\mathbf{q}(0)$ if and only if $\mathbf{q}(k)[\mathbf{I} - \mathbf{A}(k)] > 0$ implies that $\mathbf{B}(k) = \mathbf{B}(0)$ for all $k \geq 0$.

To prove sufficiency, let $\mathbf{B}(k) = \mathbf{B}(0) = \mathbf{B}$ for all $k \geq 0$. By assumption $\mathbf{B}$ has a dominant eigenvalue which is real and positive. Let the set of all eigenvalues in $\mathbf{B}$ be ordered in such a way that $b_{max} = b_1$. There exists a non-singular matrix $\mathbf{S}$ such that

$$\mathbf{B} = \mathbf{S}Db\mathbf{S}^{-1} \qquad (1A.1)$$

where $Db = $ diagonal $\{b_1, b_2, ..., b_n\}$, and where the first row of $\mathbf{S}^{-1}$, $\mathbf{s}_1^{-1}$, and the first column of $\mathbf{S}$, $\mathbf{ls}_1$, are the left and right eigenvectors of $\mathbf{B}$ corresponding to b_{max}. By the Frobenius theorem the components of $\mathbf{s}_1^{-1}$ and $\mathbf{ls}_1$ are strictly positive. From (1.3) the i-th component of $\mathbf{q}(k)$ may be defined by

$$q_i(k) = \mathbf{q}(0)\mathbf{B}^k\mathbf{e}_i \qquad (1A.2)$$

where $\mathbf{e}_i$ is the i-th unit vector. From (1A.1) this may be written

$$q_i(k) = \mathbf{q}(0)\mathbf{S}Db^k\mathbf{S}^{-1}\mathbf{e}_i \qquad (1A.3)$$

for any k and all i in $\{1, 2, ..., n\}$. (1A.3) may also be written in the form

$$q_i(k) = b_1^k\mathbf{q}(0)\mathbf{S}Dc^{-k}\mathbf{S}^{-1}\mathbf{e}_i \qquad (1A.4)$$

where

$$Dc^{-k} = \text{diag}(1, b_2/b_1, b_3/b_1, ..., b_n/b_1)^k. \qquad (1A.5)$$

Accordingly, for all i in $\{1, 2, ..., n\}$ we have in the limit:

$$\lim_{k\to\infty} \frac{q_i(k)}{q_i(k-1)} = \lim_{k\to\infty} \frac{b_1^k}{b_1^{k-1}} \frac{\mathbf{q}(0)\mathbf{S}Dc^{-k}\mathbf{S}^{-1}\mathbf{e}_i}{\mathbf{q}(0)\mathbf{S}Dc^{-(k-1)}\mathbf{S}^{-1}\mathbf{e}_i}. \qquad (1A.6)$$

Since $\mathbf{q}(0)$ is positive by assumption, since $\mathbf{s}_1^{-1}$ and $|\mathbf{s}_1$ are positive by the Frobenius theorem, and since $\lim_{k \to \infty} D\mathbf{c}^{-k} = \mathrm{diag}(1, 0, ..., 0)$, $\mathbf{q}(0)SD\mathbf{c}^{-k}S^{-1}\mathbf{e}_i$ $= \mathbf{q}(0)SD\mathbf{c}^{-(k-1)}S^{-1}\mathbf{e}_i$. Hence, defining $b^* = b_1$:

$$\lim_{k \to \infty} q_i^{(k)}/q_i^{(k-1)} = b^* \tag{1A.7}$$

for all i in $\{1, 2, ..., n\}$. Moreover

$$\lim_{k \to \infty} \mathbf{q}(k) = z\,\mathbf{s}_1^{-1} \tag{1A.8}$$

$z > 0$. If $\mathbf{B}(k) = \mathbf{B}(0) = \mathbf{B}$ for all $k \geq 0$ then the rate of growth of all resources converges to the dominant eigenvalue of $\mathbf{B}$, and the quantity vector converges to a left eigenvector of $\mathbf{B}$ corresponding to b_{max}.□

Necessity follows directly from (1.4). A semi-positive vector of residuals $\mathbf{q}(k)[\mathbf{I} - \mathbf{A}(k-1)]$ implies that, in order to satisfy (1.4c), there will exist a matrix $\mathbf{A}_\Delta(k-1)$ with at least one positive element. From (1.4b) there will exist a matrix $\mathbf{B}_\Delta(k-1)$ with at least one positive element, implying that $\mathbf{B}(k) \neq \mathbf{B}(k-1)$, and, if $\mathbf{B}(k-1)$ is indecomposable, that $SD\mathbf{b}(k-1)S^{-1} \neq SD\mathbf{b}(k)S^{-1}$. The eigenvectors and so the equilibrium structure of production corresponding to $\mathbf{B}(k)$ and $\mathbf{B}(k-1)$ will be different. So if $\mathbf{q}(k)[\mathbf{I} - \mathbf{A}(k)] > 0$ does not imply that $\mathbf{B}(k) = \mathbf{B}(0)$ for all $k \geq 0$, $\lim_{k \to \infty} \mathbf{q}(k)$ will not be an eigenvector of $\mathbf{B}(0)$.□

2. Ecological sustainability and environmental control

1 INTRODUCTION

It has become natural to think of environmental management as a problem of 'the control of resources' – to borrow the title of Dasgupta's (1982) text. Formally, the optimal control problem involves the maximization (or minimization) of some index of performance as a function of a set of state variables and control inputs, subject to the constraint posed by the natural dynamics of those state variables. There is an obvious correspondence between this and an economic problem involving the maximization of some measure of welfare (or the minimization of some measure of social cost) through the appropriation of environmental goods and services, subject to the natural dynamics of the environment. Indeed, since the important contributions of Clark (1976) and V.L. Smith (1977) the control approach to the management of renewable environmental resources has become both standard and standardized. It is now possible to point to a substantial control literature on the management of a wide range of biophysical stocks based on a well-recognized set of bioeconomic models. The optimal rate of harvest of fish species or other forms of wildlife, optimal stocking densities on rangeland, optimal felling or rotation of forests, the optimal depletion or drawoff of groundwater, optimal soil conservation and the optimal provision of wildlife reserves have, for example, all been analysed in these terms. Natural resource economics has become, in a very real sense, an application of optimal control theory (compare Conrad and Clark, 1987).

It is not, therefore, surprising that optimal control theory should provide a natural framework within which to address recent concern over the sustainability of resource use. What makes it particularly suitable is that it compels us to incorporate the dynamics of the environmental processes involved. In addition, where the effect of economic activity on the state of the environment feeds back into the decision-making process, the control framework ensures that we are confronted by the future environmental impacts of present activities. Perhaps the strongest argument for the application of a control approach to the sustainability problem is, however, a negative one. The framework compels us to think not only about what may be controlled, but also about what may not be controlled. And an understanding of the limits of environmental control would seem to be a crucial part of the development of an optimal policy.

This chapter harnesses the control framework to an analysis of the issues raised by the notion that an ecologically sustainable development strategy requires the preservation of the natural capital stock. It considers the structural and informational conditions necessary to satisfy a sustainability condition of this sort through an optimal control policy. These are given by the sufficient conditions for optimal control of the system. It also considers the potential for preservation of the natural capital stock where system controllability cannot be guaranteed. Since little attention has been paid to the nature of control solutions in economy–environment systems that are only partly controllable or partly observable, we still know relatively little about this aspect of environmental control. The chapter shows that while the preservation of natural capital is dependent on the controllability and (stochastic) predictability of the global system – neither of which can be guaranteed – it is possible to identify a control policy which will protect against the decline of current natural capital stocks irrespective of the controllability of the global system.

The chapter is divided into seven sections. The following section offers a general formulation of the environmental control problem in a market economy. Section 3 then reviews the requirement for the preservation of natural capital in terms of the Hicks/Lindahl theory of income from which it derives, and describes the conditions that the requirement imposes on the control problem. Section 4 derives the necessary and sufficient conditions for the optimization of a control problem of this form in the absence of uncertainty, and indicates the structural conditions for the controllability of the global system. Section 5 addresses the question of uncertainty, and indicates the informational requirements of optimal control in systems subject to uncertainty. Section 6 considers how the preservation of natural capital may be addressed in a global system that is neither controllable nor (stochastically) predictable. A final section offers a few concluding remarks.

2   FORMULATING THE ENVIRONMENTAL CONTROL PROBLEM

We are looking for a general formulation of the environmental control problem. Let us first define an n-dimensional state vector, $\mathbf{x}(t)$, which describes the set of all physical resources available to the system at time t. That is, $\mathbf{x}(t)$ includes both natural or environmental resources and manufactured or produced resources. The initial state of the system is denoted $\mathbf{x}(0)$ and its evolution over the interval

[0,*T*] is denoted by the state history, [$\mathbf{x}(t)$, $0 \le t \le T$]. The state history is accordingly a function of both natural and economic processes.

To begin with, we will ignore the problem of uncertainty. This is purely for expositional purposes, and we shall later relax the assumption. The dynamics of the state variables in the absence of uncertainty may be defined by the ordinary vector differential equation

$$\dot{\mathbf{x}}(t) = \mathbf{f}[\mathbf{x}(t), \mathbf{u}(t), t], \qquad 0 \le t \le T, \qquad (2.1)$$

in which $\mathbf{x}(t)$ has already been defined, and $\mathbf{u}(t)$, an *m*-dimensional 'control' vector, denotes the allocation of resources by the economic agents in the system. As the economic resources recorded in $\mathbf{u}(t)$ are a subset of the total resource base, *m* is strictly less than *n*. In the absence of uncertainty, $\mathbf{x}(t)$ and $\mathbf{u}(t)$ are known at each moment.

Equation (2.1) defines the 'equations of motion' of the system. For given initial conditions,

$$\mathbf{x}(0) = \mathbf{x}_0, \qquad (2.2)$$

it implies the state trajectory: $\mathbf{x}(t) = \mathbf{x}_0 + \int_0^T \mathbf{f}[\mathbf{x}(t), \mathbf{u}(t), t]dt; 0 \le t \le T$.

As formalized here, the general problem of optimal environmental control is to find that 'control' history, [$\mathbf{u}(t), 0 \le t \le T$], which maximizes some index of social welfare (to be defined later) over the interval [0,*T*], subject to constraints designed to assure the sustainability of the system. To clarify the meaning of 'control' in this context, note that while it is assumed that there exists an environmental authority, and while the environmental authority is defined as the control authority, it is not assumed that the environmental authority directs the allocative decisions of resource users. In a market economy $\mathbf{u}(t)$ summarizes the independent behaviour of all economic agents in the system. Nevertheless, the environmental authority is assumed to have the capacity to intervene in the decision-making processes of individual resource users in two ways: through the use of economic instruments which influence the current price of resource use (such as taxes, subsidies or charges), and through the use of regulatory instruments which restrict the current aggregate level of resource use (such as emission/extraction quotas, whether these are directly allocated or subject to tradable permits). It is beyond the scope of this chapter to discuss the more subtle differences between these two classes of control instrument. As a review of the US literature in the area (Cropper and Oates, 1989) has argued, there is enormous diversity in both economic incentives and regulatory instruments,[1] and the dividing line between them is not always clear. The way in which each instrument appears in the control problem in this chapter will accordingly imply a cleaner distinction than may be warranted in practice. The important point is, though, that given uncertainty in the system the two classes of instrument are not symmetrical.[2]

To understand the role of economic incentives in this formulation of the control problem, notice that it is taken as axiomatic that the allocation of economic resources is a function of the set of prices confronting resource users. Hence, the allocative decisions of resource users may be influenced by changing the price set. To capture this, we assume that there exists a control function,

$$\mathbf{u}(t) = \mathbf{u}[\mathbf{k}, \mathbf{p}(t), t], \quad 0 \leq t \leq T, \tag{2.3}$$

in which the arguments include both a non-zero m-dimensional vector of market prices, $\mathbf{p}(t)$, which are beyond the direct reach of the environmental authority, and a k-dimensional vector of economic incentives or control parameters, $\mathbf{k}$, which are not. It is supposed that $k \leq m$. The control parameters include, for example, standard Pigovian taxes or subsidies, user charges, licence fees, fines and other levies. The vector k is accordingly not restricted as to sign, and has the effect of modifying the price set confronting resource users: that is, it changes the structure of incentives. Given this, we can be more precise about the nature of the control problem. To the extent that environmental control is exercised through economic incentives it implies a parametric optimization problem. Social welfare is maximized by choice of $\mathbf{k}$, not by choice of $\mathbf{u}(t)$ directly.

The price vector $\mathbf{p}(t)$ describes the set of intertemporally efficient prices for all economic resources at time t, exclusive of the effects of environmental taxes, subsidies or charges. A price path, $\{\mathbf{p}(t)\}$, is said to be intertemporally efficient if and only if it satisfies a generalized Hotelling rule, under which the equilibrium price of undepleted/undepreciated/undegraded resources rises at a rate equal to the marginal productivity of capital. Equilibrium relative prices are assumed to reflect: (a) the set of property rights; (b) preferences (consumption technology), and manufactured production possibilities (production technology); and (c) the set of biophysical and geochemical processes that determine the productivity of the natural environment. All three factors are subsumed in a function $\mathbf{p}[.]$, the arguments of which are the set of all real resources in the system. That is

$$\mathbf{p}(t) = \mathbf{p}[\mathbf{x}(t), t], \quad 0 \leq t \leq T, \tag{2.4}$$

The main implication of this is that the weights governing the allocation of economic resources in the absence of environmental control is a function of the general state of nature, $\mathbf{x}(t)$. Indeed, an immediate corollary is that a constant state of nature is sufficient to ensure constant relative prices. That is, since

$\dot{\mathbf{p}}(t) = \mathbf{p_x}\dot{\mathbf{x}}(t)$, $\dot{\mathbf{p}}(t) = 0$ if $\dot{\mathbf{x}}(t) = 0$. Note that if $\dot{\mathbf{x}}(t) = 0$ the marginal productivity of capital is also equal to zero, and intertemporal efficiency is satisfied with a constant set of prices. Given the dependence of $\mathbf{p}(t)$ on $\mathbf{x}(t)$ we may characterize the environmental control problem as a closed-loop, or feedback, parametric optimization problem.

The index of performance in this closed-loop parametric optimization problem is assumed to be a measure of welfare. Specifically it is assumed that the problem is to maximize:

$$J = W[\mathbf{x}(T), T]e^{-\delta(T)T} + \int_0^T Y[\mathbf{x}(t), \mathbf{u}(t), t]e^{-\delta(t)t}dt, \qquad (2.5)$$

in which $W[\cdot]$ and $Y[\cdot]$ are strictly concave continuous functions defining social preference orderings over the set of all feasible $\mathbf{x}(t)$. $e^{-\delta(t)t}$ is a discount factor, with $\delta(t)$ a rate of discount equal to the marginal productivity of capital. $\delta(t)$ is accordingly beyond the reach of the control authority. The vectors $\mathbf{x}(t)$ and $\mathbf{u}(t)$ have already been defined.

Equation (2.5) indicates that we are dealing with a problem of Bolza, since welfare is assumed to be an algebraic function of the terminal value of the state variables, and an integral function of the state and the control variables over the whole period. The first function, $W[\cdot]$, represents the discounted 'bequest' value of both produced and natural assets left at the end of the period. Although the term is misleading in this context, it is what is sometimes referred to as the 'scrap' value of the global asset base. The second function, $Y[\cdot]$, represents the discounted flow of benefits deriving from the use of those assets in economic activity over the interval $[0,T]$. The use of the Bolza form of the problem does not involve any loss of generality, since it can be shown that a benefit function of the Bolza type can be transformed into a function with only a terminal benefit (of the Mayer type), or one with only an integral term (of the Lagrange type). It is useful primarily because it is intuitive, and fits well with the way in which the environmental problem is currently perceived. A common ethical strand in current debates on sustainable development is the necessity to ensure that the welfare of future generations is not prejudiced by the use we currently make of environmental resources. It is an idea that naturally bears many interpretations, and this is reflected in the variants of the concept of sustainability that inform this chapter. However, all of these share some notion of intergenerational equity that extends beyond the self-interest which drives overlapping generation models. At the same time, it is recognized that there are trade-offs in the welfare gains from exploiting the environment on the one side, and conserving it on the other. The less significant is $W[\cdot]$ relative $Y[\cdot]$, the more society weights the welfare gains from current income relative to the conservation of the asset base.

3 SUSTAINABILITY AND PRESERVATION OF NATURAL CAPITAL

At the core of the dominant economic approach to sustainability is the Hicks/Lindahl concept of income. Recall that Hicks (1946) had defined income to be the maximum amount which could be spent on consumption in one period without reducing real consumption expenditure in future periods. This has a fairly immediate and obvious implication in terms of the conservation of the asset base. If income is the maximum consumption expenditure that leaves society as well endowed at the end of a period as at the begining, it implies (a) the conservation of the value of the asset base, and hence (b) compensating expenditures to cover the depreciation or degradation of that base. But it also has interesting ethical implications. The only social welfare function that authorizes a strategy designed to yield a maximum sustainable level of consumption expenditure is an intertemporally egalitarian social welfare function.

This intuitive relation between the maximization of minimum period income (to serve an egalitarian intertemporal social welfare function) and the preservation of the asset base was formally demonstrated by Solow (1974, 1986), Hartwick (1977, 1978a, 1978b) and Dixit et al. (1980). All showed that given production functions with the requisite substitution properties, it would be possible to hold consumption constant despite the extraction of exhaustible resources if and only if all resource rents were reinvested in reproducible assets to maintain the total stock of capital. Given the requirements of the Hotelling rule, a corollary of this is that investment should be such as to maintain the value of the total capital stock (at optimal prices) (Solow, 1986; Mäler, 1990).

Notice that the maintenance of a constant stream of income over an infinite horizon despite the use of essential non-renewable resources is critically dependent on the interpretation given to the term 'essential', and on the substitution properties of the aggregate production function employed. Solow (1974) and Hartwick (1977, 1978a) defined an input to a process to be 'essential' if its absence implied that there could be no output from the process. At first blush this looks like a reasonable definition. It implies that in addition to any other properties of the production function, if the i-th input is essential $f[\mathbf{x}(t)] = 0$ if $x_i = 0$ for all t. It turns out, though, that whether or not the assumption that inputs are essential in this sense implies any real constraint on output depends on the remaining properties of the production function, including the substitution possibilities assumed to exist between inputs. Where the production function chosen to characterize global productive activity is Cobb–Douglas (constant elasticity of substitution (CES) with an elasticity of substitution equal to unity) as it is in Solow (1974) and Hartwick (1977, 1978a), we have the property that the average product of an essential resource has no upper bound.

As the resource tends to zero, its average product may tend to infinity, implying that its exhaustion does not constrain aggregate output in any meaningful way. Where the production function is CES with an elasticity of substitution between exhaustible resources and produced capital greater than unity, as it is in Hartwick (1978b), the exhaustion of natural resources means nothing because they cannot be essential.

The maintenance of constant consumption over an infinite time horizon in these models accordingly depends on an extraordinarily powerful set of technological assumptions, which bear no relation to the dynamic properties of real physical systems. The assumption that there exists effectively unlimited potential for substitution between natural and produced resources contradicts everything that is currently understood about the evolution of thermodynamic systems, about the complementarity of resources in system structure and the importance of diversity in system resilience (Georgescu-Roegen, 1971; Daly, 1977, 1990; Holling, 1973, 1986; Kay, 1990). Since it is assumed by Solow and Hartwick that technology is stationary and given, it is *a fortiori* assumed that the potential exists now for such substitutability. None would deny that there is some scope for substitution between produced and natural capital, but to assert that the potential for substitution is unlimited is nothing short of absurd.

It is now well understood that ecosystems tend to be locally stable over defined ranges of the biophysical stocks that comprise their component parts, and they become unstable if the biophysical stocks rise above or fall below some critical threshold. In any ecosystem having evolved a particular self-organization, there exist values of the resources involved which are 'thermodynamically' possible but which are incompatible with that self-organization. Whenever the resources of such an ecosystem are driven past certain threshold values, the system will switch from one 'thermodynamic path' to another, from one self-organization to another. Threshold values exist, for example, for the diversity of species in an ecosystem. While there may be a range of population sizes for the different species in an ecosystem over which the system remains stable, if any one population in an ecosystem falls below its critical threshold level the self-organization of the ecosystem as a whole will be radically and irreversibly altered (compare Pielou, 1975). Threshold values also exist for overall regressive succession; standing crop biomass; energy flows to grazing and decomposer food chains; mineral micro-nutrient stocks and so on (compare Schaeffer et al., 1988). Any point where the self-organizing forces of an ecosystem balance the 'disorganizing' forces of its environment is said to be an optimum operating point of that ecosystem (Kay, 1989). The climax community in an ecosystem accordingly represents such an optimum operating point. The integrity of an ecosystem is measured by its ability to maintain its self-organization through selection of a different operating point along the same thermodynamic path: that is, without undergoing the 'catastrophic' and irreversible change involved in a switch from one thermodynamic path to another. Since catastrophic change in one ecosystem necessarily changes the level of stress on other systems with which it interacts, economic activity that imposes unsustainable levels of stress on the natural environment may generate feedback effects which are themselves catastrophic.

In recognition of the incompatibility of these properties of biophysical systems and the technological assumptions of the more formal treatments of sustainable income, a view has been developed – largely due to Pearce – that the requirement for the conservation of the value of the capital stock be strengthened to include the preservation of at least components of the natural capital stock in physical terms (compare Pearce, 1987, 1988; Pearce et al., 1989; Barbier et al., 1990; Pearce and Turner, 1990). In one version of this, Pearce argues that this should take the form of a restriction on the rate of extraction of renewable resources to a rate no greater than the regeneration rate (Pearce, 1987). Elsewhere, he argues that given the high degree of uncertainty about the role of many resources in the ecosystem, and given the potential for inflicting irreversible damage through overexploitation of those resources, it is in any case prudent to conserve existing stocks 'until we have a clearer understanding of what the optimal stock is' (Pearce and Turner, 1990). It is possible to interpret the first of these as a requirement that current stocks of natural capital be maintained within the threshold levels of ecosystem stability as these are presently understood. The second is simply a requirement that the level of certain natural capital stocks should be the same at the end of the planning period as at the beginning.

Both interpretations create theoretical difficulties for the Solow/Hartwick approach which need not concern us here. What does concern us is what each implies for the general environmental control problem described in Section 2. The preservation of the natural capital stock is the more straightforward. It implies a terminal boundary condition on a subset of the resources in the global system. Specifically, it requires that a q-dimensional vector function of the terminal state,

$$\mathbf{g}[\mathbf{x}(T), T] = 0 \qquad (2.6)$$

should have prescribed values, $q < n$. Notice that it is not implied that the terminal boundary condition implies an inviolate restriction on current economic activity. That is to say, it is neither a regulatory instrument governing current aggregate levels of resource use, nor an economic instrument affecting current resource prices. It may be interpreted as a target set of resource values judged by the environmental authority to be a necessity if future generations are to have the same opportunities as the present generation. If the particular control instruments used by the environmental authority are effective, then it will be possible to satisfy (2.6). This will be referred to as a natural capital boundary condition.

The requirement that current stocks of natural capital be maintained within the threshold levels of ecosystem stability does imply that the environmental authority should constrain current levels of economic activity. Specifically, it implies control over the level of extraction of resources in order to maintain the stability of the ecosystems to which they belong. Formally, such regulation implies an *m*-dimensional vector inequality constraint on the state and control histories:

$$\mathbf{h}[\mathbf{x}(t), \mathbf{u}(t), t] \leq 0, \quad 0 \leq t \leq T. \tag{2.7}$$

Notice that this allows for either one-sided or two-sided bounds on the variable in question, depending on the specification of **h**. So, for example, $(u_i - u_{max}) \leq 0$ defines an upper bound on allocation of the *i*-th resource; $(u_{min} - u_i) \leq 0$ defines a lower bound; and $(u_i - u_{max})(u_i - u_{min}) \leq 0$ defines both upper and lower bounds. In general, the restriction on the state variables would take the form of a lower bound: $(x_{min} - x_i) \leq 0$. Equation (2.7) will be referred to as a sustainability constraint. This completes the description of the main elements of the control problem in the absence of uncertainty.

4   THE STRUCTURAL LIMITS TO ENVIRONMENTAL CONTROL

The general objective in the environmental control problem in market economies is to find that set of control parameters (or incentives) which will maximize the index of social welfare, subject to the system dynamics, as well as the natural capital boundary condition and natural capital constraint. The elements of a general control problem of this form are summarized in (2.8a) to (2.8g). Maximize$_\mathbf{k}$

$$J = W[\mathbf{x}(T), T]e^{-\delta T} + \int_0^T Y[\mathbf{x}(t), \mathbf{u}(t), t]e^{-\delta t}dt \tag{2.8a}$$

subject to

$$\dot{\mathbf{x}}(t) = \mathbf{f}[\mathbf{x}(t), \mathbf{u}(t), t], \quad 0 \leq t \leq T, \tag{2.8b}$$

$$\mathbf{g}[\mathbf{x}(T), T] = 0. \tag{2.8c}$$

$$\mathbf{h}[\mathbf{x}(t), \mathbf{u}(t), t] \leq 0 \quad 0 \leq t \leq T, \tag{2.8d}$$

$$\mathbf{x}(0) = \mathbf{x}_0, \tag{2.8e}$$

with

$$\mathbf{u}(t) = \mathbf{u}[\mathbf{k}, \mathbf{p}(t), t] \quad 0 \le t \le T, \qquad (2.8\text{f})$$

$$\mathbf{p}(t) = \mathbf{p}[\mathbf{x}(t), t] \quad 0 \le t \le T. \qquad (2.8\text{g})$$

Taking the problem in this form let us first consider the structural limits to environmental control. To approach this question, it is useful to begin by abstracting both from the natural capital boundary condition, (2.8c), and the sustainability constraint, (2.8d). We will therefore start by ignoring these equations, and to make it clear what is going on will index the reduced problem by the subscript '0'.

Bearing in mind that the chapter is concerned with what is fundamentally a methodological question raised by the sustainability debate – the limits of control under constraints of this sort – it is useful to offer a more complete derivation of the necessary and sufficient conditions for optimality than usual. Adjoining (2.8b), the equations of motion, to the reduced form of the benefit or welfare function, which we denote J_0, by the multiplier vector $\lambda_0'(t)$ (the prime denoting a transpose) we have the augmented function

$$\begin{aligned} J_0^+ = &W[\mathbf{x}(T), T]e^{-\delta T} + \int_0^T [Y(\mathbf{x}(t), \mathbf{u}(t), t]e^{-\delta t} \\ &+ \lambda_0'(t)\{\mathbf{f}[\mathbf{x}(t), \mathbf{u}(t), t] - \dot{\mathbf{x}}(t)\}]dt. \end{aligned} \qquad (2.9)$$

The Hamiltonian for the problem is

$$H_0[\mathbf{x}(t), \mathbf{u}(t), \lambda_0(t), t] = Y[\mathbf{x}(t), \mathbf{u}(t), t]e^{-\delta t} + \lambda_0'(t)\mathbf{f}[\mathbf{x}(t), \mathbf{u}(t), t]$$

implying that J_0^+ may be written in the form

$$J_0^+ = W[\mathbf{x}(T), T]e^{-\delta T} + \int_0^T \{H_0[\cdot] - \lambda_0'(t)\dot{\mathbf{x}}(t)\}dt$$

or, after integrating the last term on the RHS by parts

$$\begin{aligned} J_0^+ = &W[\mathbf{x}(T), T]e^{-\delta T} + \int_0^T \{H_0[\cdot] + \dot{\lambda}_0'(t)\mathbf{x}(t)\}dt \\ &- [\lambda_0'(T)\mathbf{x}(T) - \lambda_0'(0)\mathbf{x}(0)]. \end{aligned} \qquad (2.10)$$

Now the first variation of this function with respect to the control parameters is given by

$$\Delta J_0^+ = [W_x(t)e^{-\delta t} - \lambda_0'(T)]\Delta x(\Delta k) +$$
$$\int_0^T \{[Y_k e^{-\delta t} + \lambda_0'(t)F_k(t)]\Delta k + [Y_x(t)e^{-\delta t} + \lambda_0'(t)F_x(t) + \dot{\lambda}_0'(t)]\Delta x(\Delta k)\}dt$$

or

$$\Delta J_0^+ = [W_x(t)e^{-\delta t} - \lambda_0'(T)]\Delta x(\Delta k) + \int_0^T \{H_{0k}[\cdot]\Delta k$$
$$+ [H_{0x}[\cdot] + \dot{\lambda}_0'(t)]\Delta x(\Delta k)\}dt \qquad (2.11)$$

where $H_{0k}[\cdot] = \{\partial H_0[\cdot]/\partial k\}$, and $H_{0x}[\cdot] = \{\partial H_0[\cdot]/\partial x\}$. Selecting values of $\lambda_0(T)$ that will ensure that $[W_x(t)e^{-\delta t} - \lambda_0'(T)]$ and $[H_{0x}[\cdot] + \dot{\lambda}_0'(t)]$ are equal to zero, yields the first two necessary conditions for a maximum of J_0:

$$\dot{\lambda}_0'(t) = -H_{0x}[\cdot] = -Y_x(t)e^{-\delta t} - \lambda_0'(t)F_x(t) \qquad (2.12)$$

and

$$\lambda_0'(T) = W_x(t)e^{-\delta t}. \qquad (2.13)$$

Substituting these values into (2.11) reduces the first variation to

$$\Delta J_0^+ = \int_0^T \{H_{0k}[\cdot]\Delta k\}dt \qquad (2.14)$$

from which it is immediate that the benefit function will only be at a maximum if

$$H_{0k}[\cdot] = Y_k e^{-\delta t} + \lambda_0'(t)F_k(t) = 0 \qquad (2.15)$$

where

$$Y_k = \left\{\frac{\partial Y[\cdot]}{\partial u}\right\}\left\{\frac{\partial u[\cdot]}{\partial k}\right\},$$

$$F_k = \left\{\frac{\partial f[\cdot]}{\partial u}\right\}\left\{\frac{\partial u[\cdot]}{\partial k}\right\},$$

$$Y_x = \left\{\left[\frac{\partial Y[\cdot]}{\partial x}\right] + \left[\frac{\partial Y[\cdot]}{\partial u}\right]\left[\frac{\partial u[\cdot]}{\partial p}\right]\left[\frac{\partial p[\cdot]}{\partial x}\right]\right\},$$

$$F_x = \left\{\left[\frac{\partial f[\cdot]}{\partial x}\right] + \left[\frac{\partial f[\cdot]}{\partial u}\right]\left[\frac{\partial u[\cdot]}{\partial p}\right]\left[\frac{\partial p[\cdot]}{\partial x}\right]\right\}, \text{ and}$$

$$W_x = \left\{\frac{\partial W[\cdot]}{\partial x}\right\}.$$

The partial derivatives of the vectors **f**, **u** and **p** are conformably dimensioned Jacobian matrices. The partial derivatives of Y and W are conformably dimensioned row vectors. Equations (2.12) (2.13) and (2.15), the Euler–Lagrange equations, give the necessary conditions on $\lambda_0(t)$, $H_{0\mathbf{k}}[\cdot]$ and $H_{0\mathbf{x}}[\cdot]$ if all parts of the first variation are to be equal to zero in the neighbourhood of an optimal trajectory. Equation (2.12) gives alternative formulations of the adjoint equation. The adjoint vector, $\lambda_0'(T)$, obtained by integration back in time from the terminal or transversality condition (2.13), measures the sensitivity of the benefit function to perturbations in the state variables along an optimal trajectory at time t. The i-th component of the adjoint vector accordingly denotes the marginal benefit of the i-th resource available to the system along that trajectory. Equation (2.15) similarly gives alternative formulations of the maximum condition. It requires that the partial derivatives of the benefit function with respect to the parameters in the control function are zero when evaluated along an optimal trajectory.

Now consider what satisfaction of these conditions does and does not assure. Both the maximum condition and the adjoint vector are concerned with the impact of perturbations of the state variables and the control parameters, respectively, evaluated *along an optimal trajectory*. That is, they are estimated at $\mathbf{x}(t) = \mathbf{x}^*(t)$, and $\mathbf{k} = \mathbf{k}^*$. This implies that both are local, not global conditions. Satisfaction of (2.15) is required if the Hamiltonian is to be stationary with respect to variation in the control parameters along an optimal path, but it implies nothing about the existence of other optimal paths. Put another way, the existence of a set of incentives that maximizes social welfare while satisfying the equations of motion along some optimal development path does not mean that there are no other such paths. There may well be other optimal development paths that dominate the path for which the necessary conditions given in equations (2.12), (2.13) and (2.15) are satisfied. Second, and more importantly, the Euler–Lagrange equations are necessary, not sufficient conditions. Satisfaction of these equations says nothing about whether or not a locally optimal trajectory is in fact attainable. In the context of the particular problem discussed in this chapter, satisfaction of these equations says nothing about the ability of a control authority to use a form of parametric control to guide the system.

It is worth emphasizing this point because of the very casual way that sufficiency in the control problem is treated in the environmental control literature, and yet it is at the core of the problem. To address this, let us expand the problem by activating the natural capital boundary condition and consider whether or not it is possible to satisfy this condition through parametric control of the global system. To do this, let us take (2.8c) separately, and define the q-dimensional discounted vector function of terminal benefits associated with the conditions

$$\mathbf{J}_1 = \mathbf{g}[\mathbf{x}(T),\, T]e^{-\delta T}.$$

Adjoining the equations of motion to this by Λ_1', a $q \times n$ matrix formed from n q-vectors of Lagrangian multipliers corresponding to each of the terminal conditions in (2.8c), yields the augmented terminal benefit function

$$\mathbf{J}_1^+ = \mathbf{g}[\mathbf{x}(T),\, T]e^{-\delta \tau} + \int_0^T \Lambda_1'(t)\{\mathbf{f}[\mathbf{x}(t),\, \mathbf{u}(t),\, t] - \dot{\mathbf{x}}(t)\}dt. \qquad (2.16)$$

The corresponding Hamiltonian is then a component of the q-dimensional column vector

$$\mathbf{H}_1[\mathbf{x}(t),\, \mathbf{u}(t),\, \Lambda_1(t),\, t] = \Lambda_1'(t)\mathbf{f}[\cdot].$$

Hence $\mathbf{J}_1^+$ may be written in the form

$$\mathbf{J}_1^+ = \mathbf{g}[\mathbf{x}(T),\, T]e^{-\delta \tau} + \int_0^T \{\mathbf{H}_1[\cdot] + \dot{\Lambda}_1'(t)\mathbf{x}(t)\}dt - [\Lambda_1'(T)\mathbf{x}(T) - \Lambda_1'(0)\mathbf{x}(0)]. \qquad (2.17)$$

Proceeding as before, the first variation of (2.17) with respect to the control parameters is

$$\Delta \mathbf{J}_1^+ = [\mathbf{g}_\mathbf{x}e^{-\delta \tau} - \Lambda_1'(T)]\Delta\mathbf{x}(\Delta\mathbf{k}) + \int_0^T \{\Lambda'(t)\mathbf{F}_\mathbf{k}(t)\Delta\mathbf{k}$$
$$+ [\Lambda_1'(t)\mathbf{F}_\mathbf{x}(t) + \dot{\Lambda}_1'(t)]\Delta\mathbf{x}(\Delta\mathbf{k})\}dt$$

or

$$\Delta \mathbf{J}_1^+ = [\mathbf{g}_\mathbf{x}e^{-\delta \tau} - \Lambda_1'(T)]\Delta\mathbf{x}(\Delta\mathbf{k}) + \int_0^T \{\mathbf{H}_{1\mathbf{k}}[\cdot]\Delta\mathbf{k} + [\mathbf{H}_{1\mathbf{x}}[\cdot] + \dot{\Lambda}_1'(t)]\Delta\mathbf{x}(\Delta\mathbf{k})\}dt. \qquad (2.18)$$

Once again, selecting values for Λ_1 that will force the coefficients of $\Delta\mathbf{x}$ to zero implies that

$$\dot{\Lambda}_1'(t) = -\mathbf{H}_{1\mathbf{x}}[\cdot] \qquad (2.19)$$

and

$$\mathbf{g}_\mathbf{x}e^{-\delta \tau} = \Lambda_1'(T). \qquad (2.20)$$

This reduces equation (2.18) to

$$\Delta \mathbf{J}_1^+ = \int_0^T \{\mathbf{H}_{1\mathbf{k}}[\cdot]\Delta\mathbf{k}\}dt. \qquad (2.21)$$

If we now adjoin (2.21) to the first variation of the benefit function, J_0, with a vector of Lagrange multipliers, μ', the first variation of the general benefit function, J, is

$$\Delta J = \Delta J_0^+ + \mu' \Delta J_1^+ = \int_0^T \{ H_{0\mathbf{k}}[\cdot] \Delta \mathbf{k} + \mu' \mathbf{H}_{1\mathbf{k}}[\cdot] \Delta \mathbf{k} \} dt \qquad (2.22)$$

implying that on the optimal trajectory

$$H_{\mathbf{k}}[\cdot] = Y_{\mathbf{k}} e^{-\delta t} + \lambda_0'(t) \mathbf{F}_{\mathbf{k}}(t) + \mu' \Lambda_1'(t) \mathbf{F}_{\mathbf{k}}(t) = 0. \qquad (2.23)$$

We are now in a position to identify the structural conditions for the (parametric) controllability of the global system. To do this select $\Delta \mathbf{k} = \kappa H_{\mathbf{k}}[\cdot]'$ $= \kappa[Y_{\mathbf{k}}' e^{-\delta t} + \mathbf{F}_{\mathbf{k}}'(t) \lambda_0(t) + \mathbf{F}_{\mathbf{k}}'(t) \Lambda_1(t) \mu]$, where κ is a small positive constant, and substitute this into (2.21). We then have

$$\Delta J_1^+ = \kappa \int_0^T \{ \Lambda_1'(t) \mathbf{F}_{\mathbf{k}}(t) [Y_{\mathbf{k}}' e^{-\delta t} + \mathbf{F}_{\mathbf{k}}(t)' \lambda_0(t)] \} dt$$
$$+ \kappa \int_0^T \{ \Lambda_1'(t) \mathbf{F}_{\mathbf{k}}(t) \mathbf{F}_{\mathbf{k}}'(t) \Lambda_1(t) \mu \} dt. \qquad (2.24)$$

This variation must be equal to zero along an optimal trajectory enabling us to solve the equation for the vector of Lagrange multipliers corresponding to the terminal boundary conditions, μ', providing certain structural conditions are satisfied. Specifically, defining the matrix

$$\mathbf{Q} = \int_0^T \{ \Lambda_1'(t) \mathbf{F}_{\mathbf{k}}(t) \mathbf{F}_{\mathbf{k}}'(t) \Lambda_1(t) \} dt \qquad (2.25)$$

and the vector

$$\mathbf{r} = \int_0^T \{ \Lambda_1'(t) \mathbf{F}_{\mathbf{k}}(t) [Y_{\mathbf{k}}' e^{-\delta t} + \mathbf{F}_{\mathbf{k}}'(t) \lambda_0(t)] \} dt \qquad (2.26)$$

it follows that

$$\mu = - \mathbf{Q}^{-1} \mathbf{r}. \qquad (2.27)$$

That is, it is possible to find μ providing that $\mathbf{Q}^{-1}$ exists.

The invertibility of $\mathbf{Q}$ depends upon the rank of the constituent matrices: $\Lambda_1'(t)$, $\Lambda_1(t)$, $\mathbf{F}_{\mathbf{k}}(t)$ and $\mathbf{F}_{\mathbf{k}}'(t)$. The first two of these matrices are $q \times n$ and $n \times q$ respectively, while the last two are $n \times k$ and $k \times n$. So the dimension of $\mathbf{Q}$ is $q \times q$. If the constituent matrices are of full rank, this implies that the maximum rank of $\mathbf{Q}$ is the lesser of q and k (since $n > k, q$). Hence $\mathbf{Q}^{-1}$ exists if and only if $k \geq q$. If this inequality is satisfied, a set of optimizing control parameters can be chosen to satisfy the economic sustainability condition. If $k < q$, $\mathbf{Q}^{-1}$ will not exist, and it will not be possible to choose such parameters. One familiar implication of this is that if the constituent matrices of $\mathbf{Q}$ are of full rank, the economy–environment system will be parametrically controllable only if there are at least as many control parameters as there are resources subject to a terminal boundary condition.

The existence of the inverse of $\mathbf{Q}$ is a sufficient condition for the optimality of the problem summarized in (2.8a) to (2.8c) and (2.8e) to (2.8g).[3] If $\mathbf{Q}^{-1}$ exists, the problem is said to be 'normal'. If $\mathbf{Q}^{-1}$ does not exist it is said to be 'abnormal'. It is this normality condition which is crucial if the natural capital boundary condition is to be satisfied. What the normality condition guarantees is that the system is structurally controllable through the vector of parameters, **k**. It is possible, through those parameters, to force the system to meet condition (2.8c). The fact that $\mathbf{Q}$ is of full rank in a normal problem ensures that there exists an independent path from every state variable of interest to at least one control parameter. In terms of the environmental control problem, this means that if $\mathbf{Q}^{-1}$ exists it is possible to influence the system through the set of price incentives described by the parameters of the control function in order to preserve all of those environmental resources that are held to be crucial to global sustainability. If $\mathbf{Q}^{-1}$ does not exist then manipulation of economic incentives will leave one or more such environmental resources untouched, and therefore unprotected from degradation due to economic activity.

It is difficult to overemphasize the importance of the normality condition in the environmental control problem under a sustainability constraint, yet the condition has been almost completely ignored in the literature on environmental control. In general, attention has been focused on a limited set of necessary conditions (given by the Euler–Lagrange equations). Where sufficiency has been considered, it has been limited to the Legendre–Clebsch condition. In general, however, the literature has simply assumed controllability. This is ironical given the weight placed on controllability questions in the earlier literature on macroeconomic stabilization (compare Aoki, 1976). Yet in the economics of environmental management it is a key question as to whether the price mechanism may be harnessed in the interests of environmentally sustainable development. It is by no means clear that the environmental control problem is 'normal'. Indeed, both the weight of evidence and the logic of economy–environment systems suggest otherwise (compare Perrings, 1987). But if it is not safe to assume that the problem is normal – that the dynamic system is controllable – then it becomes important to identify the limits to environmental control and the scope for achieving alternative environmental objectives.

5   UNCERTAINTY IN THE ENVIRONMENTAL CONTROL PROBLEM

The discussion of the necessary and sufficient conditions for optimality clarifies the structural limits to environmental control under conditions of certainty. We shall return to the problem of assuring the sustainability of non-controllable systems later. At this point, however, we turn to a second source of difficulty in the environmental control problem: the uncertainty associated with the system dynamics. There are two sources of difficulty here. The first is that in a feedback control problem optimality requires the continuous measurement of state variables, and available measures may be subject to error. The second is that the system dynamics may themselves be known imperfectly, implying that feedback control will necessarily be misdirected.

If we take the difficulty created by measurement error first, it is clear that not all measurement error is fatal from a control perspective. In many cases measures may be subject only to white noise (Gaussian error). A variety of filters exist to enable the propagation of state estimates with minimum error in such cases, and such filters tend to operate reasonably well if the system under analysis is linear. Non-linearities in the system complicate matters by the effect they have on error transmission through the system. The probability density functions for stochastic effects may, for example, change as those effects are transmitted through the system. But providing that the effects are small and additive, they may be partially filtered out of non-linear systems (Stengel, 1986). The problem is altogether more difficult if errors are large and non-Gaussian, and if they are not additive.

The difficulties created by misspecification of the system dynamics are much less tractable. The misspecification of the system increases the probability that both the measures sought and the controls applied will be inconsistent with the control objectives. It is increasingly being argued that system uncertainty in the environmental control problem extends well beyond Gaussian measurement errors, and includes basic misspecifications of system dynamics. Indeed, the technological assumptions that characterize the Solow/Hartwick models are simply incompatible with any reasonable approximation of the dynamics of the global system. The result is a very large element of fundamental uncertainty about both the measures and the dynamics of the system, implying that the control authority is simply unable to form realistic expectations about the distribution of future outcomes.

The main source of uncertainty appears to be the evolutionary nature of the global system. Not all evolution creates the same amount of difficulty. Faber and Proops (1990), for example, make the point that while genotypic evolution (evolution of genetic potential) which changes the development potential of interdependent species or ecosystems is in principle unpredictable, phenotypic evolution (evolution within a genotype in response to environmental change) is not. Failure to predict phenotypic evolutionary trends may be due to the product of ignorance about the functional structure of ecosystems, but failure to predict genotypic evolutionary trends is inherent in the nature of the changes involved. Genotypic evolution is accordingly the least tractable source of system uncertainty. From a thermodynamic perspective, such genotypic evolution may be interpreted in terms of the potential for self-organizing far-from-equilibrium thermodynamic systems to undergo essentially unforeseeable and 'catastrophic' switches from one thermodynamic branch to another (Kay, 1989, 1990).

The implication of this is that the environmental control problem involves very significant error that is likely to be beyond the reach of available filter techniques. It involves the potential for novel and entirely surprising outcomes. This is not to say that knowledge of the system, or at least of parts of the system, cannot be improved over time. Estimates of the distribution of possible environmental outcomes of economic activity may well be improved through, for example, a passive Bayesian learning process. But it does imply that there is likely to remain a very large measure of fundamental ignorance about the future effects of current actions.

To get a sense of the knowledge requirements in the optimal environmental control problem, it is useful to consider a formulation of the problem suitable for the case where there exists no unique optimal trajectory. This is the case both for stochastic systems and, *a fortiori*, for systems characterized by fundamental uncertainty. The approach used in such circumstances is dynamic programming. The benefit function adopted is identical to (2.8a) save that what is optimized is some expectation of terminal and integral benefits conditional on the available state of knowledge or information set. At time T this may be written:

$$J = E\{(W[\mathbf{x}(T), T]e^{-\delta T} + \int_0^T Y[\mathbf{x}(t), \mathbf{u}(t), t]e^{-\delta t}dt)|S[0,T]\} \qquad (2.28)$$

in which $S[0,T]$ is an information set at time T that summarizes realized indirect measures of the real resource base, $[\mathbf{p}(t), 0 \leq t \leq T]$; and realized allocations of real resources, $[\mathbf{u}(t), 0 \leq t \leq T]$. That is

$$S[0,T] = \{\mathbf{p}[0,T], \mathbf{u}[0,T]\}.$$

We first define a value function, V^*, associated with (2.28) which is equal to the discounted benefit derived from the optimal parametric control of the system for the period to go to the terminal time, T. So at at a time, t_1, during the interval $[0,T]$, V^* is defined by

$$V^*(t_1) = E\{(W[\mathbf{x}^*(T), T]e^{-\delta T} + \int_{t_1}^{T} Y[\mathbf{x}^*(t), \mathbf{u}^*(t), t]e^{-\delta t}dt)|S[0,t_1]\}$$

in which $\mathbf{u}^*(t) = \mathbf{u}[\mathbf{k}^*, \mathbf{p}(t), t]$. This may be written in the form

$$V^*(t_1) = E\{(W[\mathbf{x}^*(T), T]e^{-\delta T} - \int_{T}^{t_1} Y[\mathbf{x}^*(t), \mathbf{u}^*(t), t]e^{-\delta t}dt)|S[0,t_1]\}. \quad (2.29)$$

To identify the conditions in which V^* is at a maximum at t_1, we may first expand the time derivative of $V^*(t_1)$ in series. Suppressing time indices, we have:

$$\frac{dV^*}{dt}\Delta t = E\left\{\left(\frac{\partial V^*}{\partial t}\Delta t + \frac{\partial V^*}{\partial \mathbf{x}}\dot{\mathbf{x}}\Delta t + \frac{1}{2}\left[\dot{\mathbf{x}}'\frac{\partial^2 V^*}{\partial \mathbf{x}^2}\dot{\mathbf{x}}\right]\Delta t^2 + \cdots\right)\Big|S[0,t_1]\right\}. \quad (2.30)$$

Dividing through by Δt, and equating to the derivative of (2.29) with respect to time at t_1 yields

$$0 = \max_{\mathbf{k}} E\left\{\left(Y[\cdot]e^{\delta t} + \frac{\partial V^*}{\partial t} + \frac{\partial V^*}{\partial \mathbf{x}}\dot{\mathbf{x}} + \frac{1}{2}\left[\dot{\mathbf{x}}'\frac{\partial^2 V^*}{\partial \mathbf{x}^2}\dot{\mathbf{x}}\right]\Delta t + \cdots\right)\Big|S[0,t_1]\right\}. \quad (2.31)$$

For an optimum trajectory, the expectation in (2.31) should be maximized for the interval $[T, t_1]$ through choice of the parametric control vector $\mathbf{k}$, conditioned on the available information set available at time t_1. This implies that the starting point for the maximization of (2.31) is the terminal value

$$E\{(V^*[\mathbf{x}^*(T), T]\} = E\{W[\mathbf{x}^*(T), T]e^{-\delta tT})|S[0,T]\}. \quad (2.32)$$

That is, it is the optimal value of the resource base at the terminal time, $\mathbf{x}^*(T)$, conditioned on the information set available at the terminal time, $S[0,T]$.

The difficulty here is obvious. While the optimal value of $\mathbf{x}^*(T)$ (in a 'normal' problem) will satisfy the terminal boundary or economic sustainability condition, its calculation requires the information set $S[0,T]$. In other words it requires a state of knowledge that can only be available at time T. The knowledge that is available to the control authority at any time before T is less than the knowledge required to optimize the problem. Specifically, for any time t, $0 \leq t < T$, there exists an information set $S[t+,T]$, where $t+$ is a time just greater than t, which is required for the optimization of the trajectory of $\mathbf{x}(t)$, but which is not available to the control authority. There are two possibilities to consider here. If the conditioning effect of this information is fully predictable (and if structural conditions for the controllability of the system exist) then the stochastic control of the system may still be optimal, and the economic sustainability condition may be satisfied. If the conditioning effect of $S[t+,T]$ is not fully predictable and can only be approximated, then even if the system is controllable, the control will be suboptimal and sustainability cannot be guaranteed.

Given that the environmental system is characterized by fundamental uncertainty, the available information set does not include a sufficient profile of the statistical properties of the unavailable information set to predict its conditioning effect on the future behaviour of the system. This is partly because of the existence of novel developments whose implications for the time-behaviour of the system are unclear. In a far-from-equilibrium evolutionary system, the distribution of outcomes associated with such developments cannot be inferred from the history of the system, both because of the paucity of relevant observations, and because of the effect of novelty on the system parameters. But it is also because of the indirect, noisy and incomplete character of the system observers in a market economy: the price set.

Notice that there is a close connection between the incompleteness of markets and fundamental uncertainty. In the idealized abstract market economy of Walrasian economics, it can be shown that providing that preferences are convex, continuous and monotonic, and providing that production possibilities sets are closed, bounded and strictly convex, then given perfect information there exists an intertemporal general equilibrium allocation of resources such that all markets clear for all goods and services at each instant in time, and such that there is no other allocation preferred by all agents in the economy (it is Pareto efficient). If the price of any good or service is equal to zero at equilibrium, it will be in excess supply. In this idealized abstract market economy, either market prices are perfect environmental indicators or the environment in no way constrains the economy. In reality, ignorance about what is to come precludes all but the most rudimentary futures or contingent markets. Hence equilibria can exist only for current markets. Nor can these 'temporary equilibria' be efficient except under the artifice of rational expectations (expectations consistent with the clearing of all non-existent futures or contingent markets – which is itself a denial of ignorance). As a result, a zero price attaching to an environmental good or service signifies neither that it is in excess supply, nor that its current use involves no future costs. Nor does a positive price attaching to an economic good imply an accurate measure of the social opportunity cost of that good. There may be both current and future external costs of use, current costs comprising intersectoral external costs due to the interdependence of activities reliant on a common environment (damage done to third parties which is not compensated within the existing structure of property rights); future costs comprising 'user costs' or future opportunities forgone from committing a resource to a current use (costs imposed on future generations of committing a resource in a way that deprives future users of the benefit of its use).

The incompleteness of markets, the absence of well-defined property rights, a variety of policy interventions and the distortionary effects of poverty all reduce the informational value of prices, and increase the uncertainty associated with the future effects of current actions. This does not imply that statistical knowledge of the implications of novel developments cannot improve. But it does imply that stochastic optimization of environmental systems over anything but very short time horizons will not be feasible. Moreover, even over short time horizons, stochastic optimization of the system will not be feasible unless the available information set includes the statistical properties of the conditioning effect of yet-to-be acquired knowledge.

6 ECOLOGICAL SUSTAINABILITY IN THE CONTROL PROBLEM

The last two sections have sought to identify the key difficulties in satisfying a natural capital boundary condition – due both to the absence of the structural conditions for the controllability of the system, and to the existence of fundamental uncertainty. This does not imply that the cause of environmental control to assure ecological sustainability is lost, but it does imply the need for a different approach to the problem. To see what this might be, let us first observe that where a uniquely optimal trajectory is unattainable because the system is uncontrollable, it may still be possible to achieve a degree of system stability providing that the uncontrolled (and unobserved) processes of the environment are themselves stable. Now a system may be said to be stable if a bounded input generates a bounded response. So a given ecosystem may be said to be stable if the responses to bounded exactions on or insertions into that ecosystem are themselves bounded. System stability and system sustainability are accordingly closely linked concepts. If it is possible to achieve system stability, it will in general be possible to achieve system sustainability.[4]

The important point here is that ecosystems may be stable over certain parameter ranges only. Even if such ecosystems are not themselves controllable, therefore, sustainability of the global system may be assured only if exactions on or insertions into the uncontrollable ecosystems of the environment do not drive them beyond the parameter ranges within which they are stable. The crucial indicators here are the threshold values for the populations or stocks comprising an ecosystem beyond which ecosystem stability is lost. Providing that those populations or stocks are contained within those threshold values, the global system may be said to be stabilizable to the extent that is foreseeable given the available information set.

The role of the sustainability constraint, (2.8d), is to impose direct restrictions on resource-using economic activities in order to maintain populations/resource stocks within bounds that are judged to be consistent with the stability of the ecosystem concerned. To the extent that the bounds on economic activity imposed under the constraint refer to environmental processes that are not observable or are only imperfectly observable through the price system, they must depend on direct observation. This implies the use of physical indicators both of stocks and of change in ecosystem resilience such as the number of species in an ecosystem and the relative size and distribution of the population in each species relative to its critical threshold level (compare Pielou, 1975); or changes in overall regressive succession; standing crop biomass; relative energy flows to grazing and decomposer food chains; mineral micro-nutrient stocks; and the mechanisms of and capacity for damping oscillations (Schaeffer et al.,1988; di Castri, 1987). Formally, the addition of direct observations to the information set implies that the ecological sustainability constraint vector $\mathbf{h}[\mathbf{x}(t), \mathbf{u}(t), t] \leq 0$ would be conditioned on an information set

$$S_D[0,t] = \{\hat{\mathbf{x}}[0,t], \mathbf{p}[0,t], \mathbf{u}[0,t]\} \tag{2.33}$$

which includes a direct estimate of (components of) the resources base $\hat{\mathbf{x}}(t)$.

To see the role of the ecological sustainability constraint in the environmental control problem it is convenient to return to a simple stochastic version of the problem discussed in Section 4. Since we make no special assumptions about the controllability of the system, it is convenient to disregard the natural capital boundary condition. This is the problem indexed '0' in Section 4. If we now add the ecological sustainability constraint defined by equation (2.8d) we can identify an augmented benefit function of the form:

$$J_0^+ = E\{W[\cdot]e^{-\delta T} + \int_0^T [Y[\cdot]e^{-\delta t} + \lambda_0{}'(t)\{\mathbf{f}[\cdot]$$
$$- \dot{\mathbf{x}}(t)\} + \eta_0{}'(t)\{\mathbf{h}[\mathbf{x}(t), \mathbf{u}(t), t]\}]dt \,|S_D[0,t]\} \tag{2.34}$$

with

$$\eta_0{}'(t) = \mathbf{0} \text{ if } \mathbf{c}[\cdot] < 0$$
$$\eta_0{}'(t) \geq \mathbf{0} \text{ if } \mathbf{c}[\cdot] = 0$$

$\eta_0{}'(t)$ being a vector of Lagrange multipliers adjoining the precautionary constraint to the benefit function J_0. The Hamiltonian for the problem is

$$H_0[\cdot] = Y[\cdot]e^{-\delta t} + \lambda_0{}'(t)\mathbf{f}[\cdot] + \eta_0{}'(t)\,\mathbf{c}[\cdot]$$

and the adjoint vector and transversality conditions take the form:

$$\dot{\lambda}_0'(t) = \begin{cases} -Y_x(t)e^{-\delta t} - \lambda_0'(t)\mathbf{F}_x(t), & \mathbf{h}[\cdot] < 0 \\ -Y_x(t)e^{-\delta t} - \lambda_0'(t)\mathbf{F}_x(t) - \eta_0'(t)\mathbf{H}_x(t), & \mathbf{h}[\cdot] = 0 \end{cases}$$ (2.35)

$$\lambda_0'(T) = W_x(t)e^{-\delta T}$$ (2.36)

while the maximum condition may be written

$$0 = \begin{cases} Y_k(t)e^{-\delta t} + \lambda_0'(t)\mathbf{F}_k(t), & \mathbf{h}[\cdot] < 0 \\ Y_k(t)e^{-\delta t} + \lambda_0'(t)\mathbf{F}_k(t) + \eta_0'(t)\mathbf{H}_k(t), & \mathbf{h}[\cdot] = 0. \end{cases}$$ (2.37)

Equations (2.35) to (2.37) form the Euler–Lagrange equations for our revised problem, giving the necessary conditions on $\lambda_0(t)$, $\eta_0'(t)$, $H_{0k}[\cdot]$ and $H_{0x}[\cdot]$ for optimization of the problem. Both the adjoint equation and the maximum condition now have two forms depending on whether the sustainability constraint is or is not effective along an optimal trajectory. The vector $\eta_0'(t)$ measures the sensitivity of the benefit function to the sustainability constraint. If a control is ineffective, which may be thought of as implying that a resource is non-scarce or that emission levels are within some well-defined threshold, the corresponding multiplier has a zero value. If a control is effective, the corresponding multiplier defines the marginal benefit of the relaxation of the constraint. In policy terms an 'ineffective control' translates as free access to the resource in question. An effective control translates as restricted access to the resource, whether secured by formal physical limits (quota, permits, safe minimum standards) or the use of economic instruments to meet physical limits (user fees, charges, fines and so on).

Now consider what the sustainability constraint is doing in the context of the control problem. It is well understood that the imposition of boundaries of this sort on the control instruments fully determines the optimizing control in special cases. This is true, for example, of benefit functions that do not have a well-defined maximum (or minimum). It is not, however, true in the case of the environmental control problem under discussion here. The boundaries imposed under a sustainability constraint do not necessarily determine the optimal allocation of economic resources. Nor do they necessarily affect the role of the market in securing the allocation of resources. Indeed, this depends on the degree of system controllability.

It is reasonable, from what has been said, to suppose that given available information on the global economy–environment system the structural conditions do not exist for a natural capital boundary condition to be satisfied through a parametric control programme. Put another way, there is no reason to believe that the parametric optimization of the expected value of the benefit function will generate a trajectory which both respects the maximum principle and satisfies the natural capital boundary condition. The system is neither perfectly controlled nor perfectly understood. This does not mean that all resource use may not be influenced through the price mechanism, but it does mean that some resource use is either unaffected by prices, or is influenced in an indeterminate way. The role of the sustainability constraint is to regulate the pressure on environmental resources in such a way that the parametric optimization of the system is consistent with its local stability.

7 CONCLUDING REMARKS

Sustainability constraints of this form can be thought of as precautionary constraints. The limits they impose on economic activity will depend (a) on the (local) stability of the ecosystems involved, (b) on the conjectured losses if those ecosystems should become unstable due to the effects of economic activity, and (c) on the degree of system controllability. If the structural conditions for the controllability of the global economy–environment system are not satisfied, and if the system is imperfectly observed, there exists the potential for unanticipated and 'catastrophic' effects at points far removed from the original source of damage. It is these effects that are the object of a sustainability constraint. What all sustainability constraints share is that they bound the current level of pressure imposed on particular populations, and that the bounds reflect perceptions about the potential future losses in terms of the wider system of population extinction. In terms of a simple population indicator, for example, if a species population growth function has the property that it is critically depensatory at some more or less well-defined population level (that the population will collapse with some probability if it falls below that level), then the sustainability constraint would be based on the critical depensatory point. Where it would be placed relative to the critical depensatory point would, however, depend on the perceived significance of the future welfare effects of the collapse of the population. The implication of a control approach to the management of the economy–environment system is the same as the implication of a systems approach to ecology. It is the dynamic interdependence of populations that determines the magnitude of future losses. Hence even if constraints are imposed on species populations or resource stocks, the value of those constraints should reflect not the species/stocks own-growth function, but its role in the ecosystems whose stability is to be protected.

Sustainability constraints may accordingly be thought of as analogous to the safe minimum standards that have long been a feature of engineering design.

But whether they are directly enforced as a condition of investment (compare Goodland and Ledec, 1987) or secured through some influence function involving the price mechanism, depends on the reach of the latter. That is, whether the inequalities of (2.8d) are satisfied through direct regulation or through some form of incentive-based parametric control naturally depends critically on the controllability of the system. If the resource stocks to be maintained are within the reach of the price system, then the sustainability constraint may be satisfied through some sort of economic incentive-based parametric control. If those stocks are beyond the reach of the price system, direct regulation is necessary. Indeed, it may well be that the best evidence for the uncontrollability of the global system is the prevalence of instruments of direct regulation. Transferable or non-transferable quotas in fisheries, game licences, and open and closed seasons on the predation of 'game' species are all indicators not so much of the failure of markets, as of their extraordinarily limited scope as system observers and system controllers.

NOTES

1. Sometimes styled command-and-control measures.
2. It is well known that under certain conditions price and quantity regulation *are* symmetrical, but these conditions include perfect information. In the absence of perfect information, price and quantity controls are not symmetrical (compare Weitzman, 1974). Since the environmental control problem is quintessentially a problem of control under uncertainty and ignorance as to the future environmental effects of economic activity, there is good reason to treat price and quantity controls separately.
3. In addition to the normality condition, satisfaction of two other conditions are sufficient to ensure optimality of a development path traced by the state history, [$x(t)$, $0 \le t \le T$]. The first of these is the Legendre–Clebsch condition which requires that the Hessian matrices composed of the second derivatives of the Hamiltonians with respect to the control parameters are negative definite throughout the interval [0,T]. That is

$$\left\{ \frac{\partial^2 H_i[\cdot]}{\partial \mathbf{k}^2} \right\} < 0 \qquad (2.38)$$

where $H_i[\cdot] = H_i[x^*(t), \mathbf{u}^*(t), \lambda_i^*(t), t]$. If the control problem is normal, and if the necessary conditions have been met, then (2.28) is sufficient to guarantee optimality. However, it is only locally sufficient, applying in the neighbourhood of an optimal development path. In general, if the dynamic system is non-linear, there is no reason to believe that (2.38) would hold for significant deviations from an optimal path. The second sufficiency condition is the Jacobi condition. This requires that there be no conjugate points along an optimal path, which ensures the uniqueness of that path.
4. This begs the question of what sort of system response we are interested in. The most appropriate response would seem to be in the distribution of the system parameters. This approach to the problem of ecological sustainability has been explored in Common and Perrings (1992).

REFERENCES

Aoki, M. (1976), *Optimal Control and System Theory in Dynamic Economic Analysis*, North-Holland, Amsterdam.

Barbier, E.B., Markandya, A. and Pearce, D.W. (1990), 'Sustainable agricultural development and project appraisal', *European Review of Agricultural Economics* **17**: 181–96.

Baumol, W. and Bradford, D. (1972), 'Detrimental externalities and the non-convexity of the production set', *Economica* **39**: 160–76.

Clark, C. (1976), *Mathematical Bioeconomics*, John Wiley, New York.

Common, M.S. and Perrings, C. (1992), 'Towards an ecological economics of sustainability', *Ecological Economics* **6**: 7–34.

Conrad, J. and Clark, C. (1987), *Natural Resource Economics: Notes and Problems*, Cambridge University Press, Cambridge.

Cropper, M.L. and Oates, W.E. (1989), 'Environmental economics: a survey', University of Maryland, mimeo.

Daly, H.E. (1977), *Steady-State Economics*, Freeman, San Francisco.

Daly, H.E. (1990), 'Towards some operational principles of sustainable development', *Ecological Economics* **2**: 1–6.

Dasgupta, P. (1982), *The Control of Resources*, Basil Blackwell, Oxford.

di Castri, F. (1987), 'The evolution of terrestrial ecosystems', in O. Ravera (ed.), *Ecological Assessment of Environmental Degradation, Pollution and Recovery*, Elsevier, Amsterdam.

Dixit, A., Hammond, P. and Hoel, M. (1980), 'On Hartwick's rule for regular maximin paths of capital accumulation and resource depletion', *Review of Economic Studies* **XLVII**: 551–6.

Faber, M. and Proops, J.L.R. (1990), *Evolution, Time, Production and the Environment*, Springer-Verlag, Berlin.

Georgescu-Roegen, N. (1971), *The Entropy Law and the Economic Process*, Harvard University Press, Cambridge, MA.

Goodland, R. and Ledec, G. (1987), 'Neoclassical economics and principles of sustainable development', *Ecological Modelling* **38**: 19–46.

Hartwick, J.M. (1977), 'Intergenerational equity and the investing of rents from exhaustible resources', *American Economic Review* **66**: 972–4.

Hartwick, J.M. (1978a), 'Investing returns from depleting renewable resource stocks and intergenerational equity', *Economics Letters* **1**: 85–8.

Hartwick, J.M. (1978b), 'Substitution among exhaustible resources and intergenerational equity', *Review of Economic Studies* **45** (2): 347–54.

Hicks, J.R. (1946), *Value and Capital*, Oxford University Press, Oxford.

Holling, C.S. (1973), 'Resilience and stability of ecological systems', *Annual Review of Ecological Systems* **4**: 1–24.

Holling, C.S. (1986), 'The resilience of terrestrial ecosystems: local surprise and global change', in W.C. Clark and R.E. Munn (eds), *Sustainable Development of the Biosphere*, Cambridge University Press, Cambridge: 292–317.

Kay, J.J. (1989), 'A thermodynamic perspective of the self-organization of living systems', in P.W.J. Ledington (ed.), *Proceedings of the 33rd Annual Meeting of the International Society for the System Sciences*, Edinburgh, **3**: 24–30.

Kay, J.J. (1990), 'The concept of ecological integrity, alternative theories of ecology, and implications for decision-support indicators', in CEAC, *Proceedings of the* workshop on indicators for ecologically sustainable development economics, Environment Canada, Ottawa.

Mäler, K.-G. (1990), 'National accounts and environmental resources', Stockholm School of Economics, mimeo.

Pearce, D.W. (1987), 'Foundations of an ecological economics', *Ecological Modelling* **38**: 9–18.

Pearce, D.W. (1988), 'Economics, equity and sustainable development', *Futures* **20**: 598–605.

Pearce, D.W., Markandya, A. and Barbier, E.B. (1989), *Blueprint for a Green Economy*, Earthscan, London.

Pearce, D.W. and Turner, R.K. (1990), *Economics of Natural Resources and the Environment*, Harvester-Wheatsheaf, London.

Perrings, C. (1987), *Economy and Environment*, Cambridge University Press, Cambridge.

Pielou, E.C. (1975), *Ecological Diversity*, John Wiley, New York.

Schaeffer D.J., Herricks, E. and Kerster, H. (1988), 'Ecosystem health: I. Measuring ecosystem health', *Environmental Management* **12** (4): 445–55.

Smith, V.L. (1977), 'Control theory applied to natural and environmental resources', *Journal of Environmental Economics and Management* **4**: 1–24.

Solow, R.M. (1974), 'Intergenerational equity and exhaustible resources', *Review of Economic Studies*, Symposium: 29–46.

Solow, R.M. (1986), 'On the intertemporal allocation of natural resources', *Scandinavian Journal of Economics* **88** (1): 141–9.

Stengel, R.F. (1986), *Stochastic Optimal Control*, John Wiley, New York.

Weitzman, M.L. (1974), 'Prices vs quantities', *Review of Economic Studies* **41**: 477–91.

3. Ecological resilience in the sustainability of economic development

1 SUSTAINABLE DEVELOPMENT: ECONOMICS AND ECOLOGY

There is a general consensus in the economic literature that economic development may be said to be sustainable only if the value of the aggregate capital stock is non-declining. This is implicit in the Hicks/Lindahl concept of income: the maximum amount which may be spent on consumption in one period without reducing real consumption expenditure in future periods. It admits the possibility that development based on the depletion of natural capital (environmental resources) may be sustainable, so long as (a) there exist substitutes for such natural capital, and (b) investment in those substitutes at least compensates for the loss of the natural capital (Solow, 1974, 1986; Hartwick, 1977, 1978; Dixit et al., 1980). The sense of this investment rule, the Solow–Hartwick rule, is very widely recognized, and the debate about the sustainability of economic development has instead focused on the degree of substitutability between produced and natural capital (Turner, 1988, 1992; Daly and Cobb, 1989; Daly, 1991). It is now generally agreed that there are limits to the possibilities for substitution between these two types of capital, though these limits are not very well defined, even for existing technologies. Nevertheless, at the level of principle, it is accepted that sustainable economic development implies the conservation of at least some environmental resources (Pearce, 1987; Pearce and Turner, 1990).

Which environmental resources should be conserved is another matter. There are limits to the possibilities for substitution not just between produced and natural capital, but between different types of natural capital. The historical tendency to assume that environmental resources which are substitutes in terms of human consumption are substitutes in terms of all their ecological functions may have been discarded, but it remains the case that the complementarity between species in many ecosystems is still very imperfectly understood. There is certainly some potential for substitution between species in the performance of ecosystem functions. Indeed, the resilience of ecological functions in terrestrial systems is an increasing function of the number of substitute species that can perform those functions (Schindler, 1990; Holling, 1992), but the resilience of ecological functions in many coastal and estuarine systems is not. It depends on the ability of a small number of species to operate over a wide range of conditions (Costanza et al., 1995). The ecological problem is to determine the minimum combination of resources that will enable ecosystems to function under the expected range of environmental and economic conditions. This is the same as determining the stability of ecosystem functions with respect to perturbation of the relevant environmental and economic parameters.

Conservation of irreplaceable environmental resources implies conservation of the capacity of ecological systems to provide those resources. In different ecosystems, this will have different consequences for the system components. But in all cases, it implies the protection of the stability of the system concerned with respect to potential perturbations. The point has been made elsewhere that economic sustainability and ecological resilience are 'disjoint', in the sense that maximizing the sustainable income from the exploitation of produced and natural capital will not simultaneously maximize ecological resilience. Indeed, it has been remarked that most economy–environment systems characterized by a high level of ecological resilience have not satisfied even the minimum conditions for intertemporal economic efficiency (Common and Perrings, 1992). The question I wish to explore here is related to this. How are ecological resilience, stability and the sustainability of income connected at different levels of development, and what does this signify for the economics and management of environmental resources?

The chapter introduces a way of thinking about the problem that brings to centre stage the question of where an economic–ecological system is with respect to the boundaries of local stability. The question is partly motivated by differences that have emerged between ecologists on the nature and properties of ecosystem resilience. These differences are discussed in detail below, but what makes them interesting to the problem of economic development is that they turn on the distinction between systems close to and far from equilibrium. There is a long history of conceptualizing economic development as a process characterized by evolution away from a stable equilibrium state (see, for example, Lewis, 1954; Leibenstein, 1957; Myrdal, 1957). Those ecologists who argue that the relevant concept of resilience is that applicable to systems far from equilibrium, also argue that this is precisely because economic development has driven most major ecological systems away from equilibrium. The linkages between these two lines of inquiry turn out to be highly relevant to the problem of sustainable development.

To address this question the chapter looks at three sets of issues. The first of these, considered in Section 2, concerns the general problem of economy–environment system dynamics. This section identifies the main characteristics of jointly-determined economic–ecological dynamical systems, and discusses the stability of the equilibria of such systems. Section 3 addresses the joint dynamics of produced and natural capital more formally, and stability and capital growth may be related. Section 4 focuses on the concept of resilience and its relation to the stability of the jointly-determined system. A final section offers a discussion of the implications this has for sustainable economic development.

2   ECONOMY–ENVIRONMENT SYSTEM DYNAMICS

There is a sense in which the field of ecological economics has been driven by the perception that as the economic system grows relative to its environment, the dynamics of the jointly-determined system are increasingly non-linear and discontinuous. It is this perception, more than any other, that has induced economists interested in the behaviour of the joint system to move beyond the static Walrasian approach. The flow of ideas, it should be said, has been very much from biology to economics. The mathematics of non-linear dynamical systems were applied in biology well before they were applied in economics. In the 1970s, May (1972, 1976) had observed the potential for complex behaviour in Lotka–Volterra predator–prey models. At the same time, examples of mathematical and Riemann–Hugonoit catastrophe were recorded in spruce budworm outbreaks in boreal forests (Jones, 1975). More recently, it has been shown that change in either the structure of environmental constraints or the biotic potential of a system may lead to complete alteration in the state of the system (O'Neill et al., 1989). Small adaptive moves may trigger 'avalanches' of adaptive responses among competitors (Kauffman and Johnsen, 1991). In economics, applications of the theory of non-linear dynamical systems were late in appearing, but there is now a burgeoning interest in this area (see, for example, Anderson et al., 1988; Brock and Malliaris, 1989; Puu, 1989; Rosser, 1990; Arthur, 1992; Benhabib (ed.), 1992).

There are two characteristics of jointly-determined economy–environment system dynamics that are important from the perspective of this chapter. The first is that the dynamics of the joint system reflect the structure of the connections between each subsystem. Any change in conditions generates two interlinked sets of 'general equilibrium' effects: a set of ecological effects that work themselves out in the evolution of the ecological systems concerned, and a set of economic effects that work themselves out in the evolution of the economic system. The cross-effects depend on the connectedness of the two systems, to borrow a term from ecology. The more highly connected ecological and economic systems are, the more change in one implies change in the other: the more they 'coevolve' (Norgaard, 1984). It is, however, important to appreciate that there is both a spatial and a temporal structure to the connections between the economy and its environment. It is, for example, possible for components of the joint system to be entirely unconnected viewed over one temporal or spatial horizon, but highly connected viewed over some other temporal or spatial horizon (Perrings, 1987). Moreover, the dynamics of the system vary between spatial scales (Holling et al., 1995). It turns out that the structure of the connections between the economy and its environment has a major effect on both the timing and the impact of economic change on the environment.

The second important characteristic of the dynamics of the joint system is that there exist multiple locally stable equilibria (or basins of attraction), separated by unstable equilibria (or unstable manifolds) that are defined in terms of the level or density of the state variables or components of the system. Moreover, as economic and ecological systems pass from one basin to another, so the central characteristics of the system may undergo a profound change.

The main implication of these characteristics is that the system dynamics may be neither continuous nor gradual. In ecosystems, the slow accumulation of biological capital tends to be broken by sudden shocks, and if this moves the system into another basin of attraction, the result can be irreversible or only slowly reversible. In economic systems, a very similar pattern is observed. If business cycles are the limit cycles of stable (but not asymptotically stable) equilibria, then revolutions, wars, coups and other 'events' that restructure economies are the unstable manifolds separating such equilibria. It follows that the joint system responds very differently to perturbation depending both on where either the economy or the environment are relative to the system equilibria, and on the characteristics of those equilibria. So, if a system is in the neigbourhood of a particular unstable equilibrium, or threshold, minor perturbations of its state variables may have 'catastrophic' consequences for its structure and organization. This has been observed in the management of dryland systems, for example (Walker and Noy-Meir, 1982; Walker, 1988; Westoby et al., 1989). It has also been observed in unmanaged systems. Conversely, if a system is at or close to a locally stable equilibrium, major perturbation of the same variables may have very little effect on its structure or organization.

In ecology, this characteristic has induced an approach to the analysis of system dynamics that concentrates on where an ecosystem is relative to the unstable manifolds or thresholds of the general system. This approach requires identification not of the existence and stability of equilibria, but of the capacity of a system – whether at or away from equilibrium – to absorb shocks without losing stability. This capacity is captured in the concept of ecosystem resilience. Holling (1973, 1986, 1992) has described the dynamics of ecosystems in terms of the sequential interaction between four system functions. These are exploitation – processes responsible for rapid colonization of disturbed ecosystems; conservation – the accumulation of energy and biomass; creative destruction –

abrupt change caused by external disturbance which releases energy and matter; and reorganization – mobilization of matter for the next exploitative phase.

Reorganization may be associated with a new cycle involving the same structure, or a switch to a completely different structure. If reorganization does involve a new structure, this implies that the system has crossed some threshold or unstable equilibrium, and is converging on a different locally stable equilibrium. Threshold values exist, for example, for the diversity of species in an ecosystem. There may be a range of population sizes for the different species in an ecosystem over which the system remains stable, but if any one population in an ecosystem falls below its critical threshold level, the self-organization of the ecosystem as a whole may be radically and irreversibly altered (Pielou, 1975). Threshold values also exist for overall regressive succession; standing crop biomass; energy flows to grazing and decomposer food chains; mineral micronutrient stocks and so on (Schaeffer et al., 1988). The resilience of an ecosystem is related to its ability to maintain its self-organization without undergoing the 'catastrophic' and irreversible change involved in crossing such thresholds.

Holling et al. (1995) point out that resilience of a system is defined in two rather different ways in the ecological literature. One definition is concerned with resistance to perturbation of, and speed of return to, a locally stable equilibrium (Pimm, 1984; O'Neill et al., 1989). The second is concerned with the magnitude of disturbance that can be absorbed before the system flips from one basin of attraction to another (Holling, 1973). As we shall see later, the two definitions are in fact very closely related, both being testable in terms of the properties of the Liapunov functions (if such exists) associated with each locally stable equilibrium. In both cases, resilience refers to the capacity of a system to retain its organizational structure following perturbation of some state variable from a given value (Common and Perrings, 1992). The resilience of a system is therefore conditional on the initial values of the system variables, and is relative to perturbation of one or more of those variables. It is the second definition that is explored in this chapter. If the effect of economic development is to increase the pressure on ecological systems, then the management problem is that associated with systems closer to thresholds of instability than to stable equilibria. We shall come back to this in Section 4.

3   SUSTAINABILITY AND STABILITY IN AN ECONOMY–ENVIRONMENT SYSTEM

My purpose in this section is to make the relation between development, sustainability and stability as transparent as possible. Each of these three terms will be given precise meaning later, but it is worth underlining that since they are all the subject of a large multidisciplinary literature it is not possible to capture the nuances of interpretation attaching to each. With respect to 'development', almost the only thing on which everyone agrees is that it is more than the rate of change of GDP or GDP per capita. Pearce and Turner (1990) refer to improvement in a vector of attributes including real income per capita, health and nutritional status, educational achievement, access to resources, the distribution of income and basic 'freedoms' – for which it is simply impossible to find a single index. Sustainability has been given a bewildering variety of definitions (for some of which see Pearce et al., 1989). On the face of it, stability should be the easiest to handle because there exist precise mathematical definitions, but it has been observed that the term 'ecological stability' has been used to mean the stability of so many different ecological characteristics that it is in fact very difficult to know what it implies (Kay, 1991). Given the very specific purpose of this chapter, it seems reasonable to avoid the confusion surrounding these terms by working with precise definitions.

To proceed, let us denote the vector of assets or capital available to the system at time t by $\mathbf{k} = \mathbf{k}(t)$. The i-th component of this vector, $k_i \geq 0$, denotes the non-negative value of the i-th asset or type of capital at time t. To ease discussion, let us identify two components only, which may be called produced capital, $k_p = k_p(t)$, and natural capital, $k_n = k_n(t)$. Hence:

$$\mathbf{k} = (k_p, k_n).$$

Without yet specifying the relation between these two types of capital, we may define:

Development: An economy having a stock of produced capital, k_p, will be said to be more developed than an economy having a stock of produced capital, k_p', if $k_p > k_p'$. The process of development is the process of expanding the stock of produced capital, and the level of development is measured by the value of that stock: that is, the level of development of an economy having a stock of produced capital, k_p, will be said to be approximated by k_p.

'Development' is assumed to be a function of produced capital alone. If the value of produced capital is strictly greater in one economy than another, then the first will be said to be the more developed irrespective of the value of natural capital in each economy. Similarly, if the value of produced capital in an economy is increasing over time, that economy will be said to be developing. Note that population size is not explicitly taken into account here (since I am thinking about the relation between produced and natural capital in a single closed economy), but all definitions might be set in per capita terms without loss of generality.

The main operational difference between these two types of capital is that the generation of one is controlled, while the generation of the other is not. One might want to object to the exclusion of k_n from the definition of development. The point is that k_n defines the natural endowment of the economy at a particular moment. An economy with very large natural endowments may have considerable potential for development, but it cannot be said to be developing unless that natural endowment is in the process of being converted into produced capital. Moreover, it cannot be said to be developing sustainably unless the conversion of natural capital into produced capital yields an aggregate of both natural and produced capital that is non-declining. That is, we define sustainability in the following terms:

Sustainability: An economy at any level of development, k_p, will be said to be sustainable if $\dot{k}_p + \dot{k}_n \geq 0$ for all t.

This is the Hicks/Lindahl requirement for sustainable income: that the value of the aggregate capital stock is non-declining over time. It does not imply that $\dot{\mathbf{k}} \geq 0$, since it allows individual components of $\mathbf{k}$ to be declining. However, it is immediate that a sufficient condition for the sustainability of development is that $\dot{k}_p = \dot{k}_n = 0$. Given our previous definition of development, we now have:

Sustainable development: The development of an economy may be said to be sustainable if $\dot{k}_p \geq 0$ and $\dot{k}_p + \dot{k}_n \geq 0$.

While definition of sustainable development does not restrict the sign of $\dot{k}_n$, since k_n cannot decline indefinitely it follows that in the limit, $\lim_{t \to \infty} \dot{k}_n(t) \geq 0$. Natural capital may be reduced in the development process over some finite time, but in the long run natural capital must be non-declining. This is consistent both with the Hicks–Lindahl concept of income and with the arguments of Turner, Pearce and Daly.

To approach the stability of the joint system let us first identify the equations of motion for produced and natural capital: $\dot{\mathbf{k}} = f(\mathbf{k})$. Specifically, let these be described by the differential equations:

$$\dot{k}_p = f_p(k_p, k_n) \quad f_p: K \to K$$

$$\dot{k}_n = f_n(k_n, k_p) \quad f_n: K \to K$$

in which K, the state space of the system, is an open set, and f_p and f_n are the growth functions of produced and natural capital, respectively. In general terms, if $\mathbf{k}^* = (k_p^*, k_n^*)$ is an equilibrium of these equations, it is stable if all solutions close to $\mathbf{k}^*$ remain close, and is asymptotically stable if all solutions close to $\mathbf{k}^*$ tend to $\mathbf{k}^*$. If $\mathbf{k}^*$ is asymptotically stable it is said to be a sink.[1] More particularly:

Stability: An equilibrium of the system, $\mathbf{k}^*$, will be said to be stable if there is a neigbourhood of $\mathbf{k}^*$, K', such that every solution curve, $\mathbf{k}(t)$, with its origin, $\mathbf{k}(0)$, in K' tends to $\mathbf{k}^*$. The union of all solution curves tending towards $\mathbf{k}^*$ as t tends to infinity is its basin, denoted $B(\mathbf{k}^*)$.

Stability in this sense may be characterized in terms of the properties of Liapunov function, $g: K' \rightarrow K$. Specifically if $g: K' \rightarrow K$ is a continuous function defined on a neigbourhood K' of $\mathbf{k}^*$, differentiable on $K' - \mathbf{k}^*$, then $\mathbf{k}^*$ is stable if

$$g(\mathbf{k}^*) = 0$$
$$g(\mathbf{k}) > 0 \quad \mathbf{k} \neq \mathbf{k}^*$$
$$\dot{\mathbf{k}} \leq 0 \quad \mathbf{k} \in K' - \mathbf{k}^*$$

and is asymptotically stable if

$$\dot{\mathbf{k}} < 0 \quad \mathbf{k} \in K' - \mathbf{k}^*.$$

$\dot{\mathbf{k}} \leq 0$ admits the possibility that $\mathbf{k}(t)$ will converge to a limit cycle, whereas $\dot{\mathbf{k}} < 0$ ensures that it will converge to $\mathbf{k}^*$. If a Liapunov function with these properties exists, the system characteristics it describes will be stable with respect to perturbation of the components of $\mathbf{k}$ within the neighbourhood, K'. In ecological–economic systems a natural candidate for a Liapunov function is the self-organization or structure of those systems, in the sense that one would expect that if the component parts of such systems were at equilibrium or on a limit cycle, there would be no tendency for the self-organization of the system to change.

For our purposes, the most important property of the stability or asymptotic stability of the equilibria of jointly-determined economy–environment systems is that it determines the time path of natural and produced capital only within the basins of those equilibria. Put another way, such equilibria are 'local' only. If perturbation of either produced or natural capital dislodges the system from the basin of any given equilibrium or attractor, that equilibrium will lose influence over the evolution of the system. The Liapunov function obtained for any given equilibrium may be used to estimate the extent of its basin, and so the limits within which the state variables may be perturbed before the system switches to some other basin. It is this property of Liapunov functions that we will find useful in characterizing system resilience in Section 4. First, however, let me illustrate the relation between development, sustainability and stability in the jointly-determined system.

To take things further it is necessary to impose some structure on the system dynamics. It is, however, possible to go quite a long way with minimal structure. I shall suppose the following:

i. There exists some maximum stock of natural capital fixed by the biotic potential of the system and the finite supply of abiotic resources. That is, there exists a maximum value of k_n, denoted $\bar{k}_n$, such that $\dot{k}_n > 0$ only if $k_n < \bar{k}_n$.

ii. Natural capital is essential to the creation of produced capital. That is, $k_p > 0$ only if $0 < k_n < \bar{k}_n$, and $f_p(k_p, k_n) = 0$ if $k_n = 0$. It is not possible to substitute produced capital for natural capital completely.

iii. For any given technology there exists a well-defined range of values for k_n and k_p within which accumulation of produced capital does not imply depletion of natural capital. Outside of this range, $\dot{k}_p > 0 \Rightarrow \dot{k}_n < 0$.

These very general assumptions about the relation between produced and natural capital in economy–environment systems enable us to say a good deal about the system dynamics. Consider the phase diagrams described in Figures 3.1–3. In all three the graphs of the functions $\dot{k}_p = 0$ and $\dot{k}_n = 0$ divide the values of k_p and k_n as produced and natural capital is growing or being depleted. Since a sufficient condition for the sustainability of the system is that $\dot{k}_p = \dot{k}_n = 0$, it follows that equilibria defined by the intersection of the $\dot{k}_p = 0$ and $\dot{k}_n = 0$ curves are sustainable. Each of the three figures reflects a different assumption about the development potential of the economic system. In all cases, the accumulation of capital is positive only if the stock of natural capital is positive. Figure 3.1 represents the case where the capacity of the economic system (to convert natural to produced capital) is low relative to the capacity of the ecological system (to convert produced to natural capital). Figure 3.2 represents the opposite case: where the capacity of the economic system (to convert natural to produced capital) is high relative to the capacity of the ecological system (to convert produced to natural capital). Figure 3.3 represents a median case.

Consider the system equilibria in each of these three cases. In Figures 3.1 and 3.2 there are only two equilibria: $(0,0)$ and $(0,\bar{k}_n)$. In Figure 3.1 there is an asymptotically stable equilibrium at $(0,\bar{k}_n)$, and an unstable equilibrium at $(0,0)$. That is, as $t \to \infty$, $k_n \to \bar{k}_n$ and $k_p \to 0$ for most trajectories of **k**. The development of this economy is manifestly not sustainable. Since the economic system is not large enough to secure its place in the steady state, it is 'swamped' by the ecological system. In Figure 3.2, on the other hand, both $(0,\bar{k}_n)$ and $(0,0)$ are unstable equilibria. Since the economic system is too large relative to the carrying capacity of the environment, the stock of natural capital will tend to

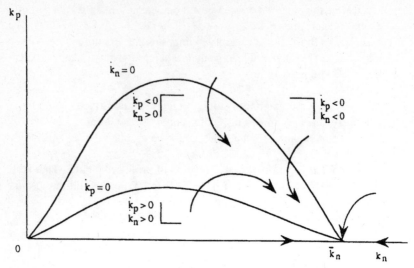

Figure 3.1   Ecological system dominates economic system

be fully depleted. Since the economic system cannot exist without natural capital, it also collapses. The development of this economy is also not sustainable.

Now take the 'codependent' system described in Figure 3.3. Aside from the cases representing, respectively, the collapse of the general system and the collapse of the economic system, $(0,0)$ and the $(0,\bar{k}_n)$, there exist equilibria, $\mathbf{k}^*$

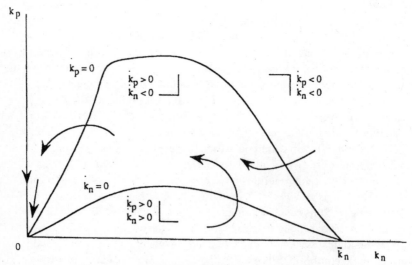

Figure 3.2   Economic system dominates ecological system

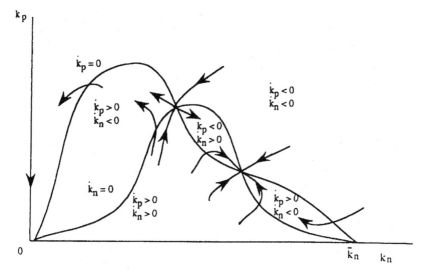

Figure 3.3 'Co-dependent' ecological and economic systems

and **k'**, at which both k_p and k_n are strictly positive. Of these, **k'** represents a higher level of development than **k***, in that $k_p' > k_p^*$: the level of produced capital at **k'** exceeds that at **k***. Both equilibria are sustainable, in that $\dot{k}_p + \dot{k}_n = 0$. However, only one, **k*** is stable (a node). The other, **k'**, is unstable (a saddlepoint). At the stable equilibrium the level of produced capital is 'low', and the level of natural capital is 'high'. At the unstable equilibrium, the position is the opposite. It follows that from a development perspective the unstable equilibrium will be preferred to the stable equilibrium.

4   RESILIENCE AND STABILITY

With this background we are now in a position to consider the relationship between resilience and stability. The concept of resilience derives from the ecological literature. It is, however, relevant to the analysis of any complex dynamical system. The observed properties of ecological systems that have prompted a re-evaluation of resilience by systems ecologists include two important features. First, change in most terrestrial systems is not continuous and gradual, but is punctuated by the sudden reorganization of the stock resources. This often occurs after long periods of apparent stability, and often after some 'exogenous' perturbation of the system. Second, ecosystems do not have single equilibria. Indeed, different equilibria define functionally different states of a system and characterize its structure and diversity. Third, the dynamics and stability of systems vary non-linearly with their scale.

The existence of multiple equilibria in natural systems invites reconsideration of their stability. In ecology this has centred on the discussion of system resilience: a concept related to but not the same as stability. Recall that resilience has been defined in two rather different ways in the ecological literature. The more 'traditional' of these two definitions focuses on the properties of the system near some stable or asymptotically stable equilibrium state (in the neighbourhood of a stable focus or node). By this definition resilience is a measure of the system's resistance to perturbation and speed of return to equilibrium (Pimm, 1984; O'Neill et al., 1989). The second definition focuses on the properties of the system further away from any stable or asymptotically stable state (in the neighbourhood of the unstable manifolds that separate the basins of different equilibria) (Holling, 1973). By this definition, resilience is a measure of the perturbation that can be absorbed before the system crosses an unstable manifold, and converges on another equilibrium state.

The second definition of resilience implicitly accepts that the multiple equilibria of ecological systems are locally stable only, and is primarily concerned to establish a measure of the limits of the local stability of each equilibrium. There is a sense in the ecological literature on this concept of resilience that as the scale or biomass of a system increases, so it becomes more susceptible to perturbation. The 'brittleness' of the system in the conservation phase may be interpreted as evidence that it is close to the limits of local stability (Holling, 1986). This notion will become relevant when we discuss the implications of resilience for economic development, but for now it is helpful to focus on the link between resilience and the limits of the local stability of system equilibria.

As has already been observed, the Liapunov function, if it exists, can be used both to characterize the system dynamics in the neighbourhood of an equilibrium state, and to ascertain the extent of the basin of that state. Hence we can use these properties of the function to explore the significance of system resilience. For simplicity, consider the case of an asymptotically stable equilibrium. The argument is first stated formally, and then intuitively.

A system at state $\mathbf{k}(t)$ in the basin of an equilibrium $\mathbf{k}^*$ may be said to be resilient (in the Holling sense) with respect to some perturbation of the state variables, denoted $\Delta(t)$, if the perturbed trajectory is convergent on $\mathbf{k}^*$: that is if $\lim_{t\to\infty}|(\mathbf{k}_i(t) + \Delta(t)) - \mathbf{k}^*| = 0$. More particularly, let $\mathbf{k}_i(t)$ be a solution lying in direction i from $\mathbf{k}^*$ in a neighbourhood $K' \subset K$ of $\mathbf{k}^*$. If $g: K' \to K$ is a Liapunov function such that $g(\mathbf{k}^*) = 0$, $g(\mathbf{k}_i(t)) > 0$, and $\dot{\mathbf{k}}_i(t) < 0$, then $\mathbf{k}^*$ is asymptotically stable, that is, $\lim_{t\to\infty}|\mathbf{k}_i(t) - \mathbf{k}^*| = 0$, and $\mathbf{k}_i(t)$. Now let $K'' \subset K$ be the closed bounded subset of K that contains all such points, $\mathbf{k}_i(t)$, in the basin of $\mathbf{k}^*$, $B(\mathbf{k}^*)$.

Let α_i define the distance in direction-i such that $|\mathbf{k}_i(t) - \mathbf{k}^*| < \alpha_i$ for all i and for all t. The α_i-neighbourhood of $\mathbf{k}^*$ is defined by

$$B_{\alpha i}(\mathbf{k}^*) = \{\mathbf{k}_i(t) \subset K | |\mathbf{k}_i(t) - \mathbf{k}^*| < \alpha_i \,\forall\, i, \text{ and } \lim_{t \to \infty} |\mathbf{k}_i(t) - \mathbf{k}^*| = 0\}.$$

K'' is simply the set of all points within the α_i-neighbourhood of $\mathbf{k}^*$: that is, $K'' = \{\mathbf{k}(t) \in B_{\alpha i}(\mathbf{k}^*)\}$.

The system at point $\mathbf{k}_i$ will be resilient with respect to perturbation in a direction that intersects the boundary of $B_{\alpha i}(\mathbf{k}^*)$ at α_j, denoted $\Delta_j(t)$, if $|\mathbf{k}_i(t) + \Delta_j(t)| < \alpha_j$. Suppose, to the contrary, that $|\mathbf{k}_i(t) + \Delta_j(t)| \geq \alpha_j$, implying that the state variables of the system lie outside the α_j-neighbourhood of $\mathbf{k}^*$. Since the α_j-neighbourhood of $\mathbf{k}^*$ includes all solutions starting in K'' for which $\lim_{t \to \infty} |\mathbf{k}_i(t) - \mathbf{k}^*| = 0$, then $\mathbf{k}_i(t) + \Delta_j(t) \notin K''$, and will not, in the limit converge on $\mathbf{k}^*$. This provides the following natural measure of system resilience.

Resilience: The resilience of a system at some point in the basin of a locally stable equilibrium, $\mathbf{k}^*$, with respect to change in any of the state variables of that system, is the maximum perturbation that can be sustained in those variables without causing the system to leave the α_i-neighbourhood of $\mathbf{k}^*$.

The importance of this measure is that it is defined both for an initial state, whether or not that is an equilibrium state, and for a specific direction of change. If the system is at $\mathbf{k}^*$, then the measure of its resilience in any given direction, i, is simply α_i. If the system is at $\mathbf{k}_i(t)$, $\mathbf{k}_i(t) - \mathbf{k}^* \neq 0$, it is the distance from $\mathbf{k}_i(t)$ along the direction of perturbation to the nearest point on the boundary of $B_{\alpha i}(\mathbf{k}^*)$ in that direction. It follows that the closer the system is to the limits of local stability – that is, to the boundary of $B_{\alpha i}(\mathbf{k}^*)$ – the less resilient it is to perturbation in the direction of the boundary.

This is shown in Figure 3.4. It is assumed that the system is at $\mathbf{k}_i(t)$, and that this is far from the stable node defined by $\mathbf{k}^*$, but lies within $B_{\alpha i}(\mathbf{k}^*)$. In the absence of perturbation, $\lim_{t \to \infty} |\mathbf{k}_i(t) - \mathbf{k}^*| = 0$. Consider the resilience of the system with respect to perturbation in two directions, i and j. The measure of system resilience in direction-i is simply $\alpha_i - \mathbf{k}_i(t)$. The measure of system resilience in direction-j is $\alpha_j - \mathbf{k}_j(t)$. If perturbation of the system in direction-j results in a fall in the value of this measure then the system may be said to have lost resilience with respect to change in that direction. If it results in a negative measure, the system may be said to have 'flipped' from one basin to another. If this is the case, the change may not be reversible, and the system will thereafter be identified with a new equilibrium.

There is a widespread perception that the state of physical systems may be associated with the equilibria to which those systems tend, simply because the

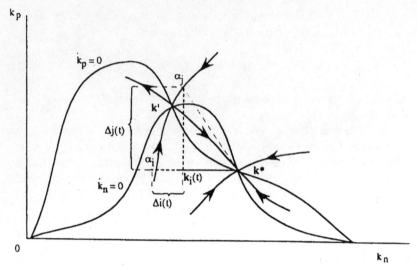

Figure 3.4   Measures of system resilience

equilibria are taken to approximate the long-term behaviour of the systems. This would imply that the steady-state measure of resilience for any state in $B_{\alpha i}(\mathbf{k}^*)$ was always α_i. However, wherever a system is far from equilibrium, this will be a highly misleading index of its ability to withstand shocks without losing self-organization. This is what Holling's concept of resilience is designed to address.

5   DISCUSSION

Let us now return to the link between resilience and sustainable economic development, the first point to make is that in an interdependent economy–environment system resilience is a property of the joint system. That is, the system equilibria are a product of the joint dynamics of both natural and produced capital, and the stability of those equilibria as well as the resilience of all possible states are characteristics of the system as a whole. Since resilience is defined with respect to perturbation in some well-defined direction, one may discuss the resilience of the joint system with respect to change in the value of natural capital, but this is not the same thing as the ecological resilience of that system. Nevertheless, it is useful to introduce discussion of the implications of this approach by focusing, once again, on the ecological literature on managed systems.

Holling (1986) has described most historical attempts to manage ecosystems as 'weak experiments testing a general hypothesis of stability/resilience', by which he means that management has been directed at minimizing the variance of some ecological variable. However, this has generally led to qualitative changes in the wider system, and has often caused that system to lose resilience. Frequently, the source of the problem has been the reduction in the diversity of communities and species within the system as a result of economic specialization on a single species, and management policies designed to achieve constant yields (Holling et al., 1995).

In terms of the development process, the phenomenon he describes represents the conversion of natural to produced capital. For purposes of this chapter, development is taken to be equivalent to the accumulation of produced capital. Since it is assumed that the growth path for produced capital is optimal by some welfare criterion, this is not overly restrictive. It does imply that economies will be considered to be more developed the greater the value of produced capital (or some measure derived from the value of produced capital, such as national income). But it does not imply that the implicit social welfare function assigns zero weight to the value of natural capital.

The distinction between produced and natural capital in the joint system is, to a very large extent, the distinction between the controlled and the uncontrolled parts of the system. Since the accumulation of produced capital is a choice variable (via investment decisions) the ratio of produced to natural capital may also be chosen, at least in so far as the behaviour of the uncontrolled ecological part of the general system is predictable. The problem identified by the ecologists lies in the fact that the dynamics of the ecological system are predictable only if the system retains its resilience: that is, only if it remains within basins whose topology is reasonably well understood. If ecological systems lose resilience, they also lose their predictability since the general topology of the basins of any new equilibria cannot be inferred in the absence of observations. The dynamics of new states of nature have to be seen before they can be understood.

The implications of the very limited structure imposed in Section 3 on the equations of motion for produced and natural capital include the following. There does exist a locally stable equilibrium for systems with these general features, $\mathbf{k}'$, and that equilibrium satisfies the requirement for sustainable development. That is, $\dot{k}_p \geq 0$ and $\dot{k}_p + \dot{k}_n \geq 0$. It is also resilient with respect to perturbation up to α_i for all i. However, it is characterized by low levels of produced capital and high levels of natural capital. This may be said to correspond to the quasi-stable equilibria long observed by development economists in subsistence or close-to-subsistence economies (see, for example, Lewis, 1954; Liebenstein, 1957; Myrdal, 1957; Fei and Ranis, 1964). The development process, through the conversion of natural capital and the accumulation of produced capital, moves the system away from such stable equilibria towards the boundaries of the surrounding basin. The highest sustainable level of development is at the equilibrium $\mathbf{k}''$. This, too, satisfies the requirements $\dot{k}_p \geq 0$ and $\dot{k}_p + \dot{k}_n \geq 0$, but it is unstable (the system has no resilience). States close to the separatrix converging on $\mathbf{k}''$ from below may exhibit some resilience in all directions, but the closer it gets, the lower is the resilience of the system with respect to perturbation towards the separatrix. That is, the smaller is the shock needed to dislodge the system on to a path along which both natural and produced capital decline in value.

To the extent that this offers a reasonable approximation of the trade-offs involved in the expansion of produced relative to natural capital, it raises a number of interesting questions about the management of environmental resources in the development process and about the sustainability of that process. The welfare gains secured through productivity improvements due to the conversion of natural capital involve a cost, and that cost is the loss of resilience in the general system. It is measured by the resources committed to protecting an unstable equilibrium and insuring against the losses caused by movement away from that equilibrium. In agriculture, for example, it is measured by the value of the increasing quantities of herbicides, pesticides, fertilizers, irrigation and other inputs needed to maintain output at or above current levels in increasingly impoverished environments. It includes the cost of relief where output fails, the cost of relocation where soils or water resources have been irreversibly damaged, and the cost of rehabilitation where damage may be partly reversible. It includes the cost of insurance against crop damage by pest or disease, along with the cost of monitoring the state of the crops, and the cost of developing new 'solutions' to the problem of novel pests and diseases. It includes, in other words, the cost of the heightened environmental management required by the choice of activity levels at or close to the threshold of resilience of the agricultural system.

The problem for policy lies in the fact that the standard indicators – market prices – do not signal whether a system is approaching the thresholds of resilience. Market prices are not adequate observers of the natural part of the system. There are various reasons for this, including the well-worn facts that many environmental resources are in the nature of public goods, that government policies exacerbate price distortions, and that the structure of property rights authorizes users to ignore the cost of their actions. They also include the facts that the poverty of resource users encourages excessively myopic behaviour, while ethnic, national, cultural and sectarian rivalries encourage excessively parochial behaviour. But at the root of the problem is a rather less well-worn fact that many of the key ecological processes are neither observable nor controllable, and that the basin boundaries are not well defined. No allocation of property rights, no reform of government pricing policies, no estimate of the willingness to pay for public goods can change this. In these circumstances, the best that can be achieved through environmental management is the stabilization of the system at sustainable levels of activity, and this is the same as the protection of system resilience (Perrings, 1991). Nor is it possible to evaluate the costs and benefits of stabilization. Since the location of the unstable manifolds that constitute the thresholds of resilience and the system dynamics beyond those thresholds are generally not known, there is a very large element of fundamental uncertainty about the cost of approaching the thresholds of resilience. The distribution of outcomes beyond the thresholds cannot be inferred from the history of the system, and certainly cannot be inferred from the current set of prices.

From the perspective of a strategy for sustainable development, the two properties of the system that are important are (i) its resilience along the development path on which it is now set, and (ii) its controllability. If the structural conditions for the controllability of the ecological components of the general system are not satisfied, and if the system is imperfectly observed, then whenever it is close to the thresholds of resilience there exists the potential for unanticipated and 'catastrophic' effects at points far removed from the original source of change. These are the 'risks' of development within a finite system. A strategy for sustainable development within a finite system is essentially a strategy for containing and insuring against these risks.

NOTE

1.   In this case, the eigenvalues of the derivative $Df(\mathbf{k}^*)$ where $\mathbf{k}^* = (k_p{}^*, k_n{}^*)$ will all have negative real parts.

REFERENCES

Anderson, P., Arrow, K. and Pines, D. (1988), *The Economy as an Evolving Complex System*, Santa Fe Institute Studies in the Sciences of Complexity V, Addison Wesley, Redwood City, CA.

Arthur, B. (1992), *On Learning and Adaptation in the Economy*, Food Research Institute, Stanford University, Stanford.

Benhabib, J. (ed.) (1992), *Cycles and Chaos in Economic Equilibrium*, Princeton University Press, Princeton, NJ.

Brock, W.A. and Malliaris, A.G. (1989), *Differential Equations, Stability and Chaos in Dynamic Economics*, North-Holland, Amsterdam.

Common, M. and Perrings, C. (1992), 'Towards an ecological economics of sustainability', *Ecological Economics* **6**: 7–34.

Costanza, R., Kemp, M. and Boynton, W. (1995), 'Scale and biodiversity in coastal and estuarine ecosystems', in C. Perrings, K.G. Mäler, C. Folke, C.S. Holling and B.-O.Janssen (eds), *Biodiversity Loss: Ecological and Economic Issues*, Cambridge University Press, Cambridge: 84–125.

Daly, H.E. (1991), 'Ecological economics and sustainable development: from concept to policy', Environment Department Divisional Working Paper No. 24, World Bank Environment Department, Washington, DC.

Daly, H.E. and Cobb, J.B. (1989), *For the Common Good: Redirecting the Economy toward Community, the Environment and a Sustainable Future*, Beacon, Boston.

Dixit, A., Hammond, P. and Hoel, M. (1980), 'On Hartwick's rule for regular maximin paths of capital accumulation and resource depletion', *Review of Economic Studies* **47**: 551–6.

Fei, J.C.H. and Ranis, G. (1964), *Development of the Labour Surplus Economy: Theory and Policy*, Yale University Press, New Haven.

Hartwick, J.M. (1977), 'Intergenerational equity and the investing of rents from exhaustible resources', *American Economic Review* **66**: 972–4.

Hartwick, J.M. (1978), 'Substitution among exhaustible resources and intergenerational equity', *Review of Economic Studies* **45**: 347–54.

Holling, C.S. (1973), 'Resilience and stability of ecological systems', *Annual Review of Ecological Systems* **4**: 1–24.

Holling, C.S. (1986), 'The resilience of terrestrial ecosystems: local surprise and global change', in W.C. Clark and R.E. Munn (eds), *Sustainable Development of the Biosphere*, Cambridge University Press, Cambridge: 292–317.

Holling, C.S. (1992), 'Cross-scale morphology geometry and dynamics of ecosystems', *Ecological Monographs* **62**: 447–502.

Holling, C.S., Schindler, D.W., Walker, B.W. and Roughgarden, J. (1995), 'Biodiversity in the functioning of ecosystems', in C. Perrings, K.G. Mäler, C. Folke, C.S. Holling and B.-O. Janssen (eds), *Biodiversity Loss: Ecological and Economic Issues*, Cambridge University Press, Cambridge: 44–83.

Jones, D.D. (1975), 'The applications of catastrophe theory to ecological systems', in G.S. Innes (ed.), *New Directions in the Analysis of Ecological Systems*, Simulation Councils, La Jolla, CA.

Kauffman, S.A. and Johnsen, S. (1991), 'Coevolution to the edge of chaos: coupled fitness landscapes, poised states, and coevolutionary avalanches', *Journal of Theoretical Biology* **149**: 467–505.

Kay, J.J. (1991), 'A nonequilibrium thermodynamic framework for discussing ecosystem integrity', *Environmental Management* **15**: 483–95.

Leibenstein, H. (1957), *Economic Backwardness and Economic Growth*, John Wiley, New York.

Lewis, W.A. (1954), 'Economic development with unlimited supplies of labour', *Manchester School* **22**: 139–91.

May, R. (1972), 'Will a large complex system be stable?', *Nature* **238**: 413–4.

May, R. (1976), 'Simple mathematical models with very complicated dynamics', *Nature* **261**: 459–67.

Myrdal, G. (1957), *Economic Theory and Underdeveloped Regions*, Duckworth, London.

Norgaard, R.B. (1984), 'Coevolutionary development potential', *Land Economics* **60**: 160–73.

Noy-Meir, I. and Walker, B.H. (1986), 'Stability and resilience in rangelands', in P.J. Joss, P.W. Lynch and O.B. Williams (eds), *Rangelands: A Resource Under Siege*, Proceedings of the Second International Rangelands Congress, International Rangelands Congress, Adelaide: 21–5.

O'Neill, R.V., Johnson, A.R. and King, A.W. (1989), 'A hierarchical framework for the analysis of scale', *Landscape Ecology* **3**: 193–205.

Pearce, D.W.P. (1987), 'Foundations of an ecological economics', *Ecological Modelling* **38**: 9–18.

Pearce, D.W. Markandya, A. and Barbier, E.B. (1989), *Blueprint for a Green Economy*, Earthscan, London.

Pearce, D.W. and Turner, R.K. (1990), *Economics of Natural Resources and the Environment*, Harvester-Wheatsheaf, London.

Perrings, C. (1987), *Economy and Environment: A Theoretical Essay on the Interdependence of Economic and Environmental Systems*, Cambridge University Press, Cambridge.

Perrings, C. (1991), 'Ecological sustainability and environmental control', *Structural Change and Economic Dynamics* 2: 275–95.

Pielou, E.C. (1975), *Ecological Diversity*, John Wiley, New York.

Pimm, S.L. (1984), 'The complexity and stability of ecosystems', *Nature* **307**: 321–6.

Puu, T. (1989), *Non-Linear Economic Dynamics*, Springer-Verlag, Berlin.

Rosser, B. (1990), *From Catastrophe to Chaos: A General Theory of Economic Discontinuities*, Kluwer, Dordrecht.

Schaeffer, D.J., Herricks, E. and Kerster, H. (1988), 'Ecosystem health: I. measuring ecosystem health', *Environmental Management* **12**: 445–55.

Schindler, D.W. (1990), 'Natural and anthropogenically imposed limitations to biotic richness in freshwaters', in G. Woodwell (ed.), *The Earth in Transition: Patterns and Processes of Biotic Impoverishment*, Cambridge University Press, Cambridge: 425–62.

Solow, R.M. (1974), 'Intergenerational equity and exhaustible resources', *Review of Economic Studies*, Symposium: 29–46.

Solow, R.M. (1986), 'On the intertemporal allocation of natural resources', *Scandinavian Journal of Economics* **88**: 141–9.

Turner, R.K. (1988), 'Sustainability, resource conservation and pollution control: an overview', in R.K. Turner (ed.), *Sustainable Environmental Management: Principles and Practice*, Bellhaven Press, London: 1–25.

Turner, R.K. (1992), 'Speculations on weak and strong sustainability', CSERGE GEC Working Paper No. 26, CSERGE and UCL, London.

Walker, B.H. (1988), 'Autecology, synecology, climate and livestock as agents of rangelands dynamics', *Australian Range Journal* **10**: 69–75.

Walker, B.H. and Noy-Meir, I. (1982), 'Aspects of the stability and resilience of savanna ecosystems', in B.J. Huntley and B.H. Walker (eds), *Ecology of Tropical Savannas*, Springer-Verlag, Berlin: 577–90.

Westoby, M., Walker, B. and Noy-Meir, I. (1989), 'Opportunistic management for rangelands not at equilibrium', *Journal of Range Management* **42**: 266–74.

4. Towards an ecological economics of sustainability

(with M.S. Common)[*]

1 INTRODUCTION

While 'sustainability' has become a watchword for much recent work in environmental economics, there remains considerable disagreement as to both the conceptual and the operational content of the term. This disagreement has various sources, including differences in disciplinary perspective, the axiomatic foundations of the dynamic models within which the concept has been explored, and the interpretation of sustainability at the policy level. Moreover, underlying many of the disputed issues is an ill-defined set of philosophical and ethical differences over the problem of both intra- and intergenerational equity. The net result is a debate in which the fundamental points at issue remain obscure. This chapter seeks to clarify matters through the development of a model of resource allocation that embraces both economic and ecological concepts of sustainability, and so helps to identify some basic operational principles of an ecological economics of sustainability. To do this it has been necessary to select from the variety of models in each of the two disciplines. We have chosen to work with the Solow/Hartwick approach from economics and the Holling approach from ecology. The former offers the most widely-used framework for addressing sustainability issues in economics. The latter, although it does not have the same status in ecology, has the double advantage that it is both cogent and obviously amenable to economic interpretation.

The approach adopted in the chapter is cross-disciplinary in that the structure of the model developed here depends on insights deriving from both ecology and economics. Since a first requirement of any economic model of natural resource allocation is that it is sensitive to the properties of ecological systems which generate the natural resources involved, the chapter is drawn into a review of those elements in the axiomatic structure of existing dynamic economic models of sustainability that are problematic from an ecological

---

[*] Mick Common is a Senior Fellow at the Centre for Resource and Environmental Studies, Australian National University, Canberra, ACT 0200, Australia.

perspective. To anticipate, we argue that while it is not necessary to sacrifice the intertemporal efficiency required by a Solow/Hartwick interpretation of economic sustainability in order to assure ecological sustainability, intertemporal price efficiency is not a necessary condition for ecological sustainability. However, we also argue that the pursuit of intertemporal efficiency on the basis of the sovereignty of the present consumer may well be inconsistent with ecological sustainability. An ethical shift away from the values that privilege consumer sovereignty may be a necessary feature of an ecological economics of sustainability. Daly and Cobb (1989) have recently arrived at a similar position via a somewhat different route.

2   ECONOMICS: SOLOW-SUSTAINABILITY

The starting point for a treatment of sustainability within the utilitarian framework of neoclassical economics is the concept of consumption. Consumption defines those goods and services which are 'taken out' of the total available goods and services generated within the global system in order to satisfy a given set of wants within the constraint posed by a given set of endowments. The concept of consumption accordingly implies two key assumptions about the nature of the economic problem. First, the notion of a given set of wants implies that there exists an exogenously-determined set of preferences (assumed to have a number of far from innocuous mathematical properties) which is both external to the productive system and invariant with respect to that system. Moreover, it implies that satisfaction of such preferences may be treated as a criterion of system performance. Second, the notion of a given set of endowments implies that there exists an exogenously-determined 'heritage' comprising both a set of resources and the property rights which map those resources into the consumer's constraint set. The set of property rights is likewise assumed to be invariant with respect to the productive system. A corollary is that the organization and technology of the productive system may also be taken to be exogenous to the economic problem.

We shall return to a discussion of these assumptions later.[1] For now our interest lies in what this concept of consumption implies for the treatment of sustainability. We begin by relating consumption and income, using the Hicks/Lindahl concept of income. Recall that in his (1946) discussion of income, Hicks canvassed three definitions. Income was defined to be the maximum amount which could be spent on consumption in one period without reducing (a) the expected capital value of prospective receipts in future periods; or (b) nominal consumption expenditure in future periods; or (c) real consumption expenditure in future periods. As has frequently been observed since, these are all definitions of sustainable net income, and they have immediate implications for the 'heritage' constraining consumption decisions. If 'income' is defined to be the maximum real consumption expenditure that leaves society as 'well off' at the end of a period as at the beginning, it presupposes the deduction of expenditures to make good the depreciation or degradation of the asset base which yields that income (compare Pearce et al., 1989). In terms of our earlier statement of the economic problem, it implies the preservation of some suitably defined capital stock with a view to ensuring that the constraint set does not tighten over time. It is accordingly income net of the expenditure needed to maintain such a suitably defined capital stock.[2]

Hicks had argued that all three definitions of income amounted to the same thing provided that both the rate of interest and prices were constant over time. If the rate of interest were to vary over time the first definition ceased to be relevant. If prices varied over time the second definition ceased to be relevant. It is of central importance to the neoclassical approach to sustainability that Hotelling (1931) had already established that a necessary condition for the efficient intertemporal allocation of exhaustible resources was that the price of an exhaustible resource should increase at the rate of interest. That is, neglecting extraction costs:

$$\dot{p}(t)\,/p_i(t) = r \qquad\qquad (4.1)$$

where r is the interest or discount rate and $p_i(t)$ is the *in situ* price of the i-th resource at time t. If the stock of capital includes both produced and (exhaustible) environmental assets, an efficient price path will be one in which the prices of *in situ* exhaustible resources change over time. While it is not possible to point to an efficiency rule governing the evolution of the rate of interest attracting similar consensus, a range of contributions by Fisher (1930), Knight (1934; 1936) and Hayek (1941) had established a relationship between the rate of interest and the marginal productivity of capital, which had similar implications. The significance of this is that the relevant definition in Hicks's gallery is the third: income is given by the maximum amount which may be spent on consumption in one period without reducing real consumption expenditure in future periods.

The translation of this definition into a theory of sustainable resource utilization involved a series of papers which sought to establish how real consumption expenditure based on the exploitation of exhaustible resources might remain constant over time. Economists have always had to work hard to find a rationalization for the principle of constant consumption. In this instance, the rationalization was provided by Solow, who used the egalitarian arguments of Rawls (1971) to propose a 'Rawlsian' maximin approach to the intertemporal distribution of consumption.[3] With this justification, Solow (1974), and later Hartwick (1977, 1978a, 1978b), Dixit et al. (1980), and Dasgupta and Mitra (1983), all considered the conditions in which real consumption expenditure might be preserved despite declining stocks of exhaustible resources. The product of their enquiry was a very simple result, now known as the Hartwick rule. The rule states that consumption may be held constant in the face of exhaustible resources only if the rents deriving from the intertemporally efficient use of those resources are reinvested in reproducible capital. That is, a necessary condition for consumption to be maintained over time is that the efficiency rents from exploiting exhaustible resources should be reinvested in non-exhaustible assets.

The intuition behind the Hartwick rule is transparent in the simplest of all cases considered by Solow (1974). Let $q = f[x]$ define net output produced under constant returns by a homogeneous stock of capital, x with initial value x_0 (we may neglect labour). Define $q = c + \dot{x}$, the sum of consumption and new investment. Then, as Solow pointed out, the maximin principle implies that $\dot{x}$ should be set equal to zero, and $x = x_0$. The optimal policy for each generation is to maintain the existing capital stock. Investment should be exactly equal to depreciation. Now the important property of a homogeneous capital stock is that each component of that stock is perfectly substitutable for all other components. If $\mathbf{x}(t)$ is defined to be a time-varying vector of heterogeneous capital stocks including exhaustible resources, this is no longer true. However, as Solow (1974) and Hartwick (1977, 1978a, 1978b) both showed, providing that there is sufficient substitutability between reproducible and exhaustible stocks, it is still possible to derive an investment rule that will maintain the productive capacity of that stock.

The proviso concerning the substitutability of reproducible and exhaustible stocks is crucial. Before we consider the Hartwick rule more closely, it is worth elaborating on the substitutability assumptions that enabled Solow and Hartwick to link the rule to sustainable consumption expenditure. We have already observed that the assumption of heterogeneous capital implies that there is less than perfect substitution between produced and natural assets. To capture this, Solow (1974), Hartwick (1977, 1978a) and Dasgupta and Mitra (1983) assumed that all inputs were 'essential' in the sense that output would be zero if any input were zero. That is, in addition to the usual properties of the production function, it was assumed that $f[\mathbf{x}(t)] = 0$ if $x_i = 0$ for all i and all t. However, whether or not the assumption that inputs are essential in this sense implies any real constraint on output depends on the substitution possibilities assumed to exist between inputs, and this depends on the form of the production function. Where the functional form chosen to characterize global productive activity is Cobb–Douglas, as it is in Solow (1974), and Hartwick (1977, 1978a), we have the extraordinary property that the average product of an essential resource has no upper bound. As the resource tends to zero, its average product may tend to infinity. Even more remarkable, where the production function is CES with an elasticity of substitution between exhaustible resources and produced capital greater than unity (for example, Hartwick, 1978b) the non-renewability of natural resources is simply irrelevant. They cannot be essential to production.

The precise form of the production function is actually irrelevant to the derivation of the Hartwick rule. However, it is crucial if application of the Hartwick rule is to be associated with constant consumption over infinite time. Indeed, the rule itself is less a criterion for sustainable development than a condition for the efficiency of intertemporal resource allocation. To see this, consider the following very general model. Let $x(t)$ denote an n-vector of the resources available to the global system at time t. $x(t)$ accordingly includes produced capital, renewable natural resources, exhaustible resources, and both 'intermediate' and 'final' consumption goods. $\dot{x}(t)$ then defines the net rate of augmentation or depletion of the corresponding components of $x(t)$. $\dot{x}_i(t) > 0$ implies that the i-th resource is expanding either through net investment (in the case of produced resources) or through natural growth (in the case of natural resources). $\dot{x}_i(t) < 0$ implies that the resource is being depleted either through depreciation (in the case of produced resources) or through extraction or degradation (in the case of natural resources). $\dot{x}_i(t) = 0$ implies that net production of the resource is zero. If it is interesting to isolate some particular class of resource, then $x(t)$ and $\dot{x}(t)$ must be partitioned appropriately. The production possibilities of the system are described by the set of all feasible pairs $[x(t),\dot{x}(t)]$, and it is assumed to be stationary, convex and continuously differentiable. In addition, let $p(t)$ denote an n-vector of prices corresponding to $x(t)$, $\dot{p}(t)$ denoting the rate of change of those prices. $p_i(t) > 0$ indicates that the i-th resource is a scarce good; $p_i(t) < 0$ that it is a bad in sufficient supply to impose costs; and $p_i(t) = 0$ that it is perceived as a non-scarce good.

A price path $[p(t),\dot{p}(t)]_{t=0}^{\infty}$ is said to be efficient if and only if it respects a generalized Hotelling rule for durable produced or natural assets. That is, denoting the rate of discount by r,[4] $[p(t),\dot{p}(t)]_{t=0}^{\infty}$ is said to be efficient if and only if

$$\dot{p}_i(t)/p_i(t) = r - \dot{x}_i(t)/x_i(t) \tag{4.2}$$

for all t and for all i. A time path for resource allocation $[x(t),\dot{x}(t)]_{t=0}^{\infty}$ is said to be efficient at prices $[p(t),\dot{p}(t)]_{t=0}^{\infty}$ if and only if, for all t, it maximizes instantaneous profit defined by:

$$\Pi(t) = p'(t)\dot{x}(t) + \dot{p}'(t)x(t) \tag{4.3}$$

$p'(t)$ denoting a row vector, the transpose of $p(t)$. It follows immediately that profit along such a time path will be at a maximum if, and only if, net investment (defined by $p'(t)\dot{x}(t)$ is equal to the imputed rents on the resource base (defined by $-\dot{p}'(t)x(t)$). More particularly, it is immediate that

$$d[p'(t)\dot{x}(t)]/dt = -d[\dot{p}'(t)x(t)]/dt \tag{4.4}$$

is a necessary condition for intertemporal efficiency in the allocation of resources. This captures the sense of the Hartwick rule: that optimal investment along an efficient time path is equal to rents on resources.

To relate the result on prices more specifically to consumption expenditure, let the vectors $\mathbf{x}(t)$ and $\mathbf{p}(t)$ be partitioned conformably to distinguish between resources devoted to consumption (subscripted c) and other resources (subscripted k), so that $\mathbf{x}(t) = [\mathbf{x}_c(t), \mathbf{x}_k(t)]$ and $\mathbf{p}(t) = [\mathbf{p}_c(t), \mathbf{p}_k(t)]$. We then have, as a condition of the maximization of profit, that

$$d[\mathbf{p}_c'(t)\dot{\mathbf{x}}_c(t)]/dt = -d(\mathbf{p}_k'(t)\dot{\mathbf{x}}_k(t)]/dt - \{d[\dot{\mathbf{p}}_c'(t)\mathbf{x}_c(t)]/dt + d[\dot{\mathbf{p}}_k'(t)\mathbf{x}_k(t)]/dt\}.$$
(4.5)

If consumption is to be constant over time, the term on the left-hand side must be equal to zero, from which it follows that

$$d[\mathbf{p}_k'(t)\dot{\mathbf{x}}_k(t)]/dt = -\{d[\dot{\mathbf{p}}_c'(t)\mathbf{x}_c(t)]/dt + d[\dot{\mathbf{p}}_k'(t)\mathbf{x}_k(t)]/dt\}.$$
(4.6)

Note that the right-hand side includes a term defining the rent on stocks of resources intended for consumption. This follows from the fact that we have insisted that prices should reflect a generalized Hotelling rule with respect to all durable assets, and stocks of resources intended for consumption fall into this category. Otherwise this restates the Hartwick rule. Moreover, since $\mathbf{p}'(t)\dot{\mathbf{x}}(t) + \dot{\mathbf{p}}'(t)\mathbf{x}(t) = d[\mathbf{p}'(t)\mathbf{x}(t)]/dt$, it is equivalent to a requirement that the value of the stock of assets is kept constant.

The important point here is that the Hartwick rule is driven by a condition on prices (the Hotelling rule), and not by a condition on the nature of the physical environment. The rule gives rise to constant consumption over infinite time in the Solow and Hartwick models – what we have called Solow-sustainability – because both authors assume that aggregate output may be maintained even as essential inputs asymptotically approach zero. However, the validity of the rule as a condition for the efficient intertemporal allocation of resources is independent of the functional form chosen to characterize productive activity.

The way in which the Hartwick rule and Solow-sustainability of consumption levels is currently being incorporated in the neoclassical approach to sustainability shows some sensitivity to the limitations of the technological assumptions made by these authors. In particular, the substitutability assumptions implicit in the sort of well-behaved neoclassical production functions adopted by Solow and Hartwick have been modified to admit the non-substitutability of certain types of natural and produced capital. It is, for example, now sometimes assumed that there exists some upper bound on the assimilative capacity of the environment to absorb wastes, and some lower bound on the level of stocks that can support sustainable development (see, for example, Barbier and Markandya, 1990). Indeed, externalities associated with the 'multifunctionality' of natural resources and the problem of irreversibility have been cited as rationales for setting the lower bound conservatively (Pearce and Turner, 1990). In addition, following the early mass-balance models of Kneese et al. (1970) it is now recognized that waste generation is an increasing function of consumption (Barbier, 1990).[5]

Nevertheless, the notion that some suitably defined stock of capital should be kept constant is a crucial component of sustainability in this approach (compare Turner, 1988; Pearce et al., 1989; Pezzey, 1989; Mäler, 1990). Moreover, while there remains some uncertainty about the appropriate definition of the stock of capital to be kept constant, there is a degree of consensus among those taking this view of sustainability that the only meaningful measure is a measure of value (compare Solow, 1986; Pearce and Turner, 1990).[6] This focus on value magnitudes is, it turns out, critically important to an understanding both of the essential features of the neoclassical approach to sustainability, and of the operational principles to which it gives rise. Recall that the price path $[\mathbf{p}(t),$ $\dot{\mathbf{p}}(t)]_{t=0}^{\infty}$ defines a set of efficiency or optimal prices. They are, accordingly, shadow prices rather than ruling market prices, capturing both the marginal extraction costs (where these are explicitly modelled) and the resource rental or marginal user costs of all assets in the global system. It is immaterial whether the resources involved are natural or produced, the optimal price will comprise the same elements in all cases. We earlier made the point that the general Hartwick rule is an arbitrage condition for the efficient intertemporal allocation of resources. What this means is that if property rights are well defined (eliminating the problem of externalities), and if all markets are competitive, then rational agents confronted by such optimal prices would allocate resources according to the rule.

The implications of this for a set of operational principles are both immediate and far-reaching. Providing that competitive agents are confronted by the full social cost of resource use, as defined by the set of optimal prices, the resulting intertemporal equilibrium allocation of resources will be Solow-sustainable. The attention then switches to the conditions in which individual resource users will be confronted by the set of optimal prices. There are two conditions here: either that there exists a complete set of markets including a complete set of contingent markets from the present date to infinity; or that all agents in the system contract in current markets on the basis of 'rational expectations' about the future course of resource prices. Since 'rational expectations' in this sense implies expectations that are consistent with the clearing of all non-existent forward or contingent markets, the two amount to the same thing. These conditions might seem excessive, but as Dasgupta and Heal (1979) show, nothing less will do. A sequence of momentary equilibria in which agents have perfect myopic foresight as to the rate of change of prices, and perfect knowledge of the current rate of interest, is not sufficient to ensure an efficient intertemporal competitive equilibrium.

3   ECOLOGY: HOLLING-SUSTAINABILITY

To approach the identification of an ecological economics of sustainability consider, again, the assumptions underpinning what we have called Solow-sustainability. These are, of course, part of the general gallery of assumptions characterizing neoclassical economics, and are not unique to the Solow/Hartwick models – even though the existence of Solow-sustainability supposes a very particular set of technological assumptions, and so a very particular selection from the neoclassical gallery. The difficulty with these assumptions from an ecological perspective lies in their treatment of the human economy in the global system. Since they ignore the fact that the human economy is an integral part of a materially closed evolutionary system, models constructed on the basis of such assumptions are necessarily blind to the dynamic implications of this fact. In fact, for more than a hundred years the dominant metaphor of economic activity has been a trophic one, in which economic agents are conceived as 'feeding off' the resources of a quiescent and independently functioning natural environment in order to satisfy an exogenously-determined set of desires up to the limits permitted by an exogenously-determined set of endowments. But except over the very shortest of time scales this is not a useful characterization of economic activity.

Human preferences and property rights are not independent of the state of nature. Indeed, there is increasingly widespread recognition in economics that the assumption of the exogeneity of preferences and property rights obstructs the further development of the discipline. Neither the structure of preferences nor the structure of property rights can any longer be left outside the domain of rational economic choice. Choices made now within a given set of preferences and rights influence the future structure of both preferences and rights. Essentially the same objection may be made with respect to the technological assumptions of the Solow/Hartwick models. Such assumptions are both inconsistent with the physical principles informing a materially closed thermodynamic system, and blind to the feedbacks due to the dynamic interdependence of human and environmental productive systems (Georgescu-Roegen, 1971). The necessity for change in the technology both of consumption (preferences) and production as a consequence of environmental change have long been recognized (compare Wilkinson, 1973; Boyden, 1987 and Common, 1988). Indeed, Perrings (1987) derives such changes as a logical necessity of the structure and dynamics of the global system. The contribution of ecologists working within a systems approach is to show how the feedbacks in an interlocking set of ecosystems may change the 'rationality' and the organizational principles of a given ecosystem.

Our starting point here is the work of Holling (1973, 1986) on the resilience and stability of ecosystems. Ecosystems, like economic systems, can be analysed in terms of the operation of principles of optimization. So, for example, Holling argues that ecosystems are characterized by discontinuous change, expressed through successional and disruptive processes, and that it is these processes which define both the organization and rationality of such systems. As an instance of this, the r and K strategies (originally identified by MacArthur and Wilson, 1967) are argued to reflect two different optimization principles: the r strategies refer to the selection of organisms during disruptive or early successional phases to maximize growth in an unconstrained environment; and the K strategies refer to those organisms selected at the climax of a successional phase for efficiency of nutrient harvest in a crowded environment. The r and K strategies are, of course, merely examples within a continuum of such strategies, but the point is that the optimization principles which underlie system organization are themselves argued to be a function of system structure and dynamics.

In order to explore the stability properties of ecosystems, Holling distinguishes between what are, in effect, two levels of stability. Stability, *per se*, he defines to mean the propensity of the populations within an ecosystem to return to an equilibrium condition (whether stationary or cyclic) following perturbation. Resilience, on the other hand, he defines to mean the propensity of a system to retain its organizational structure following perturbation. To interpret the two concepts, we note that Holling-stability is the narrower term, and refers to the stability of the system variables (the populations of organisms) in the face of disturbance. Holling-resilience is the broader term, and refers to the stability of the system parameters (organizational principles) in the face of disturbance. Resilience admits the possibility of multiple equilibrium values for the system variables, but insists on the uniqueness of equilibrium values for the system parameters.

The distinction between the terms accordingly implies a difference in the focus of analysis within an ecosystem. An ecosystem may be defined to be a community of organisms in which the effect of internal interactions between organisms dominates the effect of external events, catastrophes apart. It is legitimate to investigate either the individual populations of organisms making up the community, or the community of organisms as a whole. But the nature of the insights obtained from analysis at the micro and macro levels is very different. Nor is it symmetrical. It is not possible to derive the properties of the ecosystem as a whole from a study of one population within the ecosystem.[7] However, it is clear that the individual populations of an ecosystem will be Holling-stable only if the ecosystem is Holling-resilient. That is, the stability of the individual populations within an ecosystem presumes the stability or resilience of the ecosystem as a whole. On the other hand, Holling-resilience does not necessarily imply Holling-stability. Indeed, system resilience may be positively correlated with instability in the system populations. Since Holling-resilience is argued to be an increasing function of what is called interconnectedness or complexity within an ecosystem, Holling (1986), it may be inferred that it is an increasing function of the number of constituent populations within an ecosystem. Moreover, since ecosystems are naturally interpreted in terms of a nested hierarchy of subsystems, it seems clear that Holling-resilience is a stability concept best suited to a discussion of aggregations of communities of organisms.

To obtain a concept of sustainability from these notions of stability and resilience, it is useful to appeal to recent advances in the theory of complex thermodynamic systems. It is now understood that ecosystems which are open with respect to energy flows have a tendency to 'self-organize' within the constraints imposed by an evolutionary and fluctuating environment. Any point where the 'self-organizing' forces of the system balance the 'disorganizing' forces of the environment may be said to be an optimum operating point of that ecosystem (Kay, 1989). The climax community in an ecosystem accordingly represents one such optimum operating point. At such an operating point the individual populations of organisms within the community might be expected to be Holling-stable. However, it is recognized that consistent with a given organizational structure, there may be multiple equilibrium values for the populations within an ecosystem, each being at least locally stable. The Holling-resilience of the system may be measured by its ability to maintain its 'self-organization' or, put another way, to accommodate the stress imposed by its environment through selection of a different operating point along the same thermodynamic path without undergoing some 'catastrophic' change in organizational structure.

We refer to the notion of sustainability deriving from this as Holling-sustainability. A system may be said to be Holling-sustainable, if and only if it is Holling-resilient. This is the sense of sustainability as it has been defined with respect to agricultural systems by Conway (1985, 1987). The important feature of resilience is the capacity it implies to adapt to the stresses imposed on a system by its interdependence with other systems. In this sense, resilience preserves the options available to future generations of organisms within an ecosystem, without in any sense prescribing those options.[8]

The point made by Holling is that where the dynamics of the global system involve the discontinuous change of each component system, the resilience of each system is itself subject to change. This may occur naturally due to the interaction between ecosystems, or it may be the result of the way in which an ecosystem is exploited in the course of economic activity. Holling (1986) characterizes most historical attempts to manage ecosystems as 'weak experiments testing a general hypothesis of stability/resilience'. Management directed at minimizing the variance of some target variable has a Holling-stability goal. But, as he points out, there is overwhelming evidence that historical attempts to stabilize ecosystems in this sense, while frequently successful in terms of the short-run variance of the target variable, have led to qualitative changes in the nature of the wider system – often with adverse implications for the resilience of that wider system. In many cases, the source of difficulty lies in the reduction of the range of communities within the system as a result of an economic focus on a single species. A narrower range of communities within an ecosystem implies, among other things, a reduction in the interconnectedness or complexity that is argued to underpin the resilience of that system.

To capture the sense of Holling-sustainability formally, recall that our distinction between Holling-stability and Holling-resilience is the distinction between two classes of stability. The first requires the stability of both the (organic) variables and the (organizational) parameters of an ecosystem. The second requires the stability only of the (organizational) parameters of that system. The first class of stability is obviously stronger and more restrictive than the second. Holling-stability implies neither the phenotypic nor the genotypic evolution of the system. Holling-resilience, on the other hand, admits the evolution of systems within bounds allowed by the organizational parameters of the system. That is, it admits the phenotypic evolution of the system. As Faber and Proops (1990) have recently pointed out, this implies that the changes that may occur in what we have termed a Holling-resilient system are essentially predictable.

Holling correctly argues that the first class of stability is overly restrictive as a management concept in an evolutionary environment, where the object of analysis is a system of interdependent populations of organisms, rather than the populations themselves. Our problem here is to find a suitable logical construction to capture the second class. The first point to make is that Holling-resilience is a stability concept. Despite his reference to the qualitative insights that derive from the concept, Holling-resilience does relate to the time variation of a response to some perturbation. The primary difference between Holling-stability and Holling-resilience is in the level of analysis. Holling-stability is defined by the stability of populations within an ecosystem. Holling-resilience is defined by the stability of the ecosystem itself.

To formalize this, let us return to our earlier description of the resources of the global system at time t in terms of the n-vector $x(t)$, and note that this vector will include the populations of all organisms making up the global system. The Holling-stability of the global system would be measured by the stability of each component of $x(t)$. More particularly, if we take the Euclidean norm of the perturbations of $x(t)$, denoted $\|\tilde{x}(t)\|$, then the system may be said to be Holling-stable if it is possible to define a function $\delta(\varepsilon)$ such that if $\| \tilde{\mathbf{x}}(0) \| < \delta$, then $\| \tilde{\mathbf{x}}(t) \| < \varepsilon$, for all $\varepsilon \geq \delta > 0$ and for all $t > 0$. If $\lim_{t \to \infty} \| \tilde{\mathbf{x}}(t) \| = 0$, then the system may be said to be asymptotically Holling-stable.

To get at a concept of Holling-resilience relevant to economic decision-making, we need to have some sense of the mutual dependence of the resource stocks and the system parameters. To do this let us first define a time varying k-vector of stochastic system 'parameters', $\mathbf{z}(t)$, the joint probability density function of which at time t is denoted

$$z(t) = pr[\mathbf{z}(t)]. \tag{4.7}$$

This vector of parameters describes what we have earlier referred to as the organizational principles governing productive activity in the system. It would include, for example, indices of the effectiveness of the range of specific processes associated with entropy production in the natural system: photosynthesis, respiration, and so on. It is assumed that $z(t)$ is a function of (a) the undisturbed time path of resource stocks; and (b) perturbations in the undisturbed time path of resource stocks at time t. Formally,

$$z(t) = h[\tilde{\mathbf{x}}(t), \bar{\mathbf{x}}(t)] \tag{4.8}$$

where $\tilde{\mathbf{x}}(t)$ defines perturbations in $\mathbf{x}(t)$ due to economic activity,[9] and $\bar{\mathbf{x}}(t)$ defines the undisturbed values of $\mathbf{x}(t)$. We assume that $\bar{\mathbf{x}}(t)$ is a non-stationary random process.

Equation (4.8) accordingly reflects the assumption that the organizational principles of a system are sensitive to perturbation of the resource stocks in that system due to economic activity. An example of the sort of relation captured by this assumption would be the effects of the introduction of livestock into the semi-arid savannah ecosystems of the Sahel, eastern and south-central Africa. In all cases this has perturbed the natural balance of resource stocks in terms of both fauna and flora. On the one hand it has led to a different balance between grazing species, an expansion of domesticated cattle and goats and a contraction in herbivorous wildlife. On the other it has led to a change in the balance of vegetation: woody vegetation replacing grasses. The result has been an increase in the sensitivity of the effectiveness of the natural processes to climatic fluctuations, making the ecosystems less resilient in a Holling sense. Put another way, the effect of the perturbation of resource stocks has been a change in both the mean and the variance of the system parameters.

Stability implies that the time derivative of $z(t)$ with respect to economic perturbations of $\bar{\mathbf{x}}(t)$ is non-positive. That is:

$$\dot{z}(t) = h_x \, \dot{\tilde{x}}(t) \le 0. \tag{4.9}$$

If $\dot{z}(t) \le 0$ in the neighbourhood of the unperturbed values of the resource stocks, then the function $h[\tilde{x}(t), \, \bar{x}(t)]$ is a Lyapunov function and the neighbourhood may be said to be a stable region. It is asymptotically stable if $\dot{z}(t) < 0$. A system may be said to be locally Holling-resilient and so locally Holling-sustainable if the probability density function of the system parameters is a Lyapunov function.

Note that this does not require the stability of the elements of $x(t)$. Depending upon the nature of the function $h[\cdot]$, it is quite possible for a system to be resilient, and yet for particular components of $x(t)$ to disappear. Resilience admits the extinction of some resource stock providing that the extinction does not affect the stability of the system parameters. Holling refers to this as creative destruction. Nevertheless, since the stability of system parameters is argued on empirical grounds to be an increasing function of the diversity of populations within an ecosystem, and of the links between them, the extinction of any one species as opposed to one local population within a species will generally reduce the stability of the system parameters.

4   MODELLING THE ECOLOGICAL ECONOMICS OF SUSTAINABILITY

It should be apparent that the major difference between the models that underpin the Solow and Holling approaches to sustainability lies in the explicit or implicit axiomatic structure of the physical components of each model. The axiomatic framework of the Solow model is fundamentally blind to the properties of the physical system in which the economic system is embedded. Indeed, it contains a variety of free gifts and free disposals assumptions that insulate the model from its environment, and prevent consideration of the most important dynamic implications of resource use. The axiomatic framework of the Holling model, on the other hand, privileges the system over its component parts. The dynamic economic problem for Holling exists precisely because of the physical feedbacks that characterize the growth and decay of subsystems within the global system. The model does not exclude the possibility that economic activity may accelerate the dynamics of natural processes. Nor does it exclude the possibility that the acceleration of natural processes may lead to the irreversible change of system organization and structures.

Having said this, though, we do not want to suggest that the models represent a fundamental division between economics and ecology. The Solow approach is no more representative of all economics than the Holling approach is of all ecology. The division is between a systems or macroscopic view of the physical processes involved on the one hand, and a component or microscopic view on the other. Within the history of economic thought there is, in fact, a very strong and continuous line of economic models since the Physiocrats that are all very consciously rooted in the biophysical systems of the environment (Christensen, 1987, 1989; Cleveland, 1987; Martinez-Alier, 1987). And while some of the impetus to the development of such models was undoubtedly lost in the aftermath of the Walrasian revolution in economic thought, economists concerned with the limitations of a microscopic view of the environment have continued to insist on the importance of an axiomatic structure that respects the properties of physical systems.[10] Moreover, even within work founded on the Solow approach to sustainability it is recognized that the technological assumptions underpinning Solow-sustainability do not reflect the essential properties of the real phenomena being modelled.[11] On the other side, ecology also has examples of component (population) oriented analysis. Moreover, even among those who take a systems perspective, there is no consensus on ecosystem dynamics, although there is some recent evidence of convergence at a methodological level in the main theoretical approaches to ecosystem analysis (compare Mauersberger and Straskraba, 1987).

When we speak of an ecological economics of sustainability in terms of the Solow and Holling approaches we do not, therefore, have in mind some sort of weighted average of disciplinary concerns. The problem addressed is an economic problem in as much as it involves human activity for the satisfaction of competing human purposes. The problem is usefully conceptualized in terms of the allocation of resources in order to optimize some welfare objective over time subject to a constraint set. What characterizes our approach to this problem is not an ecological bias so much as a systems perspective. This leads us to admit the dynamic interdependence of the objectives, instruments and constraints alike – not to exclude it by assumption. Ecology is, in this sense, important because the constraint set includes the properties of the biophysical systems within which economic activity takes place. The constraint set has its own internal dynamics, and these dynamics are sensitive to the stimuli offered by the economic exploitation of the resources within an ecosystem, or of the imposition of wastes on an ecosystem. The evolution of the economy and the evolution of the constraint set are accordingly interdependent. It is not only proper, it is crucial to think in terms of Norgaard's (1984) 'co-evolution' of the economic and environmental components of the global system.

As before, let $x(t)$ denote an n-vector of the resources available to the global system at time t, and let it be defined so as to include produced capital, renewable natural resources, exhaustible resources, and both 'intermediate' and 'final' consumption goods. In addition let $\dot{x}(t)$ define the net rate of augmentation or depletion of the corresponding components of $x(t)$. We now define an m-vector of economic resources, $\mathbf{u}(t)$, the components of which are physical measures of those resources in the system which are (a) subject to rights of property, and (b) transacted in a market. Since $\mathbf{x}(t)$ is the set of resources available to the global system at time t, it follows that the components of $\mathbf{u}(t)$ are a subset of the components of $\mathbf{x}(t)$, and that $m \leq n$. As before, let the distribution of the set of system parameters, $\mathbf{z}(t)$, be defined by the probability density function $z(t) = pr[\mathbf{z}(t)]$, where $z(t) = h[\tilde{\mathbf{x}}(t), \bar{\mathbf{x}}(t)]$ from (4.8). More particularly, let

$$z(t) = h[\mathbf{x}(t) - \bar{\mathbf{x}}(t), \bar{\mathbf{x}}(t)] \tag{4.10}$$

where $\tilde{\mathbf{x}}(t) = \mathbf{x}(t) - \bar{\mathbf{x}}(t)$ indicates the difference between the disturbed and undisturbed value of resource stocks at time t. As a first approximation we define this difference to be equal to the allocation of economic resources, $\mathbf{u}(t)$. That is,[12]

$$\tilde{\mathbf{x}}(t) = \mathbf{u}(t). \tag{4.11}$$

The rate of change in resource stocks (their growth or reduction) is assumed to depend on (a) the undisturbed processes of the natural environment, (b) disturbances due to the allocation of economic resources, and (c) the probability density function of the system parameters. This gives an equation of motion for the system of the form:

$$\dot{\mathbf{x}}(t) = \mathbf{f}[\bar{\mathbf{x}}(t), \mathbf{u}(t), z(t), t]. \tag{4.12}$$

The rate of change in resource stocks is accordingly affected by the allocation of economic resources in two ways: one through a direct growth function which relates outputs to inputs; and the other through a function relating the probability density function of the system parameters to the level of resource stocks. Notice that from equations (4.10) and (4.11) the condition for the Holling-resilience of the global system becomes

$$\dot{z}(t) = h_{\mathbf{u}}{'}\dot{\mathbf{u}}(t) \leq 0. \tag{4.13}$$

$\mathbf{p}(t)$ again denotes an n-vector of prices corresponding to $\mathbf{x}(t)$, $\dot{\mathbf{p}}(t)$ denoting the rate of change of those prices. As before, positive and negative prices indicate goods and bads, respectively. A zero price for a resource is usually interpreted to mean that it is a non-scarce good, but may equally imply that it is not subject to property rights. Since resource allocation in a dynamic framework is assumed to be a function of the set of relative prices, and its evolution over time, we have

$$\mathbf{u}(t) = \mathbf{u}[\mathbf{p}(t),t]. \qquad (4.14)$$

To characterize the sustainability problem we assume a benefit or social welfare function of the form

$$J = W(T)[\mathbf{x}(T),z(T),T]e^{-rT} + \int_0^T Y(t)[\bar{\mathbf{x}}(t), \mathbf{u}(t), z(t), t]e^{-rt}dt. \qquad (4.15)$$

Welfare is assumed to be time varying, and depends on two things. The first of these is the state of the resource base together with an index of system health, the probability density function of the system parameters, at the terminal time. It is assumed that the present generation derives benefit from the state of the system it bequeaths to future generations. We shall be more precise about this when we discuss the constraint set below. The second is the income deriving from exploitation of the resource base over the 'planning' period. This depends on the productive potential of the global system, and so on the same index of system health. Welfare is discounted at the rate r (given by the marginal productivity of capital evaluated at intertemporally efficient prices).

The 'planning' period is defined by the interval $[0,T]$. It relates to the period in which it is reasonable to assume that the relation between social preferences and the state of the system may be treated as constant. That is, defining the relations $W(T) = W[z(T)]$ and $Y(t) = Y[z(t)]$, T represents the maximum time over which the functions $W[\cdot]$ and $Y[\cdot]$ represent meaningful criteria of system performance. It therefore depends on the range of institutional, technological, cultural and ethical factors which regulate both the function and its arguments. One might, however, think of T as defining the minimum of the technological and preferential 'short periods'. Once again, we shall be more precise about this when we discuss the constraint set.

The primary constraints on the optimization of welfare are given by the dynamics of the global system, described by the equation of motion (4.12), and the initial conditions in respect of resource stocks, $\mathbf{x}(0) = \mathbf{x}_0$, and prices, $\mathbf{p}(0) = \mathbf{p}_0$. The 'ecological' content in our treatment of this problem relates to the way that these system dynamics are incorporated in the decision-making process. The basis for our approach is the Holling condition for the resilience of ecosystems, which we have interpreted in equation (4.9) as a condition on the probability density function of the system parameters. Equations (4.10) and (4.11) assert that Holling-resilience and so Holling-sustainability is to be regarded as a function of the allocation of economic resources in the global system which, from (4.14), depends on the time path of resource prices. To be sure, system resilience may change independently of economic decisions, but the implication of these equations is that the natural evolution of ecosystems will also be affected by economic decisions. We believe that this formal statement of the connection between economic resource allocation and system health is both intuitive and in accordance with the historical experience that has motivated the sustainability debate.

An ecological sustainability constraint of the Holling variety is a constraint on the allocation of economic resources designed to ensure the stability of the function $z(t) = h[\bar{\mathbf{x}}(t), \bar{\mathbf{x}}(t)]$. In general, such a constraint requires only that $\dot{z}(t) = h_u'\dot{\mathbf{u}}(t)$ be non-positive. Consider, however, the functions $W(T) = W[z(T)]$ and $Y(t) = Y[z(t)]$. These state that the form of the benefit function is itself dependent on the system parameters. It is immediate, therefore, that the form of the benefit function will be constant if and only if the probability density function of the system parameters is constant. That is $\dot{W}(T), \dot{Y}(t) = 0$ if, and only if $h_u'\dot{\mathbf{u}}(t) = 0$ for all t, $0 \leq t \leq T$. The Holling-resilience of the global system is both a necessary and a sufficient condition for the existence of a constant structure of preferences.

A corollary of this is that a sufficient condition for the Holling-resilience of the global system (where we ignore natural disturbances to the distribution of the system parameters) is that $\dot{\mathbf{u}}(t) = 0$. In other words, if there is no change in the allocation of resources over time, there will be no change in the density function $z(t)$. It is easy to see from this that the emphasis in the classical growth models on the ability of a system to reproduce or replicate itself over time is rather naturally related to the notion of Holling-sustainability. If the structure and level of consumption and investment is constant, $\dot{\mathbf{u}}(t) = 0$, and if the system is resilient at time t, then it will continue to be resilient thereafter. Since the structure of consumption and investment will be constant along a classical equilibrium path, and since the level of consumption and investment will be constant if the rate of growth is zero, it follows that the zero rate of growth along an equilibrium path is sufficient to assure Holling-sustainability. Conversely, surplus and positive growth in a classical model would be inconsistent with Holling-sustainability.[13]

The secondary constraints on the optimization of welfare derive from the Hartwick arbitrage rule for the optimal intertemporal allocation of resources. The rule requires that along an optimal path $d[\mathbf{p}'(t)\dot{\mathbf{x}}(t) + \dot{\mathbf{p}}'(t)\mathbf{x}(t)]/dt = 0$ for all t. Given that the equilibrium rate of interest is identical to the internal rate of return, we have

$$0 = -\mathbf{p}'(t)\mathbf{x}(t) + [\mathbf{p}'(t)\dot{\mathbf{x}}(t) + \dot{\mathbf{p}}'(t)\mathbf{x}(t)]e^{-rt}$$

implying that

$$\mathbf{p}'(t)\mathbf{x}(t)e^{rt} = \mathbf{p}'(t)\dot{\mathbf{x}}(t) + \dot{\mathbf{p}}'(t)\mathbf{x}(t).$$

Now $d[\mathbf{p}'(t)\dot{\mathbf{x}}(t) + \dot{\mathbf{p}}'(t)\mathbf{x}(t)]/dt = 0$ implies that $d[\mathbf{p}'(t)\mathbf{x}(t)e^{rt}]/dt = 0$. Taking this last derivative and eliminating common terms, we are left with the following condition on the rate of change in the value of the resource base relative to the discount rate.

$$r\mathbf{p}'(t)\mathbf{x}(t) + \mathbf{p}'(t)\dot{\mathbf{x}}(t) + \dot{\mathbf{p}}'(t)\mathbf{x}(t) = 0. \tag{4.16}$$

We are now in a position to state the social problem in full. It is to maximize the benefit function

$$J = W[\mathbf{x}(T),z(T),T]e^{-rT} + \int_0^T Y[\bar{\mathbf{x}}(t), \mathbf{u}(t), z(t), t]e^{-rt}dt \tag{4.17}$$

subject to

$$\mathbf{f}[\bar{\mathbf{x}}(t), \mathbf{u}(t), z(t),t] - \dot{\mathbf{x}}(t) = 0 \qquad\qquad 0 \leq t \leq T \tag{4.18}$$

$$\dot{z}(t) = 0 \qquad\qquad 0 \leq t \leq T \tag{4.19}$$

$$r\mathbf{p}'(t)\mathbf{x}(t) + \mathbf{p}'(t)\dot{\mathbf{x}}(t) + \dot{\mathbf{p}}'(t)\mathbf{x}(t) = 0 \qquad 0 \leq t \leq T \tag{4.20}$$

with boundary conditions

$$\mathbf{x}(0) = \mathbf{x}_0 \tag{4.21}$$

$$z(0) = z_0 \tag{4.22}$$

$$\mathbf{p}(0) = \mathbf{p}_0 \tag{4.23}$$

and given that

$$\mathbf{u}(t) = \mathbf{u}[\mathbf{p}(t),t] \tag{4.24}$$

$$\mathbf{p}(t) = \mathbf{p}[\mathbf{x}(t), z(t),t]. \tag{4.25}$$

Since $\dot{z}(t)$ is constrained to be equal to zero, and since this is a sufficient condition for $\dot{W}(T)$, $\dot{Y}(t) = 0$, $W[\cdot]$ and $Y[\cdot]$ are shown in (4.17) as time-invariant functions. To draw out the implications of the approach as simply as possible, we once again ignore the potential for disturbances to the system from other than an economic source. This is tantamount to an assumption that $\bar{\mathbf{x}}(t) = 0$ for all t. While we would not regard such an assumption as an acceptable approximation of reality, it is useful for present purposes. The Hamiltonian for the function is

$$H[\bar{\mathbf{x}}(t), \mathbf{u}(t), z(t), r, \mathbf{p}(t)\mathbf{x}(t), \lambda(t), \mu(t), t]$$
$$= Y[\bar{\mathbf{x}}(t), \mathbf{u}(t), z(t), t]e^{-rt}dt + \lambda'(t)\mathbf{f}[\bar{\mathbf{x}}(t),\mathbf{u}(t), z(t), t] + \mu(t)r\mathbf{p}'(t)\mathbf{x}(t) \tag{4.26}$$

where $\lambda(t)$, an n-dimensional vector, and $\mu(t)$, a scalar, are Lagrange multipliers, enabling us to write the augmented benefit function in the form

$$
\begin{aligned}
J = W[\cdot]e^{-rT} + &\int_0^T \{H[\cdot]e^{-rt} + \dot{\lambda}'(t)\mathbf{x}(t) - \dot{\gamma}(t)\,z(t) - \dot{\mu}(t)\,\mathbf{p}'(t)\mathbf{x}(t)\}dt \\
&- [\lambda'(T)\mathbf{x}(T) - \lambda'(0)\mathbf{x}(0)] + [\gamma(T)z(T) - \gamma(0)z(0)] \\
&+ [\mu(T)\mathbf{p}'(T)\mathbf{x}(T)) - \mu(0)\mathbf{p}'(0)\mathbf{x}(0)]
\end{aligned} \tag{4.27}
$$

and to obtain, as necessary conditions for an optimum, the adjoint equations:

$$
\dot{\lambda}'(t) = -H_{\mathbf{x}}[\cdot] = -Y_{\mathbf{x}}(t)e^{-rt} - \lambda'(t)\mathbf{f}_{\mathbf{x}}(t) - [\mu(t)r - \dot{\mu}(t)\,][\mathbf{x}'(t)\mathbf{p}_{\mathbf{x}}' + \mathbf{p}(t)] \tag{4.28}
$$

$$
\dot{\gamma}(t) = H_z[\cdot] = Y_z(t)e^{-rt} + \lambda'(t)\mathbf{f}_z(t) + [\mu(t)r - \dot{\mu}(t)]\mathbf{p}_z'\mathbf{x}(t) \tag{4.29}
$$

$$
\dot{\mu}(t) = H_{\mathbf{px}}[\cdot] = \mu(t)r(t) \tag{4.30}
$$

together with the transversality conditions

$$
\gamma(T)z(T) = W_z(T)e^{-rT} \tag{4.31}
$$

$$
\lambda(T)\mathbf{x}(T) = W_{\mathbf{x}}(T)e^{-rT} \tag{4.32}
$$

and the maximum condition

$$
\dot{\gamma}(t)\,z_{\mathbf{u}}'(t) = Y_{\mathbf{u}}'(t)e^{-rt} + \lambda'(t)\mathbf{f}_{\mathbf{u}}(t). \tag{4.33}
$$

The adjoint vector, $\lambda(t)$, obtained by integration of (4.28) measures the sensitivity of the benefit function to variation in the system dynamics due to changes in the level of real resources, $\mathbf{x}(t)$, along an optimal trajectory. Analogously, the multipliers $\gamma(T)$ and $\mu(t)$, obtained by integration of (4.29) and (4.30), measure the sensitivity of the benefit function to variations in the indicator of system stability, and to the rate of change in the value of the resource base.

We may use these to investigate the significance of the economic efficiency condition and the ecological sustainability constraint, respectively. First, consider the adjoint equations (4.28) and (4.30). The adjoint vector, $\lambda(t)$, defines the marginal benefit of the dynamics of the real resources, and the equation describes its evolution over the interval $[0,T]$. The i-th component of the first vector on the right-hand side of (4.28) denotes the marginal benefit of the i-th real resource in the system. The i-th component of the second vector is the marginal benefit forgone of a change in the rate of growth/decay of the i-th resource. The i-th component of the last vector on the right-hand side is the marginal cost of the i-th resource weighted by the change in marginal benefit of the real discounted value of the resource base. It is this last vector that captures the effects on the evolution of $\lambda(t)$ of an intertemporal efficiency condition on prices. But notice that if condition (4.30) is satisfied, the last vector is equal to zero and the efficiency condition has no effect on the time path for $\lambda(t)$. Condition (4.30) is perfectly intuitive. It requires that along an optimal trajectory the marginal benefit from a change in the value of the resource base should grow at a rate equal to the discount rate. If the rate of discount and the rate of change of prices is out of balance with changes in the real system, the time paths of $\lambda(t)$ and hence $\mathbf{u}(t)$ will be affected. We repeat, however, that satisfaction of (4.30) is a necessary condition for the economic efficiency of an optimal trajectory. It is not a necessary condition for the ecological sustainability of that trajectory. Non-optimal prices will affect the allocation of resources through the rate of change of $\lambda(t)$, but optimal prices will not ensure the satisfaction of the constraint on $z(t)$.

To see what the impact of an ecological sustainability constraint may be, consider the second of the adjoint equations (4.29) together with the maximum condition (4.33). Substitution of the former into the latter reveals that

$$[Y_{\mathbf{u}}'(t) - Y_z(t)\, z_{\mathbf{u}}'(t)]e^{-rt} + \{\lambda'(t)\mathbf{f}_{\mathbf{u}}(t) - [\lambda'(t)\, \mathbf{f}_z(t)]z_{\mathbf{u}}'(t)\}$$
$$- [\mu(t)r - \dot{\mu}(t)]\mathbf{x}'(t)\mathbf{p}_z' = 0 \qquad (4.34)$$

which makes the effect of the ecological sustainability constraint apparent. The discounted marginal benefit of the allocation of economic resources is reduced by the impact of that allocation on the index of system stability. Similarly, the marginal forgone benefits of the allocation of economic resources are augmented by the indirect effects of economic resource allocation on the rate of growth/decay of resources through their effects on the system parameters. The impact of the price efficiency condition enters via the vector $[\mu(t)r - \dot{\mu}(t)]\mathbf{x}'(t)\mathbf{p}_z'$. Once again, along an optimal trajectory this vector will be equal to zero. The optimal allocation of resources is found by solving (4.34) for $\mathbf{u}(t)$. This presumes that $\lambda(t)$ has already been found from (4.28) and (4.29) and implies that if the price efficiency condition is not satisfied it will have both an indirect and a direct effect on the time path of $\mathbf{u}(t)$: indirectly through its effect on the adjoint vector $\lambda(t)$ in (4.28), and directly on $\mathbf{u}(t)$ in (4.34). Nevertheless, it remains the case that satisfaction of a condition for the intertemporally efficient evolution of prices is not necessary for the satisfaction of an ecological sustainability constraint.

5   CONCLUSIONS

The most striking conclusion to be drawn from this is that the concepts of Solow-sustainability and Holling-sustainability that underpin the constraint set in our approach are largely disjoint. Moreover, this conclusion is despite the dependence of prices on both real resources and some index of system health. While it is clear that change in the structure of prices due to change in the structure of real resources implies some shift in the optimal allocation of resources, it is not clear that this implies satisfaction of an ecological sustainability constraint. Nor should we expect there to be a close relationship between economic efficiency and ecological sustainability. Indeed, historically it would appear that most economies that have managed a resource base in an ecologically sustainable manner have not satisfied the minimum conditions for intertemporal economic efficiency. Such economies have typically been characterized by gross underutilization of resources; by crude rationing devices that do not facilitate adjustments at the margin; by highly ritualized gift and exchange mechanisms which preclude the law of one price. And yet, at the same time, they have operated in such a way as to minimize the pressure on the system parameters.

This is not to imply that an efficient price path is necessarily incompatible with the ecological sustainability of the system. If prices derive from the preferences of economic agents, and if preferences weight the ecologically sustainable use of resources heavily, efficient prices may also be ecologically sustainable. More particularly, from (4.13) and (4.14) we have that

$$\dot{z}(t) = h_\mathbf{u}'\mathbf{u}_\mathbf{p}\dot{\mathbf{p}}(t).$$
(4.35)

A sufficient condition for this to be equal to zero is that $\dot{\mathbf{p}}(t) = 0$. From (4.25) it follows that

$$\dot{\mathbf{p}}(t) = \mathbf{p}_\mathbf{x}\dot{\mathbf{x}}(t) + \mathbf{p}_z\dot{z}(t)$$
(4.36)

which will be zero valued along an optimal trajectory only if both terms are equal to zero. Since $\dot{z}(t) = 0$ in order to satisfy the ecological sustainability constraint, $\dot{\mathbf{p}}(t) = 0$ requires then that $\mathbf{p}_\mathbf{x}\dot{\mathbf{x}}(t) = 0$. This implies either that $\dot{\mathbf{x}}(t) = 0$, which means that the global system is stationary, or that $\dot{\mathbf{x}}(t) \neq 0$, but $\mathbf{p}_\mathbf{x}\dot{\mathbf{x}}(t) = 0$, which means that non-zero changes in the real resource base are not registered in the price set. This last case requires that the only real resources changing over time are either goods in excess supply or bads in insufficient supply to register. This hardly sounds credible. Returning to (4.35), we have two further possibilities. Either $\dot{\mathbf{u}}(t) = 0$, which means that the economy is stationary, or that $\dot{\mathbf{u}}(t) \neq 0$, but $h_\mathbf{u}'\dot{\mathbf{u}}(t) = 0$, which means that non-zero changes in the allocation of economic resources do not affect the system parameters.

It is this last option which is in a very real sense the goal of an ecologically sustainable development strategy. Providing that economic activity does not perturb the system parameters to the point where the stability (Holling-resilience) of the system or key components of that system are threatened, then the preferences/technology (and hence prices) driving economic activity may be said to be ecologically sustainable. The problem of ecological sustainability is, in this sense, to be solved at the level of preferences or technology. If the preference and production possibilities sets informing economic behaviour are ecologically sustainable, then the corresponding set of optimal and intertemporally efficient prices will also be ecologically sustainable.

This brings us to the operational *differentia specifica* of an ecological economics of sustainability. Since the conditions in which a set of optimal resource prices will be generated do not exist (and cannot exist) the operationalization of the Solow approach necessarily involves a set of second-best instruments. It turns out that for many commentators the choice of these hinges on their implications for the principle of consumer sovereignty. It is, for example, the principle of the sovereignty of the consumer of the moment (as well as fear of Hobbes's Leviathan) that lies behind most property rights solutions. Nor does it apparently matter that the principle of consumer sovereignty may compromise both economic efficiency and ecological sustainability. Athough the allocation of property rights sufficient to generate a complete set of current markets may be consistent with momentary equilibrium, it has been shown that this will generate a time path for the resources of the global system that is either infeasible or intertemporally inefficient (Dasgupta and Heal, 1979), and almost certainly ecologically unsustainable. The tendency to seek an intertemporally efficient allocation of environmental resources through price corrections based on the contingent valuation of such resources in both surrogate and simulated markets, which is such a pervasive characteristic of much recent work in environmental economics, is further evidence of the dominance of the principle of consumer sovereignty over the relevance of the instruments. To be sure, the maintenance of the value of the stock of capital is a necessary condition for Solow-sustainability, and this certainly implies the need to generate measures of the value of that stock which will enable it to be monitored over time. Indeed, this is what lies behind the development of natural resource accounts. But as Mäler (1990) points out, it is the optimal value of that stock which is at issue. There is no reason to believe that prices generated in simulated or surrogate markets are at all relevant to such a measure.

To approach the operational principles in an ecological economics approach, it is worth repeating that Solow-sustainability is a value concept deriving from an efficiency condition: the Hartwick rule. The sustainability indicators in this approach are accordingly measures of value. By contrast, Holling-sustainability is a physical concept deriving from a condition for the stability of ecosystems. The relevant indicators in this approach are accordingly a set of physical measures. In the case of Holling-stability they are population indicators.[14] In the case of Holling-resilience, they are indicators of the responsiveness in the distribution of the system parameters to perturbation in resource stocks. Notice that the size of any given population relative either to other populations or to its critical threshold size is not a sufficient indicator of the resilience of the system, although it may be a necessary component of a set of sustainability indicators. Schaeffer et al. (1988), for example, suggest the following combination of stock and response indicators: changes in the numbers of native species; overall regressive succession; changes in standing crop biomass; changes in the relative energy flows to grazing and decomposer food chains; changes in mineral micro-nutrient stocks; and finally changes in the mechanisms of and capacity for damping oscillations. A number of these are stock or population measures (the independent variables of the function $z(t) = h[\tilde{\mathbf{x}}(t), \bar{\mathbf{x}}(t)]$, but others relate to the system parameters. The key indicators in the approach are in fact the derivatives of the function with respect to the resource stocks under economic control.

An ecological economics approach requires that resources be allocated in such a way that they do not threaten the stability either of the system as a whole, or of key components of the system. If a self-regulating economic system is to be ecologically sustainable, it should serve a set of consumption and production objectives that are themselves sustainable. But this runs us up against a principle of consumer sovereignty that privileges the existing preferences and technologies. If existing preferences and technologies are not ecologically sustainable, then consumer sovereignty implies system instability. This leaves these options: if existing preferences and technologies are not ecologically sustainable, it is necessary either to regulate activity levels within the existing structure of preferences, or to change that structure of preferences, or both. The appropriate instruments – whether price manipulation, education, changes to property rights, and so on – will vary depending on institutional and other characteristics, and we do not wish to discuss them in this chapter. What we do wish to emphasize is that an ecological economics of sustainability implies an approach that privileges the requirements of the system above those of the individual. Certainly this involves ethical judgements about the role and rights of present individuals (compare Pearce, 1987). Consumer sovereignty, in such an approach, is an acceptable principle only in so far as consumer interests do not threaten the general system – and through this, the welfare of future generations. More particularly, since the valuation of resources deriving from ecologically unsustainable preferences is itself unsustainable, there is no advantage in giving special weight and special privilege to such valuations. What is important in the approach is the ability of the system to retain the resilience to cope with random shocks, and this is not served by operating as if the present structure of private preferences is the sole criterion against which to judge system performance.

NOTES

1.   The assumptions appear to have limited usefulness as a framework within which to consider the long-run economic history of man: see Common (1988).

2. The theoretical basis for this has recently been explored by Hartwick (1991).
3. It is interesting that Rawls himself deliberately shied away from the maximin principle when dealing with intergenerational equity.
4. The use of an exogenously-determined rate of discount should not be taken to imply that the determination of *r* is unproblematic. However, it is beyond the scope of this chapter to discuss the issues it raises.
5. It is of interest to note that in *The Limits to Growth*, Meadows et al. (1972) did explicitly recognize the connection between waste production and resource consumption, and drew attention to the pollution problems arising should resource stocks be larger than assumed in their base case. Although the base case itself attracted much (hostile) comment from economists, this feature of the work passed largely unnoticed by economists.
6. Nevertheless, Pearce and Turner (1990) do argue the importance of preserving certain physical assets. The significance of such a requirement in the environmental control problem is considered in Perrings (1991).
7. This is, of course, in marked contrast to Walrasian economic theory, where it is assumed that knowledge of the behaviour of individuals is sufficient to give knowledge of the behaviour of the system as a whole. Indeed, this is a fundamental point of methodological dispute between an ecological and a Walrasian or neoclassical approach to the economics of the environment.
8. We note, in passing, that while the constant consumption rule which motivates the Solow approach has a similar intent, it does constrain options in so far as it requires that a particular savings rule be followed.
9. We offer a more precise definition of this vector in Section 4 below.
10. The historical reviews cited above cover many of these. It is, however, worth signalling the most seminal contributions: those which have added a dimension of the biophysical system that turns out to have significant implications for the economic system. Of these Boulding (1966), Kneese et al. (1970), Georgescu-Roegen (1971), Clark (1976), Daly (1977) and Norgaard (1984) are perhaps pre-eminent.
11. A good example is Pearce and Turner (1990).
12. This is, of course, a strong assumption which we take to be justified by the focus of this chapter.
13. Walsh and Gram (1980) in an exposition of the viability conditions for a classical technology model, actually refer to 'sustainable outputs' and comment in a footnote as follows: 'One might imagine an economy temporarily in a position which, if it continued, would eventually be self-destroying. Pollution problems, for example, can turn otherwise viable technologies into nonviable ones. We leave this matter aside' (pp. 270–71). Cremeans (1974) and Lipnowski (1976) consider the existence and nature of an equilibrium growth path in a classical model where pollution occurs and a clean-up industry exists.
14. One population indicator consistent with Holling-sustainability is the maintenance of species diversity. This indicator considers both the number of species in an ecosystem and the relative size and distribution of the population of each species (compare Pielou, 1975). It concentrates attention on the dynamics of the size of each population relative to its critical threshold level. This approach implicitly assumes that there may be a range of population sizes over which the ecosystem remains stable, but if any one population in an ecosystem falls below its critical threshold level the 'self-organization' of the ecosystem as a whole will be radically altered. The ecosystem will become unstable. In other words it assumes the complementarity of all species in the ecosystem.

REFERENCES

Barbier, E.B. (1990), 'Alternative approaches to economic–environmental interactions', *Ecological Economics* **2**: 7–26.

Barbier, E.B. and Markandya, A. (1990), 'The conditions for achieving environmentally sustainable development', *European Economic Review* **34**: 659–69.

Barbier, E.B., Markandya, A. and Pearce, D.W. (1990), 'Sustainable agricultural development and project appraisal', *European Review of Agricultural Economics* **17**: 181–96.

Boulding, K.E. (1966), 'The economics of the coming spaceship earth', in H. Jarrett (ed)., *Environmental Quality in a Growing Economy*, Resources For the Future/Johns Hopkins Press, Baltimore: 3–14.

Boyden, S. (1987), *Western Civilization in Biological Perspective: Patterns in Biohistory*, Oxford University Press, Oxford.

Christensen, P. (1987), 'Classical roots for a modern materials–energy analysis', *Ecological Modelling* **38**: 75–89.

Christensen, P. (1989), 'Historical roots for ecological economics – biophysical versus allocative approaches', *Ecological Economics*, **1**: 17–36.

Clark, C. (1976), *Mathematical Bioeconomics*, John Wiley, New York.

Cleveland, C. (1987), 'Biophysical economics: historical perspective and current research trends', *Ecological Modelling* **38**: 47–73.

Common, M.S. (1988), '"Poverty and Progress" Revisited', in D. Collard, D. Pearce and D. Ulph (eds), *Economics Growth and Sustainable Environments*, Macmillan, Basingstoke.

Conway, G.R. (1985), 'Agroecosystem analysis', *Agricultural Administration* **20**: 31–55.

Conway, G.R. (1987), 'The properties of agroecosystems', *Agricultural Systems* **24**: 95–117.

Conway, G.R. and Barbier, E.B. (1990), *Sustainable Agriculture for Development*, Earthscan, London.

Costanza, R. (1989), 'What is ecological economics?', *Ecological Economics* **1**: 1–7.

Cremeans, J.E. (1974), 'Pollution abatement and economic growth: an application of the von Neumann model of an expanding economy', *Naval Research Logistics Quarterly* **21**: 525–42.

Cropper, M.L. and Oates, W.E. (1989), 'Environmental economics: a survey', University of Maryland, mimeo.

Daly, H.E. (1977), *Steady-State Economics*, Freeman, San Francisco.

Daly, H.E. and Cobb, J.B. (1989), *For the Common Good: Redirecting the Economy Toward Community, the Environment and a Sustainable Future*, Beacon, Boston.

Dasgupta, P. (1982), *The Control of Resources*, Blackwell, Oxford.

Dasgupta, P. and Heal, G.M. (1979), *Economic Theory and Exhaustible Resources*, Cambridge University Press, Cambridge.

Dasgupta, S. and Mitra, T. (1983), 'Intergenerational equity and efficient allocation of exhaustible resources', *International Economics Review* **24** (1): 133–53.

di Castri, F. (1987), 'The evolution of terrestrial ecosystems', in O. Ravera (ed.), *Ecological Assessment of Environmental Degradation, Pollution and Recovery*, Elsevier, Amsterdam:

Dixit, A., Hammond, P. and Hoel, M. (1980), 'On Hartwick's rule for regular maximin paths of capital accumulation and resource depletion', *Review of Economic Studies* **XLVII**: 551–6.

Faber, M. and Proops, J.L.R. (1990), *Evolution, Time, Production and the Environment*, Springer-Verlag, Berlin.

Fisher, I. (1930), *The Theory of Interest*, Macmillan, New York.

Georgescu-Roegen, N. (1971), *The Entropy Law and the Economic Process*, Harvard University Press, Cambridge, MA.

Goodland, R. and Ledec, G. (1987), 'Neoclassical economics and principles of sustainable development', *Ecological Modelling* **38**: 19–46.

Hartwick, J.M. (1977), 'Intergenerational equity and the investing of rents from exhaustible resources', *American Economic Review* **66**: 972–4.

Hartwick, J.M. (1978a), 'Investing returns from depleting renewable resource stocks and intergenerational equity', *Economics Letters* **1**: 85–8.

Hartwick, J.M. (1978b), 'Substitution among exhaustible resources and intergenerational equity', *Review of Economic Studies* **45** (2): 347–54.

Hartwick, J.M. (1991), 'Economic depreciation of mineral stocks and the contribution of El Serafy', World Bank Environment Department, Working Paper No. 4, October.

Hayek, F.A. (1941), *The Pure Theory of Capital*, Routledge & Kegan Paul, London.

Hicks, J.R. (1946), *Value and Capital*, Oxford University Press, Oxford.

Holling, C.S. (1973), 'Resilience and stability of ecological systems', *Annual Review of Ecological Systems* **4**: 1–24.

Holling, C.S. (1986), 'The resilience of terrestrial ecosystems: local surprise and global change', in W.C. Clark and R.E. Munn (eds), *Sustainable Development of the Biosphere*, Cambridge University Press, Cambridge: 292–317.

Hotelling, H. (1931), 'The economics of exhaustible resources', *Journal of Political Economy* **39**: 137–75.

Kay, J.J. (1989), 'A thermodynamic perspective of the self-organization of living systems', in P.W.J. Ledington (ed.), *Proceedings of the 33rd Annual Meeting of the International Society for the System Sciences*, Edinburgh, **3**: 24–30.

Kneese, A.V., Ayres, R.U. and d'Arge, R.C. (1970), *Economics and the Environment: A Materials Balance Approach*, Johns Hopkins Press, Baltimore.

Knight, F.H. (1934), 'Capital, time and the interest rate', *Economica* **1**, 257–86.

Knight, F.H. (1936), 'The quantity of capital and the rate of interest', *Journal of Political Economy* **44**: 433–63, 612–42.

Lipnowski, I.F. (1976), 'An input–output analysis of environmental preservation', *Journal of Environmental Economics and Management* **3**: 205–14.

MacArthur, R.H. and Wilson, O.E. (1967), *The Theory of Island Biogeography*, Princeton University Press, Princeton, NJ.

Mäler, K.-G. (1990), 'National accounts and environmental resources', Stockholm School of Economics, mimeo.

Martinez-Alier, J. (1987), *Ecological Economics*, Basil Blackwell, Oxford.

Mauersberger, P. and Straskraba, M. (1987), 'Two approaches to generalized ecosystem modelling: thermodynamic and cybernetic', *Ecological Modelling*, **39**: 161–9.

Meadows, D.H., Meadows, D.L., Randers, J. and Behrens, W.W. (1972), *The Limits to Growth*, Earth Island, London.

Norgaard, R.B. (1984), 'Coevolutionary development potential', *Land Economics* **60**: 160–73.

Norgaard, R.B. (1989), 'The case for methodological pluralism', *Ecological Economics* **1**: 37–57.

Pearce, D.W. (1987), 'Foundations of an ecological economics', *Ecological Modelling* **38**: 9–18.

Pearce, D.W. Markandya, A. and Barbier, E.B. (1989), *Blueprint for a Green Economy*, Earthscan, London.

Pearce, D.W. and Turner, R.K. (1990), *Economics of Natural Resources and the Environment*, Harvester-Wheatsheaf, London.

Perrings, C. (1987), *Economy and Environment*, Cambridge University Press, Cambridge.

Perrings, C. (1991), 'Ecological sustainability and environmental control', *Structural Change and Economic Dynamics* **2**: 275–95.

Pezzey, J. (1989), 'Economic analysis of sustainable growth and sustainable development', World Bank Environment Department, Working Paper No. 15, World Bank, Washington, DC.

Pielou, E.C. (1975), *Ecological Diversity*, John Wiley, New York.

Rawls, J. (1971), *A Theory of Justice*, Harvard University Press, Cambridge, MA.

Schaeffer, D.J., Herricks, E. and Kerster, H. (1988), 'Ecosystem health: I. Measuring ecosystem health', *Environmental Management* **12** (4): 445–55.

Solow, R.M. (1974), 'Intergenerational equity and exhaustible resources', *Review of Economic Studies*, Symposium: 29–46.

Solow, R.M. (1986), 'On the intertemporal allocation of natural resources', *Scandinavian Journal of Economics* **88** (1): 141–9.

Turner, R.K. (1988), 'Sustainability, resource conservation and pollution control: an overview', in R.K. Turner (ed.), *Sustainable Environmental Management: Principles and Practice*, Bellhaven Press, London: 1–25.

van der Ploeg, S.W.F., Braat, L.C. and van Lierop, W.F.J. (1987), 'Integration of resource economics and ecology', *Ecological Modelling* **38**: 171–90.

Walsh, V. and Gram, H. (1980), *Classical and Neoclassical Theories of General Equilibrium: Historical Origins and Mathematical Structure*, Oxford University Press, New York.

Wilkinson, R.G. (1973), *Poverty and Progress: An Ecological Model of Economic Development*, Methuen, London.

PART II

The Economic Environment and Ecological Change

5. An optimal path to extinction? Poverty and resource degradation in the open agrarian economy

1 INTRODUCTION

This chapter develops a theory of resource degradation and poverty in the agrarian economies that is independent of the Malthusian explanations common in much of the literature.[1] The empirical problem at issue is a very general one. The environmental despoliation of the Sahel and the Horn of Africa, and the destitution of much of the population of these areas in the last two decades, are not unique. The combination of rural poverty and resource degradation has in fact become a problem of increasingly severe proportions in the agriculturally- and pastorally-based economies of Africa, Asia and Latin America. Despite its enormous welfare costs and the *ex animo* concern it generates, comparatively little has so far been done to explore the causes of the problem at a theoretical level. This chapter offers a perspective on the link between resource degradation and poverty in open agrarian economies that takes as its point of departure the exhaustible nature of the basic resource in agricultural or pastoral activities – land. The results of the chapter spring both from the sensitivity of the environment to changes in the level of agricultural or pastoral activities (a physical problem) and from the intertemporal choices of agents operating near the minimum level of subsistence (an economic problem).

The focus of the chapter is the open agrarian economy. Open agrarian economies differ from closed agrarian economies primarily in the scope for accommodating uncertainty offered by environmentally conservative production strategies. In open agrarian economies the prices of inputs and outputs are set in the world market, so the level of real income is determined by factors that lie outside the control of the agents of the economy. To be sure, income changes with the same climatic factors that influence all agrarian activity, but it is also susceptible to price fluctuations. Where agrarian incomes are such that there is little surplus to forgo if the terms of trade turn against such economies, there may be few alternatives to increasing activity levels regardless of the environmental risks involved. Indeed, the interesting thing about open agrarian economies of the type described here, is that relative price shifts can lead to a positive feedback process in which increasing levels of activity lead directly to deepening poverty and resource degradation.

A concern with the potentially adverse effects of change in the economic and natural environments of open agrarian economies means that the chapter addresses questions raised in several quite distinct areas of the literature. Some of these questions have been causing concern for a considerable period. Among these, the potentially adverse effects of trade between more- and less-developed economies that has attracted the persistent attention of trade and development theorists alike – the prospect of immiserizing growth – can be traced back to the work of Friedrich List in 1837 (see List, 1966). This chapter offers explanations for such potentially adverse effects that have parallels in both the elasticity arguments of, for example, Bhagwati (1958, 1968) and the specialization loss arguments of, for example, Metcalfe and Steedman (1979). Where the arguments of this chapter diverge from those offered elsewhere is in the suggested causes of the adverse effects of trade. It is the exigencies of poverty that raise the prospect of immiserizing growth.

Because I am concerned with the time-behaviour of open agrarian economies, the chapter also touches on a related literature on the long-run dynamics of agrarian economies stimulated by Boserup's anti-Malthusian models (1965, 1981). Darity (1980) and Pryor and Maurer (1982) have both developed formal models of the intensification of subsistence production within a defined technological horizon in terms of an exogenously-determined population growth function: Darity for an open economy, and Pryor and Maurer for a closed economy. The model developed in this chapter is similarly concerned with the intensification of production within a defined technological horizon, and this is similarly taken to be a response to exogenously-determined stimuli. It nevertheless differs from the Darity and Pryor/Maurer models in certain important respects. Most obviously, it is not population growth, but the effects of change in the world economy on levels of agrarian poverty that drive the intensification of production. In addition, the period of interest is not the centuries envisaged by Boserup, Darity, or Pryor and Maurer. It is the span of a generation. I am interested in changes occurring within the rhythms of population adjustment. Agrarian producers at the minimum level of subsistence faced with exogenous price shocks cannot wait to respond by natural demographic adjustments. I am, therefore, interested in a more urgent problem altogether.

Partly because of this difference in time perspective, the model discussed in this chapter is also more directly influenced by the exhaustible nature of the natural resources exploited by rural producers. The cost of increased intensity is not just diminishing returns, it is potentially the complete collapse of the economic system. The exhaustibility of arable or pastoral resources is not, of course, directly analogous to the exhaustibility of, say, a mineral deposit. What both have in common, though, is the irrevocability or irreversibility of the changes involved. Arable or pastoral land is only renewable if agrarian activity does not involve irreversible change that makes that land useless under the technology applied. If it does involve such change it is to all intents and purposes exhaustible.[2] The chapter accordingly addresses a set of very old questions about the nature of environmental strategies in the face of exhaustible resources and technological inflexibility, posed both in economics and in anthropology.

This points towards one final set of questions addressed in this chapter concerning the connection between poverty and resource degradation, and that is the set of questions raised in Sen's (1981) seminal inquiry into the proximate causes of famine. This paper is motivated, above all, by the experience of the open agrarian economies that dominate rural sub-Saharan Africa. The famines that have decimated areas of Ethiopia, the Sahel and Mozambique, are only the most obvious signs of widespread resource degradation and poverty in these economies. The failure of trade, direct and transfer entitlements after years of 'rural development' implies that we are somehow misreading the probable effects of the commercialization of agrarian economies. This chapter suggests that the impact of any change in the economic environment of an open agrarian economy will vary both with the level of activity (the intensity of resource use within the existing technological horizon), and with the sensitivity of the natural environment to change in that level. Because perverse effects are not only possible but inevitable in certain cases, it may be useful to have a sense of the combination of circumstances that make this so.[3]

2 CHARACTERIZING THE OPEN AGRARIAN ECONOMY

The dominant characteristics of agrarian economies everywhere are a heavy reliance on agricultural or pastoral activities, and the use of a typically rudimentary technology that is constant over extended periods. Fei and Ranis have described such economies as 'essentially stagnant with nature and population vying for supremacy over long periods of recorded history. Moreover ... the prognosis for the future is likely to be "more of the same"' (1978: 2). Schultz (1964) saw this as a particular type of economic equilibrium in which the state of the arts (production functions) and preferences (utility functions) were both constant, in which the marginal physical product of all resources employed was zero, and net savings were close to zero. The last two properties were linked; the incentive to save being weak because of the low marginal physical product of capital. The longevity of the technology employed in agrarian economies was taken by Schultz to imply that the particular type of economic equilibrium he described was, in fact, stable.

This agrees with the more formal model of the closed agrarian economy constructed by Leibenstein (1957) which generated what the author called a quasi-stable equilibrium, or a stable equilibrium conditional on the economy concerned being insulated from external influences. Later attempts to model the dynamic properties of agrarian economies have been less in accord. Pryor and Maurer (1982), for example, observe that of sixty such economies researched by one of the authors, all seemed either to be at, or moving towards, a static equilibrium, making it slightly ironic that the closed agrarian economy models developed by the authors converged to *positive* growth paths in most cases, even though they recognized that under their own assumptions there had to be long-run limits to the growth of the economy. By contrast, the open economy model constructed by Darity (1980) generates a highly unstable equilibrium – a knife edge – divergence which necessarily leads either to the collapse or to the sustained growth of the system. There is at least a superficial similarity between the approaches of Darity and Leibenstein, in that the opening of the backward economies described by Leibenstein was argued to create at least the possibility of similarly sustained disequilibrium growth, but he was convinced that the closed agrarian economy was stable.

The anthropological evidence suggests that the apparent stability of closed agrarian economies was the product of a range of institutional control mechanisms designed to guarantee the economy in the face of an uncertain environment (see Herskovits, 1940; Nash, 1967; and Sahlins, 1974). Using such anthropological evidence I have argued elsewhere (Perrings, 1985) that the dominant feature of agrarian economies is the existence of institutions to limit the level of capacity utilization to environmentally sustainable levels. There is no reason to believe, however, that such economies were economically stable. Since real income and savings are both positively correlated with agriculturally favourable environmental conditions (rainfall and so on), the unregulated closed agrarian economy should be prone to exactly the same climatically-determined overgrazing and overcultivation that has been argued as a cause of resource degradation in the Sahel. The existence of institutions to restrict investment to sustainable levels appears to have been a crucial factor in the longevity of economically unstable or only locally stable closed agrarian economies.

The opening of the agrarian economies to world product markets has changed their characteristics in very important ways. Since certain input and output prices are now set in world markets, the link between real income, savings and local environmental conditions has been partly severed. More particularly, the role of traditional institutions in regulating capacity utilization has been substantially weakened, with implications both for the incentive effects of traditional communal or common property, and for the way that uncertainty is accommodated. There are now two sources of uncertainty – the environment and the world market – and the behaviour of agrarian producers is very much a function of the methods chosen to minimize risk in both areas.

In all open agrarian economies, producer strategies for minimizing risk hinge on decisions in two areas: the traditional choice as to the optimal level of activity; and a new choice between production either for direct consumption or for the market (Livingstone, 1981). The important point here is that neither the market risk nor the direct consumption risk of harvest failure are insurable except through the decisions made by agrarian producers in these two areas. Accordingly, since producers near the minimum subsistence level simply cannot take a loss below subsistence, they tend to adopt what Lipton (1968) has called 'survival algorithms': environmentally conservative practices characterized by the selection of low-value but robust crops or livestock suitable for both market production and direct consumption. They tend to avoid high market value but environmentally susceptible crops or livestock that are not directly consumable if need be (compare also Yamey, 1964). The risk-minimizing strategies of producers in the open agrarian economies accordingly bias production and consumption decisions in favour of tried practices and traditional products, and against technological innovation. Opening the agrarian economy does not therefore necessarily lead to the adoption of innovative practices, particularly where technological change is itself a source of risk (see Schultz, 1964). The costs of such technological conservatism, in terms of the specialization losses of trade, are implicitly accepted as part of the premium to be paid for the risk of participating in the world market.

A very similar set of considerations inform the savings behaviour of agrarian producers. Savings in the open agrarian economy may notionally be made in the form of either financial or real assets; money, bank deposits and the like, or grain and livestock. In fact the possibility for saving in financial assets tends to be limited by the availability of financial institutions, though the absence of such institutions may also be a consequence of the fact that the safety-oriented survival algorithms employed favour saving in real assets. Saving in real assets provides both a means of direct consumption in the case of drought (insurance against direct entitlement failure) and a degree of protection against the volatility of product prices (insurance against trade entitlement failure).[4] An important implication of this is that savings and investment decisions tend to be taken by the same agents. Real savings realized by 'household abstention' imply direct investment by the household head (Firth, 1964). Capital in the open agrarian economy is not freely mobile.

Like all other dynamic economies, the open agrarian economy is driven by savings, but it is savings out of the discretionary income of people living close to the poverty line and poverty turns out to have crucially important effects. Poverty, in this context, is subjective in the sense that it is defined by the agents' own assessment of need (see Drewnowski, 1977). For present purposes poverty may be said to exist wherever there is dissaving to maintain consumption. The degradation of natural resources – whether the devegetation of woodlands, the exhaustion of soil nutrients, the deplenishment of acquifers, or the starvation of livestock – represents dissaving of the most important assets of the agrarian economy, and there are few better indicators of the extent of rural poverty.

A final characteristic of agrarian economies worth noting relates to the intrahousehold distribution of income and division of labour. While there certainly exists a division of labour based on both age and gender, none is exempt from labour save the very old and the very young. All members are therefore assumed to belong to the household workforce. For convenience it is assumed that all have an equal claim to household income. These various characteristics are now summarized in the formal model of the open agrarian economy.

The income generated by agricultural or pastoral activity under the state of nature prevailing in period t is defined by:

$$Y_t = Q_t[b(Q_t)P_{t+1} - aP_t] \tag{5.1}$$

where Y_t denotes income; Q_t denotes the level of activity, or the level of intensity of resource use; $b(Q_t)$ denotes a unit activity level output coefficient as a function of Q_t; a denotes a constant unit activity level input coefficient; and P_{t+1}, P_t denote world prices of agrarian outputs and inputs, respectively. All except the input coefficient, a, are variable over time. Time is treated discretely since this seems to be the most natural way of dealing with production that is seasonal in nature. Income is distributed equally to all the members of agrarian labour force, which is assumed to be of constant size in the period of interest (the span of a generation). Hence

$$Y_t = Nw_t \tag{5.2}$$

where N denotes the agrarian labour force, and w_t denotes the income of each member of the labour force. Since the intensity of labour varies with the level of activity we have also

$$Y_t = Q_t n_t w_t \tag{5.3}$$

where n_t denotes the intensity of labour. The higher the level of activity the greater the intensity of agrarian labour.

Production in the agrarian economy may thus be characterized by a function relating output, $Q_t b(Q_t)$, to labour, $Q_t n_t$, and material inputs, $Q_t a$. Land is assumed to be in fixed supply and only enters the production function implicitly, via its effect on the productivity of fixed quantities of labour and material inputs used at differing levels of intensity. This enables us to capture the role of a factor of production that is not traded in the ordinary sense. The technology, in other words, reflects the fact that labour and material inputs are combined with a potentially exhaustible resource, land.

The effects of pressure on land are captured in the value of the output coefficient under different activity levels. This is taken to exhibit first increasing and then diminishing returns. Omitting the time index for the moment, the first derivatives of $b(Q)$ are positive for all Q up to some value Q_{bmax} (defined later) and are negative thereafter; the second derivatives are positive for all Q up to some value $Q < Q_{bmax}$, and are negative thereafter for most Q of interest. That is:

$b'(Q) > 0$ for all $Q \leq Q_{bmax}$
$b'(Q) < 0$ for all $Q > Q_{bmax}$
$b''(Q) >$ for all $Q \leq Q < Q_{bmax}$
$b''(Q) < 0$ for most $Q > Q$.

This allows increasing returns to scale at low levels of intensity of resource use. In general, therefore, we would expect the graph of the function to be of the form shown in Figure 5.1.

For concreteness, however, I assume the function to be of a specific, symmetrical, form.

$$b = b_{max}\exp[-\tfrac{1}{2}(Q - Q_{bmax})^2] \qquad (5.4)$$

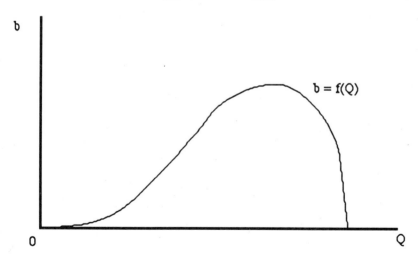

Figure 5.1   *General growth function for agrarian output*

where b_{max} denotes the maximum unit activity level output coefficient; Q_{bmax} denotes the activity level at which b attains a maximum. This function has all the required properties described above. Its graph is of the form shown in Figure 5.2.

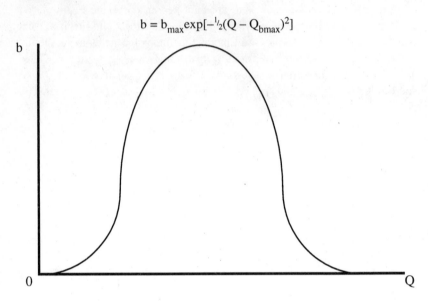

$$b = b_{max}\exp[-\tfrac{1}{2}(Q - Q_{bmax})^2]$$

Figure 5.2   Symmetric growth function for agrarian output

Although, as we have seen, changes in the level of intensity are not driven by population in the time scale of interest in this chapter, they do have similar implications for the time path of the system. Since land is regarded as an exhaustible resource there are very clear and well-defined limits to the intensity at which it can be exploited under a given technology, and a given state of nature. To reflect the effects of change in the state of nature on the value of $b(Q)$ equation (5.4) will be written in the time-indexed form:

$$b_t = b_{maxt} \exp[-\tfrac{1}{2}(Q_t - Q_{bmaxt})^2]. \tag{5.5}$$

To explore the dynamics of the open agrarian economy we need to specify the savings behaviour of agrarian producers. Total savings are defined by:

$$S_t = s_t Y_t \tag{5.6}$$

where s_t denotes the agrarian producers' propensity to save in period t. It may be positive, negative or zero. As indicated earlier savings are determined by the relation between actual income and the perceived minimum subsistence needs of agrarian producers. This may be thought of as the poverty point, and is denoted by w. The relation between savings and poverty is then described by:

$$s_t = \beta[Y_t - wN]/Y_t \qquad (5.7)$$

where β is a positive constant indicating the fixed proportion of discretionary income saved. The general propensity to save accordingly varies with the amount of income earned relative to the (subjective) poverty point. In all periods:

$$w \leq (1 - s_t)w_t. \qquad (5.8)$$

Since investment in period $t + 1$ is simply

$$I_{t+1} = Q_{t+1}aP_{t+1} \qquad (5.9)$$

the savings investment identity takes the form

$$Q_{t+1}aP_{t+1} = s_t Q_t n_t w_t. \qquad (5.10)$$

Thus, if world prices are stable, the system is driven by the interaction of two variables: the propensity to save, and the productivity of complementary factors at the prevailing level of intensity of resource use.

These two variables are not independent. More particularly the propensity to save will rise (fall) with an increase in the level of intensity of resource use for all intensity levels less than (greater than) the maximum income level. To see this, notice that the maximum income level of agricultural activity, found by setting the derivative of Y_t with respect to Q_t equal to zero, is given by

$$Q_{ymaxt} = [n_t w_t / V_t] + Q_{bmaxt} \qquad (5.11)$$

where $V_t = Q_t b_t P_{t+1}$ denotes the value of agrarian output. Taking the derivative of s_t with respect to Q_t in (5.7),

$$\frac{ds_t}{dQ_t} = \frac{\beta - s_t}{y_t}\left[n_t w_t - \left[Q_t - Q_{bmaxt}\right]V_t\right] \qquad (5.12)$$

it follows immediately from (5.11) that this will be negative for all $Q_t > Q_{ymaxt}$, and positive for all $Q_t < Q_{ymaxt}$. As average income changes with the level of activity so, too, does discretionary income, and with it the propensity to save.

This completes the description of the formal structure of the open agrarian economy model. As with any model developed at a high level of abstraction from the reality it is intended to explain, it misses much of the richness of the social and political fabric within which agrarian producers make their decisions. It does, however capture what seem to be the characteristics of agrarian economies most important to an understanding of their behaviour over time: the limited availability of grazing or arable land; the inflexibility of aggregate labour supply but the variability of the intensity of effort, the dependence on external markets for both inputs and outputs; the tendency to save real rather than financial assets (both output and land fertility) and the exhaustible nature of the principal resource. We can now consider the dynamics of the model.

3 THE DYNAMICS OF THE OPEN AGRARIAN ECONOMY MODEL

A time path for resource use in an open agrarian economy with the above characteristics may be obtained from the phase line generated by the following non-linear first-order difference equation taken from (5.10), (5.3) and (5.1):

$$Q_{t+1} = \frac{s_t}{aP_{t+1}} Q_t \left\{ b_{max\,t} \exp\left[-\tfrac{1}{2}(Q_t - Q_{b\,max\,t})^2\right] P_{t+1} - aP_t \right\}. \quad (5.13)$$

The level of activity in period $t + 1$ varies with three things: the propensity to save and the intensity of resource exploitation in period t (as we have already seen) and the change in world prices between periods t and $t + 1$. The first can be seen by taking the derivative of Q_{t+1} with respect to Q_t

$$\frac{dQ_{t+1}}{dQ_t} = \frac{\beta}{aP_{t+1}} \left[n_t w_t - (Q_t - Q_{b\,max\,t}) V_t \right]. \quad (5.14)$$

Once again, it follows immediately that the slope of the phase line deriving from (5.13) will be positive or negative as the level of agricultural activity is less than or greater than the maximum income level of intensity. The impact of prices is more easily seen if (5.14) is written in the form:

$$\frac{dQ_{t+1}}{dQ_t} = \beta\left\{(b_t / a)\left[1 - \left(Q_t - Q_{bmaxt}\right)\right] - P_t / P_{t+1}\right\}. \qquad (5.15)$$

Other things being equal, rising world prices will cause the level of activity to change more sharply. Falling world prices will have the opposite effect. Assuming constant world prices, the phase line defining the time path of the system is of the general form described in Figure 5.3. The line $Q_{t+1} = Q_t$, a 45° ray from the origin, indicates all points at which activity levels are constant. The phase line defined by the graph of $Q_{t+1} = s_t Q_t n_t w_t / aP_{t+1}$ indicates the forward difference associated with each value of Q_t. Iterative calculation of that difference from the phase line enables us to construct a time path for the system.

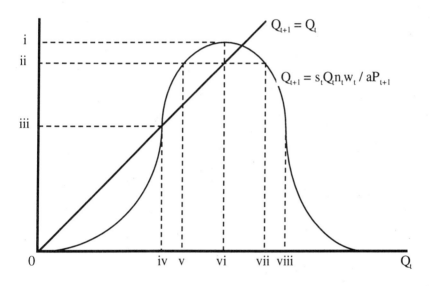

$i = Q_{ymaxt}.$
$ii = Q_{emaxt}.$
$iii = Q_{emint}.$
$iv = Q_{emint}.$

$v = Q_{bmaxt}.$
$vi = Q_{ymaxt}.$
$vii = Q_{emaxt}.$
$viii = Q_{maxt}.$

Figure 5.3   Phase line: symmetric case

In the discussion of the global and local stability of the system that follows, five values of Q_t are of interest, two of which have already been defined. Q_{ymaxt} is the maximum income level of activity. At that point the phase line has a slope of zero. Q_{bmaxt} is the maximum productivity level of activity. At that point the phase line has a slope of $s_t n_t w_t / a P_{t+1}$. Two other values of Q_t of interest lie at the intersection of the phase line with the $Q_{t+1} = Q_t$ locus. These define the steady-state equilibria of the system: that is, the levels of activity at which there is no impetus to change. Since Q_{emaxt} indicates a level of activity associated with higher average productivity than Q_{emint}, it will be referred to as the maximum income equilibrium activity level. Q_{emint} will be referred to as the minimum income equilibrium level. Notice that the latter also denotes the minimum sustainable level of activity, in the sense that any level of activity below Q_{emint} will lead to the collapse of the system. Q_{maxt} denotes the maximum sustainable level of activity in the sense that any level of activity above Q_{maxt} will similarly lead to the collapse of the system.

Global Stability

The open agrarian economy may be said to be globally stable at a particular state of nature if the maximum attainable level of activity $Q_{ymaxt+1}$ is no greater than the maximum sustainable level of activity Q_{maxt}, and to be globally unstable if this is not true. This is shown heuristically in Figures 5.4 and 5.5. Figure 5.4 illustrates the globally stable case where $Q_{ymaxt+1} < Q_{maxt}$. It can be seen that

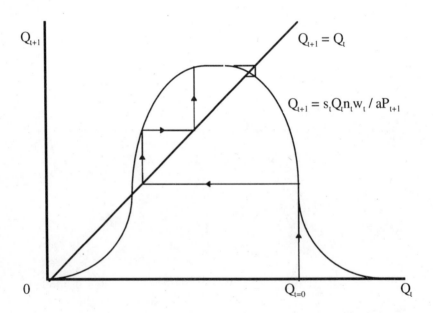

Figure 5.4   Global stability

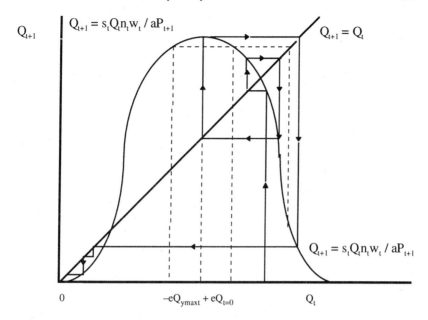

Figure 5.5   Local stability

the forward difference corresponding to every feasible activity level is sustainable, where an activity level, Q_t is defined to be feasible if $Q_{emint} \le Q_t \le Q_{maxt}$. A time path constructed for one such feasible initial level of activity, $Q_{t=0}$ is shown. Figure 5.5 illustrates the opposite case, where $Q_{ymaxt+1} > Q_{maxt}$. It can be seen that there exists a range of feasible activity levels for which the corresponding forward difference is not sustainable. Assuming an initial activity level $Q_{t=0}$ on the edge of the feasible range, Figure 5.5 shows that the time path of the system will take it into the range of unsustainable activity levels, leading to a general collapse. The system is globally unstable.

The intuition behind this should be clear. An unstable economy is one in which certain feasible levels of activity lead to unsustainable activity levels in the future. Economically, it is the rate of potential savings associated with these levels of activity that creates the problem. More particularly, the open agrarian economy will be globally stable at a particular state of nature and for a constant set of world prices if the maximum potential rate of savings per unit activity level is no greater than the ratio of maximum sustainable to maximum attainable levels of activity, and will be globally unstable otherwise.

The maximum potential rate of savings per unit activity level may be defined by $s_{ymaxt}[(b_{ymaxt}/a) - 1]$, where s_{ymaxt} and b_{ymaxt} are the savings propensities and output coefficients corresponding to the maximum income activity level, Q_{ymaxt}. The system will therefore be globally stable if:

$$s_{ymaxt}[(b_{ymaxt}/a) - 1] > Q_{maxt}/Q_{ymaxt} \qquad (5.16a)$$

for all $t \geq 0$, and will be globally unstable if

$$s_{ymaxt}[(b_{ymaxt}/a) - 1] > Q_{maxt}/Q_{ymaxt}. \qquad (5.16b)$$

Internally generated savings that cannot flow out of the system, and that lead to unsustainable levels of activity may cause the collapse of the system.[5]

Notice that global stability in the sense of this chapter does not necessarily imply that the system will converge to a steady-state equilibrium from any feasible initial activity level. The system may be convergent or it may be oscillatory. Global stability implies only that for a constant state of nature and world prices, a feasible initial level of activity will correspond to a time path in which activity levels in each period are both feasible and sustainable.

Local Stability

The local stability of the steady-state equilibria of the system depends on the absolute value of slope of the phase line at the points Q_{emint} and Q_{emaxt}. If this is less than unity, the equilibria are locally stable, if greater than unity they are locally unstable. If the steady-state equilibria are locally stable, the time path of the system will converge to the equilibrium point for any initial activity level in the neighbourhood of that point. If locally unstable, the time path of the system will diverge from the equilibrium point for any initial activity level in the neighbourhood of that point. Figure 5.4 in fact illustrates the case of a system that is both globally stable, and locally stable at Q_{emaxt}. It is locally unstable at Q_{emint}. Figures 5.6 and 5.7 illustrate two other possible cases. In Figure 5.6 the system is globally stable, but locally unstable at both the steady-state equilibria Q_{emaxt} and Q_{emint}. Small upward perturbations at Q_{emint} and small perturbations in either direction at Q_{emaxt} will lead to a sequence of irregular undamped oscillations that take activity anywhere over the range of feasible activity levels.

Figure 5.7 illustrates the case of a system that is locally stable at Q_{emaxt} but is globally unstable. In this case small perturbations about Q_{emaxt} within the range $\{Q\}_{smaxt}$, or within the range $\{Q\}_{smint}$, will lead to the reconvergence of the system. Any other level of activity will lead to the collapse of the system.

Time paths for each of these cases are illustrated in Figure 5.8. The nature of the time path in all cases depends on the technological parameters of the system, and the saving behaviour associated with any given poverty point. Phase lines reflecting the fact that productivity and savings rates are little

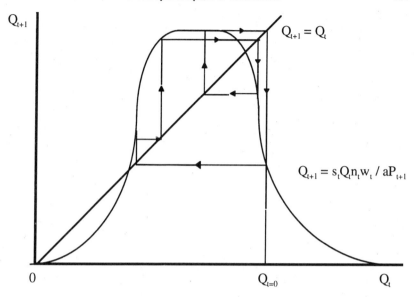

Figure 5.6   Multiple unstable equilibria in a globally stable economy

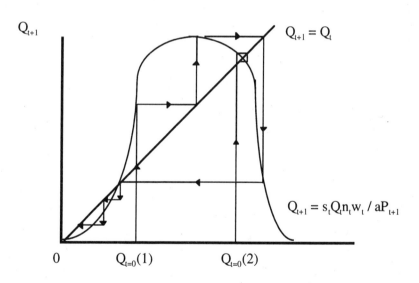

1. Initial activity level outside the locally stable ranges $\{Q\}_{smint}$ and $\{Q\}_{smint}$.
2. Initial activity level inside the locally stable ranges $\{Q\}_{smint}$ and $\{Q\}_{smint}$.

Figure 5.7   Locally stable equilibrium in a globally unstable economy

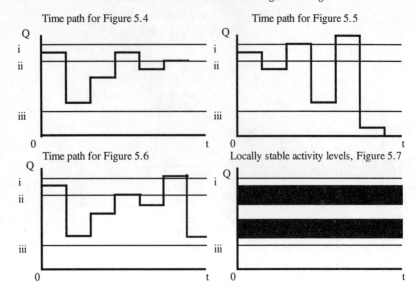

$i = Q_{max}.$
$ii = Q_{emax}.$
$iii = Q_{emin}.$

Figure 5.8   Time paths for local and globally stable cases

affected by the level of activity (a broad bell shape) are less likely to be associated with global instability than those reflecting the fact that small changes in the level of activity have significant effects on productivity and savings (a narrow bell shape). The latter indicate that diminishing returns at the intensive margin are important. The former indicate that they are not. Put another way, the more delicate is the ecological balance, the higher the probability that the system will be unstable, or at least unstable outside of a narrow range of activity levels. Many of the economies most affected by resource degradation would seem to be of this type.

4   DETERMINANTS OF THE LEVEL OF ACTIVITY

Consider, now, the potential for producers who are implementing quite rational security-oriented survival algorithms in globally unstable systems to adopt programmes of activity that may lead to the degradation and possible collapse of the resource base of the economy. We may take the closed economy first. It was argued in Section 2 that anthropological evidence suggests that producers in closed agrarian economies sought to regulate the level of capacity utilization to environmentally sustainable levels. This tendency to operate at an environmentally sustainable subsistence level which yet left considerable spare capacity suggests that such economies were institutionally held at or (proximately) above a point such as Q_{emin}, the minimum income steady-state equilibrium. Such a position would ensure that even substantial fluctuations in the environment might be accommodated without risk of nearing the upper limits of sustainable activity. It would, coincidentally, also ensure that the increasing returns to scale available in the system were just exhausted. The longevity of such systems might then be attributed to the effectiveness of a set of social institutions designed to dispose of surpluses in an environmentally benign way. These institutions might reasonably be thought of as approximating a homeostatic control mechanism.[6]

This interpretation would seem to be consistent with at least one other recent model of the agrarian economy. Although the construction of the Darity (1980) model is somewhat different from the model discussed in this chapter, the knife-edge equilibrium described by Darity is analogous to the point Q_{emin} in all the cases discussed here. The use of a homeostatic control mechanism to minimize fluctuations about this equilibrium value might explain the paradox of an apparent tendency to static equilibrium in closed agrarian economies, when those economies had the potential for at least limited growth through the intensification of resource use. That the potential for growth should be limited follows from the assumption of fixed availability of land. Of course, neither Darity nor others who have developed formal anti-Malthusian models of the agrarian economy have considered what happens when the limits of intensification are reached. That, after all, is the Malthusian end of the problem.

Without stepping outside the bounds of the closed agrarian economy, it is apparent that under such a strategy any change in the natural environment, or any weakening of the strict regulation of the level of activity will force the system away from the steady state. If the system is globally stable an increase in activity levels will lead either to undamped oscillation (if it is locally unstable) or to convergence to the maximum income steady-state equilibrium, Q_{emax}. If the system is not only locally, but globally unstable, then the results may be collective disaster. Consider the state of nature first. It should be intuitively clear that a change in environmental conditions would be sufficient to dislodge an uncontrolled economy from an unstable steady-state equilibrium. For example, drought both lowers the mean level of productivity, and increases the sensitivity of productivity to changes in activity levels. It thus changes the shape of the function (5.5). Hence a level of activity consistent with the steady state under historic environmental conditions will no longer be consistent with the steady state under the new environmental conditions. If changes in the state of nature are not adjusted to, or adjusted only with a significant lag, an apparently stable time path can very rapidly develop alarming instabilities. Where expectations are adaptive, as has been argued to be the case in agrarian economies (compare Lipton, 1968), this indicates a problem in the speed of adjustment. Hare, for example, has argued that part of the physical problem in the Sahel may be attributed to the slow rate of adjustment to changes in environmental conditions. He claims that pastoralists have tended to build up herds in wet years, but have failed to reduce those herds during times of drought. This has led to additional pressure on drought-stressed pastures and, after successive dry years, the result has been all the usual symptoms of the degradation of grazing land. Agriculturists, similarly, have extended the area of cultivation in wet years but have failed to contract that area in dry years, with similar results (Hare, 1977; see also Konczacki, 1978; and Ruddle and Manshard, 1981).

What is missed in such accounts is that stocking and cultivation decisions take place in circumstances where saving has an important insurance function, and where the opening of the economy has weakened many of the traditional controls over capacity utilization. In such circumstances, overstocking in particular makes perfect sense. As Sen (1981) has argued, it is entirely rational for individuals to overstock in times of drought for insurance purposes whenever grazing land has at least aspects of open access common property (*res nullius*). Even without the common property problem, though, there is an incentive to hold on to stock in times of drought. As we have already seen, the closer to poverty agrarian producers are, the higher the insurance premium against starvation will be. The result is, as Lipton (1968: 327–51) puts it, 'increasingly desperate insurance measures, rather than more efficient allocation procedures'.

Although failure to adapt to the natural environment may cause instability in the agrarian economy, so, too, may failure to adapt to the economic environment. The opening of the agrarian economies has typically thrust them into an economic environment which is highly uncertain, and in which they are at an enormous informational disadvantage. The result is that they are uniformly maladapted. It has long been recognized that in any move from autarky to trade there are losers and gainers, and there is no reason why the gains and losses from trade should be shared in any particular way. It is quite possible that the opening of a given economy will make all the agents of that economy worse off than under autarky. What is important from the perspective of the open agrarian economies is that the welfare effects of trade depend on two effects: the exchange effect (the impact of change in relative prices on consumption) and the specialization effect (the impact of a change in relative prices on the structure of production and choice of technique). Unlike the exchange effects of trade which are generally assumed to be positive, the specialization effects may be positive or negative. More particularly, the specialization effects may be positive only if there exists a choice of technique. Where the specialization losses outweigh the exchange gains, it is possible that income will be less under trade than under autarky (compare Metcalfe and Steedman, 1979). Given the risk-minimizing strategies of agrarian economies it is not at all clear that the exchange effects of trade will be positive, and it is almost certain that the specialization effects will be negative. It has already been remarked that the main evidence of the risk averseness of agrarian producers in the face of considerable climatic and market uncertainty is their commitment to tried practices. It is exactly this which makes them susceptible to specialization losses, since it prevents them from producing efficiently under post-trade relative prices.

The result is that the commercialization of agriculture has made the open agrarian economies of sub-Saharan Africa, in particular, more rather than less vulnerable to the exigencies of poverty. Environmental uncertainty has been augmented by market uncertainty. Exchange rate and price fluctuations are, potentially, at least, just as damaging as rainfall fluctuations. Indeed, Sen's whole thesis rests on the proposition that it is failure of trade entitlements (a market phenomenon) and not direct entitlements (food availability decline) that best explains many of the recent famines in Africa. Extreme poverty has occurred without any change in the aggregate output of food.

Famine due to the collapse of trade entitlements is bad enough. What is worse is that a failure of trade entitlements has highly damaging future effects on the physical system which threaten to make poverty not occasional but endemic. More particularly, where poverty due to unfavourable price movements raises the level of activity, it may lead to damped or persistent oscillations if the economy is globally stable, but to total collapse if the economy is globally unstable. In other words, a failure of trade entitlements in the present may cause a permanent decline of food availability in the future. To see this, consider the output and input price elasticities of agrarian activity. From equations (5.7) and (5.13) the output price elasticity of agrarian activity is simply

$$\frac{dQ_{t+1}}{dP_{t+1}} \cdot \frac{P_{t+1}}{Q_{t+1}} = \frac{\beta V_t}{s_t Y_t} - 1 \qquad (5.17)$$

while the input price elasticity is

$$\frac{dQ_{t+1}}{dP_t} \cdot \frac{P_t}{Q_{t+1}} = -\frac{\beta I_t}{s_t Y_t}. \qquad (5.18)$$

If $s_t > 0$ the algebraic signs of these elasticities are unambiguous and as expected: (5.17) is positive, and (5.18) is negative. Notice, though, that both turn on the savings propensity, s_t, and this is a function of the level of subjective poverty (the difference between actual income Y_t and the minimum subsistence income wN. From (5.7) s_t is positive or negative as Y_t is greater than or less than wN. The response of producers to changes in either input or output prices will therefore be perverse wherever they are in subjective poverty, implying dissaving to maintain consumption levels. When the need to stave off starvation governs all current production decisions it may be expected that people will ignore the future consequences of these decisions. If the price of output falls, or the price of inputs rises, and if this drives agrarian income below the poverty line (the minimum subjective subsistence level) agricultural activity will rise to compensate – even if the future costs approach infinity. Poverty may be expected to drive up their rate of time preference to the point where all that matters is consumption today.

The future of agrarian producers in these circumstances depends on whether or not the system is globally stable. If it is globally unstable the level of activity will be driven to the point where the environment is irreversibly damaged, in terms of its usefulness under the existing technology. This does not imply an irrational approach on the part of agrarian producers to intertemporal choice. It merely implies that intertemporal decision-making is dominated by the exigencies of the present. Defining a discounted consumption stream over T periods to be

$$PV\{Y_t\}T = \hat{I}_t[1 - s_t Y_t][1 + d]^{-t}, t = 0, ..., T. \tag{5.19}$$

If $[1 - s_0] Y_0] = wN$ ($\beta = 1$) with $s_0 < 0$, and Y_0 set residually, it implies that the endogenously-determined discount rate (or minimum rate of time preference), d, will be found in the solution to

$$s_0 Y_0 = Y_0 + \hat{I}_t[1 - s_t]Y_t[1 + d]^{-t}, t = 1, ..., T. \tag{5.20}$$

d accordingly denotes a poverty-determined rate of discount. Even if the choice of Q_0 does drive the economy on to an unsustainable time path, the future costs of present decisions will necessarily be fully discounted. It will always be preferable to starve tomorrow rather than today. Consequently, irrespective of the 'rationality' of expectations, rational intertemporal choice that raises current output at the cost of future output may lead the agents of globally unstable open agrarian economies to collapse.

If we think of the consumption path of people facing such a collapse as the product of a sequence of discrete production decisions similar to that described in (5.20), it will be similar to that in Figure 5.9 where C denotes consumption, C denotes the irreducible subjective poverty line, $C_{t=i}$ the consumption path selected in period t, and C_t, the outer envelope of the $C_{t=i}$, the actual consumption path over the relevant time horizon.

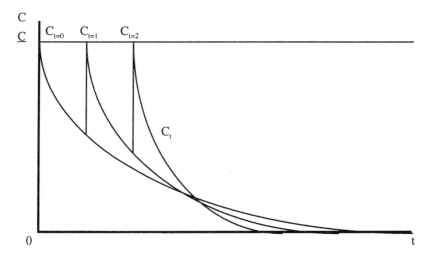

Figure 5.9   Consumption path in a collapsing system

The effect of such a sequential approach is that the poverty-determined discount rate is driven higher and higher with each decision. This is, in fact, similar to the consumption paths that Strotz (1955–56) described for 'spendthrifts' – those with perversely high rates of time preference – in that in each period the costs of present activity are deferred to a later date. Strotz saw this as a problem of inconsistency in optimal intertemporal consumption plans made at successive dates. In the present case, however, it represents quite consistent and rational behaviour. Bearing in mind that the agents concerned are assumed to be in subjective poverty, they will seek to maximize the number of periods in which minimum subsistence needs are satisfied, and to do this through choice of activity levels, the future costs of which are an indirect measure of their willingness to dissave. In other words they will try to stay alive for as long as possible. Nor is there reason to believe that the consumption paths selected will be anything other than optimal. The final value of consumption may well be zero, implying extinction, but this does not mean that agrarian producers are not doing the best they can given the state of nature and range of options open to them.[7]

5   CONCLUDING REMARKS

Famine is evidence of extreme poverty. Since the work of Sen (1981) we may be reasonably confident that it is not necessarily evidence of the collapse of agricultural or pastoral output – food availability decline. This chapter suggests, however, an even more disturbing causal relationship between extreme poverty and the state of agricultural or pastoral resources in open agrarian economies that is worth further study. It now seems clear that the dynamics of open agrarian economies are rather more complex than the early (quasi) stable equilibrium models of such as Leibenstein would suggest, and that causality between poverty and resource degradation can run both ways. We have seen, for example, that a collapse in the trade entitlements of agrarian producers may prompt them to increase the level of intensity with which the land is exploited even if this imposes costs in terms of reduced productivity in the future. In the extreme case where the system is both locally and globally unstable, these costs can be fatal. Indeed, if we apply the logic of exhaustible resource theory to the problem, given the distorting effects of poverty, we cannot avoid the conclusion that in the Sahelian and similar cases people have set themselves on to what Pearce (1988) has called an 'optimal path to extinction'.

The collective response has been to avert disaster so far as possible by emergency relief, but this will do nothing to avert a recurrence of the problem in the future. Yet if the source of the problem is the opening of agrarian economies dependent on fragile ecological systems, the solution ought to lie in the arena of trade and transfers. The compensation principle is, for example, a powerful ally in arguments for aid in cases where the gains from trade are uniformly negative for one country. By this principle trade will always be superior to autarky since there exists a system of transfers that would ensure that everyone could be made better off. But the compensation has to be made if trade is not to impoverish rather than enrich. The appropriation of the gains from trade in the advanced industrial economies, with occasional disbursements of aid or emergency relief to the traditional agrarian economies in times of famine, is no guarantee against the collapse of the latter. The problem, as Sen points out, lies in the entitlements of agrarian producers in these economies. It is of crucial importance to secure a set of entitlements – whether by appeal to the compensation principle or not – that will provide those producers with the incentives to operate at sustainable levels, and to search out forms of insurance against environmental fluctuations that do not themselves undermine the potential gains from trade.

NOTES

1.   See, for widely differing examples of works that assign final responsibility for environmental degradation to population expansion, Eckholm (1976) and Ruddle and Manshard (1981). The arguments of this chapter are consistent with population-induced changes in activity levels, but are concerned with a shorter time frame than is ordinarily assumed in population-driven models. They would also lend support to the claims of those such as Kates et al. (1977), that the relation between resource degradation and population expansion is non-monotonic. It is increasingly recognized that there may be other factors in resource degradation that are more important than population expansion, implying that the proximate causes of resource degradation

– overstocking and overcultivation – bear no systematic relation to population increase (compare Repetto and Holmes, 1983, and Pearce, 1988). This investigates one set of such factors.

2. Dryland ecosystems tend to be particularly vulnerable to increasing resource use. Vegetational cover tends to be sparse, and soils tend to be poor in organic matter and nutrients. Devegetation can result in damage from which recovery, in the sense of a return to existing conditions, may never occur. More particularly, greater exposure of the surface of the soil results in lower water retention, encouraging sheet and gully erosion, and reducing the productivity of economically useful plants (see Ruddle and Manshard, 1981). It is also argued that reduction in surface vegetation may have climatic effects. It may increase surface albedo (reflectivity of solar radiation), and this may cause the air to lose heat radiatively, and so to descend, losing relative humidity in the process (Charney, 1975; Hare, 1977).

3. The chapter does not, therefore, address the link between resource degradation and technological change. It is worth noting, however, that many of the most commonly cited instances of technological change – the introduction of deep wells, for example – may be interpreted as the intensification of activity within a given technology.

4. Recently the savings of agrarian producers in terms of real assets has been interpreted by Ravallion (1987) as speculative hoarding, but this misses the insurance role of real savings in economies where most producers are close to the minimum level of subsistence.

5. Since it is assumed that world prices are constant, implying that $Pt = P_{t+1}$ for all $k \geq 0$, (5.16a) may be written in the form

$$Q_{\mathrm{max}t} \geq Q_{\mathrm{ymax}t} \, [s_{\mathrm{ymax}t}/aP_{t+1}][b_{\mathrm{ymax}t}P_{t+1} - aP_t]$$

and since the right-hand side of this equation is just $Q_{\mathrm{ymax}t+1}$, the maximum attainable level of activity, the proposition merely restates the conditions for the global stability of the system.

6. See Perrings (1987) for a more detailed discussion of the potential for homeostatic control in an evolutionary system.

7. Given the objective described in the text, such a time path would not contradict Bellman's principle of optimality. The latter requires that whatever the initial state and decision are, the remaining decisions at any point in the path must constitute an optimal policy with regard to the state resulting from the first decision. Each segment of the time path must itself be optimal, no matter what has gone on before. In this case the optimal policy requires quite simply that the individual maintain consumption at the minimum subsistence level by dissaving for as long as possible.

REFERENCES

Bhagwati, J.N. (1958), 'Immiserizing growth: a geometrical note', *Review of Economic Studies* **25**: 201–5.

Bhagwati, J.N. (1968), 'Distortions and immiserizing growth: a generalization', *Review of Economic Studies* **35**: 481–5.

Boserup, E. (1965), *The Conditions of Agricultural Growth: The Economics of Agrarian Change Under Population Pressure*, George Allen & Unwin, London.

Boserup, E. (1981), *Population and Technology*, Basil Blackwell, Oxford.

Charney, J. (1975), 'Dynamics of deserts and drought in the Sahel', *Quarterly Journal of the Royal Meteorological Society* **101**: 193–202.

Darity, W.A. (1980), 'The Boserup theory of agricultural growth: a model for anthropological economics', *Journal of Development Economics* **7**: 137–57.

Drewnowski, J. (1977), 'Poverty: its meaning and measurement', *Development and Change* **8**: 183–208.

Eckholm, E.P. (1976), *Losing Ground: Environmental Stress and World Food Prospects*, W.W. Norton, New York.

Fei, J.C.H. and Ranis, G. (1978), 'Agrarianism, dualism, and economic development', in S.P. Singh (ed.), *Underdevelopment to Developing Economies*, Oxford University Press, New York: 1–42.

Firth, R. (1964), 'Capital, saving and credit in peasant societies: a viewpoint from economic anthropology', in R. Firth and B.S. Yamey (eds), *Capital Saving and Credit in Peasant Societies*, Allen & Unwin, London: 15–34.

Ghai, D. and Radwan, S. (eds), (1983), *Agrarian Policies and Rural Poverty in Africa*, International Labour Organization, Geneva.

Hare, F.K. (1977), 'Climate and desertification', in *United Nations Conference on Desertification, Desertification: Its Causes and Consequences*, Pergamon Press, Oxford: 63–168.

Herskovits, M.J. (1940), *The Economic Life of Primitive Peoples*, Alfred Knopf, New York.

Kates, R.W., Johnson D.L. and Haring, K.J. (1977), 'Population, society and desertification', in *United Nations Conference on Desertification, Desertification: Its Causes and Consequences*, Pergamon Press, Oxford: 261–318.

Konczacki, Z.A. (1978), *The Economics of Pastoralism: A Case Study of Sub-Saharan Africa*, Frank Cass, London.

Leibenstein, H. (1957), *Economic Backwardness and Economic Growth*, Wiley, New York.

Lipton, M. (1968), 'The theory of the optimising peasant', *Journal of Development Studies*: 327–51.

List, F. (1966), *The National System of Political Economy*, Augustus Kelley, New York.

Livingstone, I. (1981), 'Supply responses of peasant producers: the effect of own-account consumption on the supply of marketed output', in *Development Economics and Policy: Readings*, George Allen & Unwin, London: 272–6.

Metcalfe, J.S. and Steedman, I. (1979), 'A note on the gain from trade', in I. Steedman (ed.), *Fundamental Issues in Trade Theory*, Macmillan, London: 47–63.

Nash, M. (1967), 'The social context of economic choice in a small society', in G. Dalton (ed.), *Tribal and Peasant Economies*, University of Texas Press, Austin: 524–38.

Pearce, D.W. (1988), 'The economics of natural resource degradation in developing countries', in R.K. Turner (ed.), *Sustainable Growth and Environmental Management: Principles and Practice*, Pinter, London: 103–17.

Perrings, C. (1985), 'The natural economy revisited', *Economic Development and Cultural Change* **34** (4): 829–50.

Perrings, C. (1987), *Economy and Environment: A Theoretical Essay on the Interaction of Economic and Environmental Systems*, Cambridge University Press, Cambridge.

Pryor, F.L. and Maurer, S.B. (1982), 'On induced economic change in precapitalist societies', *Journal of Development Economics* **10**: 325–53.

Ravallion, M. (1987), *Markets and Famines*, Oxford University Press, Oxford.

Repetto, R. and Holmes, J. (1983), 'The role of population in resource depletion in developing countries', *Population and Development Review* **9** (4): 609–32.

Ruddle, K. and Manshard, W. (1981), *Renewable Natural Resources and the Environment: Pressing Problems in the Developing World*, Tycooly International for United Nations University, Dublin.

Sahlins, M. (1974), *Stone Age Economics*, Tavistock Press, London.

Schultz, T.W. (1964), *Transforming Traditional Agriculture*, Yale University Press, New Haven.

Sen, A. (1981), *Poverty and Famines: An Essay on Entitlement and Deprivation*, Oxford University Press, Oxford.

Strotz, R.H. (1955–56), 'Myopia and inconsistency in dynamic utility maximization', *Review of Economic Studies* **XXIII**: 165–80.

Yamey, B.S. (1964), 'The study of peasant economic systems: some concluding comments and questions', in R. Firth and B.S. Yamey (eds), *Capital Saving and Credit in Peasant Societies*, George Allen & Unwin, London: 376–86.

6. Industrial growth, rural income and the overexploitation of land in the dual economy

1 INTRODUCTION

One result of the chronic failure of the countries of sub-Saharan Africa to assure food security under a range of climatic conditions has been a reappraisal of the growth-through-industrialization strategy that has dominated policy in those countries in the post-war period. Ever since Lewis published his seminal (1954) paper on growth in the dual economy, it has been an article of faith that development in countries of the sub-Saharan African type implies the expansion of the modern industrial sector using resources drawn from the traditional agricultural sector. But while the importance of industrialization to the development process is still not questioned, the implications of industrialization for the sustainability of agricultural performance are coming under increasingly close scrutiny. A succession of surveys in the mid-1980s showed that industrial growth had not only failed to stimulate agricultural growth in sub-Saharan Africa, it had also been associated with a chronic decline in average agricultural output (FAO, 1985; UN,1986; and IMF,1987; World Bank, 1987). Since then the World Bank and the IMF have launched a direct attack on the interest rate and agricultural price policies associated with the industrialization strategy of those countries where industrial export revenue has been insufficient to service current debts. They have alleged a systematic bias against agriculture – citing the taxation of agricultural exports; procurement prices below the border prices for exports and import substitutes under monopsonistic marketing arrangements; and low interest rate structures that discourage agricultural savings. More importantly, they have made the removal of such a bias a condition of structural adjustment finance (Commander (ed.), 1989).

The World Bank and IMF initiatives are designed to stimulate agricultural output by providing appropriate microeconomic incentives to farmers. Given the results of earlier work on the supply responsiveness of farmers elsewhere (for example, Behrman, 1968), the initiatives have assumed that improved producer prices will lead to the expansion of agricultural supply, and will provide both the incentives and the resources to conserve the agricultural resource base (see, for example, Bond, 1983; Cleaver, 1985, 1988; Barbier, 1988). To date, however, evidence on the impact of the initiatives has been very mixed. A number of countries have revised exchange rate policy, and have introduced the principle of export parity pricing for major cash crops – but there has been no continent-wide trend towards this objective (Mosley and Smith, 1989). Indeed, in most less-developed economies agriculture continues to be 'penalized' by the protection of the industrial sector, either directly or through the overvaluation of the exchange rate (Barbier, 1989). Moreover, even where price regimes have been liberalized, the supply responsiveness of farmers in sub-Saharan Africa has been muted. The short-run price elasticity of supply of individual cash crops has been shown to be positive and sometimes high, but long-run aggregate supply elasticities are generally very low, and in some cases even negative (Green, 1989; Perrings, 1989a; Rao, 1989).

This evidence raises two sets of questions about the sustainability of agriculture in sub-Saharan Africa. The first relates to the microeconomic problem of individual supply responses, and the resource implications of the particular responses observed in sub-Saharan Africa. It is widely recognized that price responsiveness is more tightly constrained by institutional factors in sub-Saharan Africa than it is in, for example, south-east Asia (Delgado and Mellor, 1984; Lipton, 1987; Junankar, 1989). The fact that a substantial proportion of goods and services are not traded, and cannot be traded under existing institutions, is argued to limit the scope for influencing farmers' production strategies solely through price adjustment (Ghai and Smith, 1987; Beynon, 1989). Additionally, constraints on the supply of basic natural resources limit the capacity of those who do participate in the market to respond to price incentives. As Addison and Demery (1989) point out, raising the return on productive assets will not help if people do not have access to those assets. Moreover, even where farmers do have access to productive assets, the lack of infrastructure – both real and financial – may limit their capacity to respond to the incentives offered by changing real returns on those assets (Addison and Demery, 1989; Beynon, 1989). As yet, however, very little attention has been paid to the short- or long-run environmental effects of changing incentives. Indeed, the nature of the linkages between producer prices, agricultural supply responses, and natural resource effects has yet to be identified – though there are good prima facie reasons to suppose that a positive supply response will be associated with significant environmental effects. In many parts of sub-Saharan Africa it has been argued that poorer farmers cannot increase productivity at the extensive margin simply because they do not have access to land (Feder and Noronha, 1987). But the evidence is that such expansion of agricultural output as has occurred has been at the extensive rather than the intensive margin. It has involved movement into increasingly marginal climatic, vegetational or topographical conditions, and the potentially adverse environmental implications of expansion of cultivation in forested, hilly or semi-arid conditions are well established (Barbier, 1988; Pearce et al.,1988; Mosley and Smith, 1989).

The second set of questions raised by the evidence are logically prior to questions about farmer responses. They concern the linkages between the general strategy of growth through industrialization, and the prices which guide the allocative decisions made by farmers. These questions ask what the strategy means for agricultural incentives, and so for agricultural resource utilization. They are also concerned with the scope for, and nature of, agricultural price liberalization under the strategy. Unlike the issue of supply responsiveness, these questions have attracted very little attention at an empirical level, and almost no attention at a theoretical level. While the properties of the dual economy model of industrialization in an agrarian economy are the subject of a continuing literature, attention remains fixed on the well-researched issue of unemployment (see, for example, Feldman, 1989).

Given the increasing attention being paid to the sustainability of development strategies, and given also the consensus that appropriate incentives are crucial to the sustainable utilization of natural resources, both sets of questions are important. This chapter is, however, mainly concerned with the broader issue of the linkages between agricultural incentives and the development strategies applied in dual economies. To explore these linkages, it considers the implications of a model of the dual economy for the utilization of resources in the agricultural sector. The model is a variant of the dual economy model originally due to Lewis (1954), but owing its current form to later contributions by, *inter alia*, Fei and Ranis (1964, 1978), Harris and Todaro (1970), Cordon and Findlay (1975) and Basu (1980).

The model has been adjusted in two ways. First, it includes a non-standard specification of labour costs in the agricultural sector. This is intended to capture the peculiar characteristics of Lewis's 'traditional sector' in respect of employment, productivity and the distribution of the product. That is, it is assumed that labour is not hired at a productivity-related wage, and that the product is distributed between all those available to work whether they are working or not. The standard specification of labour costs in later versions of the model fail to capture these characteristics. Second, the model allows for the link between increases in aggregate supply and land utilization observed by Pearce et al. (1988) and Mosley and Smith (1989). That is, it relaxes the assumption that the area of arable or grazing land available is fixed, and allows for expansion at the extensive margin. The strict meaning of land scarcity in this context is that expansion at the extensive margin involves movement on to land of progressively inferior quality.

The chapter is concerned only with the relation between certain key price and quantity variables in the dual economy at and away from equilibrium. It does not attempt to model the dynamic processes involved in agricultural or ecological change, nor does it attempt to model the growth path of the industrial sector. The question of the long-run sustainability of resource utilization is therefore addressed only indirectly, through the link between agricultural price policy and the utilization of labour in the agricultural sector. The chapter shows the conditions in which agricultural resources will be exploited to the point where the marginal physical product of labour is zero or even negative. It is assumed that in such conditions, the probability that those resources will be degraded in the long run is increased.

The chapter is in six sections. The following section offers a very brief review of the characteristics and development of the dual economy model which has underpinned the strategy of growth through industrialization in the post-war years. It also indicates which assumptions of the model have been adjusted during its development and why. Section 3 describes a model of industrial profits in a dual economy. Section 4 discusses the implications of the model for the link between industrial wages, agricultural productivity and agricultural employment, and establishes the rationale for an anti-agricultural bias in dual economies pursuing a strategy of growth through industrialization. Section 5 then considers the implications of an anti-agricultural bias for the utilization of agricultural resources. A final section discusses the significance of different price regimes and farmer responses for the sustainability of the agricultural sector.

2   CHARACTERIZING THE DUAL ECONOMY

The main characteristics of the idealized dual economy are well understood, and so may be listed with little elaboration. There are assumed to be two distinct sectors: a traditional agricultural sector on the one side, and a modern industrial sector on the other. Following convention, these will be referred to as the agricultural and industrial sectors, but it is important to emphasize that the key difference between the two lies in the terms 'traditional' and 'modern'. The term 'industrial' is in fact a catch-all for the whole of the non-traditional sector of the economy, and so covers various non-manufacturing resource-based activities including commercial agriculture. It is held to constitute an 'enclave' in the agricultural sector, implying that it is in some way insulated from the agricultural sector. More particularly, it is supposed that while labour and products flow freely between the sectors, capital does not. Thus, while there is a tendency for wages/average rural incomes and prices to equalize across the economy, the rate of profit in the two sectors will differ. The presumption here is that agricultural capital is relatively immobile, partly because of the nature of property rights in agricultural assets, and partly because of the absence of financial intermediaries. The fact that most land is subject to common or communal tenure, for example, means that it cannot be sold. Similarly, the fact that there are few financial institutions – indeed few financial assets – inhibits the mobilization of rural savings.

The agricultural sector in the dual economy is characterized by land scarcity and labour abundance, together with a stagnant technology that is inappropriate to the factor endowments of the sector. Since agricultural expansion in many land-scarce economies has taken place at the extensive margin, land scarcity in the dual economy is more Ricardian than is implied by the Fei–Ranis version of the model. Expansion of arable or rangeland brings ever more marginal land into use. Labour abundance implies the existence of a labour surplus. This is indicated by the fact that even though technology is labour intensive relative to that in the industrial sector, it still yields a zero or negative marginal physical product of labour at full employment.

The existence of a labour surplus creates a pool of labour which is available to the industrial sector at no cost, in terms of forgone output, to the agricultural sector. In the Lewis model of the labour market in a dual economy, industrial labour is supplied at a constant real wage greater than the average rural income (the opportunity cost of industrial labour). This is the constant institutional wage hypothesis. Employment in the industrial sector is held to expand up to the point at which the marginal revenue product of industrial labour is equated with the marginal cost of that labour. The main inference of the model follows directly. Until such time as the labour surplus is exhausted, the expansion of the industrial sector leads to a rising profit share in national income, a rising savings ratio (since industrialists are assumed to save at higher rates than farmers), increasing levels of investment, and hence an accelerating rate of growth.

The most frequently questioned of these characteristics has been the constant institutional wage hypothesis. The hypothesis was implicitly challenged in the Harris–Todaro two-sector model, in which the supply of industrial labour was held to depend on the level of unemployment in the system. This has given rise to what is now referred to as the Harris–Todaro equilibrium condition for the labour market, in which the differential between the industrial and agricultural wages (industrial wages and average agricultural income in this chapter) is a function of the relative size of the industrial and agricultural labour forces and the level of unemployment in the system.

The Harris–Todaro equilibrium condition challenges the assumption that the industrial wage is invariant with respect to changes in the level of agricultural employment and unemployment. The more general underlying assumption that the characteristics of the agricultural sector are independent of the characteristics of the industrial sector has also been been challenged from a structuralist perspective. It has been widely claimed that the dual economies observed by Lewis in the post-war years, particularly in sub-Saharan Africa, were each the product of a unique history in which the characteristics of both sectors had evolved together. The agricultural sector was itself the product of a development process, and did not reflect some sort of original state (see, for example, Arrighi, 1970). More particularly, it has been argued that the characteristics and role of the agricultural sector in dual economies of the Lewis type have, historically, been the product of government intervention.

Lewis had certainly acknowledged the potentially damaging effects of intervention in the agricultural sector, but he suggested that the failure of growth in the industrial sector to stimulate the agricultural sector was evidence of pathological conditions unique to the developing countries whether the government coerced or helped the traditional sector (1976, 1979). Lewis's structuralist critics, like Myrdal before them, argued that far from being evidence of a pathological condition, agricultural decay was necessary in order to maintain the crucial labour supply and wage control functions of the agricultural sector.

To see how such intervention may work requires a clear sense of the decision-making process within the agricultural sector, and here the characterization of the dual economy has typically been very weak. One important dimension to the contrast Lewis drew between the 'capitalist' relations of the modern sector and the 'pre-capitalist' relations of the traditional sector, is the differing rules governing employment and the distribution of the product in each sector. This dimension has, however, been lost in the later versions of the dual economy model. The kin-based production units of the traditional sector – the traditional family farm – are in fact much closer in spirit to the labour-managed firm than to the standard profit-maximizing firm assumed in the later versions of the dual economy model. But unlike the labour-managed firm, however, the number of claimants to the net product is, to all intents and purposes, independent of any employment decisions made by the traditional family farm. Labour is not hired. Nor is it paid a wage related to its marginal product. Moreover, since (by assumption) there exists a labour surplus, the opportunity cost of adding members of the labour pool to the agricultural labour force is zero. In its characterization of this aspect of the agricultural sector, this chapter appeals to the now extensive anthropological literature on the organization of labour and the distribution of the product in pre-capitalist economies (reviewed in Perrings, 1985).

3   INDUSTRIAL PROFITS IN AN AGRARIAN ECONOMY

Whether government intervention in the agricultural sector of the dual economy is seen as a pathological condition or not, it is clear that intervention has been endemic in the economies of reference. Industrial wages have not been determined exogenously – as the constant institutional wage hypothesis would have us believe – but have been jointly determined with the industrial rate of profit, and the level of agricultural income. Agricultural productivity has not been independent of the growth of the industrial sector: agricultural output, employment and the industrial wage have been endogenously, not exogenously, determined. What this suggests is that the utilization of the resource base in the agricultural sector is also a function of price policy developed in support of industrial growth. It becomes interesting to consider, therefore, both how the supply and the supply price of industrial labour are determined in these circumstances, and what the implications of variations in the supply price of industrial labour are for the use made of natural resources in the agricultural sector. It is still useful to think of the industrial wage as a function of the opportunity cost of industrial labour, average rural income, but there is no reason to believe that this will be constant. Nor is there any reason to believe that it will be independent of either agricultural price policy, or agricultural employment. The main features of a model that enables us to consider these problems are described below.

It is assumed that both sectors produce tradables, although whether they are actually traded is a separate issue. The agricultural sector produces crops/livestock for sale and/or for direct consumption. The industrial sector produces competitive manufactured goods (a catch-all for the range of products of modern sector enterprises) for sale. Both sectors employ material inputs at the world price net of the combined effects of tariffs and the exchange rate. In addition, however, the agricultural sector employs non-tradable natural resources collectively called 'land'. Capital is assumed to be immobile between the two sectors, and there is no tendency to the equalization of rates of return on the assets employed in each sector. The labour force in both sectors derives from the rural population, and labour is assumed to be freely mobile between the sectors. The industrial wage rate is related to average rural income, and is equal to average rural income when unemployment is equal to zero (the Harris–Todaro condition). Average rural income is given by total income in the agricultural sector averaged over the whole of the economically active and inactive rural population. For convenience, population is assumed to be stationary, though extension of the model to include population increase is trivial.

The general form of the production function assumed in the industrial sector is standard. The production function assumed in the agricultural sector is less so. Agricultural output is held to be a function of labour, capital and land, but the latter is regarded as a function of the level of agricultural employment. This is intended to capture the stylized fact that in conditions of labour surplus an increase in employment within the area over which a family farm has rights, means the expansion of farm activities on to more marginal land. The technology is assumed to be stationary. A fixed input-variable output, discrete-time, dynamic model of production in the open agrarian economy is described in

Perrings (1989b). The present model is more general in terms of the technological assumptions made, but given the specific aims of the chapter it is not dynamic.

The core of the model comprises two identities describing the income of each of the two classes of asset-holder, industrialist and farming kin-group; two behavioural equations describing production possibilities in the two sectors, the production functions; and an equilibrium condition relating the industrial wage and average agricultural income. The income of each of the two classes of asset-holder are described by:

$$Y = px - rk - vz \tag{6.1}$$

$$\Pi = \pi\chi - \rho\kappa - \omega\lambda \tag{6.2}$$

in which

$$x = x(k, L, z(L)) \tag{6.3}$$

$$\chi = \chi(\kappa, \lambda) \tag{6.4}$$

define agricultural and industrial output, respectively, and:

Y = income of farmers;
Π = income of industrialists (profits);
k = material inputs in the agricultural sector;
κ = material inputs in the industrial sector;
L = labour inputs in the agricultural sector;
λ = labour inputs in the industrial sector;
z = land inputs in the agricultural sector (a function of the level of agricultural employment);
p = price of agricultural output;
π = price of industrial output;
r = price of material inputs in the agricultural sector;
ρ = price of material inputs in the industrial sector;
v = price of agricultural land;
w = average rural income;
ω = industrial wage; and
u = unemployment.

Since it is assumed that labour is not hired in the agricultural sector, the costs in equation (6.1) exclude a wage bill component. It would be straightforward to extend the model to cover the case where an agricultural labour market has developed, accommodating individuals who have no rights of access to land or other assets. That is not, however, the case being considered in this chapter.

The prices of tradables in both sectors are net of taxes, tariffs or subsidies:

$$p = ep^*(1 - tx)$$
$$r = er^*(1 + tk)$$
$$\pi = e\pi^*(1 - t\chi)$$
$$\rho = e\rho^*(1 - t\kappa)$$

where

e = the exchange rate;
p^* = the world price of agricultural output;
t_χ = the net effect of the exchange rate and agricultural export taxes;
r^* = the world price of agricultural material inputs;
t_k = the net effect of the exchange rate and tariffs on imports of agricultural material inputs;
π^* = the world price of industrial output;
t_χ = the net effect of the exchange rate and industrial export taxes;
ρ^* = the world price of industrial material inputs; and
t_κ = the net effect of the exchange rate and tariffs on imports of industrial material inputs.

The 'price' of land, v, is given by the institutional price, v_i, plus effective land taxes or subsidies, v_t. That is

$$v = v_i + v_t.$$

So, for example, if agricultural land is held in common property ($v_i = 0$), and is subject to open access ($v_t = 0$), $v = 0$. On the other hand if agricultural land is held in common property ($v_i = 0$), but access is regulated through user charges ($v_t > 0$), $v = v_t$. The two sectors are linked through the labour market by the equilibrium (Harris–Todaro) condition:

$$w = \frac{Y(\lambda + u)}{\lambda(L + u)}. \tag{6.5}$$

This defines the industrial wage as a function of agricultural income, unemployment, and the relative size of the industrial and agricultural labour forces. Since we are holding population fixed, we may normalize by setting the total population equal to unity, such that:

$$1 = L + \lambda + u \tag{6.6}$$

and since average agricultural income is defined by:

$$w = Y/(L + u) \tag{6.7}$$

equation (6.5) may be written in the form

$$\omega = w(1 - L)/\lambda. \tag{6.8}$$

Equations (6.5) and (6.8) make the scope for anti-agricultural biases to serve the interests of industrial growth immediately clear. The industrial wage varies directly with average rural income, although the relation is mediated by the level of unemployment. Since industrial profits vary inversely with industrial wages, a strategy of development through industrialization implies an incentive to intervene in the production decisions of farmers in a way that redistributes income away from those assumed to save at a low rate and towards those assumed to save at a high rate – for the usual Kaldor–Pasinetti reasons.

The instruments commonly used to adjust the functional distribution of incomes are a set of taxes – formal or informal export taxes on output and import tariffs on inputs. Tax and tariff regimes are maintained that will confer benefits on the industrial sector through the effect on the wage rate. Indeed, the tax wedge in agricultural income provides a direct lever on the industrial wage: industrial wages being affected in very similar ways by changes in either the taxation of agricultural outputs, or tariffs on agricultural inputs. Specifically, if we write equation (6.5) in the form

$$\omega = \{[ep^*(1 - t_x)x - er^*(1 + t_k) - (v_i + v_t)z](1 - L)\}/\lambda(1 - \lambda) \tag{6.9}$$

it is immediate that for agricultural exports,

$$d\omega/dt_x = -ep^*x(1 - L)/[\lambda(1 - \lambda)]; \tag{6.10}$$

for imported material inputs,

$$d\omega/dt_k = -er^*k(1 - L)/[\lambda(1 - \lambda)]; \tag{6.11}$$

and for land,

$$d\omega/dv_t = -z(1 - L)/[\lambda(1 - \lambda)]. \tag{6.12}$$

An increase in taxes on agricultural output and tariffs on agricultural inputs, or an increase in the user charges on land will, *ceteris paribus*, have the effect of driving industrial wages down, and so industrial profits up. The effective limits to the admissible level of taxes and tariffs are given by the 'no-trade' point: the point at which producers choose to opt out of the market, producing either for direct consumption or for parallel markets. Given the very high proportion of tradable goods in sub-Saharan Africa that are transacted outside formal markets, there is reason to believe that tax and tariff regimes have been fully exploited in this regard.

4 AGRICULTURAL EMPLOYMENT, RURAL INCOME AND INDUSTRIAL PROFITS

Consider first the link between agricultural productivity and agricultural employment. The agricultural production function, $x = x(k, L, z(L))$, is constructed on the assumption that there is no technological change. Material inputs and labour are both combined with land which has all the usual properties of a potentially exhaustible resource. If 'underexploited' the marginal physical product of agricultural labour will be positive and increasing, if 'overexploited' the marginal physical product of agricultural labour will be negative. The total physical product of agricultural labour, described in Figure 6.1, reflects these properties. The assumption of 'surplus' labour is reflected in the location of the 'full employment' locus: $L + u = 1 - \lambda_0$. This is located to the right of the highest point on the total physical product curve to indicate the existence of what Fei and Ranis called a 'redundant population'. What it implies is that for a given level of industrial employment, and for a given set of land resources, the rural population sharing in the agricultural product is greater than the population which could be productively employed.

The 'average rural product' is given by the slope of a ray from the origin to the point on the full employment locus $L + u = 1 - \lambda_0$ associated with the level of output corresponding to the actual level of employment. Notice that for all except the maximum level of total physical product there exist two levels of employment corresponding to the same 'average rural product'. We can thus define two measures of excess human capacity in the system: open and disguised unemployment. Open unemployment characterizes that section of the rural population who are not economically active. Disguised unemployment characterizes those who are economically active, but who could be withdrawn without affecting average rural income. In Figure 6.1, if current employment were L_0, open unemployment would be given by $u = 1 - \lambda_0 - L_0$, and underemployment by $L_0 - L_1$.

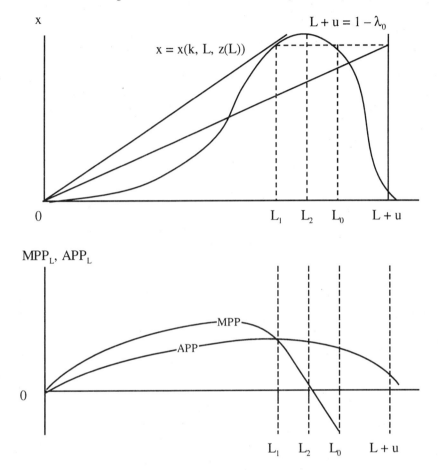

Figure 6.1   Total, average and marginal physical product of agricultural labour

The objective of the agricultural sector derives from the assumption that total agricultural income is distributed between all members of the rural population. Accordingly, if the agricultural population is fixed, average rural income will be maximized at the point where total distributable income is greatest. This results in familiar first-order conditions: the equalization of the marginal revenue product and marginal cost of labour. From (6.1), (6.3) and (6.6) the first-order conditions for the maximization of w with respect to L require that:

$$p(x_L + x_z z_L) - vz_L = 0. \tag{6.13}$$

$p(x_L + x_z z_L)$, the marginal revenue product of labour, reflects both the direct effect on output of a change in employment and the indirect effect on output of a change in land utilization due to a change in employment. vz_L, the marginal cost of labour, reflects the cost of bringing additional land into use as agricultural employment increases. It is an indirect cost. By assumption there are no direct costs of labour. Note that these first-order conditions suppose that the rural population is fixed, implying that an increase or reduction in agricultural employment results in an equivalent reduction or increase in open unemployment (that is, $du/dL = -1$). The first-order conditions for the maximization of average rural income where this is not the case will be discussed later. Equation (6.13) indicates that if there exists a labour surplus, and if land is held in common property with no user charges: that is, $u > 0$ and $v_i + v_t = 0$, the optimal level of employment will be that at which the marginal physical product of agricultural labour is equal to zero – L_2 in Figure 6.1.

To show the importance of the assumption that $du/dL = -1$, let us take two other cases: the first where $dw/du = 0$, implying that the unemployed do not share in the distribution of agricultural income (the labour-managed firm case); the second where $du/dL = 0$, implying that a fall in agricultural labour does not result in a rise in unemployment in the system. In both these cases the optimal level of employment will be that at which the average rural income is equated with the difference between the marginal revenue product and the marginal cost of agricultural labour – marginal agricultural income. Assuming $v_i + v_t = 0$, this would be at L_1 in Figure 6.1. In these two cases, the first-order conditions would require that

$$p(x_L + x_z z_L) - vz_L - w = 0. \tag{6.14}$$

These conditions look rather closer to the conditions one would expect under a standard specification of labour costs, and standard distributional assumptions. They help to underline the importance of the distributional assumptions of this chapter. Under the assumption that the unemployed do share in the distribution of the net agricultural product, it is not possible for a traditional family farm to change the average income of its members by changing the number of people with some claim on the net income generated by the farm. It follows that the existence of a labour surplus in the dual economy influences both average rural income (6.7), and, since average rural income is the opportunity cost of industrial labour, the industrial wage (6.8).

Taking open unemployment first, since $w\lambda = w(\lambda + u)$, it follows that $w \geq w$, and that $w = w$ if and only if $u = 0$. Under the assumption that migration is costless, industrial wages and average rural income will be equal if and only if there is no open unemployment in the system (the probability of finding industrial employment is equal to unity in a Harris–Todaro sense). Underemployment has a similar effect to unemployment, in that positive underemployment depresses average rural income, and so industrial wages. But the mechanism is different. Where open unemployment depresses average rural income by adding unproductive claimants to the total physical product, underemployment depresses average rural income directly by reducing the total physical product. This follows directly from the definition of underemployment as comprising that section of the agricultural workforce which could be withdrawn with no effect on average rural income. The existence of underemployment implies that the marginal physical product of agricultural labour is negative – as at L_0 in Figure 6.1.

The industrial wage rate accordingly varies with agricultural employment, underemployment and unemployment, as well as with the relative input and output prices which determine the value of the agricultural product. To approach the link between industrial wages, profits and agricultural employment, consider the general relation between income growth in the two sectors. Using (6.1), (6.3) and (6.5) to (6.8), and holding prices constant, the total differential of (6.5) is:

$$d\omega = [(1 - L)/(1 - \lambda)][(px_L + px_z z_L - vz_L - w)dL - wdu]$$
$$- \omega[1 - \lambda/(1 - \lambda)]d\lambda/\lambda + [(1 - L)/\lambda]dw \qquad (6.15)$$

in which the expression $[(px_L + px_z z_L - vz_L - w)dL - wdu]$ will be equal to zero at the optimal level of agricultural employment. Depending on the distributional rules either $du/dL = -1$ or $du/dL = 0$. In the first case conditions (6.13) apply. In the second case conditions (6.14) apply.

Let us now define the proportional growth of the industrial and agricultural labour forces to be,

$$\underline{L} = -\eta \underline{w} \qquad (6.16)$$

$$\underline{\lambda} = -\epsilon \underline{\omega} \qquad (6.17)$$

where

$\underline{L} = dL/L$
$\underline{\lambda} = d\lambda/\lambda$
$\underline{w} = dw/w$
$\underline{\omega} = d\omega/\omega$

and where $-\eta$ and $-\epsilon$ are the demand elasticities for agricultural and industrial labour, respectively. Using (6.8), (6.16) and (6.17), (6.15) may be written in the form

$$\underline{\omega} = \underline{w}\, \frac{1 - \eta(L/\lambda)(\Omega/w)}{1 - \varepsilon[1 - \lambda/(1-\lambda)]} \tag{6.18}$$

where

$$\Omega = [(1 - L)/(1 - \lambda)][(px_L + px_z z_L - vz_L - w)dL - wdu/dL].$$

Equation (6.18) is analogous to the Cordon–Findlay equation (Cordon and Findlay, 1975; Feldman, 1989), in that it defines the relation between the growth of industrial wages and the growth of rural income in dual economies. Unlike the Cordon–Findlay equation, however, the algebraic sign of (6.18) does not turn on the elasticity of demand for industrial labour alone. The expression $[1 - \lambda/(1 - \lambda)]$ may be positive or negative depending on the size of the industrial labour force relative to the rural population. More particularly, $[1 - \lambda/(1 - \lambda)] < 0$ if $2\lambda > (1 - \lambda)$. The smaller the industrial labour force as a proportion of the total population, the higher the elasticity of demand required to switch the sign of the equation from positive to negative.

Certainly, the higher the elasticity of demand for industrial labour, and the higher the level of industrial unemployment, the greater will be the probability that growth in industrial wages will vary inversely with growth in average rural income. In general, however, evidence on both employment levels and demand elasticities suggests that industrial wages in dual economies may be expected to vary directly with average rural income. Indeed, this turns out to be the main source of difficulty in the liberalization of agricultural price regimes. In addition, while $\Omega = 0$ at equilibrium levels of agricultural employment – ensuring that the numerator is positive, disequilibrium in the agricultural labour market opens up the possibility of other results.

To see the link between industrial profits and agricultural employment more directly, consider the derivative of (6.5) with respect to L:

$$d\omega/dL = \Omega/\lambda\{1 - \varepsilon[1 - \lambda/(1 - \lambda)]\}. \tag{6.19}$$

It is clear that industrial profits will respond positively to changes in the level of agricultural employment away from equilibrium. As with (6.18) the sign of this derivative depends on the elasticity of demand for industrial labour and the size of the industrial labour force relative to the total population. But it also depends on Ω. At the optimal level of agricultural employment $\Omega = 0$, indicating a plateau in the industrial wage function. Moreover, since $d^2\omega_b/d\lambda^2$ is of the same sign d^2w/dL^2, and since $d^2w/dL^2 < 0$ at the critical value of L, the industrial wage is maximized at the level of agricultural employment at which average rural income is maximized. By the same reasoning, industrial profits are minimized at that level of agricultural employment. Specifically, the first derivative

$$d\Pi/dL = -\Omega/\{1 - \varepsilon[1 - \lambda/(1 - \lambda)]\} \tag{6.20}$$

is equal to zero at the critical value of L, while the second derivative is of the opposite sign to d^2w/dL^2 at that value. More generally, a change in the economically active proportion of the rural population is by itself sufficient to change the industrial rate of profit (by changing the industrial wage rate) irrespective of what is happening to relative prices in either the industrial or agricultural markets.

An associated set of effects worth identifying are the feedback effects of a change in the level of industrial employment. Since industrial labour is drawn from the rural population it follows that a change in the level of industrial employment will have a direct impact on average rural income, whether or not it is associated with change in agricultural productivity. But the strength of this impact will depend on whether industrial labour is drawn from the economically active or inactive populations. There are two cases to consider.

In the first case, if industrial workers are drawn from the economically active rural population ($du/d\lambda = 0$), then

$$d\Pi/d\lambda = \pi\chi_\lambda - \omega\{[\lambda/(1 - \lambda)] - \Omega/\omega\} \tag{6.21}$$

where $\pi\chi_\lambda$ denotes the value of the marginal physical product of industrial labour. (6.21) will be maximized where the value of the marginal physical product of industrial labour is equal to the direct and indirect marginal cost of employing an additional unit of industrial labour. The marginal cost of industrial labour comprises both the direct wage costs and the indirect effect (positive or negative) on industrial wages of a change in the level of agricultural employment. If the difference between the value of the marginal physical product and marginal cost of agricultural labour is greater than average rural income, an increase in industrial employment will be associated with falling wage rates, and vice versa.

In the second case, if industrial workers are drawn from the economically inactive rural population ($dL/d\lambda = 0$), there are two indirect effects on industrial profits. The first is the effect on industrial wages of a change in the size of the economically inactive rural population sharing in an agricultural product of fixed amount. If unemployment falls as industrial employment rises, average rural income and so industrial wages rise, causing industrial profits to fall. The second is the effect of a change in open unemployment on the differential between industrial wages and average rural income. In this case, if unemployment falls the differential will narrow so increasing the industrial profits associated with a given level of average rural income. The two effects accordingly work in opposite directions. From the derivative

$$d\Pi/d\lambda = \pi\chi_{\lambda} - \omega\{[\lambda/(1-\lambda)] - w/\omega[1 - (1-L)/(1-\lambda)]\} \qquad (6.22)$$

we can see that the relative strength of the two effects depends on the relative importance of industrial and agricultural employment. If $L > \lambda$, then $[1 - (1 - L)/(1 - \lambda)] > 0$, and the net indirect effect on industrial profits will be negative. On the other hand, if $L < \lambda$, the net indirect effect on industrial profits will be positive. For a given level of agricultural employment greater than the level of industrial employment, rising industrial employment (falling unemployment) will cause industrial profits to rise. For a level of agricultural employment less than or equal to the level of industrial employment, rising industrial employment will have the opposite effect.

Since W includes the expression $w[(1 - L)/(1 - \lambda)]dL/du$, (6.22) differs from (6.21) only in the absence of a term capturing the effect of a change in the value of the marginal physical product of agricultural labour. Accordingly, whether the marginal costs of industrial labour are raised or lowered by drawing additional labour from the rural population depends in the first case ($du/d\lambda = 0$) on the effect of a change in agricultural employment on the marginal physical productivity of agricultural labour, and in the second case ($dL/d\lambda = 0$) on the relative size of the two sectors.

5   ANTI-AGRICULTURAL BIASES AND AGRICULTURAL RESOURCE UTILIZATION

Consider now the implications of the anti-agricultural biases observed in sub-Saharan Africa for the utilization of real resources in the agricultural sector. It should be recalled that wage restraint in this model of the dual economy is secured by restricting average agricultural income. Industrial wages are assumed not to be determined on a cost-of-living basis, but by reference to the opportunity cost of industrial labour. The presumption here is that even if the cost of living is formally a part of wage calculations under an incomes policy, average agricultural income remains a *de facto* point of reference in wage determination. Food price controls, for instance, operate through their effect on agricultural income, rather than on the urban cost of living.

This suggests a very particular interpretation of the term 'agricultural bias'. Specifically, agricultural prices are said to be biased if they reduce average agricultural income below the level that would obtain under the same distribution of the agricultural product at socially efficient prices – export and import parity prices in the case of tradable, and prices equal to marginal social cost in the case of non-tradable. In other words, an anti-agricultural bias implies non-neutral intervention in respect of both input and output prices. The existence of monopsonistic purchasing prices below export parity prices, for example, may or may not indicate the existence of an anti-agricultural bias, depending on the pricing of agricultural inputs. If tradable inputs are subsidized, and non-tradable inputs are priced below marginal social cost, monopsonistic pricing may be associated with higher agricultural incomes and industrial wages than would obtain under socially efficient prices.

The anti-agricultural biases alleged to exist in sub-Saharan Africa relate almost exclusively to distortions in the cost of tradable inputs and outputs due to the monopsonistic pricing of outputs, monopolistic pricing of inputs, and the income-depressing effects of taxes and tariffs. Throughout the literature virtually nothing is said about the cost of non-tradable – range and arable land in particular. Yet this is the source of the uncertainty that leads Pearce et al. (1988) to question the environmental effects of changes in producer prices. From the first-order conditions for the maximization of average rural income where income is distributed to all members of the rural population, (6.13), agricultural employment will increase up to the point where the marginal cost and marginal revenue product of labour are equal. The marginal revenue product of labour is simply the value of the (tradable) direct and indirect marginal physical product of labour, $p(x_L + x_z z_L)$. The marginal cost of labour comprises the indirect costs of bringing additional (non-tradable) land into use, vz_L. Under the structure of property rights existing in much of sub-Saharan Africa, land held in communal ownership is zero priced, implying that $vz_L = 0$, and therefore that the optimal use of agricultural resources will be that at which the marginal physical product of labour is equal to zero. This is not affected by the level of the output price, p. Nor, more importantly, is it affected by the deregulation of the price of traded agricultural inputs and outputs. If agricultural output prices are raised to export parity levels, average agricultural income and so industrial wages will both be raised, but optimal resource use will remain unchanged.

The limited scope for output price liberalization to stimulate an expansion in agricultural output in these circumstances is obvious. So, too, are the adverse effects of output price liberalization on industrial profits. From (6.1) it is immediate that average rural income will remain constant in the face of a change in revenue, only if there is an exactly compensating change in costs. If output prices are decontrolled, while input prices are fixed, average agricultural incomes and hence industrial wages will rise (providing that equation (6.18) is positive in sign). This, in turn, will mean a reduction in the competitiveness of the industrial sector. While it is possible to seek compensating increases in the cost of tradable inputs – interest rates, fuels, fertilizers and the like – the experience of the countries of reference here suggests both that the level of employment of such inputs is low, and that their elasticity of demand is high. Price liberalization that is not associated with the introduction of user charges on non-tradables in common property will tend to reduce industrial profits.

There are two important qualifications to this, however, and it is these qualifications which have perhaps the most significance for agricultural resource utilization. The first derives from the fact that industrial wages (and so industrial profits) are also sensitive to the relative magnitudes of the industrial labour force and the economically active agricultural population. Equations (6.21) and (6.22) show this for the case where change in the level of unemployment is due to the growth of the industrial labour force. But industrial wages also respond to change in unemployment caused by change in the economically active proportion of the rural population. Specifically

$$d\omega/du = (w/\lambda)\{1 - [(1 - L)/(1 - \lambda)]\} - (\Omega/\lambda). \tag{6.23}$$

Equation (6.23) indicates that industrial wages will fall with a fall in unemployment providing that the economically active rural population is greater than the industrial labour force. What this means is that policies which reduce open unemployment by stimulating the expansion of agricultural employment will cause industrial profits to rise. The implications of this will be considered later. The second qualification derives from the fact that agricultural productivity, too, is sensitive to changes in the economically active proportion of the rural population, and is affected differently by changes in the level of productive employment and underemployment. Specifically, the expansion of underemployment – indicated by a negative marginal physical product of labour – implies a direct reduction in both agricultural output (and so agricultural revenue), and open unemployment.

From (6.13), positive underemployment in the agricultural sector will exist if and only if the marginal cost of labour is negative. From the assumption that $z_L > 0$, the marginal cost of labour, $(x_L + x_z z_L)$, will be negative if and only if $v < 0$. In the case where arable and pastoral land is held in common property, suggesting that $v_i = 0$, $v < 0$ implies that $v_t < 0$: user charges for land are negative. Negative user charges imply the existence of subsidies which make it privately profitable for individual farmers to work land even where the marginal physical product of labour is negative. There are, in fact, a wide range of examples of subsidies that are readily interpretable as negative user charges in the agricultural sector in sub-Saharan Africa; ploughing and land clearance grants being perhaps the most obvious examples. In terms of the model of the dual economy discussed here, the lower the level of open unemployment in an economy with a relatively small industrial sector, and the higher the level of underemployment, the lower will be the industrial wage rate.

Price intervention which lowers input prices relative to output prices does not necessarily affect industrial profits adversely (a) if it is associated with change in any of the real variables influencing the relation between industrial wages and average rural income (agricultural employment and unemployment) or (b) if it results in the direct reduction of agricultural output (underemployment). The second effect is particularly important. Underemployment implies that x_L, x_z, and v are all negative. If a subsidy on land use, vz_L, exceeds the output losses associated with that use, $(px_L + px_z z_L)$, expansion of the economically active proportion of the agricultural population will actually increase industrial profits.

6   THE SUSTAINABILITY OF RESOURCE USE

To conclude, let us return to the question that has motivated this chapter: the sustainability of agricultural resource utilization under a strategy of growth through industrialization. Using a simple equilibrium model of the dual economy that is well adapted to the identification of trade-offs in the economy (but which lays no claim to capturing the essential features of dynamic processes), the chapter has considered what the implications of industrial growth are for the performance of the agricultural sector. Since average rural income is the opportunity cost of industrial labour in such an economy, the conflict of interest between the industrial and agricultural sectors is quite intuitive. The systematic bias against agriculture observed by the World Bank and the IMF may then be interpreted as the other side of a strategy of development through industrialization. Rural poverty may be interpreted as the outcome of policies suggested by the strategy. The question is whether the distributional implications of the strategy have any clearly identifiable significance for the sustainability of the agricultural sector.

The context within which this question is posed is the IMF/World Bank adjustment programme for low-income, highly-indebted, dual economies. The programmes are implicitly critical of most of the agricultural policies associated with the industrializing growth strategy. They are explicitly critical of the policy of depressing the prices paid to producers by monopsonistic marketing boards, and the liberalization of agricultural pricing policy is a major part of the programme. There is a certain irony in the fact that having driven down agricultural incomes through the manipulation of agricultural input and output prices in the interests of containing industrial wages, successive governments in many low-income countries have watched the emergence of a tenuous, makeshift, competitive local industrial sector in which the implicit subsidy on wages is not the source of extraordinary investment funds for the expansion of the sector, but the sole reason for its existence. To the extent that increases in average agricultural income feed through into industrial wages, higher producer prices will tend to be seen as threatening to such an industrial sector. Indeed, this remains one of the strongest reasons for the unwillingness of many governments to allow producer prices to rise to world levels. It is also one of the strongest reasons for considering alternative forms of wage restraint once producer prices have risen.

Agricultural bias, in the sense of this chapter, may be said to exist whenever input and/or output prices are modified in such a way as to reduce the average agricultural income stream below the level that would hold under a marginal social cost pricing rule. In the case of tradables, the appropriate prices under this rule are 'border' prices. In the case of non-tradables, the appropriate prices are given by the marginal social cost of the resource, where the marginal social cost reflects the sum of the direct, external and user costs. The marginal social cost of a natural resource such as grazing land, for example, includes not just the direct costs to the user of bringing that land into use, but also any uncompensated costs visited on others using the same resource, together with the future opportunities forgone by committing the resource to a particular use now.

Anti-agricultural bias in respect of tradables is typically associated with output prices below export parity prices, and input prices above import parity prices. In respect of non-tradables the position is a little more complicated. A particular feature of the price structure of agriculture in much of sub-Saharan Africa has been the implicit subsidy on agricultural land offered by traditional (common or communal) land tenure systems. Land has been almost universally priced below its marginal social cost, and in most cases has been 'free'. One result of this is that the resource has been overutilized in an economic sense. Indeed, we have seen that where land is zero priced under such land tenure systems, the optimal level of agricultural employment will be that at which the marginal physical product of labour is zero. This is certainly what was assumed in earlier versions of the dual economy model (for example, Fei and Ranis, 1964). In this chapter, the price of agricultural land is defined as the sum of an 'institutional' price – equal to zero for common property regimes – and a user charge. The term 'user charge' covers the sum of all direct charges, such as grazing or water fees, and all subsidies associated with the use of land. Where subsidies exceed any direct charges, the user charge is negative. Because of the effect that negative user charges have on privately optimal employment (and productivity) levels, we have the paradoxical result that cash grants to farmers can reflect an anti-agricultural bias.

This follows from the fact that bias is judged in terms of an income stream. It is important to consider the effect of the agricultural price regime on the long-run performance of the sector. The question of the sustainability of resource use (and hence the sustainability of an income stream) under common property regimes turns on the user charge. User charges that are less than the marginal social cost of land, imply that the resource will be overutilized in an economic sense. This does not, of course, necessarily imply that it will be overutilized in an ecological sense (Barrett, 1989). For all renewable natural resources there exist levels of exploitation that are sustainable. If the level of exploitation lies outside this range, however, the resource will be depleted or degraded – due to the exhaustion of soil nutrients, erosion, devegetation or the like. Ecological overutilization supposes the depletion or degradation of renewable resources. Nevertheless, if a resource is appropriately priced, economic and ecological overutilization should be highly correlated. An anti-agricultural bias that rests on incentives to overutilize agricultural resources in an economic sense will tend to be ecologically unsustainable.

For this reason it is worth paying special attention to the impact of land-use subsidies on the industrial wage. Overutilization of land through underemployment of agricultural labour depresses industrial wages by reducing real output, open unemployment – and so the differential between rural income and industrial wages. Wherever industrial profits are under pressure (whether through the effect of agricultural ouput price liberalization or not) and wherever industrial profits are privileged under the general development strategy, there is an incentive to intervene in the agricultural sector to restrain average agricultural incomes. If intervention encourages the overutilization of natural resources, it increases the probability of the degradation of those resources.

REFERENCES

Addison, A. and Demery, L. (1989), 'The economics of rural poverty alleviation', in Commander (ed.): 71–89.

Arrighi, G. (1970), 'Labour supplies in historical perspective: a study in the proletarianization of the African peasantry in Rhodesia', *Journal of Development Studies* **6** (3): 197–234.

Barbier, E.B. (1988), 'Sustainable agriculture and the resource poor: policy issues and options', LEEC Paper No. 2.

Barbier, E.B. (1989), 'Cash crops, food crops and sustainability: the case of Indonesia', *World Development* **17** (6): 879–95.

Barrett, S. (1989), 'On the overgrazing problem', LEEC Paper No. 7.

Basu, K. (1980), 'Optimal policies in dual economies', *Quarterly Journal of Economics*, August, 187–96.

Behrman, J.R. (1968), *Supply Response in Underdeveloped Agriculture*, North-Holland, Amsterdam.

Beynon, J.G. (1989), 'Pricism v. structuralism in sub-Saharan African agriculture', *Journal of Agricultural Economics* **40** (3): 323–35.

Bond, M.E. (1983), 'Agricultural responses to prices in sub-Saharan African countries', IMF Staff Papers No. 30.

Cleaver, K. (1985), 'The impact of price and exchange rate policies on agriculture in sub-Saharan Africa', World Bank Staff Working Paper No. 728.

Cleaver, K. (1988), 'The use of price policy to stimulate agricultural growth in sub-Saharan Africa', Paper presented to the 8th Agricultural Sector Symposium on Trade, Aid, and Policy Reform for Agriculture.

Commander, S. (ed.) (1989), *Structural Adjustment and Agriculture: Theory and Practice in Africa and Latin America*, ODI, London.

Cordon, W.M. and Findlay, R. (1975), 'Urban unemployment, intersectoral capital mobility and development policy', *Economica*, February: 59–78.

Delgado G.L. and Mellor J.W. (1984), 'A structural view of policy issues in African agricultural development', *American Journal of Agricultural Economics* **66** (5): 665–70.

Feder, G. and Noronha, R. (1987), 'Land rights systems and agricultural development in sub-Saharan Africa', *World Bank Research Observer* **2** (2):.

Fei, J.C.H. and Ranis G. (1964), *Development of the Labor Surplus Economy: Theory and Policy*, R.D. Irwin, Homewood, Ill.

Fei, J.C.H. and Ranis, G. (1978), 'Agrarianism, dualism, and economic development', in S.P. Singh (ed.), *Underdevelopment to Developing Economies*, Oxford University Press, Oxford: 1–42.

Feldman, D.H. (1989), 'The trade-off between GNP and unemployment in a dual economy', *Southern Economic Journal* **56** (1): 46–55.

Food and Agriculture Organization (FAO) (1985), *The State of Food and Agriculture 1984*, FAO, Rome.

Ghai, D. and Smith, L.D. (1987), *Agricultural Prices, Policy and Equity in sub-Saharan Africa*, Lynne Rienner, Boulder, Colo.

Green, R.H. (1989), 'Articulating stabilization programmes and structural adjustment', in Commander (ed.): 35–54.

Harris, J.R. and Todaro, M.P. (1970), 'Migration, unemployment and development: a two sector analysis', *American Economic Review*, March: 126–42.

International Monetary Fund (IMF) (1987), *World Economic Outlook*, IMF, Washington, DC.

Johnson, O.E.G. (1989), 'The agricultural sector in IMF stand-by arrangements', in Commander (ed.): 19–34.

Junankar, P.N. (1989), 'The response of peasant farmers to price incentives: the use and misuse of profit functions', *Journal of Development Studies* **25** (2): 169–82.

Lewis, W.A. (1954), 'Economic development with unlimited supplies of labour', *The Manchester School of Economic and Social Studies* **22** (2): 139–91.

Lewis, W.A. (1958), 'Unlimited labour supply: further notes', *The Manchester School of Economic and Social Studies* **26**: 1–32.

Lewis, W.A. (1976), 'Development and distribution', in A. Cairncross and M. Puri (eds), *Employment, Income Distribution and Development Strategy: Problems of the Developing Countries*, Macmillan, London: 26–43.

Lewis, W.A. (1979), 'The dual economy revisited', *The Manchester School of Economic and Social Studies* **47** (3): 211–29.

Lipton, M. (1987), 'Limits of price policy for agriculture: which way for the World Bank?', *Development Policy Review* **5** (2):.

Mosley, P. and Smith, L. (1989), 'Structural adjustment and agricultural performance in sub-Saharan Africa 1980–1987', *Journal of International Development* **1** (3): 321–55.

Pearce, D.W., Barbier, E.B. and Markandya, A. (1988), 'Environmental economics and decision-making in sub-Saharan Africa', LEEC Paper No. 1.

Perrings, C. (1985), 'The natural economy revisited', *Economic Development and Cultural Change* **33** (4): 829–50.

Perrings, C. (1989a), 'Debt and resource degradation in low income countries: the adjustment problem and the perverse effects of poverty in sub-Saharan Africa', in H. Singer and S. Sharma (eds), *Economic Development and World Debt*, Macmillan, London:

Perrings C. (1989b), 'An optimal path to extinction? Poverty and resource degradation in the open agrarian economy', *Journal of Development Economics* **30**: 1–24.

Rao, J.M. (1986), 'Agriculture in recent development theory', *Journal of Development Economics* **22**: 41–86.

Rao, J.M. (1989), 'Agricultural supply response: a survey', *Agricultural Economics* **3** (1): 1–22.

United Nations (UN) (1986), *World Economic Survey 1986: Current Trends and Policies in the World Economy*, United Nations, New York.

World Bank (1987), *World Development Report 1986*, Oxford University Press for the World Bank, Oxford.

7.   Stress, shock and the sustainability of resource use in semi-arid environments

1   INTRODUCTION

The close links between agricultural and economic growth in many low-income countries during a decade of 'crisis' has prompted a widespread theoretical and empirical reappraisal of the dynamics of agricultural sector performance. Increasingly, attention is being focused on the determinants of the microeconomic decisions of resource users, and specifically on the role of incentives in encouraging the sustainable use of such resources. As Pearce et al. (1988) put it: 'Africa's economic crisis' is due to 'Africa's agricultural crisis', and it is becoming increasingly apparent that Africa's agricultural crisis is fuelled by the environmental effects of a set of incentives that encourage the myopic use of resources. The emphasis in much of the recent work is accordingly on the generation of an appropriate economic environment, and the necessary enabling institutions (compare Repetto, 1986, 1989; Warford, 1989).

What is not clear is what an 'appropriate' economic environment implies. One strand of the literature is dominated by the presumption that it implies an intertemporally efficient set of prices. Indeed, much of the recent work on incentives for the sustainable use of environmental resources argues for the liberalization of prices on these grounds (compare Bond, 1983; Cleaver, 1985, 1988; Barbier, 1988, 1989b). However, it turns out that efficiency in the allocation of resources is neither necessary nor sufficient for ecological sustainability. There is no reason to believe that a set of prices which is intertemporally efficient will induce a more ecologically sustainable use of resources than one which is not. The use of border prices as proxies for the social opportunity cost of tradable resources in the small open economy, for example, offers no guarantee against the degradation of the domestic resource base.

This chapter explores the link between the economic environment and ecologically sustainable use of resources in the case of livestock farming in semi-arid lands in the context of an infinite horizon stochastic control model of range management in semi-arid lands. A characteristic feature of the problem being modelled here is the high degree of uncertainty about the productivity of environmental assets, due to the considerable variation in both temperature and rainfall. Since variance in rainfall tends to rise as the mean falls, uncertainty in rain-fed agriculture is greater in the arid and semi-arid areas than it is elsewhere. Agricultural systems in such areas are more frequently subject to climatic shocks, and their ability to continue to function in the face of these is an important measure of the sustainability of the management strategies being pursued (Conway, 1987; Barbier, 1989a). The value of the approach is that it makes it easy to trace the the longer-term effects of allocations that are optimal under the present price structure through the feedback mechanisms registered in the model. This makes it possible to test the effects of a given price structure over time. Moreover it makes it possible to test for the sensitivity of the natural environment to change in the price structure. While there is reason to believe that the longer-term effects of current price regimes do give cause for alarm in the semi-arid lands, there are few attempts to incorporate those long-term effects in an analysis of price policy. This is one way of handling the problem. More importantly, it is a way of addressing the question of what are the properties of an ecologically sustainable 'economic environment'.

The chapter is organized in seven sections. The following section discusses the ecological component of the model, and clarifies the assumptions made about range and herd dynamics in the absence of control. Section 3 elaborates the economic problem addressed, and derives the equations required for the construction of an optimal policy. A simulation to illustrate the construction of an optimal policy is presented in Section 4. The policy, its influence on the time paths of the state variables in both the deterministic and stochastic cases, and the properties of those time paths under varying values for the ecological and economic parameters of the system, is illustrated in a numerical example in Section 5. Section 6 examines the policy implications of the model, and a final section offers some concluding remarks.

2   THE ECOLOGICAL MODEL

Three characteristics of the pastoral economy are assumed to be essential to the specification of the ecological component of a bioeconomic model of range-land use. The first is that current changes in herd size and the level of offtake affect future range-land carrying capacity. This means both that the current carrying capacity of range land is not independent of the history of range-land use, and that current herd size is not independent of the past evolution of carrying capacity. It is this interdependence of population and carrying capacity which makes the problem somewhat different from the many other renewable resource problems analysed in control terms.[1] The second characteristic is that the system evolves through periodic change. The 'process noise' that randomizes the time paths of herd size and carrying capacity is the product of variance in rainfall. Moreover, the effect of variance in rainfall on herd size and carrying capacity is not instantaneous, but occurs with a seasonally-determined lag. Accordingly, time is treated discretely, rather than continuously, with a year being the natural interval. The third characteristic is that there is a very large measure of uncertainty attached to the future value of the state variables – herd size and carrying capacity. As has already been remarked, the carrying capacity of range land and the growth rate of the herd are both a function of rainfall, which has an extremely high variance in semi-arid areas. This characteristic makes the problem an intrinsically stochastic one.

To reflect these essential characteristics while preserving simplicity, the structure of the model developed here differs in certain respects from existing pastoral models. Carrying capacity is assumed to change over time with changes both in the degree of grazing pressure, and in climatic conditions. The relation between carrying capacity and grazing pressure is defined within the model. The relation between carrying capacity and factors exogenous to the model, such as rainfall, is captured by random variation of the ecological parameters of the model. Just how the regeneration of the range is expected to change with variation in endogenous factors will be discussed later, but the important point is that the ecological model should reflect the fact that herd growth, the impact of herd size on range-land vegetation, and the recuperative powers of the range are interdependent, and are all sensitive to climatic conditions.

The ecological system in isolation is formally assumed to be globally stable, in that the vegetative cover of the range is assumed to converge to some well-defined maximum value (the climax vegation) regardless of the severity of shocks due to either temporary climatic variation or overgrazing. This implies that it will regenerate in the same way irrespective of the degree of damage inflicted on both the soil and its vegetative cover through overgrazing, once the herd is removed. Put another way, it is formally assumed that nothing is irreversible: the system is non-evolutionary. This is clearly a very strong assumption, which does not correspond to reality. However, it serves the purpose of the chapter. Leaving the evolutionary nature of the ecological system to one side, and abstracting from the significance of herd and range composition, the remaining characteristics of pastoral systems are captured in the following equations of motion. The sequences $\{x_t\}$ and $\{k_t\}$ describe the time paths of the herd and the carrying capacity of the range. Both are measured in terms of livestock units, and both may be thought of as the natural endogenous variables of the system. $\{x_t\}$ and $\{k_t\}$ are generated by the following first-order forward recursions:

$$x_{t+1} - x_t = \alpha_r x_t (1 - x_t/k_t) - u_t \qquad (7.1)$$

$$k_{t+1} - k_t = \beta_t k_t (1 - k_t/k_c) - \gamma_t(x_t - u_t) \qquad (7.2)$$

in which

x_t = herd size at time t $(0 \le x_t \le k_c)$;
k_t = carrying capacity at time t $(0 \le k_t \le k_c)$;
k_c = maximum carrying capacity of the range;
u_t = offtake at time t (in the most general case $-k_c \le u_t \le x_t$);
α_t = the net growth rate of the herd on the range $(-1 \le \alpha_t)$;
β_t = the rate of regeneration of the range $(-1 \le \beta_t)$;
γ_t = the rate of depletion of the range due to the herd $(\gamma_t \le 1)$.

The state variables, x_t and k_t are restricted to non-negative values. Offtake, u_t, may in principle be positive or negative. If offtake is positive (implying that livestock is being drawn off the range) it is limited to values less than or equal to the size of the herd. If offtake is negative (implying that the range is being restocked) it is limited to values less than or equal to the maximum carrying capacity of the range. In the absence of supply restrictions or other constraints, restocking will generally be a part of an optimal strategy in a stochastic environment.

The time-behaviour of the ecological system depends on the ecological parameters, α_t, β_t and γ_t. Note that the time-behaviour of non-linear difference equations similar to (7.1) and (7.2) tends to be rather complex. Ignoring offtake, if α_t and β_t were assumed to be positive constant parameters (as they would be in the deterministic case), the size of the herd and the carrying capacity of the range would converge to equilibrium values if $0 < \alpha_t, \beta_t \le 2$. Moreover, convergence would be asymptotic for $0 < \alpha_t, \beta_t \le 1$, and through damped oscillation for $1 < \alpha_t, \beta_t \le 2$. But for $\alpha_t, \beta_t \ge 2$ the sequences $\{x_t\}$ and $\{k_t\}$ would be non-convergent, and if $\alpha_t, \beta_t > 2.57$, would exhibit 'chaotic' behaviour. In the general case where α_t and β_t are not restricted to positive values, and are time varying, the properties of the system will change depending on the current value of α_t. $\{x_t\}$ and $\{k_t\}$ may converge on some positive growth path over some time segments, may converge on zero over others, or may be entirely non-convergent.

In this chapter, α_t, β_t and γ_t are defined as stochastic parameters. That is, they are independently distributed random variables with means α, β and γ, and variances σ_α^2, σ_β^2 and σ_γ^2. The system is thus subject to 'process noise'.[2] To get a sense of the likely values for the mean and variance of α_t, we need to consider both the ecological and the institutional determinants of herd growth. Recall that the focus of the chapter is range land in semi-arid areas, which includes much of the Sahel and south-central and south-western Africa. Institutionally, these areas tend to be dominated by more or less regulated common property regimes. The main source of variance in α_t is rainfall, assumed here to be independent of changes in the vegetative cover of the range.[3] This affects both the net natural rate of increase of the herd, and the rate at which animals are moved or migrate into or out of a particular range. The net natural rate of increase is a function of both fertility and mortality in the herd, each of which tends to be highly sensitive to the level of rainfall for most species herded in these areas. Pastoralism in most semi-arid areas involves the managed movement of herds between ranges, depending on the state of the vegetative cover – the pattern being facilitated by open-access common property regimes. But there is also some autonomous movement both of livestock and of competing ungulates. This implies that while α will tend to have a value somewhere near the long-run mean net natural rate of increase of the herd itself, it will be subject to considerable variance. Indeed, given the influence that rainfall has on herd fertility, mortality and migration, fluctuation in rainfall has historically led to dramatic swings in herd sizes on a given range from one period to the next. It has also led to dramatic shifts in the species composition of the herd, although no attempt is being made to model this here.

The mean and variance of β_t capture the net natural rate of increase of the vegetation consumed by the herd on the range land of interest. As in the case of herd growth, there are a number of different effects involved here. Clearly, there is a positive correlation between rainfall and the growth of graze or browse, but where there is a short-run shift in species composition within the vegetative cover from edible grasses to woody biomass, or from edible to non-edible grasses, this will show up as a decrease in vegetative cover, even though total biomass may have increased. Similarly, where climatic conditions associated with increasing vegetative biomass also favour the growth of populations of competitors to the herd (other ungulates or insects, say), the graze or browse available to the herd may decrease. This is a very real problem in many of the semi-arid areas of sub-Saharan Africa, which are also populated by highly mobile, highly fluctuating herds of antelope, and are subject to depredation by insect swarms. An additional complication arises if edible grasses are not the climax vegetation of the area, but this problem is set aside in this chapter. Once again, while β will tend to have a value somewhere near the long-run, mean, net natural rate of regeneration of the range, it will be subject to considerable variance.

As a result of the variance of α_t and β_t, the time-behaviour of the recursions (7.1) and (7.2) may be extremely complex – even in the absence of offtake. The herd growth function may have normal compensatory, overcompensatory, depensatory and critical depensatory properties for similar herd sizes at different periods.[4] There is no reason to believe that normal compensatory growth (which leads asymptotically to convergence to equilibrium values for both herd size and range carrying capacity) will be encountered in reality. Indeed, it is more likely that growth will be overcompensatory (leading either to convergence via damped oscillations, or to non-convergent oscillation). But it is also perfectly possible for the growth function to be critically depensatory (leading to the collapse of the herd) where carrying capacity falls sharply over consecutive periods.

In general, change in the size of the herd will vary directly with change in the level of grazing pressure given by the ratio x_t/k_t. In general, that is, overgrazing will lead to a decline in the size of the herd. However, it is important to add that since the natural rate of growth of both herd and carrying capacity is assumed to fluctuate, and since negative values for α_t and β_t are admissible, this will not necessarily be the case. In the absence of offtake/restocking, the difference $x_{t+1} - x_t$ will be negative if $\alpha_t x_t(1 - x_t/k_t) < 0$, which will occur either if $(1 - x_t/k_t) < 0$ and $\alpha_t > 0$; or if $(1 - x_t/k_t) > 0$ and $\alpha_t < 0$. The first alternative implies that the future size of the herd will decline where pressure is increasing on range that is currently being overgrazed. The second option implies that future herd sizes may fall (due to disease or drought, say) where the range is not currently being overgrazed. Moreover, since $x_{t+1} - x_t > 0$ if $(1 - x_t/k_t) < 0$ and $\alpha_t < 0$, future herd sizes may rise where the range is being currently overgrazed in an ecological sense, providing that herd pressure on the range is falling. Similarly, the carrying capacity of the range in the uncontrolled case may decline for various reasons. $\beta_t k_t(1 - k_t/k_c) - \gamma_t(x_t - u_t) < 0$ if either $\beta_t > 0$ and depletion is greater than regeneration, or if $\beta_t < 0$. The fact that herd size may exceed the carrying capacity of the range in any one year is not, therefore, a necessary condition for declining carrying capacity in the next year. Future carrying capacity may fall or rise due to climatic changes independently of current herd densities.

The net growth of the herd in any given period (7.1) is equal to the difference between offtake and the natural growth of the herd, given the degree of grazing pressure, x_t/k_t. The net growth in the carrying capacity of the range (7.2) is the difference between the net depletion of the vegetative cover of the range as a consequence of the stocking decision, and the natural rate of regeneration of the range. Offtake accordingly has both direct and indirect effects on the size of the herd. If livestock are drawn off in the current period, the current size of the herd is reduced but the future growth potential of the herd is improved due to the effect on the carrying capacity of the range via the damage function $-\gamma_t(x_t - u_t)$.

Maximization of the growth function (7.2) with respect to current carrying capacity shows that the maximum rate of regeneration of the range is $k_t = k_m = 1/2k_c$. The maximum sustainable yield of the range is the point at which the net rate of depletion of the range due to grazing is equal to the maximum rate of its regeneration. From (7.1) and (7.2), the size of the herd corresponding to the maximum sustainable yield is given by:

$$x_m = (k_c/4\alpha_t)\{-(1 - \alpha_t) \pm [(1 - \alpha_t)^2 + 2\alpha_t\beta_t/\gamma_t]^{1/2}\} \qquad (7.3)$$

and the maximum sustainable level of offtake is given by

$$u_m = \alpha_t x_m(1 - x_m/k_m) = x_m - 1/2(\beta_t/\alpha_t)k_m. \qquad (7.4)$$

3   THE ECONOMIC PROBLEM

Without yet describing the economic environment within which pastoral activity takes place, it is possible to write a general form of the optimization problem involved. Pastoralists are assumed to maximize welfare over an infinite horizon through choice of the level of offtake, and subject to the properties of the physical system. That is, the problem is to:

$$\max_{\{u_t\}} \sum_{t=0}^{\infty} \rho^t W(x_t, k_t, u_t) \qquad (7.5a)$$

subject to

$$\dot{x}_{t+1} - x_t = \alpha_t x_t(1 - x_t/k_t) - u_t \qquad (7.5b)$$

$$k_{t+1} - k_t = \beta_t k_t(1 - k_t/k_c) - \gamma_t(x_t - u_t) \qquad (7.5c)$$

$$x_0 > 0 = x(0) \qquad (7.5d)$$

$$k_0 > 0 = k(0) \qquad (7.5e)$$

$$-k_c \leq u_t \leq x_t \qquad (7.5f)$$

$$x_t, k_t \geq 0 \qquad (7.5g)$$

where $\rho = [1/(1 + \delta)]$ denotes a discount factor, with δ being the rate of discount. The remaining variables and parameters have already been defined.

The solution to this problem provides a decision rule which fixes the optimal offtake policy under whatever range management strategy is in use. This chapter describes the results of an equilibrium strategy (with restocking).[5] The current value Hamiltonian for the problem is:

$$H(x_t, u_t, \lambda_t) = W(x_t, k_t, u_t) + \rho\lambda_{t+1}\{\alpha x_t(1 - x_t/k_t) - u_t\}$$
$$+ \rho\zeta_{t+1}\{\beta k_t(1 - k_t/k_c) - \gamma(x_t - u_t)\} \qquad (7.6)$$

with first-order conditions:

$$0 \qquad = H_{ut} \qquad = W_{ut} - \rho\lambda_{t+1} + \rho\zeta_{t+1}\gamma \qquad (7.7a)$$

$$\rho\lambda_{t+1} - \lambda_t \quad = -H_{xt} \qquad = -W_{xt} - \rho\lambda_{t+1}\alpha(1 - 2x_t/k_t) + \rho\zeta_{t+1}\gamma \qquad (7.7b)$$

$$\rho\zeta_{t+1} - \zeta_t \quad = -H_{kt} \qquad = -W_{kt} - \rho\lambda_{t+1}\alpha x_t^2/k_t^2 - \rho\zeta_{t+1}\beta(1 - 2k_t/k_c) \qquad (7.7c)$$

$$x_{t+1} - x_t \quad = H_{\rho\lambda t+1} \quad = \alpha x_t(1 - x_t/k_t) - u_t \qquad (7.7d)$$

$$k_{t+1} - k_t \quad = H_{\rho\zeta t+1} \quad = \beta k_t(1 - k_t/k_c) - \gamma(x_t - u_t) \qquad (7.7e)$$

$$x_0 \qquad = x(0) \qquad (7.7f)$$

$$k_0 \qquad = k(0) \qquad (7.7g)$$

$$u_t \qquad \in U.$$

If a steady-state solution exists, such that $\lambda_t = \lambda_{t+1}$, and $\zeta_t = \zeta_{t+1}$, (7.7a), (7.7b) and (7.7c) may be used to define a steady-state 'rule' for determining the optimal level of grazing pressure. Defining the ratios:

$$\kappa_t \equiv k_t/k_c \qquad (7.8a)$$

$$\psi_t \equiv x_t/k_t \qquad (7.8b)$$

$$\omega_{xt} \equiv W_{xt}/W_{ut} \qquad (7.8c)$$

$$\omega_{kt} \equiv W_{kt}/W_{ut} \qquad (7.8d)$$

solving (7.7b) and (7.7c) for the steady-state values of λ and ζ from, and inserting these into (7.7a) yields the quadratic:

$$0 = \psi_t^{*2}\alpha\gamma(1+\omega_{xt}) - \psi_t^{*}2\alpha[\beta(1-2\kappa_t) - \omega_{kt}\gamma - \delta] + \omega_{kt}\gamma(1 - \alpha + \delta)$$
$$+ [\beta(1-2\kappa_t) - \delta][\omega_{xt} + \alpha - \delta]. \qquad (7.9)$$

ψ_t^{*}, a positive root of the quadratic, defines the optimal level of grazing pressure. Given ψ_t^{*}, the optimal herd size corresponding to k_t is obtained directly, and the optimal offtake is simply that which adjusts the herd size to its optimal value. It is defined by:

$$u_t{}^* = x_{t-} \psi_t{}^* k_t.$$
(7.10)

The ecological effects of the optimal offtake policy will depend on the level of grazing pressure generated by the optimal policy. Two measures of overgrazing may be identified: an economic measure and an ecological measure. Economic overgrazing implies that the actual level of grazing pressure exceeds the optimal level of grazing pressure. Ecological overgrazing, on the other hand, implies that the actual level of grazing pressure exceeds the level of grazing pressure at the maximum sustainable yield. Whether optimal grazing pressure is greater or less than the level of grazing pressure at the maximum sustainable yield depends on the parameters of the system – both economic and ecological. If relative prices are such that it is optimal to 'mine' the range, then the optimal grazing pressure will exceed the maximum sustainable grazing pressure. On the other hand if relative prices are consistent with the sustainable use of the resource, the optimal grazing pressure will be less than or equal to the grazing pressure at the maximum sustainable yield.

Economic overgrazing will accordingly be said to exist wherever $(\psi_t/\psi_t{}^*) - 1 > 0$, ψ_t being the current level of grazing pressure and $\psi_t{}^*$ being the optimal level of grazing pressure. Ecological overgrazing will be said to exist wherever $(\psi_t/\psi_m) - 1 > 0$, ψ_m being the level of grazing pressure at the maximum sustainable yield of the range. Since $\psi_t{}^*$ may be greater than, less than, or equal to ψ_m, it follows that whether a system is overgrazed in an ecological sense does not necessarily imply anything about whether it is overgrazed in an economic sense. But if the optimal level of grazing pressure is equal to or greater than the level of grazing pressure at the maximum sustainable yield, economic overgrazing will imply ecological overgrazing. The advantage of this formulation of the problem is that it makes it easy to test the sensitivity of the level of grazing pressure (and hence presence or absence of ecological overgrazing) to variation in the economic environment. This is illustrated in the following set of simulations.

4   A SIMULATION

To illustrate the construction of an optimal policy, we need to specialize the welfare function further. It is convenient to assume a welfare function of simple additive separable form. The problem described in (7.5a) to (7.5g) then becomes:

$$\max_{\{u_t\}} \sum_{t=0}^{\infty} \rho^t \left(pu_t - cx_t - rk_t \right)$$
(7.11a)

subject to

$$x_{t+1} - x_t = \alpha_t x_t (1 - x_t/k_t) - u_t \tag{7.11b}$$

$$k_{t+1} - k_t = \beta_t k_t (1 - k_t/k_c) - \gamma_t (x_t - u_t) \tag{7.11c}$$

$$x_0 > 0 = x(0) \tag{7.11d}$$

$$k_0 > 0 = k(0) \tag{7.11e}$$

$$-k_c \leq u_t \leq x_t \tag{7.11f}$$

$$x_t, k_t \geq 0. \tag{7.11g}$$

p in (7.11a) denotes the (constant) net producer price, c denotes the net benefits of livestock holdings or inventory, and r denotes the cost of range access. The net producer price is simply the price per livestock unit at the point of sale net of the costs of transport to the point of sale. The net benefit of inventory is more complicated, largely because the role of livestock in pastoral economies goes far beyond the production of beef, lamb or goatmeat. The maintenance of livestock does involve costs (which may be an increasing function of the level of grazing pressure), but it also provides significant benefits to its owners in the form of draft power, animal products, the status it confers, the insurance it provides against adverse climatic conditions, and the fact that it is 'privileged currency' in bridewealth and other important social transactions. What c approximates in (7.11a), therefore, is the difference in the unit value of benefits and costs of holding one livestock unit. The cost of range access may be thought of as a productivity related charge for the right to graze animals on the range. That is, the charge is higher the greater the carrying capacity of the range. Where there exist markets for land, it is the price of land. Where pastoralism is based on communal grazing areas it is the sum of all costs associated with preserving traditional rights.

Given (7.11a) it follows that the ratios ω_{xt} and ω_{kt} are just the marginal real-product cost/benefit of livestock holdings, and the marginal real-product cost of carrying capacity. In the baseline case in this numerical example it is assumed that p, c and r have the values:

$p = 1$
$c = -0.3$
$r = 0.03.$

It is further assumed that the mean values of the ecological parameters are:

$\alpha = 0.3$
$\beta = 0.1$
$\gamma = 0.2.$

that the initial conditions (7.11d) and (7.11e) are

$x_0 = 50$
$k_0 = 100$

and that the mean maximum carrying capacity of the range is:

$k_c = 200.$

The initial conditions in the example have been selected to correspond to the case where a herd of unsustainable size is introduced to a range regenerating at the maximum rate. This implies that there is ecological overgrazing (in the sense that the current level of grazing pressure exceeds the level of grazing pressure associated with the maximum sustainable yield of the range). The economic environment is such that the net benefit of inventory is positive, but less than the net price of offtake. The cost of range access is assumed to be small relative to both. The ecological parameters and the maximum carrying capacity of the range are assumed to vary with rainfall: maximum carrying capacity, herd growth and the rate of range regeneration varying directly with rainfall, and the rate of range degradation varying inversely with rainfall. In this case, rainfall is assumed to be stochastic. The case where rainfall is cyclic is considered in Perrings (1993). This gives rise to the 'histories' for the ecological parameters (α_t, β_t and γ_t), and the size of the herd corresponding to the maximum sustainable yield of the system (MSYH) reported in Table 7.1.

The control sequence for this case is constructed sequentially. Given the initial value of the state variables, x_0 and k_0, optimal offtake is calculated on the basis of the expected values of the ecological parameters, α, β and γ. Then, using *ex post* observations on the actual values of these parameters, α_t, β_t and γ_t, along with the equations of motion (7.1) and (7.2), x_1 and k_1 are found, and so on. The resulting control policy is summarized in Table 7.2.

Recalling that it is assumed that the range is initially being overgrazed in an ecological sense, the time paths for offtake, herd size, carring capacity and income are quite intuitive. The early periods mark a sharp adjustment in herd size through high rates of offtake. This reduces the level of overgrazing, but too late to avert a reduction in the carrying capacity of the range. The result is a phase during which optimal herd size, carrying capacity, offtake and income are all below the stochastic equilibrium of the system. This is followed by a recovery phase. Nevertheless, given the economic environment, ecological overgrazing is a persistent feature of the optimal strategy in the baseline case. These trends are shown in Figures 7.1 to 7.3. Figure 7.1 graphs the time paths for the state and control variables, and illustrates very clearly the 'overshoot' involved in adjustment to the initially very high levels of ecological overgrazing.

Table 7.1   Values of ecological parameters and the maximum sustainable yield size of the herd

Period	α_t	β_t	γ_t	MSYH	Period	α_t	β_t	γ_t	MSYH
1	0.35	0.12	0.17	50.7	16	0.26	0.09	0.23	20.2
2	0.23	0.08	0.27	13.6	17	0.34	0.11	0.18	48.2
3	0.11	0.04	0.56	1.3	18	0.69	0.23	0.09	278.1
4	0.33	0.11	0.18	43.7	19	0.33	0.11	0.18	42.3
5	0.49	0.16	0.12	125.0	20	0.35	0.12	0.17	51.7
6	0.17	0.06	0.34	6.0	21	0.27	0.09	0.22	23.5
7	0.20	0.07	0.30	9.6	22	0.32	0.11	0.19	39.9
8	0.15	0.05	0.40	3.6	23	0.24	0.08	0.25	16.2
9	0.26	0.09	0.23	20.8	24	0.35	0.12	0.17	49.7
10	0.33	0.11	0.18	41.8	25	0.28	0.09	0.21	27.2
11	0.45	0.15	0.13	103.7	26	0.30	0.10	0.20	32.7
12	0.20	0.07	0.30	9.2	27	0.25	0.08	0.24	17.5
13	0.25	0.08	0.24	19.4	28	0.32	0.11	0.19	39.0
14	0.43	0.14	0.14	91.6	29	0.25	0.08	0.24	17.7
15	0.31	0.10	0.19	35.7	30	0.20	0.07	0.30	9.2

The relationship between the ecological and economic overgrazing generated by the strategy is shown in Figure 7.2. This figure nicely illustrates the lagged effect of ecological overgrazing on economic overgrazing: if the range is being overgrazed ecologically in one period (implying that the actual grazing pressure exceeds the maximum 'sustainable' grazing pressure of the range), this induces a reduction in the optimal level of grazing pressure in the next period, and an increase in the level of offtake. The reduction in optimal grazing pressure relative to actual grazing pressure shows up as an increase in the level of economic overgrazing.

The third figure in this sequence graphs the income stream associated with the optimal control policy, and shows how it matches changes in herd size. The important point to note here is that while current income is highest during those periods in which the range is being overgrazed, this is unsustainable in two quite different senses. First, the high level of herd densities is ecologically unsustainable in the sense that it is inconsistent with the existing carrying capacity of the range, and a fall in carrying capacity implies a fall in herd densities.

Table 7.2 A sequential control policy: deterministic case

Period	k_t	x_t	u_t	x_t/k_t	$(x/k)^*$	Economic overgrazing	Ecological overgrazing	Income
1	100	50	1	0.50	0.49	0.01	0.18	12.67
2	98	58	10	0.59	0.49	0.21	2.38	24.45
3	88	53	13	0.61	0.46	0.31	15.76	26.10
4	65	43	19	0.66	0.37	0.78	0.72	29.82
5	66	29	4	0.44	0.38	0.17	−0.41	11.00
6	71	33	4	0.46	0.40	0.14	3.56	11.61
7	63	32	9	0.50	0.36	0.39	2.63	16.46
8	59	26	6	0.44	0.33	0.32	5.22	12.39
9	52	22	7	0.42	0.28	0.48	0.80	12.03
10	52	18	3	0.35	0.28	0.24	−0.06	7.32
11	53	18	3	0.34	0.30	0.16	−0.48	6.53
12	58	21	2	0.37	0.33	0.11	1.74	6.79
13	54	22	5	0.40	0.30	0.32	0.80	10.16
14	54	20	4	0.37	0.30	0.24	−0.40	8.25
15	58	21	2	0.37	0.33	0.13	0.10	7.13
16	58	23	4	0.40	0.33	0.19	0.73	8.90
17	57	23	4	0.40	0.33	0.24	−0.02	9.67
18	59	23	4	0.40	0.34	0.18	−0.66	8.75
19	69	30	3	0.43	0.39	0.09	0.14	9.34
20	69	33	5	0.47	0.39	0.20	0.09	13.03
21	71	33	5	0.47	0.40	0.19	0.86	13.14
22	68	33	6	0.48	0.39	0.24	0.33	14.16
23	68	32	5	0.47	0.39	0.20	1.36	12.90
24	65	31	7	0.47	0.37	0.27	0.13	13.74
25	66	30	5	0.45	0.38	0.19	0.60	11.61
26	65	30	5	0.46	0.37	0.23	0.44	12.40
27	65	29	5	0.45	0.37	0.21	1.16	11.86
28	62	28	6	0.45	0.36	0.26	0.26	12.24
29	63	27	4	0.43	0.36	0.20	1.05	10.70
30	60	26	5	0.43	0.35	0.26	2.23	11.44

It follows that the income deriving from inventory or livestock holdings in these periods is unsustainable. Second, the income deriving from offtake is unsustainable in the same sense as the income deriving from the mining of any

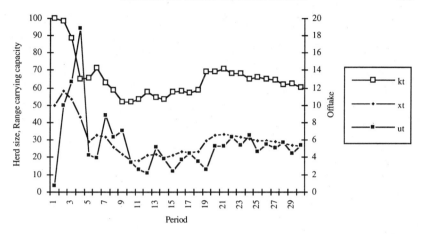

Figure 7.1   Time paths for herd size, carrying capacity and offtake (the state and control variables): baseline case

natural resource is unsustainable. That is, since the optimal rate of offtake exceeds the natural rate of herd growth, the high level of current income represents the consumption of capital. Of course, this says nothing about the potential for converting the 'rents' from mining the resource into some other form of reproducible capital via the Solow–Hartwick rule. But it does say that the level of agricultural income associated with the adjustment phase is unsustainable.

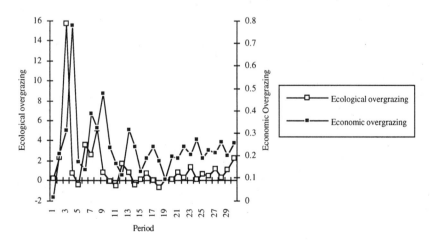

Figure 7.2   Rates of economic and ecological overgrazing: baseline case

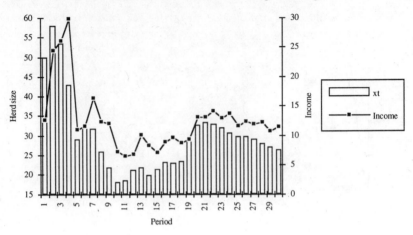

Figure 7.3   Income and herd size: baseline case

Before considering the sensitivity of the ecological sustainability of the optimal policy to change in the economic environment, it is useful to have a sense of how the optimal policy depends on the ecological parameters. Accordingly, the following sequence of figures reports the impact of variation in each of the ecological parameters around the values assumed in the baseline case on (i) grazing pressure (Figures 7.4a, 7.4b, 7.4c) and (ii) income (Figures 7.5a, 7.5b, 7.5c).

Taking the impact on grazing pressure first, the first point to make is that variation in the mean value of each of the ecological parameters affects grazing pressure in very different ways. Variation in the mean rate of herd growth (Figure 7.4a) has a significant effect on the volatility of grazing pressure but little effect on the (stochastic) equilibrium level of grazing pressure. Convergence on the equilibrium level of grazing pressure is non-monotonic for all feasible rates of herd growth, but low rates of herd growth are associated with greater extremes of grazing pressure than high rates of herd growth. Variation in the mean rate of range degradation (Figure 7.4c), on the other hand, has a significant effect on the equilibrium level of grazing pressure, but little effect on the volatility of the convergence path. The equilibrium level of grazing pressure is a monotonically decreasing function of the mean rate of range degradation due to grazing: the higher the mean rate of range degradation, the lower is the equilibrium level of grazing pressure. In neither case does variation in the ecological parameters affect the existence of an ecologically sustainable equilibrium – since there always exists an offtake policy that will 'balance' the ecological effects of both herd growth and range degradation. But the same is not true of the mean rate of range regeneration. An increase in the mean rate of range regeneration (Figure 7.4b) implies both a fall in the equilibrium level of grazing pressure and a rise in its volatility. Indeed, in the particular economic environment of the baseline case, the sensitivity of grazing pressure to variation in the rate of range regeneration is such that a fairly modest rise in the latter is sufficient to induce an economic collapse.

It is important to underline two things here. The first is that the collapse of the pastoral economy as a consequence of rise in the rate of range regeneration

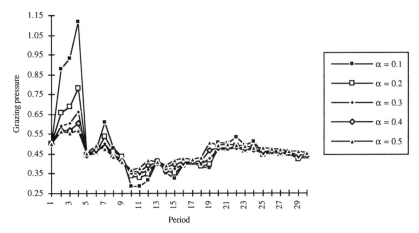

Figure 7.4a   Sensitivity of grazing pressure to the rate of herd growth: baseline case

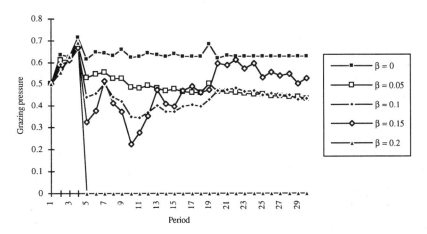

Figure 7.4b   Sensitivity of grazing pressure to the rate of range regeneration: baseline case

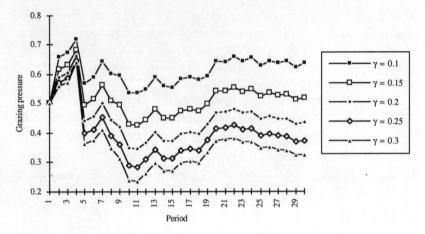

*Figure 7.4c   Sensitivity of grazing pressure to the rate of range degradation:
baseline case*

is due to the volatility of the state variables. Although a sustainable stochastic
equilibrium may exist for the system at higher values of β, it is not attainable
given the initial conditions. This implies that the stochastic equilibrium is
locally stable only, and the initial conditions lie outside the limits of such local
stability. The second thing is that the sensitivity of grazing pressure to variation
in the rate of range regeneration is not independent of the economic environment.
That is, although a value of β equal to 0.2 induces an economic collapse in the
baseline case, it would not necessarily do so under any other set of relative prices.

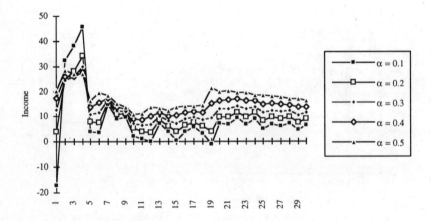

Figure 7.5a   Sensitivity of income to the rate of herd growth: baseline case

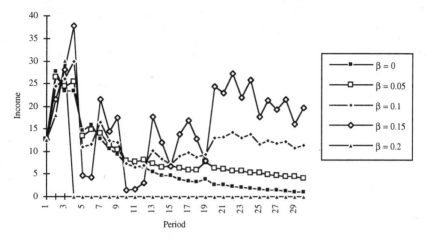

Figure 7.5b   Sensitivity of income to the rate of range regeneration: baseline case

Now consider the sensitivity of income to variation in the ecological parameters in the baseline case. Figures 7.5a, 7.5b and 7.5c report the impact on income of the same changes in α, β and γ_t recorded in Figures 7.4a, 7.4b and 7.4c. The results mirror the results in respect of grazing pressure, and once again the instructive case is the second. The stochastic equilibrium income associated with the optimal strategy is an increasing function of the rate of herd growth, and a decreasing function of the rate of range degradation. In respect of the latter (Figure

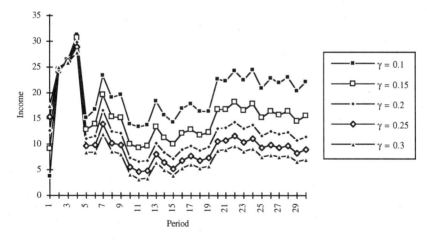

Figure 7.5c   Sensitivity of income to the rate of range degradation: baseline case

7.5b) a rise in the rate of range regeneration lifts both the mean and variance of the level of current income. At very low rates of range regeneration the equilibrium income is very low, but so, too, is the volatility of income. Conversely, as β rises so does both the equilibrium income and its volatility. Under the initial conditions and economic environment assumed in the baseline case, if β rises too far the economic system collapses and income falls to zero. There is therefore a range of values for β within which livestock farming is viable, given the economic environment. What is important from a policy perspective, however, is that it turns out that the range may be contracted or extended by change in the economic environment.

5   ECOLOGICAL SUSTAINABILITY AND THE ECONOMIC ENVIRONMENT

The economic environment in this case is defined by the set of relative 'prices', p, c and r, and the rate of discount, δ. Just as the relative 'prices' reflect much more than a set of market indicators, so the rate of discount reflects much more than an interest rate. Since there is reason to believe that the rate of discount is a decreasing function of income and wealth, particularly at low absolute levels of both (Perrings, 1989a), variation of the rate of discount may be used to test the ecological sensitivity of an optimal strategy to change in income or wealth. This section reports the implications of variation in the economic environment for grazing pressure, ecological overgrazing and income. From a policy perspective, the exercise is of interest as a means of testing the ecological implications of different regimes of user charges/taxes – whether this is motivated by the goal of aligning private and social costs or not. It has already been remarked that stochastic equilibrium values for the state and control variables may be identified only if the ecological parameters of the system lie within well-defined ranges. Parameter values outside of these ranges imply either the instability or local stability of the stochastic equilibrium of the system. It has also been remarked that the interdependence of the ecological and economic parameters means that change in one, changes the response of the system to the others. Hence the values of the economic parameters of the system – the economic environment – affect the system's response to fluctuations in the ecological parameters – the natural environment.

Considerable attention has been paid in recent years to changing the economic environment in agriculture in the low-income countries, by removing what has been seen as a systematic bias against the sector evidenced by high levels of taxation of agricultural exports; artificially depressed procurement prices; and the protection of the industrial sector, either directly or through the overvaluation of the exchange rate. In so far as the improvement of procurement prices raises agricultural incomes, the argument that liberalization of the price system generates the means to conserve the resource base is well founded. It is not quite as clear that it creates the incentive to do so, although higher producer prices in this model are associated with higher rates of offtake, and so lower levels of grazing pressure. To see how a change in the different components of the economic environment affects grazing pressure, Figures 7.6a–7.6d graph the time paths for grazing pressure under different values for relative 'prices'.

Figure 7.6a shows the sensitivity of grazing pressure to variation in the net price of offtake, an increase in which implies either a rise in producer prices or a fall in transport costs. The effect is very clear: grazing pressure being a monotonically decreasing function of the net benefits of offtake. The implications of this are considered later. Figures 7.6b and 7.6c show the sensitivity of grazing pressure to variation in the net benefit of inventory and the cost of range access, respectively. These indicate that an increase in either the net benefit of inventory or the cost of range access has a very pronounced impact on the volatility of grazing pressure and a less-pronounced but direct impact on the stochastic equilibrium values of herd size and carrying capacity. As has already been remarked, if the stochastic equilibrium is locally stable only, an increase in the volatility of grazing pressure may be as prejudicial to the sustainability of production as a rise in the equilibrium level. This is shown in Figure 7.6b, in which the increased level and volatility of grazing pressure associated with rising levels of net herd benefits result in the economic collapse of the system.

Figure 7.6d reports the effects on grazing pressure of variation in the rate of discount. Given that change in the discount rate can be treated as an indirect measure of change in the endowment of livestock farmers, this may be the most interesting case. It turns out that grazing pressure is minimal at both very low and very high rates of discount, and that it reaches a maximum at some intermediate rate. The low level of grazing pressure at high rates of discount follows from the fact that in this case the herd is optimally 'mined' in the early periods to boost current consumption. The low level of grazing pressure at low rates of discount is caused by the opposite effect. Low levels of offtake result in high levels of ecological overgrazing, which then reduce the carrying capacity of the range and force down grazing pressure. It follows that grazing pressure in the second case will be more volatile than in the first.

The degree of ecological overgrazing associated with these changes in the economic environment is indicated in Table 7.3. The baseline case in each part of this table has been boxed for clarity. Positive values indicate positive ecological overgrazing, that is, grazing pressure above the grazing pressure associated with the maximum 'sustainable' yield of the range at current climatic conditions. Negative values indicate grazing pressure below the maximum sustainable pressure. Since the maximum sustainable grazing pressure has

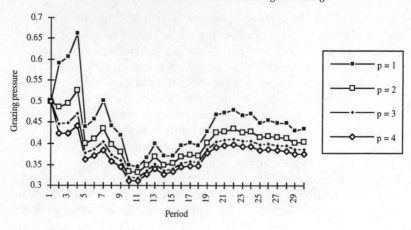

Figure 7.6a   Sensitivity of grazing pressure to producer prices: baseline case

been assumed to vary directly with rainfall, there may be large swings in the degree of ecological overgrazing irrespective of whether there has been any change in herd size. The table indicates that the changes in grazing pressure associated with variation in the economic environment do provide a good guide as to the relative ecological impacts of different economic environments, although they do not indicate the degree of ecological overgrazing associated with a given change in grazing pressure. Once again, both the volatility and the the stochastic equilibrium level of ecological overgrazing is shown to be a

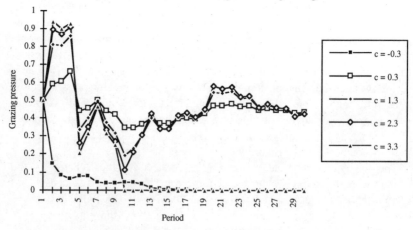

*Figure 7.6b   Sensitivity of grazing pressure to the net benefits of livestock
holdings: baseline case*

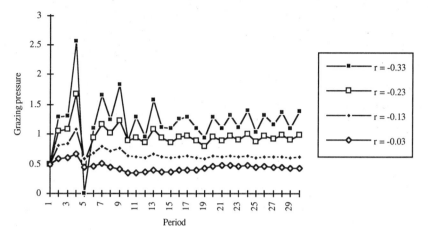

Figure 7.6c   Sensitivity of grazing pressure to the costs of range access: baseline case

decreasing function of producer prices, and an increasing function of the costs of range access and the net benefits of inventory or livestock holdings. As in the case of grazing pressure, the degree of ecological overgrazing is a non-monotonic function of the discount rate. To the extent that the discount rate is a function of the income and assets of livestock farmers, this also indicates that ecological overgrazing is a similarly non-monotonic function of income.

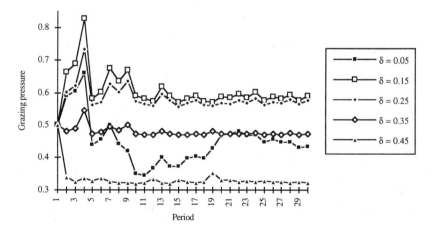

Figure 7.6d   Sensitivity of grazing pressure to the discount rate: baseline case

Table 7.3 Sensitivity of ecological overgrazing to the economic environment

a.	Net benefits of offtake				b.	Net benefits of inventory			
Period	$p = 1$	$p = 2$	$p = 3$	$p = 4$	$c = -0.3$	$c = 0.3$	$c = 1.3$	$c = 2.3$	$c = 3.3$
1	0.18	0.18	0.18	0.18	0.18	0.18	0.18	0.18	0.18
2	2.38	1.79	1.55	1.43	−0.16	2.38	3.63	4.13	4.39
3	15.76	12.69	11.43	10.75	1.25	15.76	21.29	23.11	23.99
4	0.72	0.37	0.23	0.15	−0.84	0.72	1.24	1.37	1.43
5	−0.41	−0.46	−0.50	−0.52	−0.90	−0.41	−0.55	−0.65	−0.72
6	3.56	3.10	2.86	2.72	−0.23	3.56	3.01	2.50	2.16
7	2.63	2.15	1.92	1.79	−0.70	2.63	2.59	2.45	2.37
8	5.22	4.58	4.24	4.04	−0.46	5.22	4.30	3.76	3.47
9	0.80	0.63	0.54	0.48	−0.85	0.80	0.36	0.16	0.07
10	−0.06	−0.11	−0.14	−0.17	−0.89	−0.06	−0.49	−0.70	0.00
11	−0.48	−0.50	−0.52	−0.54	−0.94	−0.48	−0.65	−0.68	0.00
12	1.74	1.61	1.51	1.45	−0.74	1.74	1.27	1.29	0.00
13	0.80	0.66	0.58	0.53	−0.94	0.80	0.80	0.91	0.00
14	−0.40	−0.43	−0.46	−0.47	−0.98	−0.40	−0.45	−0.44	0.00
15	0.10	0.05	0.01	−0.01	−0.98	0.10	0.01	0.01	0.00
16	0.73	0.61	0.54	0.50	−0.99	0.73	0.77	0.83	0.00
17	−0.02	−0.09	−0.13	−0.15	−1.00	−0.02	0.02	0.06	0.00
18	−0.66	−0.68	−0.70	−0.71	−1.00	−0.66	−0.66	−0.66	0.00
19	0.14	0.07	0.03	0.01	−1.00	0.14	0.18	0.20	0.00
20	0.09	−0.01	−0.06	−0.09	−1.00	0.09	0.28	0.35	0.00
21	0.86	0.69	0.61	0.56	−1.00	0.86	1.13	1.23	0.00
22	0.33	0.20	0.14	0.10	−1.00	0.33	0.53	0.60	0.00
23	1.36	1.16	1.06	0.99	−1.00	1.36	1.60	1.65	0.00
24	0.13	0.03	−0.03	−0.06	−1.00	0.13	0.24	0.27	0.00
25	0.60	0.48	0.42	0.38	−1.00	0.60	0.65	0.64	0.00
26	0.44	0.32	0.26	0.22	−1.00	0.44	0.51	0.52	0.00
27	1.16	1.00	0.91	0.85	−1.00	1.16	1.22	1.22	0.00
28	0.26	0.16	0.11	0.08	−1.00	0.26	0.29	0.28	0.00
29	1.05	0.92	0.84	0.79	−1.00	1.05	1.01	0.97	0.00
30	2.23	2.01	1.88	1.80	−1.00	2.23	2.21	2.18	0.00

Table 7.3   continued

c. *Cost of range access*   d. *The discount rate*

Period	$r =$ -0.33	$r =$ -0.23	$r =$ -0.13	$r =$ -0.03	$\delta =$ 0.05	$\delta =$ 0.15	$\delta =$ 0.25	$\delta =$ 0.35	$\delta =$ 0.45
1	0.18	0.18	0.18	0.18	0.18	0.18	0.18	0.18	0.18
2	6.40	5.02	3.69	2.38	2.38	2.81	2.44	1.76	0.94
3	35.11	28.91	22.42	15.76	15.76	18.09	16.21	12.57	7.98
4	5.66	3.35	1.82	0.72	0.72	1.16	0.91	0.42	-0.13
5	-1.00	-0.30	-0.20	-0.41	-0.41	-0.22	-0.25	-0.37	-0.56
6	9.96	8.43	5.81	3.56	3.56	5.01	4.71	3.76	2.36
7	10.93	7.46	4.76	2.63	2.63	3.89	3.54	2.58	1.34
8	16.45	13.34	9.08	5.22	5.22	7.93	7.46	5.80	3.50
9	6.85	4.26	2.25	0.80	0.80	1.87	1.72	1.14	0.38
10	1.40	1.37	0.70	-0.06	-0.06	0.59	0.54	0.27	-0.14
11	0.94	0.40	-0.07	-0.48	-0.48	-0.13	-0.15	-0.30	-0.52
12	6.18	5.35	3.55	1.74	1.74	3.29	3.18	2.51	1.48
13	6.09	3.90	2.04	0.80	0.80	1.78	1.68	1.16	0.44
14	0.80	0.52	0.02	-0.40	-0.40	-0.04	-0.07	-0.24	-0.48
15	2.27	1.55	0.78	0.10	0.10	0.70	0.66	0.40	-0.02
16	4.45	3.15	1.71	0.73	0.73	1.54	1.48	1.05	0.41
17	2.15	1.38	0.54	-0.02	-0.02	0.44	0.41	0.15	-0.22
18	-0.06	-0.24	-0.49	-0.66	-0.66	-0.51	-0.52	-0.60	-0.72
19	1.49	1.12	0.58	0.14	0.14	0.52	0.49	0.28	-0.06
20	1.99	1.22	0.47	0.09	0.09	0.37	0.33	0.10	-0.23
21	3.31	2.53	1.46	0.86	0.86	1.30	1.23	0.86	0.30
22	2.67	1.70	0.78	0.33	0.33	0.65	0.60	0.31	-0.10
23	4.66	3.59	2.16	1.36	1.36	1.96	1.88	1.39	0.65
24	2.34	1.41	0.54	0.13	0.13	0.44	0.39	0.14	-0.23
25	2.69	2.13	1.17	0.60	0.60	1.06	1.02	0.68	0.17
26	3.19	2.05	0.97	0.44	0.44	0.86	0.81	0.49	0.03
27	4.57	3.45	1.96	1.16	1.16	1.81	1.74	1.27	0.57
28	2.83	1.79	0.76	0.26	0.26	0.67	0.63	0.33	-0.09
29	4.25	3.29	1.86	1.05	1.05	1.75	1.69	1.24	0.55
30	9.28	6.40	3.59	2.23	2.23	3.39	3.29	2.52	1.40

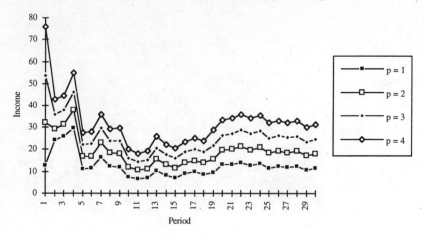

Figure 7.7a   Sensitivity of income to producer prices: baseline case

The next sequence of figures, 7.7a to 7.7d, shows the sensitivity of income to change in the economic environment. The two figures worth particular mention in this case are 7.7b and 7.7d, which record the effects of the net benefits of inventory and the discount rate, respectively. In Figure 7.7b, higher net benefits of inventory do have a strongly positive effect on income in the short run, but this is at the cost of pressure on the range which is unsustainable, given the climatic shocks to which the system is subject. The result is that income falls

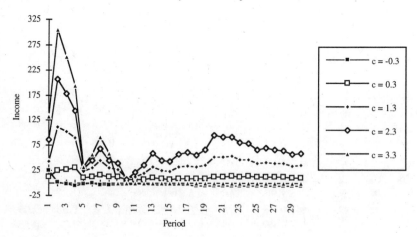

Figure 7.7b   Sensitivity of income to the net benefits of livestock holdings: baseline case

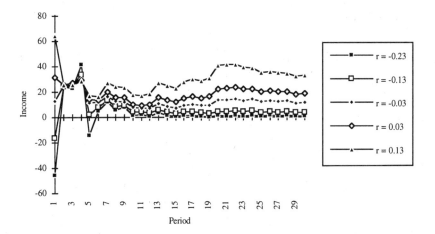

Figure 7.7c   Sensitivity of income to the costs of range access: baseline case

to zero. Figure 7.7d shows, again, the very clear short-run benefits of the optimal policy under high rates of discount. But it also shows how short-lived these benefits are. Moreover, even though the lower herd sizes associated with high rates of discount do generate longer-term benefits, these are largely irrelevant from the point of view of the decision-maker – since the net present value of the income stream associated with the optimal policy is a decreasing function of the rate of discount.[6]

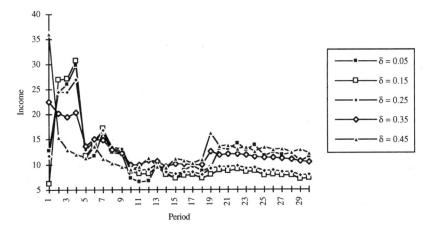

Figure 7.7d   Sensitivity of income to the discount rate: baseline case

6   POLICY IMPLICATIONS

It was earlier argued that the approach adopted in this chapter may be used to test the ecological impact of policy-induced change in the economic environment within which pastoralists operate. More particularly, it was argued that it may be possible to test the short- and long-term ecological effects of different regimes of user charges, taxes or subsidies. The argument rests on the presumption that it is possible to approximate the system sufficiently closely so that the time paths generated within the model constitute reasonable predictions of system behaviour.

There are a number of difficulties with this presumption. It requires, for example, specification of the representative private objective function, and the private perception of the constraint set against which that objective function is optimized. This is not an area in which there is any consensus in the economic, or the anthropological or the range management literature. Nor is it an area that has been taken very seriously in the past. The application of range management models designed for the US livestock sector to sub-Saharan Africa has been commonplace for some time (compare ILCA, 1978), but is singularly inappropriate. Most pastoral economies in the region are not based on single commodity (meat) production. Indeed, a key feature of pastoralism in the low-income countries is that livestock yield a number of products of which meat may or may not be the most important. Moreover, many of the joint products of livestock are not transacted in the market place, but are either directly consumed, or exchanged in a variety of non-market transactions. A range management model should, at the very least, recognize the mix of benefits that characterizes pastoral production in the low-income countries.

Approximation of the system also requires specification of the feedbacks that operate in any given rural economy. Since the behaviour of the system is highly sensitive to certain ecological parameter values, it is important to have realistic estimates of these parameters. A good deal of work has been done on range management systems in the semi-arid environments, and reasonably precise estimates exist for rates of soil and vegetation loss associated with different herd intensities (see, for example, Abel, 1990, and Biot, 1990). But the sensitivity of herd intensities to change in economic or institutional parameters is still very little understood. The available evidence on resource user responses to changes in the private cost of resources is complicated by the strength of income (or scale) effects in price responses, particularly among those resource users at the lower end of the income scale. The available evidence on supply elasticities in the agricultural economies of the semi-arid areas is highly ambiguous. It cannot even be assumed, for example, that elasticities will always be of the expected algebraic sign (compare Rao, 1989; Perrings 1989b). Nevertheless, even if the predictions generated by a heuristic model of the sort discussed in this chapter may not be assumed to be 'right' for any particular rural economy, they make it possible to make a number of general points about the ecological implications of change in the economic environment.

For any range with a positive regeneration rate in all time periods, and for any reasonable objective function, there exists a vector of relative 'prices' at which the stochastic equilibrium herd density will be ecologically sustainable. That is, there exists a vector (c^T, r^T, p^T) such that

$$0 = \psi_t^{*2} \alpha\gamma(1+(c^T/p^T)) - \psi_t^{*}2 \alpha[\beta(1 - 2\kappa_t) - (r^T/p^T)\gamma_\_\delta]$$
$$+ (r^T/p^T)\gamma(1 - \alpha + \delta) + [\beta(1 - 2\kappa_t) - \delta][(c^T/p^T) + \alpha - \delta]$$

has a positive root. It is not as clear that the equilibrium density will be attainable for given far-from-equilibrium initial conditions, since this depends on the stability of the equilibrium. However, there exists both a vector of relative prices (c^T, r^T, p^T), and a set of initial conditions (x_0^T, k_0^T) such that there exists a stochastic equilibrium which is both ecologically sustainable and attainable. This last merely implies that if such an equilibrium is locally stable only, then (x_0^T, k_0^T) lies inside the limits of local stability. This indicates that providing only that natural climatic shocks are not so severe that they would cause the collapse of the range, there exists an economic environment and an endowment of livestock that is consistent with the ecologically sustainable use of the range. It says nothing about the economic sustainability of pastoralism, nor does it say anything about the efficiency of the resulting allocation. It says only that there exist policy regimes that will guarantee the ecological sustainability of resource use.

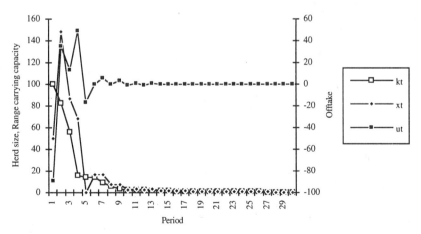

Figure 7.8   Herd size, carrying capacity and offtake: communal grazing case

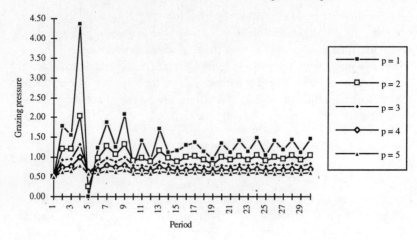

Figure 7.9   Sensitivity of grazing pressure to output prices: communal grazing case

Consider, for example, a case that is typical of a number of communal grazing lands. Suppose that output prices are depressed ($p = 1$), the cost of range access is zero ($r = 0$), the net benefits of livestock holdings are very high relative to the net benefits of offtake ($c = 2$), and pastoralists' endowments are such that the rate of discount is high ($\delta = 0.25$). The optimal policy for the baseline case in these circumstances involves persistent and highly volatile ecological overgrazing, with herd size, carrying capacity and income being driven to zero (see Figure 7.8). However, as Figures 7.9 and 7.10 and Table 7.4 indicate, a

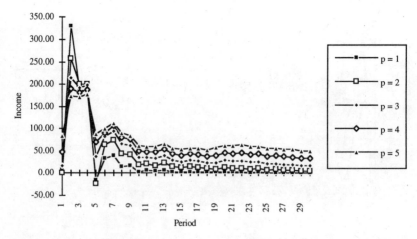

Figure 7.10   Sensitivity of income to output prices: communal grazing case

variation in the economic environment involving an increase in producer prices is sufficient in this case to reverse both the damage done to the carrying capacity of the range through overgrazing, and the decline in incomes.

Table 7.4   *The sensitivity of ecological overgrazing to output prices: communal grazing case*

Period	$p = 1$	$p = 2$	$p = 3$	$p = 4$	Period	$p = 1$	$p = 2$	$p = 3$	$p = 4$
1	0.2	0.2	0.2	0.2	16	4.8	2.5	1.2	0.5
2	8.5	4.0	2.1	1.0	17	2.4	1.0	0.3	−0.2
3	41.2	24.0	14.1	8.4	18	0.0	−0.3	−0.6	−0.7
4	9.4	2.2	0.6	−0.1	19	1.6	0.9	0.4	0.0
5	−1.0	−0.1	−0.3	−0.5	20	2.2	0.9	0.2	−0.2
6	11.4	6.8	4.2	2.5	21	3.5	2.0	1.0	0.3
7	12.8	5.8	3.0	1.4	22	3.0	1.3	0.4	−0.1
8	16.8	11.1	6.6	3.7	23	4.9	3.0	1.6	0.7
9	8.2	3.2	1.4	0.4	24	2.7	1.0	0.3	−0.2
10	1.0	1.1	0.4	−0.1	25	2.7	1.7	0.8	0.2
11	1.2	0.2	−0.2	−0.5	26	3.6	1.5	0.6	0.1
12	6.0	4.6	2.8	1.6	27	4.8	2.8	1.5	0.6
13	7.0	3.0	1.4	0.5	28	3.2	1.3	0.5	−0.1
14	0.8	0.3	−0.2	−0.5	29	4.4	2.7	1.5	0.6
15	2.6	1.2	0.5	0.0	30	10.3	5.1	2.9	1.5

Notice that the statement that there exists both a vector of relative prices *and* a set of initial conditions such that a sustainable stochastic equilibrium exists and is attainable, implies that change in the set of relative prices may not be sufficient to address the problem. That is, if the stochastic equilibrium of the system is locally stable only, given both the natural and economic environments, it may not be attainable unless the endowments of pastoralists are adjusted to bring them within the stable range. The collapse of herds during periods of drought may be thought of as just such an adjustment, but the point being made here is that adjustment of pastoralists' endowments may also need to be a deliberate part of policy.

On the adjustment of relative prices, notice also that for welfare functions of the general form discussed in this chapter, output prices offer the most effective of the available levers on grazing pressure. This is partly because of their well-defined effect on stocking decisions. But it is also because of the empirical fact that output prices are more readily influenced by policy than the other available levers. An increase in the net price of offtake both raises producer incomes and reduces the optimal size of the herd. It depends very heavily on a single price, the producer price, which may be easily 'controlled' in a market environment where government or parastatal meat-processing and -marketing boards are at the very least market leaders, and frequently monopsonists. A reduction in the cost of range access has a similar effect as an increase in producer prices in this model, but wherever grazing lands are in communal property (there are no markets for land) the cost of range access is not a well-defined price amenable to intervention by the government. The producer price is. There may be arguments for promoting the development of markets for grazing land, but in the absence of such markets the lever is not really available. Similarly, although a reduction in the net benefits of inventory reduces both the volatility and the equilibrium level of grazing pressure, many of the benefits of inventory are non-market benefits which depend on cultural, social and institutional factors. To be sure, the costs of inventory do depend on input subsidies which are within the purview of policy. But the overall balance between benefits and costs is related to policy in a much more complicated and opaque way than other 'prices' in the model, and includes factors that are entirely beyond the reach of policy.

For various reasons, agricultural policy in the low-income countries has tended to focus on other levers. This is partly because of the widespread adoption of a policy of import-parity producer prices, supposedly motivated by considerations of efficiency.[7] This has had the effect of removing or weakening government influence on the behaviour of pastoralists through the price of offtake. It has not restricted intervention in the agricultural sector, but has meant that governments have tended to intervene via the set of prices that determine the net benefit of inventory rather than via producer prices. Wherever the objective of intervention has been income support (as it has in many countries during the past decade), this has meant policies which have raised the net benefits of inventory relative to offtake. Given their impact on grazing pressure, the model discussed in this chapter suggests that such policies would be expected to lead to increasing rather than decreasing environmental damage.

7   CONCLUDING REMARKS

At the most general level, this chapter has argued that the economic environment within which decisions are made is critically important to the sustainability of resource-based activities in a stochastic natural environment. It is the economic environment which determines the effect of environmental shocks on such activities. So, for example, if relative prices dictate optimal herd densities greater than the maximum sustainable herd density, the herd will be more prone to collapse in the face of climatic shocks than if relative prices dictate optimal herd densities less than the maximum sustainable herd density. If we can use the ecological concept of resilience in a slightly unusual context, this is to say that the economic environment determines the resilience of the managed ecological system (the pastoral system) in the face of climatic shocks. Although I have made the very strong assumption that the underlying natural ecological system is globally stable (that the range will regenerate no matter how degraded it is), the managed ecological system has the more recognizable characteristic that it is locally stable only. If the size of the herd or the carrying capacity lies outside a certain range, then the time paths for both will not be convergent under an optimal policy. Given any set of ecological parameter values, the economic environment determines both the properties of the stochastic equilibrium, and the limits of its stability.

It follows that if the economic environment may be influenced, it will in turn be possible to influence the sustainability of resource-based economic activities: that is, economic activities that involve the management of ecological systems. So administered prices, user fees, taxes, subsidies and transfers may all be used to underwrite the resilience of resource-based activities by adjusting the economic environment. Notice that nothing is being said about the efficiency of prices that are consistent with the sustainability of resource-based activities. There is no reason to believe that it will always be socially optimal to exploit renewable natural resources on a sustainable basis, but this is not the point. An approach such as that used in this chapter enables us to ask two questions. First, for any given control problem, initial conditions, state of nature (set of ecological parameters) and economic environment (set of economic parameters), does an optimal policy involve the extinction of one or more populations? Second, if the activity is not sustainable under the given conditions, what are the properties of (a) an economic environment and (b) the initial endowments at which it would be sustainable? The first question may be asked of any set of relative prices, whether these correspond to the social opportunity cost of resource use or not. The point is to understand the implications of the interaction of economic and natural environments, not to identify a set of optimal Pigouvian taxes.

NOTES

1. For a formal description of which, see Clark (1976) and Conrad and Clark (1987).
2. In reality, grazing systems are usually also subject to 'observation noise'. That is, the state variables x_t and y_t will tend to be observed only with some error. However, we may ignore this additional source of uncertainty here.
3. Various short-term climatic effects of local change in surface vegetation have been conjectured by climatologists (compare Charney, 1975) but it seems reasonable to assume that rainfall variation is independent of the state of the range.
4. The best discussion of these various properties of biological growth models is still Clark (1976).
5. For a discussion of the environmental implications of other strategies, see Perrings (1993).
6. In the baseline case, the net present value of the income stream generated under an optimal policy at the different rates of discount tested is as follows:

δ = 0.05	δ = 0.15	δ = 0.25	δ = 0.35	δ = 0.45
208.53	102.21	69.065	53.167	44.885

7. The problem with this is that border prices (at equilibrium exchange rates) define only the lower bound of the social opportunity cost of resource use. In general, the social opportunity cost of agricultural products will be strictly greater than their border prices.

REFERENCES

Abel, N.O.J. (1990), 'Destocking and communal pastures in Southern Africa: is it worth it?', Proceedings of the technical meeting on savanna development and pasture production, ODI, Woburn.
Barbier, E.B. (1988), 'Sustainable agriculture and the resource poor: policy issues and options', LEEC Paper No. 2.
Barbier, E.B. (1989a), 'The contribution of environmental and resource economics to an economics of sustainable development', *Development and Change* 20: 429–59.
Barbier, E.B. (1989b), 'Cash crops, food crops and sustainability: the case of Indonesia', *World Development* 17 (6): 879–95.
Biot, Y. (1990), 'How long can high stocking densities be sustained?', Proceedings of the technical meeting on savanna development and pasture production, ODI, Woburn.
Bond, M.E. (1983), 'Agricultural responses to prices in sub-Saharan African countries', *IMF Staff Papers*, 30.
Clark, C.W. (1976), *Mathematical Bioeconomics: The Optimal Management of Renewable Resources*, John Wiley, New York.
Cleaver, K. (1985), 'The impact of price and exchange rate policies on agriculture in sub-Saharan Africa', World Bank Staff Working Paper, No. 728.
Cleaver, K. (1988), 'The use of price policy to stimulate agricultural growth in sub-Saharan Africa', Paper presented to the 8th Agricultural Sector Symposium on Trade, Aid, and Policy Reform for Agriculture.
Conrad, J. and Clark, C. (1987), *Natural Resource Economics: Notes and Problems*, Cambridge, Cambridge University Press.
Conway, G.R. (1987), 'The properties of agroecosystems', *Agricultural Systems* 24 (2): 95–117.
Dyson-Hudson, N. (1984), 'Adaptive resource use by African pastoralists', in di Castri et al. (eds), *Ecological Practice*, UNESCO, Paris.
ILCA (1978), *Mathematical modelling of livestock production systems: application of the Texas A. & M. production model in Botswana*, ILCA, Addis Ababa.
Mosley, P. and Smith, L. (1989), 'Structural adjustment and agricultural performance in sub-Saharan Africa 1980–1987', *Journal of International Development* 1 (3): 321–55.
Pearce, D.W., Barbier, E.B. and Markandya, A. (1988), 'Environmental economics and decision-making in sub-Saharan Africa', LEEC Paper No. 1.
Perrings, C.A. (1989a), 'Debt and resource degradation in low income countries: the adjustment problem and the perverse effects of poverty in sub-Saharan Africa', in H. Singer and S. Sharma (eds), *Economic Development and World Debt*, Macmillan, London.
Perrings, C.A. (1989b), 'An optimal path to extinction? Poverty and resource degradation in the open agrarian economy', *Journal of Development Economics* 30: 1–24.

Perrings, C.A. (1993), 'Pastoral strategies in sub-Saharan Africa: the economic and ecological sustainability of dryland range management', Paper prepared for the Environment Department, World Bank.

Rao, J.M. (1989), 'Agricultural supply response: a survey', *Agricultural Economics* **3** (1): 1–22.

Repetto, R. (1986), *World Enough and Time*, Yale University Press, New Haven.

Repetto, R. (1989), 'Economic incentives for sustainable production', in G. Schramme and J.J. Warford (eds), *Environmental Management and Economic Development*, Johns Hopkins for the World Bank, Baltimore: 69–86.

Warford J.J. (1989), 'Environmental management and economic policy in developing countries', in G. Schramme and J.J. Warford (eds), *Environmental Management and Economic Development*, Johns Hopkins for the World Bank, Baltimore: 7–22.

PART III

Uncertainty, Innovation and Choice

8. Reserved rationality and the precautionary principle: technological change, time and uncertainty in environmental decision-making

1 INTRODUCTION

In recent debates over the problem of global climate change there has been strong support for the application of a 'precautionary principle'.[1] There is, however, no consensus on what the principle means for decision-making under uncertainty, either generally or in the context of specific issues such as global climate change. While it is clear that a precautionary principle implies the commitment of resources now to safeguard against the potentially adverse future outcomes of some decision, it is not clear how this should be related to the uncertainty associated with those outcomes. The sort of decisions in which the precautionary principle is currently being invoked are those for which the probability distribution of future outcomes cannot be known with confidence. Indeed, all that may be known is that the probability of distant but potentially catastrophic outcomes is positive – even if there is no information on the precise nature, timing or incidence of those outcomes. They are outcomes against which it is impossible to insure commercially because there are insufficient data on which to estimate an expected value for future losses within acceptable limits of confidence. This implies two sources of difficulty. First, it is not *a priori* clear what relationship should exist between 'safeguard' resources committed now and the expected value of such outcomes. Second, since the principle implies the commitment of public resources, it concerns collective decision-making, and so raises the familiar difficulties associated with collective responsibility for future generations.

The main concern of the chapter is with the first source of difficulty. More particularly, the chapter is concerned with the precautionary element in decision-making under uncertainty, and with the relationship between decision-making processes reflecting a precautionary principle and more conventional minimax and stochastic approaches. Specifically, the chapter considers the estimation of future environmental costs where there is a high degree of uncertainty about the nature, incidence and timing of those costs, and where the set of possible effects includes outcomes that may be catastrophic for future generations. It is argued that the application of a precautionary principle in these circumstances implies a reservation on the expected value of those costs. Put another way, decision-makers applying a precautionary principle will reserve their position on data for which the expected value (taken with whatever risk-aversion coefficient applies) is judged to be an inappropriate measure. By analogy with the concept of bounded rationality developed to deal with decision-making under uncertainty in the industrial context (compare Williamson, 1985), we may refer to this phenomenon as reserved rationality.

The chapter is in five sections. The following section addresses the second source of difficulty identified: the ethical issues raised by the responsibility borne by present generations for the welfare of future generations. Section 3 returns to the main concern of the chapter and introduces a formal framework within which to consider the problem of decision-making under incomplete information. A fourth section then considers the decision-making process under the precautionary principle, and a final section discusses the link between reserved rationality in decision-making under uncertainty and the commitment to safeguard resources under the precautionary principle.

2   DISCOUNTING, VALUATION AND THE TREATMENT OF FUTURE GENERATIONS

One of the strongest arguments in favour of the precautionary principle is that environmental effects that are both distant in time (are visited only on future generations), and thought to occur with low probability, necessarily receive little attention in decision models focusing on the discounted expected value of future effects. The prospect of catastrophe in such cases is necessarily assigned a weight close to zero. The ethical questions this raises concern the right of present generations to put at risk not just the marginal benefits to future generations of access to a particular resource or ecosystem, but the very survival of those generations. There are two main questions at issue: the first concerns the rate of discount, the second concerns the valuation of resources under the current structure of property rights.

The rate of discount is an issue for the simple reason that discounting implicitly involves ethical judgements both about intertemporal or intergenerational equity, and about the appropriate treatment of uncertainty. The social discount rate is a measure of the rate at which it is considered socially desirable to substitute consumption in the present for consumption in the future. It accordingly involves a judgement about the responsibility that the present generation should bear for future generations. At positive discount rates an unsustainable development strategy may well be judged to be optimal – implying, at the very least, indifference to the welfare of future generations. Indeed, as has been pointed out elsewhere, the impoverishment of future generations as a result of the profligacy of present generations in such cases is not just an incidental, but a desirable outcome of the decision-making process (compare Dasgupta and Heal, 1979). At zero discount rates, on the other hand, a development strategy will only be judged to be optimal if it yields a constant income stream in all periods. The optimality criterion of intertemporally egalitarian social welfare functions, the maximization of the minimum period income, implies a strategy that delivers maximum constant income.

Moreover, a positive discount rate implies a judgement about the responsibility of present generations for potentially catastrophic impacts about which there is a high level of uncertainty. Since uncertainty tends to be greater, the greater the time horizon of the decision-maker, positive discount rates act to screen uncertainty out of the information relevant to the decision-making process (Perrings, 1987). The more the future is discounted, the fewer the uncertain future effects that are relevant to the optimization problem, and the fewer the data that will be sought in its solution. Decisions taken on the basis of data relating to a short time horizon will accordingly tend to yield more unexpected effects than decisions taken on the basis of data relating to a longer time horizon. This is partly because in any given resource-based activity the rate of depletion of both renewable and non-renewable resources, and/or the rate of emission of pollutants, are increasing functions of the discount rate. In the depletion problem, a low discount rate implies that more of an exhaustible resource will be left in the environment for future extraction than under a high discount rate. In the pollution problem, a low discount rate implies that less of the pollutant will be emitted in the present than under a high discount rate. The build-up of pollutants will proceed at a slower pace. The effect of discounting in this case is thus both to increase the potential for unexpected future costs, and to eliminate those costs from present consideration. We shall return to this later.

Historically, economists have taken very different positions on the ethics of discounting. Ramsey, Pigou, and Harrod – representing the mainstream view between the 1920s and the 1950s – were all strongly critical of the ethical judgements involved in positive discount rates. Subsequently, however, the sovereignty of the present generation of consumers has been invoked both to deny any role for the state in securing the welfare of future generations, and to assert the propriety of discounting (compare Marglin, 1963). Indeed, those economists who continue to hold that sustainable development implies discount rates at or close to zero are in a small minority. The arguments of Randers and Meadows (1973) and Myrdal (1975) against the rights of individuals to inflict harm on future generations through myopic behaviour are still reflected in the work of Daly (Foy and Daly, 1989), though he acknowledges that sustainability cannot be guaranteed by adjustments to the discount rate alone. Leaving the impatience of sovereign consumers to one side, the main factor in this shift in perception on the ethics of discounting is the recognition that a positive rate of growth of services in the system 'authorizes' the discounting of the future at that rate. The argument against the rates of discount embodied in current real rates of interest is then an argument about the actual or potential growth rate of the system, and the position taken by those seeking to integrate the environment in the analysis of economic systems is that the marginal efficiency of capital assessed over the current capital base (which excludes natural capital) is a highly misleading proxy for the growth potential of the whole system (which includes natural capital) (compare Daly, 1973; Perrings, 1987).

It should be said that this is not necessarily an argument for zero rates. Although it has long been recognized that discount rates greater than the natural rate of regeneration of an environmental resource will lead to the depletion of that resource, it is now also argued that discount rates that are too low may result in unsustainable levels of investment in environmental resource-using activities (compare Pearce et al., 1989). There is, in fact, a strong argument that the discount rate should not be manipulated to achieve intergenerational equity goals, and that these goals should be satisfied directly through intergenerational transfers (Norgaard and Howarth, 1990). The argument is well founded in the sense that the welfare of future generations may be compromised by the adoption of unsustainable discount rates. But it should not be taken to mean that we may ignore the intergenerational equity implications of specific rates. We should not, for example, be blind to the potential costs imposed on future generations by the adoption of real interest rates that bear no relation to the productive potential of the global system – that are intertemporally inefficient. Real interest rates that are excessive in these terms not only invite the depletion of stocks of natural capital, they also ensure that no matter how catastrophic the future environmental effects of present activities are thought to be, they will be irrelevant if they lie beyond a generation in the future.

The second set of ethical questions raised by this class of problems concerns the impact of the structure of property rights on the valuation of resources. Under existing property rights environmental resources are not allocated on the basis of their social cost: their full intertemporal opportunity cost. Property rights tend to be such that resource users are confronted by the direct costs of resource use only, and are able to ignore the other important components of intertemporal opportunity cost: intersectoral costs (intratemporal external costs) and user costs (intertemporal external costs) (see Pearce and Markandya, 1989). The fact that an activity imposes uncompensated costs on future generations poses as much of an ethical problem as the fact that it imposes uncompensated costs on other members of the present generation. Certainly, there is scope for both intergenerational and intragenerational transfers to effect compensation in the two cases, but whereas it is possible to assign property rights in a way that ensures that intratemporal external costs are accounted for, the same is not true for all intertemporal external costs.

While the existence of overlapping generations means that continuous costs known with certainty can be compensated in intergenerational transactions, the same is not true of discontinuous and uncertain costs which might be borne in the distant future. First, there exist no means for estimating such costs directly. Much effort has gone into the estimation of the value placed by the present generation on future access to a resource (its option and existence value), but the class of problems requires the estimation of costs actually to be borne by future generations, not the future costs to be borne by the present generation(s). It is not possible to apply hedonic price or contingent valuation methods in such cases. Second, there exists no means of allocating property rights to unborn generations in any meaningful way. The net result is that such user costs will be taken into account only in so far as the present generation(s) feel an ethical responsibility for the generations to come.

3   DECISION-MAKING UNDER INCOMPLETE INFORMATION

The problem of determining the optimal use of resources under uncertainty belongs to the general class of problems of decision-making under incomplete information. How the problem is framed in any given circumstance will depend on the sense in which information is incomplete. If information is incomplete only in the sense that it is not known which of a well-defined set of outcomes will eventuate, but that the probability of each outcome is known, then the problem is one of decision-making under risk. If information is incomplete in the sense that it is not known in advance whether the outcome will belong to a particular set, nor is it known in advance what the probability of each outcome in that set is, then the problem is one of decision-making under uncertainty.[2] It is a characteristic of decision-making under risk that no new relevant information is acquired in the course of time. By contrast, it is a characteristic of decision-making under uncertainty that new information is acquired over time.

Uncertainty will typically exist where some activity, or a constituent part of some activity, is without historical precedent. It will not then be possible to predict the set of outcomes of such activities, let alone the probability of each outcome in that set. That is, the future states of nature associated with such activities and the probability of occurrence of the future states of nature will be unknown at the moment the activities are undertaken. However, as the constituent parts of an economic activity are undertaken, a historical record of their outcomes will be built up, so changing the boundary between the known and unknown outcomes of the activity as a whole. Repeated enumeration of events makes possible the development of increasingly robust predictions. Symmetrically, as the limits of what is 'known' in a probabilistic sense change, so too does the list of outcomes of the remaining aspects of the activity. Hence the decision-making process will itself evolve sequentially in response to the changing information available to the decision-maker, and to the decision-maker's changing perceptions of that information.

To provide a framework for the discussion of decision-making under the precautionary principle, this section specifies a model of sequential decision-making under incomplete information in two variants: stochastic and minimax. Each variant requires sufficient initial information to initiate an iterative decision-making process, although the nature of such information requirements differs in the two cases. Each also allows the acquisition of new information at successive stages of the process. Formally, the two variants are very similar.

Let the state of knowledge of the system at time t be denoted W_t and assume perfect recall of all observations before time t. Hence W_t gives the history of all observations on the system up to time t. The evolutionary nature of the system is such that new unanticipated (and unanticipatable) observations are added in each period. Hence, W_t may be said to be observable at W_{t+1}, but W_{t+1} is not observable at W_t. This is known as the monotonic property of knowledge: the future is not knowable on the basis of the past history of the system. Further, let all actions depend on the state of knowledge at the time they are made, and define an action in time t as $u_t = u(W_t)$. A rule specifying u_t for all t is called a policy, and may be denoted $\upsilon = \{u_t\}$. From the monotonic property of knowledge, u_t may be said to be observable given W_{t+1}, but not to be observable given W_t. That is, W_t specifies the history of observations on the system *before* u_t is undertaken. The problem is to determine an optimal policy in circumstances where each action has implications that are not observable at the time the action is undertaken.

To specialize this general problem, let the social objective be to minimize the environmental costs, C, of a policy, υ, for the use of natural resources, given the developing history of the ecosystem, $\{W_t\}$. Incomplete information in this case follows from the fact that C is a function of quantities that are not observable at the moment each action is undertaken.

In the stochastic approach to the problem, the initial estimate of these environmental costs is the expected value of those costs conditional on the observed history of the system at time zero 0 and on the adoption of policy υ, denoted $E_\upsilon(C\,|W_0)$. The initial informational requirements of this approach are accordingly quite severe. It requires a stochastic model of the environmental damage function, which assumes knowledge of the probability distribution of future environmental costs. The optimal policy in such a case is the one that minimizes average environmental costs over variation in the unobserved part of the history of the system.

In the minimax approach to the problem, the initial estimate of environmental costs is the 'maximum' of C, conditional on the observed history of the system at time 0 and adoption of policy υ, which may be written $M_\upsilon(C|W_0)$. Uncertainty about environmental costs in this case is rendered tractable by assigning a 'worst-case' value to C, given W_0. The optimal policy in the minimax case is the one that minimizes the maximum environmental costs over variation in the unobserved part of the history of the system.

Mathematically, the stochastic and minimax variants are similar, and the results carry over readily from one to the other. Taking the minimax example and assuming a finite horizon, T, the 'worst-case' costs of policy υ from time t are defined as

$$H_M(\upsilon,W_t) = M_\upsilon(C|W_t). \tag{8.1}$$

From the fact that u_t is observable at W_{t+1}, this may be written in the form of the recursion

$$H_M(\upsilon,W_t) = M_\upsilon[H_M(\upsilon,W_{t+1})|W_t]. \tag{8.2}$$

The implication of the finite horizon, T, is that the costs of the policy υ at time T are independent of u_T, so that

$$H_M(\upsilon,W_T) = H_M(W_T). \tag{8.3}$$

Defining $G_M(W_t)$ to be the minimum of $H_M(\upsilon,W_t)$ over all possible u_t, this yields the optimality equation

$$G_M(W_t) = \inf_{u_t} M[G_M(W_{t+1})|W_t,u_t] \tag{8.4}$$

with terminal condition

$$G_M(W_T) = H_M(W_T). \tag{8.5}$$

The values of u_t that minimize the maximum environmental costs for all t in (8.4), conditional on the state of knowledge in each period, define the optimal policy, υ^*. It can be shown[3] that with such a policy $H_M(\upsilon^*,W_t) \leq H_M(\upsilon,W_t)$ for all υ, all t, and all W_t.

The stochastic version of this problem is entirely analogous, with the optimality equation identical to (8.4) except that the maximizing operator, M, is replaced by the expectation operator, E. That is, we have:

$$G_E(W_t) = \inf_{ut} E[G_E(W_{t+1}) | W_t, u_t] \qquad (8.6)$$

with terminal condition

$$G_E(W_T) = H_E(W_T). \qquad (8.7)$$

The minimizing value of u_t in (8.6) is optimal, and defines the minimum expected environmental costs over all policies, conditional on the state of knowledge at each point in time. This completes our description of a sequential decision-making framework under incomplete information.

4   DECISION-MAKING UNDER THE PRECAUTIONARY PRINCIPLE

The class of problems for which the precautionary principle is advocated includes those in which both the level of fundamental uncertainty and the potential costs (or stakes) are high. This places such problems in the realm of what Funtowicz and Ravetz (1990) have referred to as 'second order science', where 'traditional' science is argued to be 'inadequate' and ethical judgements are argued to be 'ubiquitous'. The precautionary principle does indeed involve a highly normative judgement about the responsibility borne by present generations towards future generations. Nor can this be captured in existing models of rational decision-making. Nevertheless, the gulf between such 'second order' problems as global climate change where the precautionary principle is invoked and the more mundane sequential decision-making problems for which dynamic programming techniques were devised is not so wide that the techniques themselves are irrelevant. As Section 3 has shown, neither the stochastic nor the minimax variant of the decision-making model is formally privileged over the other. Yet the minimax variant does, as we shall see, imply a normative judgement about the appropriate attitude to uncertainty. Indeed, there is a strong sense among some economists that a minimax approach is, for this reason, less rational than an expected value approach (compare Mäler, 1989a, 1989b).

The link between the precautionary principle and the 'worst-case' orientation of the minimax approach is quite intuitive. The precautionary principle requires the commitment of resources now to safeguard against the potentially catastrophic future effects of current activity. It is those effects which provide a point of reference for the principle, and it is natural to think of them as the 'worst-case' effects. But it is important to clarify how the 'worst case' is arrived at in conditions of incomplete information, where the range and distribution of outcomes is not in fact known in advance. The 'worst case' identified in the minimax approach cannot be the most extreme of a known range of outcomes, since the range of outcomes is not known. Nor can it be the worst imaginable case. It is always possible to construct a story in which the worst-case environmental costs approach infinity for any policy, but such a construction would not only paralyse all activity, it would fail utterly to discriminate between different policies. Since it has to be believable enough to command the attention of decision-makers, an operational 'worst case' must be something else.

Recent work in the theory of decision-making under uncertainty by Katzner (1986, 1989) suggests that what we now interpret as the maximum cost in the minimax approach may better be represented by Shackle's concept of the focus loss of a decision.[4] In the Shackle approach it is argued that decision-makers conjecture a set of future states associated with any given action, and form an opinion on non-probabilistic grounds about the degree of disbelief they would have in the occurrence of each state (compare Shackle, 1955, 1969). More particularly, to each future state they attach a measure of the potential surprise that they imagine they would experience if that state actually occurred. Since these measures can be mapped into the closed interval [0,1] they are obviously akin to a subjective probability distribution. The set of choice options – in this case the set of policies available to the decision-maker – is ordered by an 'attractiveness function' that registers the power of each outcome to command the attention of the decision-maker. In this case, the outcomes of interest are the environmental costs of each option, and the cost which becomes the reference point for the decision-maker is the focus loss of the decision. Outcomes will typically attract greater attention, the smaller the potential surprise they involve and the greater the extent of the damage involved. Potentially catastrophic effects will, however, only seize the decision-maker's attention if the prospect of their occurrence excites minimal disbelief.

A point of central importance here is that the 'worst' outcome or focus loss of a decision is adopted as the point of reference in the decision-making process whenever the data are judged to be insufficient to support a decision on expected values. This will happen wherever the decision-maker is unable to accept the data, whether because it is objectively scarce or because of the overriding importance attached to protecting some population placed at risk by the activity. The scarcity of data is closely associated with the evolutionary nature of the global system, and with technologically innovative uses of environmental resources. It follows that in almost any activity data will be scarce with respect to certain outcomes. However, whether any data set is regarded with confidence by the decision-maker will depend on ethical judgements they may make about the weight attached to the welfare of those affected. Inadequate data will often be accepted as the basis of decisions where the welfare implications of a bad decision are trivial. This is the notion of bounded rationality. On the other hand, data that look very solid to scientists may be treated as suspect by decision-makers if the welfare costs associated with adverse outcomes are unacceptable, regardless of the objective probability of such adverse outcomes. We shall return to this point later. In both cases decision-makers will tend to reserve their position by taking an initially cautious stance – using the 'worst case' or focus loss as their point of reference. We may refer to this as reserved rationality.

The main implication of this discussion is that decisions involving uncertain environmental effects on future generations will tend to contain elements of both approaches, the balance reflecting both the degree to which the activity has historical precedents and the ethical environment within which it is made. The estimate of environmental costs of activities will tend to comprise two broad parts: the expected value of the environmental costs of those constituent actions for which the data set is sufficient to identify the set of all possible outcomes; and the focus loss of those constituent actions for which this is not true. The present value of such costs is obtained by discounting both parts at the appropriate rate. The stochastic case addresses the first data set, providing a rule for assigning probabilities to each of the set of outcomes for which the mean and variance is supplied by the decision-maker. The minimax or focus loss case addresses the second data set, identifying the focus environmental damage associated with each policy used by the decision-maker (analogous to the subjective expected value of the environmental damage function). The finite horizon stochastic and minimax cases can thus be thought of as two extremes of a spectrum of criteria of environmental costs, in which choice of the most appropriate criterion must rest both on the nature of the data base, and on the institutional and ethical conditions under which the policy is devised.

To see the implications of this for the theory of decision-making under incomplete information let us first redefine

$$M_\upsilon(C\,|W_t) = E_\upsilon(C - V\,|W_t) \tag{8.8}$$

where $V < 0$ is the compensating variation in cost involved in the reserve position: that is, the reduction in expected environmental costs that would be necessary to compensate the decision-maker for adopting the reference costs $E_\upsilon(C\,|W_t)$. The reference costs might, for example, be estimates of the effects of global warming offered by the scientific community on the basis of model simulations. In other words, the reference costs are defined by the expected value of the *available* cost estimates. Equation (8.8) merely asserts that it is possible to define a relation between the 'worst-case' outcome or focus loss of an action, and the expected value of the outcomes of that action.

Now suppose that the decision-maker chooses to reserve judgement on a subset only of the current state of knowledge on the global system, U_t. The rest of the current state of knowledge, the complement of U_t in W_t, denoted $\hat{U}_t$, is treated 'at face value'. We can then define the expected augmented costs, C^+, of the policy υ at time t given W_t as

$$E_\upsilon(C^+ | W_t) = E_\upsilon[(C - V | U_t) + (C | \hat{U}_t)]. \tag{8.9}$$

These augmented costs are merely the expected costs of the policy, plus the compensating variation in cost required for outcomes associated with data in respect of which decision-makers wish to reserve their position. Let $H_E^+(\upsilon, U_t, \hat{U}_t)$ denote such expected augmented costs. We then have

$$H_E^+(\upsilon, U_t, \hat{U}_t) = E_\upsilon[H_E^+(\upsilon, U_{t+1}, \hat{U}_{t+1}) | U_t, \hat{U}_t]. \tag{8.10}$$

The optimal policy will be the one that minimizes this.

To see what this policy is, we need to be more specific about costs. Define augmented costs from time t to time T as C^{+t}, implying that $C^+ = C^{+0}$, and let these be generated recursively by the function:

$$C^{+t} = \phi[U_{t+1}, \hat{U}_{t+1}, C^{+t+1}] \tag{8.11}$$

with terminal condition

$$C^{+T} = \phi[U_T, \hat{U}_T]. \tag{8.12}$$

If the minimum expected augmented cost is given by

$$G_E^+(U_T, \hat{U}_T) = \inf_{ut} E[C^{+t} | U_t, \hat{U}_t, u_t] \tag{8.13}$$

then the optimality equation takes the form

$$G_E^+(U_T, \hat{U}_T) = \inf_{ut} E[\phi(U_{t+1}, \hat{U}_{t+1}, G_E^+ (U_{t+1}, \hat{U}_{t+1})) | U_t, \hat{U}_t, u_t] \tag{8.14}$$

with terminal condition

$$G_E^{+T} (U_T, \hat{U}_T) = \phi (U_T, \hat{U}_T). \tag{8.15}$$

The minimizing u_t in (8.14) for all $t < T$, U_t, and $\hat{U}_t$, defines the optimal policy, υ^*, under which $H_E^+(\upsilon^*, U_t, \hat{U}_t) \leq H_E^+(\upsilon, U_t, \hat{U}_t)$ for all $t \leq T$, U_t, $\hat{U}_t$ and υ.

Indeed, this follows directly. Since environmental costs are independent of policy at time T,

$$H_E^+(\upsilon^*, U_T, \hat{U}_T) = H_E^+(\upsilon, U_T, \hat{U}_T).$$

For time less than time T,

$$
\begin{aligned}
H_E^+(\upsilon, U_t, \hat{U}_t) &= E_\upsilon[H_E^+(\upsilon, U_{t+1}, \hat{U}_{t+1}) \,|U_t, \hat{U}_t] \\
&\geq \inf_{u_t} E[H_E^+(\upsilon^*, U_{t+1}, \hat{U}_{t+1}) \,|U_t, \hat{U}_t, u_t] \\
&\geq \inf_{u_t} E[H_E^+(\upsilon^*, U_{t+1}, \hat{U}_{t+1}) \,|U_t, \hat{U}_t, u_t^*] \\
&= H_E^+(\upsilon^*, U_t, \hat{U}_t).
\end{aligned}
\tag{8.16}
$$

Moreover

$$
\begin{aligned}
H_E^+(\upsilon^*, U_t, \hat{U}_t) &= \inf_{u_t} E[\phi(U_{t+1}, \hat{U}_{t+1}, G_E^+ (U_{t+1}, \hat{U}_{t+1})) \,|U_t, \hat{U}_t, u_t^*] \\
&= G_E^+(U_T, \hat{U}_T).
\end{aligned}
\tag{8.17}
$$

Once again, the model is similar to both the stochastic and the minimax variants. The only difference is that the state of knowledge is now divided between knowledge which is accorded provisional or reserved status, U_t, and knowledge accorded confirmed status, $\hat{U}_t$. The optimal policy will be that which minimizes (a) the focus losses of activities for which the distribution of outcomes has reserved status in the decision-making process, and (b) the expected losses of all other activities.

The identification of only two such categories of knowledge is, of course, an abstraction from the complexity of the real world, where there exists a continuum of subtly distinct qualities of knowledge, but it serves our purpose. Knowledge accorded provisional status in this case is that on which the decision-maker chooses to reserve judgement. Knowledge accorded confirmed status is that which the decision-maker is content to evaluate on an expected value basis. Neither subset of the global state of knowledge will be constant over time. New observations on the state of the system may be expected to induce decision-makers to vary the proportion of the data set on which they wish to reserve their position. Indeed, if new observations on the system are not surprising they will lead decision-makers to revise upwards the judgement they make about their understanding of the system, and U_t will tend to be reduced relative to $\hat{U}_t$. On the other hand, if new observations on the state of the system are surprising, they will tend to have the opposite effect. Decision-makers will become less confident of their understanding of the global system. Notice, though, that there is no reason to believe that the acquisition of new knowledge by itself necessarily improves understanding of the global system – except in the negative sense of persuading us that we understand less than we thought.

It is a characteristic of the increasing flow of observations on the state of the global system that it does contain surprises. The emission of greenhouse gases is not new, but the notion that they might have the capacity to damage global life-support systems is. Destruction of rainforest is not new, but the notion that it may contribute to climate change is. As our knowledge of the global system increases, so, too, does our uncertainty about the long-term implications of present economic activity. Combined with the uncertainty caused by the rapid pace of change in the technology of resource use, this suggests that the increasing flow of information does not in fact leave information any more complete. The problem for decision-makers does not get any easier. Not only is the perceived range and severity of the possible environmental effects of economic activity expanding, so, too, is their gestation period.

5   RESERVED RATIONALITY AND THE PRECAUTIONARY PRINCIPLE

The notion of reserved rationality describes those decision-making processes where ignorance as to the probability distribution of outcomes, and so ignorance as to the magnitude of potential losses, makes it natural to proceed cautiously – to safeguard initially against the possibility of unexpectedly severe future costs. It seems quite intuitive that where policies have the potential to destroy crucial life-support systems it is prudent to leave some margin for error as one learns the outcomes of the policy. But there is mounting evidence that decision-making reflects this property in a much wider set of circumstances. In economic experiments, for example, it has been found that where subjects are given a substantial sum initially, and where they have no personal experience from which to construct a probability distribution of outcomes during experiments involving repeated trials, their initial strategies will be designed to minimize maximum loss – even where those subjects have been advised of the expected value of the outcome in advance. However, as the subjects build up personal experience over a sequence of trials, their strategies tend to move towards the maximization of expected value.[5] All that is required is that a (subjectively) valued asset be subject to a threat of unknown dimensions.

The relation between the notion of reserved rationality and the precautionary principle is equally intuitive. The principle requires that allowance be made for the potential, though uncertain, future losses associated with the use of environmental resources. Consider that component of the expected augmented costs of policy υ associated with the uncertain knowledge in W_t, $E_\upsilon(C - V | U_t)$. We have defined this to be the focus loss of actions informed by U_t. The difference between this and the expected or reference costs of the same policy represents the decision-maker's allowance for error in the expected costs. In the language of Shackle, $E_\upsilon(-V | U_t)$ is a measure of those costs of the policy, over and above the expected costs, which would cause the decision-maker no surprise. An efficient intertemporal allocation of resources in these circumstances requires that the expected benefits of the policy exceed the expected costs by $E_{\upsilon}(-V\,|U_t)$. This, then, defines the upper bound on the value of resources that may be committed as preventive expenditures under the precautionary principle.[6]

It is, finally, worth repeating that there is a very strong normative, ethical content to these expenditures. Recall that there are two elements to the focus loss of a policy: the first is a set of conjectured outcomes which would cause greater or lesser disbelief to the decision-maker. The second is a set of weights on those outcomes reflecting the ethical judgement of the decision-maker as to the importance of the incidence and timing of those outcomes. These weights may not be explicit. They may be implicit in the 'attractiveness function' which draws the decision-maker's attention to some outcomes rather than others. But whether implicit or explicit, they indicate the importance of equity issues in fixing the value of the safeguard allowance under a precautionary principle. A common thread in the various interpretations of sustainable development in the wake of the Brundtland Report is the necessity to preserve the options available to future generations. Intergenerational equity, in this view, will be satisfied if the activities of the present generation do not impose irreversible costs on future generations. This principle can be interpreted as saying that if it is known that an action may cause profound and irreversible environmental damage which permanently reduces the welfare of future generations, but the probability of such damage is not known, then it is inequitable to act as if the probability is known. The decision on whether to accept the expected or reference costs of a policy involving fundamental uncertainty is, in this sense, a function of the ethics underpinning an intertemporal social welfare function.

NOTES

1. This was, for example, the main recommendation of the conference on Sustainable Development, Science and Policy, Bergen, May 1990.
2. The distinction between risk and uncertainty in this chapter is Knightian, in the sense that it emphasizes the difference between those cases in which the set of possible outcomes and the probability of those outcomes is known in advance, and those cases in which it is not.
3. By reasoning analogous to that in the steps before equation (8.16).
4. See also Perrings (1989).
5. W. Schultze, personal communication.
6. It should be clear, therefore, that it is the precautionary principle and the reserved rationality that underpins it, which lies behind the environmental bonds recommended elsewhere for innovative activities with uncertain future environmental effects (compare Perrings, 1989; Costanza and Perrings, 1990).

REFERENCES

Costanza, R. and Perrings, C.A. (1990), 'A flexible assurance bonding system for improved environmental management', *Ecological Economics* **2** (1): 57–76.

Daly, H.E. (1973), 'The steady state economy: towards a political economy of biophysical equilibrium and moral growth', in H.E. Daly (ed.), *Towards a Steady State Economy*, W.H. Freeman, San Francisco: 149–74.

Dasgupta, P.S. and Heal, G.M. (1979), *Economic Theory of Exhaustible Resources*, Cambridge University Press, Cambridge.

Foy G. and Daly, H.E. (1989), 'Allocation, distribution and scale as determinants of environmental degradation: case studies of Haiti, El Salvador and Costa Rica', World Bank, Environment Department Working Paper No. 19.

Funtowicz, S.O. and Ravetz, J.R. (1990), 'Global environmental issues and the emergence of second order science', Paper presented at the ISEE Conference, The Ecological Economics of Sustainability, Washington.

Katzner, D.W. (1986), 'Potential surprise, potential confirmation and probability', *Journal of Post Keynesian Economics* **9**: 58–78.

Katzner, D.W. (1989), 'The comparative statics of the Shackle–Vickers approach to decision-making in ignorance', in T.B. Fomby and T.K. Seo (eds), *Studies in the Economics of Uncertainty: in honour of Joseph Hadar*, Springer-Verlag, Berlin.

Mäler, K.-G. (1989a), 'Risk and the environment: an attempt to a theory', Stockholm School of Economics, Research Paper No. 6390.

Mäler, K.-G. (1989b), 'Environmental resources, risk and Bayesian decision rules', Stockholm School of Economics, Research Paper No. 6391.

Marglin, S.A. (1963), 'The social rate of discount and the optimal rate of investment', *Quarterly Journal of Economics* **77**: 95–112.

Myrdal, G. (1975), *Against the Stream*, Vintage Books, New York.

Norgaard, R.B. and Howarth, R.B. (1990), 'Sustainability and the rate of discount', Paper presented at the ISEE Conference, The Ecological Economics of Sustainability, Washington.

Pearce, D.W. and Markandya, A. (1989), 'Marginal opportunity cost as a planning concept in natural resource management', in G. Schramm and J.J. Warford (eds), *Environmental Management and Economic Development*, Johns Hopkins University Press for the World Bank, Baltimore:

Pearce, D.W., Markandya, A. and Barbier, E.B. (1989), *Blueprint for a Green Economy*, Earthscan, London.

Perrings, C.A. (1987), *Economy and Environment*, Cambridge University Press, New York.

Perrings, C.A. (1989), 'Environmental bonds and environmental research in innovative activities', *Ecological Economics* **1**: 95–110.

Randers, J. and Meadows, D. (1973), 'The carrying capacity of our global environment: a look at the ethical alternatives', in H.E. Daly (ed.), *Toward a Steady State Economy*, W.H. Freeman, San Francisco.

Shackle, G.L.S. (1955), *Uncertainty in Economics*, Cambridge University Press, Cambridge.

Shackle, G.L.S. (1969), *Decision, Order and Time in Human Affairs*, Cambridge University Press, Cambridge.

Williamson, O.E. (1985), *The Economic Institutions of Capitalism*, Free Press, New York.

9. Environmental bonds and environmental research in innovative activities

1 INTRODUCTION

Decision-making under ignorance is now a well-established – though not yet a core – area of microeconomic theory (see Shackle, 1955, 1969; Arrow and Hurwicz, 1972; Katzner, 1986, 1988a, 1988b and Vickers, 1987). Little has yet been done to explore its significance for the management of environmental problems arising from economic activities. Given that many of the environmental effects of economic activities are unknown and unknowable in advance, however, it would appear to be an area in which the theory might usefully be applied. It is certainly of interest to understand how ignorance about future environmental costs might be accommodated in the decision to undertake innovative activities, and this chapter addresses one aspect of such a problem. In particular, it addresses the decision-making process of environmental authorities faced with innovative private economic activities with uncertain future environmental effects.

The necessity for decisions taken in historical, irreversible time, to have unanticipated future effects is well recognized. It is also well recognized that ignorance as to the future outcomes of present activities depends in large part on whether there exists a statistical record of the outcomes of similar activities in the past. It is quite intuitive that the difficulty of predicting the future outcomes of present activities will be greater the fewer the historical precedents for those activities. Activities for which there exist no historical precedents have been referred to by Shackle (1955, 1969) as 'crucial'. Because there exist no observations of the historical outcomes of Shackle-crucial activities, there is no basis on which to identify their possible outcomes or to construct a probability distribution for those outcomes. The only source of statistical information on the future effects of such activities is the experimental (often basic) research done in advance of their introduction. This has not stopped such activities from being undertaken, of course. But it has meant that the information on which decisions have been made has been of a non-probabilistic kind: the conjectured costs and benefits of the activity.

The problem addressed in this chapter arises from the fact that in the absence of non-market incentives there is no reason to believe that experimental research conducted by the agents proposing such innovative activities will include all relevant potential future costs. Because the activities are historically unique there is no basis on which to establish *ex ante* markets in all potential future effects, hence there may be a range of unexpected social costs or benefits. Since the weakness of such markets opens up the possibility of 'Thalidomide-type' surprises, it is worth considering whether there exists an incentive to research that will ensure that all socially relevant questions are asked about the future external effects of activities with no or few historical precedents. A passive learning process of the type discussed by Opaluch (1984) will certainly add information on the effects of innovative activities as those effects emerge, but it will not uncover in advance the possibility of future social costs, unless there exist adequate incentives to research those costs.

This chapter considers the use of sequentially-determined environmental bonds as incentives to research the socially interesting outcomes of innovative activities, recommended in Perrings (1987). Environmental bonds of one sort or another have long been used to encourage socially desirable methods of waste disposal in activities where the existing waste disposal technologies have a range of social effects, some more harmful than others. Environmental bonds have not previously been considered as research incentives, but it turns out that they are well suited to the purpose. The social insurance aspect of the bond is retained. This is, however, augmented by an uncertainty premium relating to the conjectured future social costs of the activity and since this leads to the sequential determination of the bond, it offers a direct incentive to undertake experimental research.

The chapter approaches the construction of the bond in stages. Section 2 considers the problem of decision-making under ignorance as to the future external effects of activities incorporating some historical precedents. This covers certain issues previously addressed in the environmental economics literature by Dasgupta and Heal (1979) and Bockstael and Opaluch (1983), but focuses on work on the theory of decision-making under ignorance – particularly that of Shackle (1955, 1969) and Katzner (1986, 1988a, 1989). It suggests a measure of the value of uncertain future environmental effects which is a composite. In all cases it rests on an expected present social value of those future effects known to occur with some probability. On to this is grafted a measure of the conjectured present social value of the remaining uncertain outcomes. Section 3 introduces the familiar concept of the environmental bond that has developed out of the materials-use fee first recommended by Mill (1972) and Solow (1971), and relates it to the second part of this measure. The intention is to fix the value to society of permitting innovative activities to proceed without research into possible future environmental costs. Sections 4 and 5 discuss the research incentive in such bonds and Section 6 offers some concluding remarks.

2   DECISION-MAKING UNDER IGNORANCE OF THE FUTURE ENVIRONMENTAL EFFECTS OF INNOVATIVE ACTIVITIES

No activity is wholly innovative, wholly without historical precedent. Even the most pathbreaking activities rest on, or at least include, constituent actions which have been undertaken in the past. This means that while Shackle and Katzner quite properly point to the blanks in our knowledge of the future effects of innovative activities, there remains a kernel of accumulated evidence about the effects of constituent actions conducted within well-established boundary conditions. So long as the boundary conditions are reproduced, that evidence enables a probabilistic prediction of the outcome of similar actions in the future. Moreover, the more frequently an action has been replicated in the past the more confidence we may have in the probabilities attached to its outcomes in the future.

There remain, however, those constituent actions for which there exist no historical precedents, or for which the boundary conditions change as a result of the activity. It may not be possible to predict the set of outcomes of such actions, let alone the probability of each outcome in that set. Conditions of this sort give rise to the problem of decision-making under ignorance, since they require the decision-maker to cope with real uncertainty (in the sense of Knight, 1921) as opposed to risk. No longer is it reasonable to assume that the collection of future states of nature or the probabilities of occurrence for the future states of nature is known. Nor is it reasonable to suppose that agents make decisions 'as if' they know the collection and probability distribution of those states of nature.

Ignorance here is a product both of our existence in 'historical' time (Katzner, 1988b), and of the irreversibility of the entropic processes at the heart of economic activity (Georgescu-Roegen, 1971; Perrings, 1986, 1987). In historical time, only the past and the present may be observed and recorded, and neither can yield more than partial knowledge about the future. In a world governed by the laws of thermodynamics, the irreversibility of entropic processes ensures that the system will necessarily evolve through a sequence of states that are not predictable from its history.

Yet economic agents do make decisions in the face of ignorance about the future states of the world that may result from those decisions. Moreover, they do seek to do this in a rational way – to make sure that their decision is the 'best' of all possible decisions. Despite the fact of their ignorance about the future states of the world, despite the fact that they cannot even guess at everything that might happen, decision-makers sift through a set of options and come down in favour of one. The theory of decision-making under ignorance addresses the question of how courses of action are selected when decision-makers have insufficient information to identify the probability of occurrence of the outcomes of those courses of action.

To approach the construction of a measure of the present value of the future environmental effects of innovative economic activities, it may be useful to summarize very briefly the characteristics of the process of decision-making under ignorance (for a rigorous statement of which, see Katzner, 1988a, 1989). The central assumption underpinning this approach is that decison-makers conjecture an admittedly incomplete set of future states, and form an opinion (on non-probabilistic grounds) about the degree of disbelief they would have in the occurrence of each option. They then act on this opinion. More particularly, to each subset of the incomplete list of future states of the world associated with any one activity, the decision-maker attaches a measure of the potential surprise that he/she imagines he/she would experience if it actually occurred. As with a probability distribution, all subsets are mapped into the closed interval [0,1] by the potential surprise function. The decision-maker is faced with the problem of selecting from a collection of utility-yielding or profit-yielding choice options, subject to the potential surprise of the future states of the world associated with each choice option.

The set of choice options is ordered by what Shackle refers to as an 'attractiveness function' that registers the power of the outcome of each option to command the attention of the decision-maker. An option attracting the attention of the decision-maker may generate outcomes that are more appealing (implying that they confer gains) or less appealing (implying that they impose costs). For each option the decision-maker's attention will be drawn to two values: one associated with the least potentially surprising but most *appealing* outcome; and the other with the least potentially surprising but most *unappealing* outcome. The former is sometimes referred to as the 'focus gain', and the latter as the 'focus loss' of a decision. These are parallel but not identical to the expected benefits and expected costs of a risky decision. The focus gain describes the least unbelievable conjectured gains of an option. The focus loss describes the least unbelievable conjectured costs.

Accordingly, the power of an outcome to fix the attention of the decision-maker depends both on the utility or profit functions of decision-makers that order those outcomes, and on their uncertainty avidity/indifference/aversion (which need bear no particular relation to their risk avidity/indifference/aversion). Outcomes will attract greater attention, the smaller the potential surprise involved if decision-makers are uncertainty averse, and the larger the potential surprise involved if decision-makers are uncertainty avid. So, for example, if the outcomes associated with a decision to construct nuclear power plants include the potential losses associated with a meltdown, and if the occurrence of a meltdown causes minimal potential surprise, then for an uncertainty-averse agent that would be the focus or conjectured loss of the decision (irrespective of the supposed probability of a meltdown).

The important feature of this approach to decision-making is not that the decision-maker's attention is drawn most strongly towards the prospect of unlimited gains or catastrophic losses. It is that whether such prospects lead to the corresponding choice option depends on the degree of disbelief the decision-maker has in their occurrence, noting that the degree of disbelief or the potential surprise of an outcome is not equal to one minus the probability of that outcome. To pursue the example of the last paragraph, the Chernobyl meltdown may have had no effect on the probability of similar outcomes in similar plants (supposing that data existed to calculate such a probability), but it has had a major effect on the degree of disbelief that people have in the occurrence. Indeed, it is precisely where probabilities cannot be inferred that potential surprise informs decisions.

A second feature of decision-making under ignorance is that it is of necessity subject to revision. It is a continuous process, rather than a discrete act. In terms of the concern of this chapter, the undiscounted value of the future environmental costs of innovative activities used by the decision-maker will comprise two parts. The first is the expected value of the environmental costs of those constituent actions for which the data set is sufficient to estimate a probability distribution. The second is the focus or conjectured losses of those constituent actions for which the lack of historical precedent compels the decision-maker to search out the least surprising but most unappealing outcome. The present value of such costs is obtained by discounting both parts at the appropriate rate. It therefore depends on four factors: (i) the (subjective) probability of each of an exhaustive list of outcomes of choice options with respect to those constituent actions with historical precedents; (ii) the potential surprise associated with each of an incomplete list of outcomes of choice options with respect to those constituent actions without historical precedents; (iii) the utility or profit function that explains the power of each option to command the attention of the decision-maker; and (iv) the rate of discount.

None of these factors is independent of time. Traditionally, we treat the preferences and discount rate of the decision-maker *as if* they were invariant over time, but it is intuitive that neither of the remaining factors can be constant over time. As the constituent actions of an economic activity are undertaken a historical record of their outcomes will be built up, so changing the boundary between the known and unknown outcomes of the activity as a whole. The development of a history for each action is the basis of the Bayesian approach to the acquisition of probabilistic 'knowledge'. Repeated enumeration of events makes possible the development of increasingly robust hypotheses.

More interestingly, as the limits of what is 'known' in a probabilistic sense change, so, too, does the list of outcomes of the remaining Shackle-crucial aspects of the activity. This may affect the potential surprise associated with the outcomes that are left, although it would be wrong to suggest that the potential surprise function would be affected in any determinate way. Outcomes may be added or dropped from the list without in any way changing the potential surprise associated with what is left. In all cases, however, the decision-making process will itself evolve over time in response to the changing information available to the decision-maker, and to the decision-maker's changing perceptions of that information. It is these two characteristics of decision-making under ignorance – that it rests on conjectured gains and losses, and that it is a continuous process rather than a discrete act – which determine the properties of the bonds discussed in this chapter.

3   THE GENERAL CHARACTERISTICS OF AN ENVIRONMENTAL BOND

Following the insights in the work of Boulding (1966) and Ayres and Kneese (1969) as to the significance of the law of conservation of mass for the waste disposal problem, Mill (1972) and Solow (1971) separately advanced the idea of a 'materials-use fee' to be levied on specified environmental resources at a rate equal to 'the social cost to the environment if the material were eventually returned to the environment in the most harmful way possible' (Solow, 1971: 498–503). The fee was initially seen to be equivalent to the refundable deposit long used to encourage the recycling of potentially environmentally harmful products. In other words, it provided an incentive for private users of environmental resources to dispose of waste products in a socially preferred way. The fee was prompted by considerations similar to those behind the use of Pigouvian taxes for pollution control including, in particular, the non-existence of an enforceable contractual obligation on the users of a resource to perform in a predictable way. Where the purchaser of a resource was contractually free to dispose of it in any of a number of ways, each with different known effects, the materials-use fee provided an incentive to adopt the least socially harmful method of disposal. The fee, now commonly referred to as an environmental bond, has subsequently been recommended wherever direct observation and detection of environmental damage are impossible or extremely difficult (compare Baumol and Oates, 1975, 1979).

To establish the basis for the particular bonds recommended here it is useful to recall that whatever the form of the levy or subsidy attached to an expected environmental external effect, it may be interpreted first of all as a premium for social insurance against losses due to acts of commission or omission. Losses due to acts of commission are the consequence of negative external effects, losses due to acts of omission are the positive external effects forgone if a programme of activity generating such effects is not undertaken. In the case of non-innovative activities the data set may be assumed to be sufficiently rich that the expected value of an external effect is known, and the premium may be accurately computed. In the case of innovative activities, however, this is not true, and the levy may be expected to perform a rather different role.

More particularly, the environmental bond recommended here would have the following overlapping functions in respect of innovative activities:

i.   it would register the value placed by the environmental authority on allowing an innovative activity to proceed without further research;
ii.   it would provide an incentive to innovating firms to research the future effects of their own activities;
iii. since the bond would yield interest income it would generate public research funds in direct proportion to the public concern about the future effects of innovative activities;
iv.   it would determine the timing of an innovative activity;
v.   it would encourage sufficient advance experimental research to eliminate, so far as is possible in an uncertain world, catastrophic but unsurprising conjectured outcomes; and
vi.   it would insure society against the irreducible residuum of conjectured but unsurprising losses.

The motivation for introducing a bond with these funtions is quite simple. Where the conjectured losses caused by any activity with potential future environmental effects are substantial, care should be taken in constructing a reliable data set on which to found decisions, and the decision-maker should be confident that the resources exist to meet the worst believable case – the focus loss. Focus losses that are insignificant warrant neither extensive initial investigation, nor comprehensive insurance. Focus losses that are catastophic demand both a major research effort, and the mobilization of resources to meet the worst case.

The incentive effects of the bond will be considered later. Before doing so it is worth underscoring the fact that although there will always exist a residuum of uncertainty in innovative activities, it is possible to limit that residuum through experimental research on those constituent actions of an innovative activity for which the actual boundary conditions can be both predicted and simulated. Even in activities with a large innovative element it is possible to build up a history for each of several constituent actions through experimental research under a range of boundary conditions that approximate the real environment within which the activity is to take place – adding something to what is known, with some probability, about the future effects of the activity.

4 THE INCENTIVE TO RESEARCH IN THE ENVIRONMENTAL BOND

The environmental bond discussed here is designed to stimulate research into the future effects of innovative activities. In this respect its most important characteristic is that it would vary over time with the conjectured or focus losses associated with the innovative (or unprecedented) aspects of activities. The research incentive in the bond derives from the fact that its value would change with the state of knowledge on the future effects of the activity. Given that the cost of the bond to the innovator would be proportionate to the value of the bond, and given that the value of the bond would be a function of the information available to the environmental authority, there would be a private incentive to increase investment in the acquisition of information wherever this was expected to reduce the value of the bond.

A construction of the measure of the undiscounted value of the future environmental costs of innovative activities is offered in the appendix to this chapter for the discrete time, fixed coefficient case. This measure, denoted $Z_i(k,t)$, defines the external costs of activity expected to occur in period k, as estimated or conjectured in period t. This measure would be the basis for any bond imposed by an environmental authority as security against such effects. If the activity had innovative aspects, the measure $Z_i(k,t)$ would comprise two parts: one part relating to the expected losses due to the non-innovative parts of the activity, and one part relating to the conjectured or focus losses due to the innovative parts of the activity.

The bond imposed by the environmental authority would, similarly, depend on the same two things. Let $W_i(k,t)$ denote the bond levied in period t on the i-th activity, for effects expected to occur in period k. We then have:

$$W_i(k,t) = f[EZ_i(k,t) + CZ_i(k,t)], f' > 0, f(0) = 0; \qquad (9.1)$$

where EZ_i denotes the expected value of the environmental costs of the non-innovative parts of activity i, and CZ_i denotes the conjectured value of the environmental costs of the innovative parts of the same activity. If the bond were imposed on an activity undertaken at time 0, this implies that it could be revised up to k times before it was surrendered or returned, that is, $t = 0, ..., k$.

Assuming that transactions costs were zero, the cost of the bond to the firm which is required to post it would equal the revenue to the environmental authority with which it was posted. In period t this would be $rW_i(k,t)$, r denoting the rate of interest. The bond would accordingly generate resources to research the future outcomes of present activities in two rather different ways.

First, interest income on the bond would provide a fund for public research that would vary directly with the severity of the conjectured costs of an activity. The greater the focus loss of a decision to undertake the activity, the greater the resources that would be committed to improving the quality of public information on its potential outcomes.

Second, the incentive to minimize the private cost of the bond would prompt innovators to commit resources to private research. This arises from the fact that while the bond would be set by the environmental authority (or body arbitrating between the environmental authority and the innovating firm), its value in any one period would not be independent of the research conducted by the innovating agent(s).

Consider the second incentive. The total undiscounted private cost of the bond to the agent undertaking activity i during the life of the bond would be:

$$\sum_t rW_i(k,t) + W_i(k,k); \ t = 0, ..., k.$$

This is just the sum of the opportunity cost of the bond plus its value at the surrender date. Since the value of the bond in each period would be, in part, a function of private research expenditures in previous periods, a profit-maximizing firm would increase its own research expenditures up to the point at which the marginal expenditure on research equalled the expected marginal reduction in the cost of the bond.

Assume, without loss of generality, a single-period lag between research expenditures and adjustment in the size of the bond. The value of the bond in period t, $W_i(k,t)$, would then vary independently with both public and private expenditures on research in period $t-1$, $rW_i(k,t-1)$ and $R_i(k,t-1)$, respectively. Thus

$$W_i(k,t) = g[rW_i(k,t-1)] + h[R_i(k,t-1)]. \qquad (9.2)$$

In principle the sign of both g' and h' should be indeterminate, since research into the possible future effects of innovative activities should be open to all results. In practice, however, environmental research suffers acutely from the problem of moral hazard and h', in particular, would tend to be non-positive. In other words, privately-funded research would tend to downplay the environmental costs of innovative activities. While there may be a problem of moral hazard on both sides, it is assumed that private agents have no insight into the effect of public research on the value of the bond. The net expected benefits to the firm of private expenditure on research in a two-period problem, $E\pi_i(t+1,t)$, would then be the reduction in the expected cost of the bond due to private research findings, $r\{h[R_i(k,t-1)] - Eh[R_i(k,t)]\}$, less the costs of that research, $R_i(k,t)$. That is

$$E\pi_i(t+1,t) = r\{h[R_i(k,t-1)] - Eh[R_i(k,t)]\} - R_i(k,t) \qquad (9.3)$$

from which it is immediate that the first-order conditions for the maximization of the expected net benefits require that

$$-r\frac{d}{dR_i(k,t)} Eh[R_i(k)] = 1 \qquad (9.4)$$

or that private research expenditure in period t should increase up to the point where it is equal to the reduction in the expected cost of the bond in period $t+1$. For more complicated cases the same holds true. Profits will be maximized where the marginal costs and benefits of research are equalized.

5   ADVANCE RESEARCH AS A SEARCH PROCESS

A second aspect of the private research incentive in the bonds proposed in this chapter concerns the role of the bond in stimulating or stopping advance research. Advance research is that research on the future effects of an innovative activity undertaken before the activity is launched. In other words it is research that may be expected to modify the value of the bond that would be levied at some future date if the activity were to take place at that date. It may therefore be thought of as testing the economic feasibility of the proposed activity.

To take a very simple case, assume that the technical coefficients of production are fixed. The expected revenue of a firm considering launching an innovative activity in period t is

$$y_i(t)\mathbf{b}_iE\mathbf{p}(t+1),$$

where $\mathbf{b}_i$ denotes the vector of output coefficients in activity i, $y_i(t)$ denotes the planned level of activity, and $E\mathbf{p}(t+1)$ denotes the expected output price vector. Expected costs in the same period are

$$y_i(t)\mathbf{a}_iE\mathbf{p}(t),$$

where $\mathbf{a}_i$ denotes the vector of input coefficients in the activity, and $E\mathbf{p}(t)$ denotes the expected input price vector. If the activity involves environmental costs on which a bond is payable, expected profits in period t would be

$$E\pi_i(t) = y_i(t)[\mathbf{b}_i E\mathbf{p}(t+1) - \mathbf{a}_i E\mathbf{p}(t)] - rEW_i(k,t). \qquad (9.5)$$

For a single-period programme of production, if $E\pi_i(t) \geq ry_i(t)\mathbf{a}_i E\mathbf{p}(t)$ the activity is expected to be economic, and will be undertaken. If $E\pi_i(t) < ry_i(t)\mathbf{a}_i E\mathbf{p}(t)$ it is expected to be uneconomic, and will not be undertaken. For a multiperiod programme of production the story is similar, with the present value of the programme required to be greater than or equal to the discounted opportunity cost of the capital invested – described in period t by $ry_i(t)\mathbf{a}_i E\mathbf{p}(t)$.

The role of the bond in this case is similar to the observed wage offer in a job search process. It determines when the firm should stop its advance research into the future effects of an innovative activity and launch that activity. Staying with the single-period programme of production for ease of exposition, it follows from (9.5) that for the programme to be expected to be economic it is required that

$$EW_i(k,t) \leq {}^{1/}\!_r y_i(t)[\mathbf{b}_i E\mathbf{p}(t+1) - (1+r)\mathbf{a}_i E\mathbf{p}(t)]. \qquad (9.6)$$

If (9.6) does not hold the programme will be expected to be uneconomic in period t, and the firm will not consider implementing it. The term on the right-hand side of (9.6) accordingly represents the maximum value of the bond consistent with the expected profitability of the programme in period t. Only if the expected value of the bond is less than or equal to this maximum value will the firm consider implementing the programme. Only if the actual value of the bond levied by the environmental authority is less than or equal to the expected value of the bond will a programme under consideration actually be implemented.

The analogy of this to a search problem is obvious. Denoting $F[\pi_i(t)]$ to be the maximum return attainable on a programme under consideration for implementation in period t, and $\overline{W}_i(k,t)$ to be the maximum acceptable value of the bond equal to the right-hand side of (9.6), we have:

$$F[\pi_i(t)] = y_i(t)[\mathbf{b}_i E\mathbf{p}(t+1) - \mathbf{a}_i E\mathbf{p}(t)] - \min[W_i(k,t); EW_i(k,t)]. \qquad (9.7)$$

The maximum attainable return is the expected profits from production less the minimum of the actual or expected value of the bond. The decision rule is quite simple. If $W_i(k,t) > \overline{W}_i(k,t) \geq EW_i(k,t)$, the actual value of the bond is greater than its maximum acceptable value, the firm will not implement the programme and will continue to research its future costs (or will consider abandoning it altogether). If $W_i(k,t) \leq EW_i(k,t) \leq \overline{W}_i(k,t)$ the firm will implement the programme. The environmental authority would thus have an instrument for delaying innovative activity conjectured to have negative future social costs where it was thought that further research was desirable.

6 CONCLUDING REMARKS

It is widely held that the external effects of information, together with problems of appropriability and moral hazard, ensure that competitive markets will lead private agents to avoid investment in basic research, and to overspecialize in applied research (compare Dasgupta and Heal, 1979). This creates particular problems in innovative activities with environmental effects that are conjectured to occur with some delay. These delays are significant for a number of reasons. The most important of these is that they heighten uncertainty and so encourage a myopic vision of the future. The more myopic the vision of competitive agents, the less the incentive to undertake basic experimental research. Moreover, the more that private rates of time preference are driven above the social rate of time preference, the lower the probability that internalization of external effects by the assignment of private property rights will be socially optimal (Fisher,1981; Seneca and Taussig, 1984; Perrings, 1987).

Since there is no reason to believe that private agents will invest in experimental research at socially optimal levels in cases where the external effects of current activities may be significantly delayed, it is worth considering whether there exist incentives to ensure that due weight is given to the social importance of research in innovative activities. This chapter constructs a measure of the present social value of the future expected and potential external effects of non-innovative and innovative activities, respectively, and treats this as a proxy for the social value of research. It is suggested that this measure forms the basis for the sequential calculation of environmental bonds.

Given the motivation of the chapter, two properties of such environmental bonds turn out to be of particular interest. First, by implicitly weighting the 'worst case' or the maximum conjectured loss associated with any activity at unity, the bonds enable a risk-averse society to signal to private agents the social value placed on advance experimental research in cases where the outcome is uncertain. Second, given that the expected value of the future external effects of activities is contingent on the set of current relative prices facing the agents undertaking those activities, the bonds enable the environmental authority to change the distribution of outcomes by changing current relative prices. These properties would seem to make the bonds useful both in preventing innovators from evading the potential costs of activities undertaken in ignorance, and of avoiding the worst of those potential costs.

Finally, it is worth noting that the irreducible uncertainty of innovative activities in an evolutionary system means that there will always exist the possibility of surprise. The environmental bonds recommended in this chapter would not eliminate this possibility, but they would provide the incentive to firms to anticipate so far as possible the future outcomes of present activities, regardless of the time horizon employed in their own planning process.

REFERENCES

Arrow, K.J. and Hurwicz, L. (1972), 'An optimality criterion for decision-making under ignorance', in C.F. Carter and J.L. Ford (eds), *Uncertainty and Expectations in Economics*, Augustus M. Kelly, Clifton, NJ: 1–11.

Ayres, R.U. and Kneese, A.V. (1969), 'Production, consumption and externalities', *American Economic Review* **59**: 282–97.

Baumol, W.J. and Oates, W.E. (1975), *Economics, Environmental Policy, and the Quality of Life*, Prentice Hall, Englewood Cliffs, NJ.

Baumol, W.J. and Oates, W.E. (1979), *The Theory of Environmental Policy*, Prentice Hall, Englewood Cliffs, NJ.

Bockstael, N.E. and Opaluch, J.J. (1983), 'Discrete modelling of supply response under uncertainty: the case of fishery', *Journal of Environmental Economics and Management* **10**: 125–37.

Boulding, K.E. (1966), 'The economics of the coming spaceship earth', in H. Jarrett (ed.), *Environmental Quality in a Growing Economy*, Johns Hopkins University Press, Baltimore: 3–14.

Dasgupta, P.S. and Heal, G.M. (1979), *Economic Theory and Exhaustible Resources*, Cambridge University Press, Cambridge.

Fisher, A.C. (1981), *Resource and Environmental Economics*, Cambridge University Press, Cambridge.

Georgescu-Roegen, N. (1971), *The Entropy Law and the Economic Process*, Harvard University Press, Cambridge, MA.

Katzner, D.W. (1986), 'Potential surprise, potential confirmation and probability', *Journal of Post-Keynesian Economics* **9**: 58–78.

Katzner, D.W. (1988a), 'The Shackle–Vickers approach to decision-making in ignorance', University of Massachusetts, Amherst, mimeo.

Katzner, D.W. (1988b), 'The role of empirical analysis in the investigation of situations involving ignorance and historical time', University of Massachusetts, Amherst, mimeo.

Katzner, D.W. (1989), 'The comparative statics of the Shackle–Vickers approach to decision-making in ignorance', in T.B. Fomby and T.K. Seo (eds), *Studies in the Economics of Uncertainty: in Honour of Joseph Hadar*, Springer-Verlag, Berlin.

Knight, F.H. (1921), *Risk, Uncertainty and Profit*, Houghton-Mifflin, Boston, MA.

Meade, J.E. (1952), 'External economies and diseconomies in a competitive situation', *Economic Journal* **62**: 54–67.

Mill, E.S. (1972), *Urban Economics*, Scott Foreseman, Glenview, Ill.

Opaluch, J.J. (1984), 'Dynamic aspects of effluent taxation under uncertainty', *Journal of Environmental Economics and Management* **11**: 1–13.

Perrings, C. (1986), 'Conservation of mass and instability in a dynamic economy–environment system', *Journal of Environmental Economics and Management* **13**: 199–211.

Perrings, C. (1987), *Economy and Environment: A Theoretical Essay on the Interdependence of Economic and Environmental Systems*, Cambridge University Press, Cambridge.

Seneca, J.J. and Taussig, M.K. (1984), *Environmental Economics*, Prentice-Hall, Englewood Cliffs, NJ.

Shackle, G.L.S. (1955), *Uncertainty in Economics*, Cambridge University Press, Cambridge.

Shackle, G.L.S. (1969), *Decision, Order and Time in Human Affairs*, Cambridge University Press, Cambridge.

Solow, R.M. (1971), 'The economists' approach to pollution control', *Science* **173**: 498–503.

Vickers, D. (1987), *Money Capital in the Theory of the Firm*, Cambridge University Press, Cambridge.

APPENDIX

Let the technology of the i-th economic activity in the period k be described by the n-dimensional time-indexed row vectors of input and output coefficients, $\mathbf{a}_i(t)$ and $\mathbf{b}_i(t)$. The level of activity in period t is denoted $y_i(t)$. Assume that m components of these vectors, $m \leq n$, refer to economic (positively valued) inputs and outputs, and that the remaining $n - m$ components refer to non-economic (zero-valued) inputs and outputs. The latter describe inputs and outputs for which there exist no well-defined private property rights – for whatever reason. We can thus identify a corresponding time-indexed vector of prices, $\mathbf{p}(t)$, m components of which are positive, all others being equal to zero. Since the list of economic inputs and outputs is incomplete for $m < n$, there are up to $n - m$ inputs and outputs which are unobserved through the price system. If these non-economic inputs or outputs are linked backwards or forwards to other economic activities we have the familiar problem of external effects.

Consider the construction of measures for these effects. Let us first take only those activities or aspects of activities for which there exist some historical precedents. Assume that the delay between the external effect of activity i on activity h is k periods. This defines the 'time-distance' between the activities. A unit increase in the current level of activity in i may be assumed (on the basis of historical experience) to generate a set of s possible outcomes in activity h in period k. That is, we can identify a set of S values for the output vector $\mathbf{b}_h(k)$ dependent on the level of activity $yi(0)$. We may denote this set of values $\mathbf{b}_{hi}^s(k,0)$, $s = 1, ..., S$. It is subject to the probability distribution $P_{hi}^s = P[\mathbf{b}_{hi}^s(k,0)]$ with $P_{hi}^s > 0$, and $\sum_s P_{hi}^s = 1$. We thus have complete (historically acquired) knowledge of the set of outcomes possible for activity h in period k as a result of the level of activity in i in period 0. From this it is possible to define the output losses or gains associated with that level of activity. We denote these output losses or gains

$$E\Delta\mathbf{b}_{hi}^s(k,0) = E\mathbf{b}_h^s(k,0) - E\mathbf{b}_{hi}^s(k,0), \qquad (9\text{A}.1)$$

where $E\mathbf{b}_h^s(k,0)$ is expected output in activity h if the level of activity in i were currently zero, and $E\mathbf{b}_{hi}^s(k,0)$ is expected output in activity h when the activity in i is at its actual level.

We may now use this measure to establish the value to society of the general environmental external effects of activity i in period k. Let $x_{hi}(k,0)$ denote the welfare cost of the risk of loss of output in activity h in period k as a result of the current level of activity i. Further, let the weighting factor for the risk attached to expected future environmental external effects be a function, ϕ, of this welfare cost. The (undiscounted) expected social value of the external effect of the current level of activity in i on h at time k, denoted by $EZ_{hi}(k,0)$, may accordingly be defined as follows:

$$EZ_{hi}(k,0) = y_h(k)[E\Delta\mathbf{b}_{hi}^s(k,0)\ \phi(x_{hi}(k,0))]E\mathbf{p}(k+1) \qquad (9A.2)$$

where $y_h(k)$ is the planned level of activity in h at time k, and $E\mathbf{p}(k+t)$ is the expected output price vector at time k.

To obtain a present social value for the general future external effects of the activity i at time k, we need only to discount this and to sum over all affected downstream activities. That is

$$EZ_i(k,0) = \Sigma_h EZ_{hi}(k,0)$$
$$= \{\Sigma_h y_h(k)\ [E\Delta\mathbf{b}_{hi}^s(k,0)\phi(x_{hi}(k,0))]E\mathbf{p}(k+1)(1+r)^{-k}. \qquad (9A.3)$$

Now consider the corresponding measure for the external effects of innovative activities, in which decision-makers are in ignorance about the outcomes of those activities. There is no basis on which to construct a probability distribution for the effects of current activity in i on any other activity since there are no historical precedents. We have seen that in such cases decision-makers will have their attention drawn to the focus loss or focus gain of the activity – to the least unbelievable conjectured losses or gains from the activity. So for the effects of current innovative activity in i on activity h at time k we may identify two additional physical measures: $C_L\Delta\mathbf{b}_{hi}(k,0)$, which describes the focus loss, and $C_G\Delta\mathbf{b}_{hi}(k,0)$, which describes the focus gain.

We have already assumed that there exists an expected output potential for the activity h in period k when $y_j(0) = 0$, and have denoted this $E\mathbf{b}_h^s(k,0)$. There are thus four cases of interest:

i.   if $C_G\Delta\mathbf{b}_{hi}(k,0) = C_L\Delta\mathbf{b}_{hi}(k,0) = E\mathbf{b}_h^s(k,0)$ current activity in i will be conjectured to have no effect on activity h in period k;

ii. if $E\mathbf{b}_h^s(k,0) > C_G\Delta\mathbf{b}_{hi}(k,0) \geq C_L\Delta\mathbf{b}_{hi}(k,0)$ current activity in i will be conjectured to have negative effects on activity h in period k;

iii. if $C_G\Delta\mathbf{b}_{hi}(k,0) \geq C_L\Delta\mathbf{b}_{hi}(k,0) > E\mathbf{b}_h^s(k,0)$ current activity in i will be conjectured to have positive effects on activity h in period k; and

iv. if $C_G\Delta\mathbf{b}_{hi}(k,0) > E\mathbf{b}_h^s(k,0) > C_L\Delta\mathbf{b}_{hi}(k,0)$ current activity in i will be conjectured to have effects that may be either positive or negative.

In each of the last three cases there will be potential gain in improving the quality of the information required to make a decision. By similar construction to (9A.3), and assuming uncertainty aversion, the conjectured present social value of the environmental costs of the current level of the i-th activity occurring at time k is:

$$C_L Z_i(k,0) = \sum_h C_L Z_{hi}(k,0)$$
$$= \{\sum_h y_h(k)[C_L \Delta \mathbf{b}_{hi}(k,0)]E\mathbf{p}(k+1)\}(1+r)^{-k}, \; i = 1, ..., m. \qquad (9A.4)$$

This may be interpreted as the focus or conjectured loss associated with the unresearched implementation of the *i*-th activity in the present period. Accordingly, for activities with both innovative and non-innovative aspects the appropriate measure is ungainly but straightforward

$$EZ_i(k,0) + C_L Z_i(k,0)$$
$$= \{\sum_h y_h(k)[E\Delta \mathbf{b}_{hi}^s(k,0)\phi(x_{hi}(k,0))$$
$$+ C_L \Delta \mathbf{b}_{hi}^s(k,0)]E\mathbf{p}(k+1)\}(1+r)^{-k}. \qquad (9A.5)$$

This last measure will be the relevant one wherever there do not exist sufficient observations to estimate an expected value for the future costs of present activities within acceptable limits of confidence. In all such cases the expected present social value of the future effects of current activities should be augmented by the conjectured losses associated with the Shackle-crucial or innovative aspects of those activities.

10. Biodiversity, sustainable development and natural capital

1 INTRODUCTION

What criteria should govern collective decisions which, by changing the mix of biotic resources, change the opportunities available to all future generations? Such decisions are characterized by fundamental uncertainty about the long-run ecological implications of biodiversity change. They also raise questions about the ethics of depleting a common resource that contains the genetic blueprint for the stock of natural capital available to all future generations. The future effects of species extinction are neither known in a probabilistic sense, nor free of ethical judgements. What may be known are the net benefits to the present generation from exploitation of existing biota under current preferences. But the social opportunity cost of the exploitation of existing biota includes the opportunities forgone or gained by future generations from the resulting change in a biotic resource base that is yet to exist, and under technologies and preferences yet to be determined. It is a problem of decision-making under ignorance about both the physical and the economic implications of current actions.

Part of the problem lies in the irreversibility of change. Errors in the management of global biotic resources cannot, in general, be undone. But irreversibility is not always a source of difficulty. We can no more recapture the services of ecosystems lost through the 'development' of Manhattan in the 17th century, than we can the genetic uniqueness of *didus ineptus* (the dodo) hunted to extinction in the course of the 'development' of Mauritius in the same period. The loss of biodiversity involved in both instances is just as irreversible. But the regret we might now feel at the loss will be very different in the two cases. Biodiversity loss does not always serve the future ill. Indeed, the enormous worldwide growth in material production over the last three centuries is largely based on the specialization of natural resource use, and so on the loss of biodiversity. While it can be argued that many of the future costs of past specialization in the use of biotic resources were consistently ignored, and are only now beginning to be understood, it is also very clear that much biodiversity loss has improved the human condition.

The net result is that we cannot be sure what the current global assault on biodiversity implies for the wellbeing of future generations. Although we are in the midst of an extinction 'spasm' that has prompted massive demands for the preservation of species, it is not at all clear that this is what we should be doing. Indeed, a decision to preserve the biotic *status quo* may very well condemn future generations to progressive impoverishment, especially in the light of the continuing expansion of the global human population. Although growth at the extensive margin in tropical megadiversity zones is the single greatest current cause of species extinction, it may very well be that growth is a necessary condition for the protection of biodiversity in the future. Growth based on extension of the agricultural frontier in Amazonia, Central America or Central Africa is destroying both habitats and the species that those habitats support at an unprecedented rate. But without growth in the personal incomes of the poorest two-thirds of the world's inhabitants, and without a demographic transition that depends on growth in personal incomes, there is little hope of halting the march into the world's remaining forested areas.

Many of the choices to be made in these circumstances are social choices. That is, society cannot abdicate responsibility for the future impact of present decisions by leaving the problem to the mercy of private decisions based on current market signals. The pervasiveness of intertemporal environmental externalities and the equity implications of the intergenerational redistribution of assets it implies, obliges society to make collective decisions about the loss of biotic diversity. Reliance on an incomplete set of current markets will not do. But if society is to make choices that affect future generations, it is important that those choices are sensitive both to the limitations on our understanding of the dynamical behaviour of the biosphere, and to the ethical dimensions of those choices.

I take the ethic that guides the decision process in this case to be defined, in the broadest sense, by spirit of the Brundtland Report (WCED, 1987). This is not the only ethic that links environmental care with the wellbeing of future generations, but it is one that has sufficiently deep roots in the history of social philosophy and a wide enough measure of popular support that it is at least credible. In what follows, therefore, the touchstone for any principle of social choice is whether it satisfies Brundtland in the sense that it is consistent with both meeting the needs of present generations and preserving the opportunities available to future generations. That is, the touchstone for any principle of social choice is whether it is sustainable in the sense of Brundtland.

The chapter reduces the collective decision process into its simplest components, and constructs corresponding principles of collective choice that may be used to test for the sustainability of development in the face of biodiversity loss. The decision problem breaks down, as I have observed elsewhere, into aspects over which the current generation exercises some control, and aspects over which it does not (Perrings, 1991a, 1991b). Confronted with a given set of biotic resources, a given technology and a given preference ordering over the set of all alternatives, the current generation can choose the 'best' outcome in terms of the set of foreseeable opportunity costs. But the opportunities lost by future generations of resource users as a result of a change in the mix of biotic resources depend on the preferences and technologies not now available. The present generation can opt to limit its forward vision, either by truncating the time horizon over which it evaluates the opportunity costs of the options before, or by discounting those costs at a high enough rate. But it is stuck with the responsibility that comes with the fact that present actions do change the opportunities available to all future generations. This, it turns out, is very closely related to an intratemporal problem discussed in the social choice literature – the role of freedom of choice in the ranking of sets of opportunities under incomplete information about preferences (Pattanaik and Xu, 1990; Sen, 1991).

The chapter is divided into five sections. To approach the decision problem, the next section discusses the requirements of a sustainable development process, and the implications of a change in biodiversity for that process. A third section then considers the link between biodiversity, the set of opportunities open to society, and the value of natural and produced capital, and states the principles of social choice that seem to be consistent with sustainability in the sense of Brundtland. A fourth section derives sufficient conditions for the sustainability of development on the basis of these principles, and a final section offers some concluding remarks.

2 DEVELOPMENT, BIODIVERSITY AND OPPORTUNITY

As a first approximation we may take development to be given by any welfare-improving change in the set of opportunities open to society, where the set of opportunities is given by the potential uses to which the available assets may be put. Although development is often approximated by the change in per capita GDP, it is now conventional to ask for a more general index which takes into account measures of the 'quality of life' – educational attainment, nutritional status, access to basic freedoms, spiritual welfare and so on. Pearce and Turner (1990), for example, take development to be given by positive change in any of the components of a vector of the attributes that society values. This would include increases in per capita GDP, but it would also depend on improvements in health and nutritional status, educational achievement, access to resources, the distribution of income and basic freedoms. Such approaches recognize that the market value of consumption may not be a good measure of the welfare: one involving an increase in the value to society of a given set of opportunities, the other involving an expansion in the set of opportunities. Development may be satisfied by any of the following: an expansion in the set of opportunities open to society without reduction in the instrumental or use value of those opportunities; an increase in the instrumental value of the opportunities available to society without reduction in the range of opportunities; or both.

Since a positive rate of change in per capita GDP may be positively correlated with an expansion in the opportunity set, the traditional proxy for development may not be wholly misleading. However, much of what is currently recorded as economic growth – the accelerated mining of non-renewable resources, or increasing defensive expenditures against environmental degradation – is actually evidence of declining future opportunities. Development is clearly not the same as economic growth. Indeed, wherever economic growth has the effect of narrowing the range of opportunities, it may be said to be development-retarding or regressive. Development is accordingly conceptualized as any evolutionary process which extends either or both of the set of opportunities available to society and the instrumental value of those opportunities.

In any given society, and for any given set of opportunities, the alternatives open to society may be ranked according to some preference ordering over those alternatives. There will exist an indirect function which defines the welfare yielded as the best alternative from the set of all alternatives. The relative value of each alternative under this preference ordering lies in the utility or welfare it yields to society: that is, value is instrumental. Using such criteria it is also possible for society to rank distinct sets of opportunities – to judge whether the best outcome in the set of opportunities available today, for example, is better or worse than the best outcome of other sets of opportunities that may be available in the future. In other words, using a set of weights of the sort that lies behind Pearce and Turner's vector of attributes, one generation may compare present and future opportunity sets in terms of the best outcome in each.

The limitation of this comparison lies in the fact that one generation's ranking between distinct sets of opportunities is based on its own preference ordering of the alternatives in each opportunity set. No generation can know the preference ordering that will inform the ranking that another as yet unborn generation might make among the same opportunity sets. What this means is that opportunities will have value to future generations of producers and consumers in ways that cannot be assessed in instrumental terms by the present generation. If opportunity sets are to be ranked in this case, it will have to be on some non-instrumental (ethical) basis.

One basis suggested by the debate since Brundtland is the freedom of choice offered by different opportunity sets, where freedom of choice is equivalent to the range of alternatives in each set. That is, the present generation may discriminate between present and future opportunity sets on the basis of the number of options offered in each set. In the absence of a common preference ordering between generations, it is the range of choice that counts. While the present generation may be certain that development implies more automobiles, tobacco, open heart surgery, theme parks, nuclear power stations and fewer wetlands, tropical moist forests and semi-arid savannas, it is not at all clear that future generations will take the same view. Hence a process which narrows the range of choice open to future generations by locking them in to the combination preferred by the present generation might satisfy a ranking between present and future opportunity sets by the preference ordering of the present generation, but it would violate a ranking in which the range of alternatives in each opportunity set is a factor. That is, while it might satisfy a ranking between present and future opportunity sets on instrumental grounds, it would violate a ranking grounded in the principle of freedom of choice.

Biotic diversity derives its instrumental value to human society in two ways. Specific organisms have properties that make them of direct (actual or potential) use in production or consumption activities. In addition, the mix of organisms and their role in a variety of ecological functions makes them of indirect (actual or potential) use to producers and consumers who depend in some way on those ecological functions. Actual use gives rise to what is normally referred to as use value, while potential use gives rise to what is normally referred to as option, quasi-option or scientific value. The first of these is the value of the option to make use of the resource in the future (Weisbrod, 1964), the second the value of the future information made available through the preservation of a resource (Arrow and Fisher, 1974; Henry, 1974; Fisher and Hanneman, 1983), and the third the value of organisms as scientific resources (Krutilla, 1967).

For a small number of species the direct value of the chemical or physical properties which make them useful as sources of food, drugs, construction materials, clothing and so on is reasonably closely approximated by the market price. For many other species, however, their direct value is known only to a small group of users, usually indigenous to the area from which such species derive, and is not closely approximated by a market price. The biophysical basis of the indirect value of biodiversity is even less well understood, and even less well captured in the market price of species. The basis of the indirect value of species lies in their individual role in food webs (Paine, 1980), in solar fixation, and the regulation of ecosystem processes (Westman, 1990), as well as in the collective contribution of the diversity of genes, genotypes, species and communities to ecosystem functions (Solbrig, 1991). This is, however, an area in which little is now known with certainty. There is also no reason to believe that the indirect value of species is reflected in either the current set of market prices, or the private valuation of species for which there exist no markets. The private valuation of a species is given by the value of the goods and services which the consumer is prepared to forgo by committing the species to some particular use: that is, its opportunity cost to the private user. Since much of the indirect value of a species accrues to agents other than the direct user, and since there exist no markets for the indirect effects of an increase or decrease in most species, that indirect value will be external to the private valuation of the species.

With respect to the non-instrumental value of biodiversity, it is intuitive that the set of opportunities associated with a stock of biotic resources is an increasing function of the diversity of those resources. The genetic diversity of existing biota fixes the range of the properties of existing species which, though not now valuable, may have value under future preferences and technologies. It also fixes the evolutionary potential of species, and so the potential range of valuable properties of future species. Put another way, the genetic diversity of existing biota is what limits the range of alternative uses of future biota to future generations. An increase in diversity, *ceteris paribus*, implies an increase in the opportunity sets available to future generations. Symmetrically, a decrease in diversity, *ceteris paribus*, implies the reverse.

Environmental economists have devoted considerable effort to uncovering the basis of the non-instrumental value of biotic resources. It has been argued at various times to include bequest value (Krutilla, 1967) and the value conferred simply by the existence of a resource (Pearce and Turner, 1990). Both notions come close to capturing the value to current generations of the range of opportunities available to future generations. Neither implies the ranking of opportunities in terms of the preference ordering of the current generation. Weisbrod's option value and Fisher and Hanneman's quasi-option value are both concerned with the potential value of existing biota to existing users, given the current preference ordering. In other words, they are instrumental values.

Mäler (1992) has argued that the instrumental or use values and non-instrumental or non-use values of environmental resources can be accommodated within a single preference relation, providing that it is separable in the two sorts of value. If we are considering some biotic resource, he suggests that if utility can be written as the sum of one function of the resource alone, and a second function which is not additive separable in the same resource and all other goods and services, then the non-use value of the resource is the value associated with the first term, and the use value of the resource is the value associated with the second term. In other words, the non-instrumental value attached to some species by an individual is independent of any use he/she may or may not make of that resource. It is independent, therefore, of any direct value-based preference ordering of the set of all alternatives. Writ large, what this implies is that the value of the mix of species to society can likewise be reflected by a separable function, in which the non-instrumental value of biodiversity is independent of the use that society makes of it. To be consistent with the definition of development adopted here, the non-instrumental value of biodiversity would be constrained to be an increasing function of the number of species. That is, it would be constrained to be an increasing function of the existence of species. It is interesting that authors taking a quasi-theological view on the problem have something of this sort in mind (compare Daly and Cobb, 1989; Blasi and Zamagni (eds), 1991).

3   BIODIVERSITY, NATURAL CAPITAL AND SUSTAINABLE DEVELOPMENT

It is well understood that the definition of (Hicksian) income[1] on which all economic analysis of the sustainability problem is based embodies a notion of sustainability. The maximum flow of benefits from the exploitation of some asset base is defined to be income only if it leaves intact the capacity of that asset base to yield a similar flow of benefits in the future. This implies that true income is maximum sustainable income. It is not a priori clear why Hicksian income should be a goal of policy, though there does exist a social welfare function that generates Hicksian income as an optimal outcome. A Rawlsian or intertemporally egalitarian social welfare function is satisfied only if the level of welfare of successive generations is the same (viewed from the perspective of the first generation) (Solow, 1974; Hartwick, 1977). Most recent treatments of the problem of sustainable development are less restrictive in the form of intertemporal social welfare function assumed, but all require that the welfare successive generations gain from the exploitation of the resource base is at least as great as the welfare of the current generation (compare Turner, 1988; Pearce et al.,1989; Pezzey, 1989; Pearce and Turner, 1990). As one would expect, the two requirements are slightly different in the implications they have for the value of the asset base. Constant welfare requires that the value of the asset base be constant over time, whereas non-declining welfare implies that the value of the asset base be non-declining (Solow, 1986).

To approach the link between development (as it has been defined in this chapter), welfare and the value of the asset base, it will be useful to make these conditions more precise. Let us first define the set of all possible produced and natural assets over the time horizon of interest, T, to be K_T, the number of elements in which, denoted $\#K_T$, is n. That is, there are a maximum of n produced and natural assets available to the economic system over this period. Let us further define the alternative combinations of these n assets by the power set, $\Pi(K_T)$. Any element of $\Pi(K_T)$, $K_i(t) \in \Pi(K_T)$ denotes an opportunity set, the cardinality of which is n at most: that is, $\#K_i(t) \leq n$. This last means that the opportunity sets between which society chooses include some opportunity sets for which the range of assets is narrower than in others. Since biodiversity loss implies a reduction in the range of assets available to society, it also implies a reduction in the cardinality of the corresponding opportunity sets. $K_i(t)$ defines the discounted net benefit (welfare) of the alternatives in the opportunity set evaluated at time t. This is generated by a social preference ordering on K_T that is both reflexive and transitive, and that enables society to rank opportunity sets within $\Pi(K_T)$ and over T. If $K_j(t + s) \geqslant K_i(t)$ the j-th opportunity set at time $t + s$ may be said to offer at least as high a level of welfare as the i-th opportunity set at time t. Hence the criteria of non-declining welfare and non-declining asset value will be satisfied for a society exercising choice over opportunity set i at time t only if $K_j(t + s) \geqslant K_j(t)$ for any i and for all $s \in \{1, ..., T - t\}$.

My interest lies in the significance of biodiversity in the ranking of opportunity sets implied by this relation. More particularly, my interest is in the conditions for one set of opportunities to offer at least as high a level of welfare as another, and in the role of the stock of biotic resources in the satisfaction of those conditions. To characterize the axioms of social choice for this problem, it may be useful to think in terms of three cases: where the only value of assets to society is instrumental, where the only value of assets to society is non-instrumental, and where the value of assets to society has both instrumental and non-instrumental components. The first might be thought to correspond to the case of the hedonistic but sovereign consumer who asks not what he/she can do for the future but what the future has done for him/her. The second might be thought to correspond to the case of the ascetic altruist on his/her deathbed. The third might be thought to correspond to some improbable combination of the two. In breaking down the decision problem into its simplest components, we need to consider the principles corresponding to the instrumental and non-instrumental value of opportunities, and these three cases may make it easier to motivate each principle.

The Instrumental Value of Biotic Resources and the Axioms of Social Choice

If all assets have only instrumental value, it has been shown that where the capital stock includes exhaustible or depletable natural resources, a necessary condition for the value of capital to be non-declining is that the rents deriving from resource depletion should be reinvested in reproducible capital to compensate for the user costs of depletion (Hartwick, 1977, 1978, 1991). This is the Hartwick rule. The intuition behind it is quite clear: if the loss of biotic resources has a social opportunity cost in terms of forgone benefits of future use, this should be compensated by an equivalent gain in produced assets. The net user cost of the depletion of biotic resources should be zero. Sufficiency requires a rather stronger set of conditions, including that there exist substitutes for all biotic resources with instrumental value. That is, the Hartwick rule will be effective in maintaining the use value of the asset base where certain biotic assets are deleted from the list providing that there exist substitutes capable of delivering equally valued services. Similar conditions have been derived for other models of growth with exhaustible resources (compare Kemp and Long, 1984).

I shall consider the physical implications of biodiversity loss later. What is important about these conditions for the non-declining value of the asset base is that if biotic resources are valued for the services they offer under a given set of preferences and technology, then any set of resources yielding the same services will be as valuable. That is, there exists a focus to each opportunity set which enables the decision-maker to rank that opportunity set against others regardless of the particular mix or absolute number of resources in each. The focus is an index of the instrumental value of the opportunity set to society. One way of thinking about the focus of the i-th opportunity set at time t, $f(K_i(t))$, is that it is the dominant element in $K_i(t)$ given the social preference ordering of the alternatives it contains. But this is not the only possibility. If the opportunity set comprised the elements of some ecosystem, for example, its focus might be a particular indicator species. More generally, if the opportunity set were characterized by fundamental uncertainty, its focus would be the outcome with the most power to attract the decision-maker's attention – the focus gain of the opportunity set (compare Katzner, 1986, 1989; Perrings, 1991a).[2]

Since the foci of opportunity sets are a function of social preferences, if there is a change in the composition of the alternatives under some opportunity set that does not affect its focus, that change will be irrelevant to the decision-making process. So, for example, the deletion or addition of a species that has no effect on the instrumental value of the services yielded by some ecological system would be irrelevant to the wellbeing of the society using that ecosystem. This gives rise to the following principle of social choice.

Axiom of focus
A1:   For all $K_j(t + s) \neq K_i(t) \in \Pi(K_T)$ and for all $s \in \{0, ..., T - t\}$, if #K_j $(t + s) =$ #$K_i(t)$, $f(K_j(t + s)) \sim f(K_i(t))$ implies that $K_j(t + s) \sim K_i(t)$.

This says that if society is indifferent ($\sim$) between the foci of any two distinct opportunity sets of equal cardinality, it will be indifferent between the opportunity sets themselves. It implies the irrelevance of socal preferences between alternatives that do not affect the focus of the opportunity sets being compared. If society is to rank a world of automobiles and bears against a world of automobiles and bearskin rugs, for example, and if automobiles are the focus of each set of alternatives, it is irrelevant that society might prefer live bears to dead ones.

A second axiom merely extends this idea. It says that adding or deleting alternatives that are irrelevant to the focus of compared opportunity sets does not change the ranking of those opportunity sets. The axiom corresponding to this is an extension of Bossert et al.'s (1992) weak independence principle, and is named accordingly.

Axiom of weak independence

A2i: For all $K_h \in \Pi(K_T) \backslash (K_j(t+s) \cup K_i(t))$ such that $f(K_j(t+s)) > f(K_h(t+s))$ and $f(K_i(t)) > f(K_h(t))$, $K_j(t+s) > K_i(t)$ implies that $K_j(t+s) \cup K_h(t+s) > K_i(t) \cup K_h(t)$; and

A2ii: For all K_h contained in $(K_j(t+s) \cup K_i(t))$ such that $f(K_j(t+s)) > f(K_h(t+s))$ and $f(K_i(t)) > f(K_h(t))$, $K_j(t+s) > K_i(t)$ implies that $K_j(t+s) \backslash K_h(t+s) > K_i(t) \backslash K_h(t)$

where $>$ implies strict preference. The first of these says that if any set of opportunities, not a subset of the i-th opportunity set at time t or the j-th opportunity set at time $t + s$, is added to these opportunity sets, and if its focus is dominated by the foci of the opportunity sets to which it is being added, then it will not change the ranking of those sets. The second says that if any set of opportunities which is a subset of the i-th opportunity set at time t and the j-th opportunity set at time $t + s$, is deleted from these opportunity sets, and if its focus is dominated by the foci of the opportunity sets from which it has been deleted, then it will not change the ranking of those sets. By this axiom, non-declining welfare and non-declining asset value are both consistent with a change in the number and composition of species.

It follows that there is nothing in an instrumental valuation that privileges the existence of species. At the same time, however, there is nothing that precludes the preservation of species. If there exist no substitutes for some species of indirect value, then the preservation of that species will be required under an instrumental approach. It is the substitutability of species that determines their preservation value. There is certainly a high degree of substitutability between species in terms of their direct instrumental value (think of plants as photosynthesizers, or animals as protein sources). But plants and animals also perform a range of ecological functions of indirect value in which the possibilities for substitution between species is much reduced (think of keystone or critical-link species). In such cases, a change in the balance between the species in an ecosystem, whether or not this involves species deletion, may induce changes in the dynamics of that system that have far-reaching consequences for the ecological services available to society.

Ecosystems typically evolve in a process of discontinuous change, involving both successional and disruptive processes, and driven by a complex set of feedbacks. They are, in other words, typically complex, non-linear, discontinuous, feedback systems. The points of discontinuity in such systems occur around a set of system thresholds, which mark the limits of system resilience. Note that an ecosystem is said to have lost resilience whenever a change in its environment disrupts the system to the extent that its internal organization breaks down. Loss of resilience implies the (generally irreversible) loss of a systems ability to maintain functions in the face of exogenous stress and shock (compare Holling, 1973, 1986).[3] It turns out to be important for the instrumental value of future resources for two reasons. First, loss of resilience implies a qualitative change in the structure and functioning of the system, and so in the nature of ecological services it delivers – the source of its instrumental value to society. Second, even if the qualitative changes in ecological functions caused by loss of resilience are not economically significant, the disruption of an ecological system is frequently associated with a reduction in its biological productivity, and so a quantitative reduction in the ecological services it delivers. For both reasons, maintenance of the resilience of ecosystems delivering instrumentally valued services for which there are no ready substitutes is as necessary to the sustainability of the economic system as the Hartwick rule (Perrings, 1991b; Common and Perrings, 1992).

The link between resilience and biodiversity is very direct. Holling (1986) has argued that resilience is an increasing function of the complexity of ecosystems, where complexity refers both to the number of constituent populations in a system and to the interdependence between them. This implies that the ability of an ecosystem to coevolve with its environment depends on the breadth of evolutionary options open to it. Its resilience, like the riskiness of any portfolio of assets, rises as the diversity of its constituent populations increases. That is, resilience is an increasing function of the size of the opportunity set. In such cases, even an instrumental valuation of natural capital will require maintenance of the size of the opportunity set: maintenance, that is, of species within the thresholds of system resilience. This is reflected in arguments for the protection of some upper bound on the assimilative capacity of the environment to absorb wastes, and some lower bound on the level of biotic stocks that can support sustainable development (Barbier and Markandya, 1990). Indeed, the 'multifunctionality' of biotic resources and the irreversibility change associated with loss of ecosystem resilience have been cited as reasons to set such bounds conservatively (Pearce and Turner, 1990).

The Non-instrumental Value of Biotic Resources and the Axioms of Social Choice

What of the non-instrumental value of biotic resources: the bequest and existence values referred to earlier? How do these enter the collective decision-making process? The Hicks criterion implies that if the welfare of future generations is assessed on the basis of an intertemporal social welfare function rooted in the present, then future generations should be at least as well off as the present generation by the standards of the latter. If all generations could be assumed to share the preference ordering of the present generation, and in the absence of fundamental uncertainty, this condition would be satisfied if, for all $s \in \{1, ..., T-t\}$, there exist reachable $K_j(t+s)$ such that $f(K_j(t+s)) \geqslant f(K_i(t))$, where $f(K_i(t))$ is the focus of the opportunity set currently subject to choice. Put another way, the non-declining welfare and non-declining value conditions will be satisfied if there is a path between opportunity sets such that, given choice of $K_i(t)$, there exist opportunity sets over the whole time horizon which are attainable, and under which society will be at least as well off in instrumental value terms as at time t.

As we have already seen, the non-instrumental value of biotic resources has a number of facets, but a common feature is that the value assigned to species is unrelated to the use currently made of those species. Since an intertemporal comparison of opportunity sets based on instrumental value takes the current preference ordering of society as the yardstick for comparison, it does depend on the use currently made of biotic resources. The problem considered in this section exists because the social preference ordering of future generations over the universal set of alternatives cannot be known. Hence it cannot be assumed that satisfaction of the condition $f(K_j(t+s)) \geq f(K_i(t))$ will ensure that future generations are no worse off than the present generation. What is needed is a criterion that is independent of the specific uses to which biotic resources are now put.

This problem is very similar to the role of freedom of choice addressed in the choice literature by Pattanaik and Xu (1990), Sen (1991), and Bossert et al. (1992). The problem discussed in this literature concerns the ranking of opportunity sets based on considerations of freedom of choice, where freedom of choice is equivalent to the range of options open to the individual, and is given by the number of elements in the opportunity set over which the individual has to choose. Hence if one opportunity set has more elements (more choice) than another, it is said to involve more freedom than the other. The notion that freedom is given by the range of choice is an intuitive one, but there is a difference in the approach to the problem taken by Sen, who argues that preferences are important in defining the areas over which individuals wish to exercise choice, and Pattanaik et al., who argue that freedom is independent of the preferences of the individual. It is the second approach that is relevant in the context of this chapter.

The justification for regarding freedom as independent of preferences (at least in some cases) is illustrated by Bossert et al. (1992) in terms of the following simple example. Suppose that an individual is confronted by two opportunity sets, X and Y, each consisting of only one element. Suppose that the element in X is preferred to that in Y. Clearly X will dominate Y in terms of the indirect utility of the two alternatives. But X and Y both involve exactly the same range of choice – none at all. The individual may be better off in utility terms with X than with Y, but it is not obvious that they are better off in terms of the freedom they enjoy. The problem considered in this chapter is slightly different, but may also be posed in terms of a similar simple example. Suppose that there are no common elements in two opportunity sets, X and Y, available to two individuals, A and B. Suppose further that X has one element, that Y has two elements, and that individual A is indifferent between the two sets. If B's preferences are unknown to A, but A is charged with ranking the two opportunity sets on behalf of B, which set dominates? In this case it is not at all obvious whether X or Y would leave B better off in utility terms, but it is quite clear that Y offers greater freedom of choice.

In the biodiversity problem, future generations are not in a position to determine which out of all possible opportunity sets in $\Pi(K_T)$ they would prefer. They are stuck with an inheritance from the present generation that depends on current use of assets. So, for example, current strategies that involve the widening and deepening of human capital extend the future opportunities. Conversely, current strategies involving the destruction of tropical moist forest narrow future opportunities. The present generation is, in a very important sense, responsible for determining which opportunity sets are available to future generations. Using the social preference ordering of the first generation, it is possible to rank opportunity sets over time in a way that establishes which reachable future opportunity sets have at least as high a (discounted) instrumental value to the present generation as the current opportunity set. But since it cannot know the social preferences of future generations, the present generation cannot determine which of these opportunity sets will yield the greatest instrumental value to future generations. All that it can know is the freedom of choice associated with each opportunity set. Freedom of intergenerational choice accordingly provides a means of ranking opportunity sets that is independent of any ranking that may be obtained from application of the preference orderings of different generations.

Freedom of choice, in this sense, is identical to the cardinality of the opportunity sets, $K_i(t)$. If $\#K_i(t + s) = \#K_i(t)$ then the opportunity sets $K_j(t + s)$ and $K_i(t)$ have the same range of choice. The principle implied by this (analogous to Bossert et al.'s simple monotonicity principle) is reflected in the following axiom:

Axiom of choice
A3:   For all $K_j(t + s) \neq K_i(t) \in \Pi(K_T)$, and for all t, $s \in \{0, ..., T\}$, $\#K_j(t + s) >$ $\#K_i(t)$ and $f(K_j(t + s)) \sim f(K_i(t))$ implies that $K_j(t + s) > K_i(t)$.

If the j-th opportunity set at time $t + s$ offers greater freedom of choice than the i-th opportunity set at time t, and if the foci of each are equally preferred, then it will also offer a higher level of wellbeing. In other words, independent of the time at which it is being assessed, if one opportunity set involves a greater range of opportunities than another which is as valuable in instrumental terms, then it offers a higher level of wellbeing.

Notice that since future opportunities depend on the underlying list of assets, and since the cardinality criterion weights all alternatives associated with a particular list of assets equally, this axiom has a strong preservationist bias in certain cases. If two opportunity sets are compared, each having the same focus, and identical except for the fact that a species which is irrelevant to that focus has been deleted from one, the opportunity set without the deletion will dominate the opportunity set with the deletion. The axiom does not preclude a trade-off between produced and natural capital. But it does imply that any strategy involving the deletion of species will be at least as good as a preservationist strategy only if the number opportunities lost through depletion are more than compensated by the number of opportunities gained through the introduction of produced assets or the expansion of other species. This is very different to the implications of the axiom of focus, by which alternatives that do not affect the focus of an opportunity set are irrelevant to its ranking. By the axiom of focus, the deletion of lesser-valued species and the addition of inferior alternatives have no bearing on the valuation of any opportunity set. By the axiom of choice, they are crucial.

An even more important characteristic of the axiom of choice is that the criterion by which opportunity sets are ranked is independent of time. The cardinality of opportunity sets is not sensitive to the rate of discount. In other words, the axiom of choice insists that a necessary condition for non-declining welfare is a non-declining range of choice. Since the global system is evolutionary, and since there does exist potential for substitution between resources, the axiom of choice does not require the preservation of existing opportunities. But it does require that changes in the set of opportunities should not diminish the freedom of choice open to future generations.

4   THE PRINCIPLES OF SOCIAL CHOICE AND THE SUFFICIENT CONDITIONS FOR THE SUSTAINABILITY OF DEVELOPMENT

Development was defined in Section 2 as a process by which human welfare is improved over time. The process was argued to have two components: the expansion of the set of opportunities open to society, and the growth of the instrumental value of the asset base. It is now evident that the axioms of social choice discussed above are directly related to these components, and may be used to establish the sufficient conditions for the sustainability of the development process.

Before addressing this, however, consider for a moment a slightly different question. What conditions are sufficient to assure not development but the absence of regression – the stationary state. In other words, what conditions are sufficient to assure that welfare is constant over time: the Hicks criterion. By the axiom of choice, for all $K_j(t + s) \neq K_i(t) \in \Pi(K_T)$ and for all $s \in \{0, ..., T - t\}$, if $\#K_j(t + s) = \#K_i(t), f(K_j(t + s)) \sim f(K_i(t))$ implies that $K_j(t + s) \sim K_i(t)$. That is, if distinct opportunity sets offer the same freedom of choice if society is indifferent between the foci of those opportunity sets, then welfare will be constant over time. But what if opportunity sets are not distinct? What if we consider the preservation of the existing set of opportunities? In this case it turns out that the sufficient conditions include what may be interpreted as a very stringent restriction on the social rate of time preference. Consider the following proposition.

P1:   If there exist $K_i(t) \in \Pi(K_T)$ such that $f(K_i(t + s)) \sim f(K_i(t))$ for all $s \in \{1, ..., T - t\}$, and if the relation $\geqslant$ satisfies the axiom of focus, then $K_i(t + s) \sim K_i(t)$.

That is, if there exist opportunity sets such that the foci of those sets are equally preferred when evaluated over the whole time horizon, then those opportunity sets will yield a constant level of welfare. Since the cardinality of $K_i(t)$ is independent of time, $\#K_j(t + s) = \#K_i(t)$ for all $s \in \{1, ..., T - t\}$. Let this cardinality be equal to m, and define the opportunity sets $K_j'(t + s) = K_j(t + s)\backslash f(K_j(t + s))$ and $K_i'(t) = K_i(t)\backslash f(K_i(t))$, both of cardinality $m - 1$. If $f(K_j(t + s)) \sim f(K_i(t))$, then by the axiom of focus, $f(K_j(t + s))\cup K_j'(t + s) \sim f(K_i(t))\cup K_i'(t)$, and hence $K_i(t + s) \sim K_i(t)$ for all $s \in \{1, ..., T - t\}$ which is what we want. But consider what the restriction $f(K_i(t + s)) \sim f(K_i(t))$ implies. Recall that the function $K_i(t)$ discounts the instrumental value of the opportunity set K_i. If the rate of discount is strictly positive then $f(K_i(t)) > f(K_j(t + s))$: present wellbeing will be preferred to future wellbeing. Hence $f(K_i(t + s)) \sim f(K_i(t))$ only if the future benefits of an opportunity set are discounted at the zero rate. So if simple preservation of the set of opportunities is to be consistent with a constant level of welfare, the rate of discount is constrained to be equal to zero.

Sustainable development requires something more than maintenance of the status quo, whether that is conceived in terms of a set of opportunities or a level of welfare. In this case we are interested in the conditions for welfare to be strictly increasing over time. Consider the following propositions:

P2:   If there exist reachable $K_j(t + s)$ such that $\#K_j(t + s) = \#K_i(t)$ and $f(K_j(t + s)) > f(K_i(t))$, and if the relation $\geqslant$ satisfies the axiom of focus, then $K_j(t + s) > K_i(t)$; and

P3:   If there exist reachable $K_j(t + s)$ such that $\#K_j(t + s) > \#K_i(t)$ and $f(K_j(t + s)) \sim f(K_i(t))$, and if the relation $\geqslant$ satisfies the axioms of weak independence and choice, then $K_j(t + s) > K_i(t)$.

The first says that if there exist opportunity sets that are reachable from $K_i(t)$, that offer the same freedom of choice but that have a focus of greater value than $K_i(t)$, then there exists a development path along which welfare will be strictly increasing. The second says that if there exist opportunity sets that are reachable from $K_i(t)$, the foci of which are equally preferred, but that offer greater freedom of choice than $K_i(t)$, then there exists a development path along which welfare will be strictly increasing.

Both are quite intuitive, and can be verified very shortly. First consider the case where $\#K_j(t + s) = \#K_i(t)$ and $f(K_j(t + s)) > f(K_i(t))$. Suppose, as before, that the cardinality of $\#K_j(t + s) = \#K_i(t) = m$, and define the opportunity sets $K_j '(t + s) = K_j(t + s)\backslash f(K_j(t + s))$ and $K_i'(t) = K_i(t)\backslash f(K_i(t))$, both of cardinality $m - 1$. Since $f(K_j(t + s)) > f(K_i(t))$, by the axiom of focus $f(K_j(t + s))\cup K_j'(t + s) > f(K_i(t))\cup K_i'(t)$, and hence $K_j(t + s) > K_i(t)$. The preservation of the range of choice combined with an increase in the value of the focus of successive opportunity sets is sufficient to assure a development path along which welfare will be strictly increasing.

The second case is only a little more complicated. If $\#K_j(t + s) > \#K_i(t)$, and $f(K_j(t + s)) \sim f(K_i(t))$, there exists a set of opportunities, $K_0 = K_j(t + s)\backslash K_i(t)$, which does not contain the focus of either opportunity set. It follows from the axiom of choice that $f(K_j(t + s))\cup K_0 > f(K_i(t))$, and from the axiom of weak independence that $f(K_j(t + s))\cup K_0\cup K_i(t)\backslash f(K_i(t)) > f(K_i(t))\cup K_i(t)\backslash f(K_i(t))$. From P1, $K_j(t + s) \sim f(K_j(t + s))\cup K_0\cup K_i(t)\backslash f(K_i(t))$, hence by transitivity of f, $K_j(t + s) > K_i(t)$. That is, if there exist reachable opportunity sets that offer strictly greater freedom of choice, and have the same the focus as the set $K_i(t)$, there exists a development path that will yield strictly increasing welfare over time.

These propositions help us to think about the sufficient conditions for sustainable development in the case where $\#K_j(t + s) < \#K_i(t)$ and $f(K_j(t + s)) > f(K_i(t))$ (or the opposite). Indeed, something of this kind probably better characterizes reality than conditions of the type indicated in P2 and P3. While the instrumental value of the opportunities available to the present generation may be growing (albeit very slowly during the current recession), the range of options open to future generations is narrowing with the destruction of more and more biotic resources. It is not intuitively obvious what conditions of this sort mean for the sustainability of the development process. In such a case the states, $K_j(t + s)$ and $K_i(t)$ are non-comparable under the axioms of focus, weak independence and choice. Neither instrumental value nor freedom of choice is privileged over the other. Nor is there is any scope for a trade-off between these two factors. In this case, a minimal condition for $K_j(t + s)$ to be part of a sustainable development strategy, is for the opportunity set $K_j(t + s)$ to be augmented by some set, $K_h(t + s)$, equally preferred to the opportunities lost from the current opportunity set, such that $\#(K_j(t + s) \cup K_h(t + s)) = \#K_i(t)$. In particular:

P4:   If there exist reachable $K_j(t + s)$ such that $\#K_j(t + s) < \#K_i(t)$ and $f(K_j(t + s)) > f(K_i(t))$, if there exist $K_i''(t) \sim K_h(t + s) \in \Pi(K_T) \backslash K_j(t + s)$ such that $\#K_i''(t) = \#K_h(t + s) = (\#K_i(t) - \#K_j(t + s))$, and if the relation $>$ satisfies the axioms of focus and weak independence, then $(K_j(t + s) \cup K_h(t + s)) \sim K_i(t)$.

If $\#K_j(t + s) < \#K_i(t)$ and $f(K_j(t + s)) > f(K_i(t))$ there exists an opportunity set $K_i'(t)$ such that $\#K_j(t + s) = \#K_i'(t)$, with $f(K_i(t)) \in K_i'(t)$. By the axiom of weak independence $f(K_j(t + s)) \cup K_i'(t) \backslash f(K_i(t)) > f(K_i(t)) \cup K_i'(t) \backslash f(K_i(t))$, and by the axiom of focus, $f(K_j(t + s)) \cup K_i'(t) \backslash f(K_i(t)) \sim f(K_j(t + s)) \cup K_j(t + s) \backslash f(K_j(t + s))$. It follows that $f(K_j(t + s)) \cup K_i'(t) \backslash f(K_i(t)) \sim K_j(t + s)$, and by transitivity of $>$, $K_j(t + s) > f(K_i(t)) \cup K_i'(t) \backslash f(K_i(t))$. Let $K_i''(t) = K_i(t) \backslash K_i'(t)$. If there exists $K_h(t + s) \sim K_i''(t)$, then by the axiom of focus, $K_j(t + s) \cup K_h(t + s) > f(K_i(t)) \cup K_i'(t) \backslash f(K_i(t)) \cup K_i''(t)$. Hence $K_j(t + s) \cup K_h(t + s) > (K_i(t))$. The proposition states that a sufficient condition for a reachable opportunity set that does not offer the same freedom of choice as the current opportunity set to be on a sustainable path, is for that set to be augmented by a range of choice of equal size and (present) value to that lost from the current opportunity set. If the loss of biotic diversity implies a narrowing of the options open to future generations, even though positive rates of economic growth signal an increase in the instrumental value of opportunities now available, sustainability requires that those options be restored or replaced with options of comparable value.

5   CONCLUSIONS

The burden of these propositions is that any development path will be sustainable if it offers either an increase in the range of choice, holding the discounted instrumental value of the opportunities open to society constant, or an increase in the discounted instrumental value of the opportunities open to society holding the range of choice constant. Current preference is one criterion for non-declining welfare, the range of choice is another. Aspects of the axiom of choice are present in the treatment of natural capital in some existing models of intertemporal resource allocation. It has already been remarked that Mäler (1992) argues that the existence of use and non-use value implies the separability of individual utility functions. I have elsewhere characterized the social optimization problem, in control terms, as one in which society seeks to maximize welfare over a finite period as the sum of an algebraic function of the terminal value of the state variables (bequest or existence value) and an integral function of the state and the control variables (use value); where the state variables are the set of all assets available to society and the control variables are the resource allocations made by society (Perrings, 1991b).[4] Both these and analogous approaches accordingly imply that there exists a set of benefits from natural biotic resources that do not in any way depend on their use in economic processes. But both also retain the notion that current preferences determine the relative non-instrumental value of such resources. Even the most significant recent work on the non-instrumental valuation of collections of different objects requires some structure of preferences to determine the criterion of distance between objects (compare Weitzman, 1991a, 1991b). But the axiom of choice is blind to preferences providing that future opportunity sets are no worse than present opportunity sets under the preference ordering of the present generation, and expansion of opportunities is welfare improving.

The ethical content of the axiom of choice lies in the implication that expansion in the set of choices available to future generations is a benefit to the present generation. In this sense the axiom captures the spirit of Brundtland very well. It insists that a necessary condition for the sustainability of development is that future generations do not forfeit freedom of choice as a result of the activities of the present generation. Hence, if the present generation is committed to the principle of sustainability, it implies that it should accept the responsibility that is the obverse of the right of choice conferred on future generations. It should be said that it is not a right that is necessarily burdensome to the present generation. Bossert et al. (1992) make the point in respect of the role of freedom in individual choice, that if an agent has the power to choose the outcome corresponding to some opportunity set, then he/she cannot lose by adding an alternative to that opportunity set, even if that alternative is strictly worse than existing alternatives. In terms of the biodiversity problem discussed here, an analogous argument is that if the present generation has the power to determine the outcome corresponding to a given opportunity set, it cannot be made worse off by retaining an alternative (some species of plant or animal) that is strictly worse than all other alternatives under the current preference ordering: that is, that has no effect on the focus of the opportunity set.

It is worth underlining the fact that while the axiom of choice does have a preservationist bias in some cases, it does not privilege the preservation of existing opportunities. Sustainable development is incompatible with the maintenance of the status quo. In an evolutionary system, the economic and ethical problems converge in the need to maintain that level of biodiversity which will guarantee the resilience of the ecosystems on which human consumption and production depend. Indeed, this is the central goal of a strategy of biodiversity conservation. It requires neither the preservation of all species, nor the maintenance of the environmental status quo. Where economic activity changes the level or composition of biodiversity, it requires that the opportunities forgone by future generations be compensated, and any change in biotic diversity that affects the flow of ecological services on which this and subsequent generations depend is affected by this principle.

This said, the weight of available evidence suggests that the loss of biotic diversity that so exercised the world's attention at the United Nations Conference on Environment and Development is compromising the interests of future generations precisely because it is narrowing the range of options open to those generations. There is no evidence that any care is being taken to assure that the accelerating destruction of biota by the present generation will not limit the range of choice open to future generations. Indeed, all available evidence indicates just the opposite. Biota are being destroyed to maintain consumption, not to promote investment. Options are being narrowed, not expanded. Perhaps it is unrealistic to expect anything different. Since much of the threat to biodiversity comes from people driven by poverty, one would expect them to be driven by the exigencies of the present. Yet many of the best examples of social protection of the rights of future generations come from societies – the so-called primitive societies – which are poor in terms of material consumption. Admittedly, such societies respect the axiom of choice more through the preservation of options than through the generation of alternatives, but the point is that care for the rights of future generations is not the prerogative of the rich. Something very much like the axiom of choice has informed collective decision-making in a wide range of societies over a long period of time. It may have become lost in the consumption-oriented individualism of many existing societies, but that is merely to demarcate the battleground for those who do worry about the effects of biodiversity loss.

NOTES

1. Hicksian income is defined as the maximum amount that can be spent on consumption in one period without reducing real consumption expenditure in future periods (Hicks, 1946).
2. The concept of focus gain derives from Shackle (1955, 1969). It may be interpreted in this case as the least-surprising outcome of a decision process based on an opportunity set about which there is fundamental uncertainty.
3. More precisely, resilience defines the ability of the system to accommodate the stress imposed by its environment through selection of a different operating point along the same thermodynamic path without undergoing some 'catastrophic' change in organizational structure.
4. The specific problem considered in Perrings (1991b) is as follows:

maximize$_k$

$$J = W[\mathbf{x}(T),T]e^{-\delta T} + \int_0^T Y[\mathbf{x}(t),\mathbf{u}(t),t]e^{-\delta t}dt$$

subject to

$$\backslash O(\mathbf{x},\cdot)(t) = f[\mathbf{x}(t),\mathbf{u}(t),t], \quad 0 \le t \le T,$$
$$g[\mathbf{x}(T), T] = 0$$
$$\mathbf{x}(0) = \mathbf{x}_0,$$

with

$$\mathbf{u}(t) = \mathbf{u}[k, \mathbf{p}(t), t] \quad 0 \le t \le T,$$
$$\mathbf{p}(t) = \mathbf{p}[\mathbf{x}(t),t] \quad 0 \le t \le T,$$

where $\mathbf{x}(t)$ is a vector of state variables (the assets available to society); $\mathbf{u}(t)$ is a vector of control variables (the allocation of resources); $W[\cdot]$ defines the bequest or existence value of assets at the terminal date, and $Y[\cdot]$ defines the use value of those assets during the time horizon of interest. $\mathbf{f}[\cdot]$ defines the equations of motion of the system, and $\mathbf{g}[\cdot]$ a set of terminal boundary conditions (restrictions on the admissible value of assets bequeathed to the next generation). $\mathbf{p}[\cdot]$ is a price vector, and $\mathbf{k}$ a vector of control parameters.

REFERENCES

Arrow, K.J. and Fisher, A.C. (1974), 'Environmental preservation, uncertainty, and irreversibility', *Quarterly Journal of Economics* **88** (2): 312–19.

Barbier, E.B. and Markandya, A. (1990), 'The conditions for achieving environmentally sustainable development', *European Economic Review* **34**: 659–69.

Blasi, P. and Zamagni, S. (eds) (1991), *Man–Environment and Development: Towards a Global Approach*, Nova Spes International Foundation Press, Rome.

Bossert, W., Pattanaik, P.K. and Xu, Y. (1992), 'Ranking opportunity sets: an axiomatic approach', unpublished paper.

Common, M. and Perrings, C. (1992), 'Towards an ecological economics of sustainability', *Ecological Economics* **6**: 7–34.

Daly, H. and Cobb, J.B. (1989), *For the Common Good*, Beacon Press, Boston.

Fisher, A.C. and Hanneman, W.M. (1983), 'Option value and the extinction of species', Working Paper No. 269, Giannini Foundation of Agricultural Economics, University of California, Berkeley.

Hartwick, J.M. (1977), 'Intergenerational equity and the investing of rents from exhaustible resources', *American Economic Review* **66**: 972–4.

Hartwick, J.M. (1978), 'Investing returns from depleting renewable resource stocks and intergenerational equity', *Economics Letters* **1**: 85–8.

Hartwick, J.M. (1991), 'Economic depreciation of mineral stocks and the contribution of El Serafy', World Bank Environment Department, Working Paper No. 4, October.

Henry C. (1974), 'Investment decisions under uncertainty: the irreversibility effect', *American Economic Review* **64**: 1006–12.

Hicks, J.R. (1946), *Value and Capital*, Oxford University Press, Oxford.

Holling, C.S. (1973), 'Resilience and stability of ecological systems', *Annual Review of Ecological Systems* **4**: 1–24.

Holling, C.S. (1986), 'The resilience of terrestrial ecosystems: local surprise and global change', in W.C. Clark and R.E. Munn (eds), *Sustainable Development of the Biosphere*, Cambridge University Press, Cambridge: 292–317.

Katzner, D.W. (1986), 'Potential surprise, potential confirmation and probability', *Journal of Post Keynesian Economics* **9**: 58–78.

Katzner, D.W. (1989), 'The comparative statics of the Shackle–Vickers approach to decision-making in ignorance', in T.B. Fomby and T.K. Seo (eds), *Studies in the Economics of Uncertainty in Honour of Joseph Hadar*, Springer-Verlag, Berlin.

Kemp, M. and Long, N.V. (1984), *Essays in the Economics of Exhaustible Resources*, North-Holland, Amsterdam.

Krutilla, J.V. (1967), 'Conservation reconsidered', *American Economic Review* **57** (4): 778–86.

Mäler, K.-G. (1992), 'Multiple use of environmental resources: the household production function approach', Beijer Discussion Paper No. 4, Beijer Institute, Stockholm.

Paine, R.T. (1980), 'Food webs: linkage interaction strength and community infrastructure', *Journal of Animal Ecology* **49**: 667–85.

Pattanaik, P.K. and Xu, Y. (1990), 'On ranking opportunity sets in terms of freedom of choice', *Recherches Economiques de Louvain* **56**: 383–90.

Pearce, D.W., Markandya, A. and Barbier, E.B. (1989), *Blueprint for a Green Economy*, Earthscan, London.

Pearce, D.W. and Turner, R.K. (1990), *Economics of Natural Resources and the Environment*, Harvester-Wheatsheaf, London.

Perrings C. (1991a), 'Reserved rationality and the precautionary principle: technological change, time and uncertainty in environmental decision-making', in R. Costanza (ed.), *Ecological Economics: The Science and Management of Sustainability*, Columbia University Press, New York: 153–67.

Perrings, C. (1991b), 'Ecological sustainability and environmental control', *Structural Change and Economic Dynamics* **2** (2): 275–95.

Pezzey, J. (1989), 'Economic analysis of sustainable growth and sustainable development', World Bank Environment Department Working Paper No. 15, World Bank, Washington, DC.

Sen, A.K. (1991), 'Welfare, preference and freedom', *Journal of Econometrics* **50**: 15–19.

Shackle, G.L.S. (1955), *Uncertainty in Economics*, Cambridge University Press, Cambridge.

Shackle, G.L.S. (1969), *Decision, Order and Time in Human Affairs*, Cambridge University Press, Cambridge.

Solbrig, O.T. (1991), 'The origin and function of biodiversity', *Environment* **33**: 10.

Solow, R.M. (1974), 'Intergenerational equity and exhaustible resources', *Review of Economic Studies*, Symposium, 29–46.

Solow, R.M. (1986), 'On the intertemporal allocation of natural resources', *Scandinavian Journal of Economics* **88** (1): 141–9.

Turner, R.K. (1988), 'Sustainability, resource conservation and pollution control: an overview', in R.K. Turner (ed.), *Sustainable Environmental Management: Principles and Practice*, Bellhaven Press, London: 1–25.

Weisbrod, B. (1964), 'Collective consumption services of individual consumption goods', *Quarterly Journal of Economics* **77**: 71–7.

Weitzman, M.L. (1991a), 'On diversity', Discussion Paper No. 1553, Harvard Institute of Economic Research, Cambridge, MA.

Weitzman, M.L. (1991b), 'A reduced form approach to maximum likelihood estimation of evolutionary trees', unpublished paper, Harvard Institute of Economic Research, Cambridge, MA.

Westman, W.E. (1990), 'Managing for biodiversity: unresolved science and policy questions', *BioScience* **40**: 26–33.

World Commission on Environment and Development (WCED) (1987), *Our Common Future*, Oxford University Press, Oxford.

Postscript: ecology, economics and ecological economics

1 INTRODUCTION

Kenneth Boulding was given to the composition of verse at odd moments. During a short break in a meeting on the research agenda for ecological economics in Washington, DC he penned the following lines:

> We need to make no apology
> For thinking about world ecology
> For mere economics
> Is stuff for the comics
> Unless we can live with biology.

The question I wish to consider here is how ecology and economics are combined in the approach now referred to as ecological economics. The evolution of theory in the sciences is generally driven by the existence of a problem or set of problems which existing science is ill-adapted to address. This is the case with ecological economics. The set of problems that have stimulated the ecological–economics approach are all linked to two common perceptions. The first is that the dynamics of economic systems are not independent of the dynamics of the ecological systems that constitute their environment. While there are different degrees of interdependence between economic and ecological systems, it is increasingly hard to find either ecological processes that are not impacted by economic activities, or economic activities that are not just mediated but constrained by the natural environment. And the dynamics of both ecological and economic systems reflect this interdependence. The second common perception is that as economies grow relative to their environment, this affects the dynamics of both. More particularly, as the dynamics of the jointly-determined system become increasingly discontinuous, the closer economic systems get to the limits of the 'assimilative' and 'carrying' capacity of the environment.

Neither joint system dynamics nor threshold effects have been adequately addressed by existing economic and ecological theory, and yet the interdependence of ecological and economic systems has never been more

232

apparent. Ecologists interested in the evolution of stressed ecosystems and economists interested in the development of economies operating close to the limits of assimilative capacity of their environment have not been able to appeal to a body of research in their respective disciplines which satisfactorily addresses this problem. In part this is because the problem has just not been posed before. But I believe that it is also because both disciplines have, over the last one hundred years at least, developed a very strong focus on the equilibrium properties of the systems under study, and that this has precluded many questions about the behaviour of those systems away from equilibrium.

It is worth remarking that essentially the same general problem about the time-behaviour of disequilibrium systems is stimulating analogous developments in both the natural and social sciences other than ecology and economics. Nor is ecological economics the only response within economics. Developments in the theory of non-linear economic dynamics, endogenous growth, technical change and preferences share a similar stimulus. The emergence of ecological economics can be seen to be part of a widespread reappraisal of the theory of complex dynamical systems. It is directly concerned with the implications of such system dynamics for the economic process, the role of the price system, and the allocation of non-marketed environmental resources. We shall argue that these implications are far-reaching: affecting not only the construction of the economic problem, but also the valuation of environmental resources, and the identification of policy options and instruments. It is, however, worth re-emphasizing that while the specific intellectual motivation of ecological economics is the perception that economic models need to be able to accommodate the complex time-behaviour of stressed ecological systems, a similar general motivation lies behind several other concurrent developments in economics.

2   THERMODYNAMIC AND BIOECONOMIC MODELS OF ECONOMY–ENVIRONMENT INTERACTIONS

There are two closely related themes in the intellectual development of ecological economics. The first is reflected in work on the structure of joint ecological–economic systems. It is reflected both in changes in the description of the physical dimensions of the joint system, and in the treatment of externality in the economic representation of that system. The second is reflected in work on the evolution of ecological–economic interactions, and on the significance of the relative scale of the economy and its environment for the evolutionary process. Historically, they have been carried in two distinct literatures: one on the thermodynamics of the physical system, and the other on the population dynamics of the biological system. Both literatures have called on the mathematics of non-linear systems.

In the first literature are a number of contributions whose primary concern has been that the physical relations underlying most economic models are incompatible with the laws of thermodynamics (Boulding, 1966; Georgescu-Roegen, 1971; Odum, 1971; Daly, 1973; Ayres and Nair, 1984). Two conclusions of relevance to the development of ecological economics were drawn from the early thermodynamic models. First, since perfect recycling of resources is precluded on thermodynamic grounds, the conservation of mass condition was taken to imply that the potential for growth of output is finite (Georgescu-Roegen, 1971, 1973). Second, since the conservation of mass condition ensures the generation of residual materials in any 'productive' process implying that this is increasing function of the growth of the economic system, and since residuals are seldom inert, higher rates of growth imply higher rates of change in the processes of the environment (Ayres 1972, 1978; Perrings, 1987). Indeed, the relation between the scale of economic activity and the nature of change in ecological systems is one of the *differentia specifica* of ecological economics. Daly has persistently argued both that economic growth beyond the 'carrying capacity' of the biosphere will lead to environmental collapse, and that there exists no feedback mechanism to ensure that an unregulated market economy will not exceed the carrying capacity of its environment (see, for example, Daly, 1968, 1973, 1991). The strong support he has received from biologists may be identified as one of the origins of ecological economics (Vitousek et al., 1986; Costanza, 1989; Ehrlich, 1992).

The most telling legacy of the early thermodynamic models has been in the development of an approach to dynamical ecological–economic systems in which the equilibrium focus of both traditional economics and traditional ecology has been displaced by a focus on multiple equilibria, and the traverse between them. This has been a consequence of developments outside economics, including aspects of the work of physicists on far-from-equilibrium systems and of mathematicians on complex dynamical systems. It is a direct result of this that ecological economics focuses on sustainability as distinct from equilibrium.

Aside from the thermodynamic models, the most important foundation of ecological-economics is to be found in bioeconomics – coincidentally one of the cornerstones of orthodox renewable resource economics. Bioeconomics is itself grounded in what Lotka termed biophysical economics. The difficulty with bioeconomic and biophysical economic models from an ecological–economics perspective is that while they do incorporate the dynamics of the environmental resources being exploited, they ignore almost all important feedback effects between the economic process and the ecological system from which those resources derive. By depleting one population, it is possible to disrupt a wide range of economically important ecological services including, for example, the maintenance of the composition of the atmosphere, amelioration of climate, operation of the hydrological cycle including flood controls and drinking water supply, waste assimilation, recycling of nutrients, generation of soils, pollination of crops, provision of food, as well as the maintenance of particular species and landscapes (Ehrlich and Mooney, 1983; Ehrlich and Ehrlich, 1992). It is obvious, for example, that timber harvest can affect the hydrology on which timber production depends (indeed, this is sometimes taken into account in forestry models), but there are many other less obvious feedbacks that have not been taken into account.

What ecological economics adds to bioeconomics are the insights to be had from recent developments in community and systems ecology. There are two sets of results that are important to the development of ecological economics. One concerns the link between the spatial and temporal structure of co-evolutionary hierarchical systems. The other concerns the link between the resilience and evolution of ecosystems. On the first of these, it has been shown that the dynamics of fitness 'landscapes' reflects their interdependence: adaptive moves by one organism deform the landscapes of those organisms with which it interacts. Moreover, small adaptive moves may trigger 'avalanches' of co-evolutionary response (Kauffman and Johnsen, 1991). It is not yet clear how the transition between orderly and chaotic states in ecosystems is related to changes in scale as it is, for example, in turbulent fluid flows. There is, however, reason to believe that the spread of the effects of perturbation depends on spatial structure of ecosystems and that for terrestrial systems, at least, ecosystem dynamics are scale dependent.

The second set of results focuses on the link between resilience, discontinuous change and the evolution of ecosystems, where ecosystem resilience is a measure of the ability of the system to absorb stress or shock without losing its self-organization, that is, *sensu* Holling (1973, 1986). Interestingly, the mathematics of non-linear dynamical systems were applied in biology (and especially in ecology) well before they were applied in economics. Examples of mathematical and Riemann–Hugonoit catastrophe had been observed in spruce budworm outbreaks in boreal forests in the 1970s (Jones, 1975). Later work on dryland systems explored the role of catastrophe in the dynamics and management of the system (Walker and Noy-Meir, 1982; Walker, 1988; Westoby et al., 1989). It also demonstrated the propensity for stressed systems to flip from one thermodynamic branch to another: grazing pressure beyond some critical threshold, for example, induced a non-reversionary switch in vegetation type (Perrings and Walker, 1995). The framework within which such dynamics have been analysed is the 'four box' model developed by Holling (1973, 1986, 1987) in which the dynamics of ecosystems is described in terms of the sequential interaction between four system functions. These are exploitation (processes responsible for rapid colonization of disturbed ecosystems);

conservation (the accumulation of energy and biomass); creative destruction (abrupt change caused by external disturbance which releases energy and matter); and reorganization (mobilization of matter for the next exploitative phase). Reorganization may be associated with a new cycle involving the same structure, or a switch to a completely different structure.

By now, the parallels between these theoretical developments in ecology and economics are striking. Economists have recently become interested in the dynamics of complex non-linear systems (Anderson et al., 1988; Brock and Malliaris, 1989; Puu, 1989; Goodwin, 1990; Arthur, 1992; Benhabib (ed.), 1992). Indeed, there are now numerous applications of non-linear dynamics in economics, particularly to problems in finance where there is an interest in endogenizing fluctuations (see, for example Scheinkman and LeBaron, 1989; Hommes, 1991; Granger and Terasvirta, 1992). What is particularly interesting is that the approach is rationalized in terms of the recognition that complex non-linearity is now generally accepted as a useful way of approaching the description of real phenomena in the natural sciences, and especially in epidemiology, biology and ecology (Brock, 1992).

To summarize, there appear to be three distinct but related strands in the development of ecological economic models. The first is to be found in the realization not just that the economy and its environment are jointly-determined systems, but that the scale of economic activity is such that this matters. The second is to be found in the perception that the dynamics of the jointly-determined system are characterized by discontinuous change around critical threshold values both for biotic and abiotic resources, and for ecosystem functions. The third lies in the recognition that the stability of the jointly-determined system depends less on the stability of individual resources than on the resilience of the system – or the ability of the system to maintain its self-organization in the face of stress and shock. Each of these strands affects the valuation of environmental resources. Each also affects the nature of the policy response, both in terms of the target of that response and the instruments required to meet them.

3   THE *DIFFERENTIA SPECIFICA* OF ECOLOGICAL ECONOMICS

Let me take the first two of these strands together: scale and discontinuity. The implications of ignoring the ecological effects of economic activity would be less significant in a world with a smaller human population and consequential level of economic activity than currently exists. So long as the depletion of ecological resources and the generation of ecologically significant waste lies inside the carrying and assimilative capacity of the system, local effects tend to remain local and the dynamics of ecological systems tend to remain predictable. It is a widespread perception in the ecological–economics literature, however, that at current rates of population growth and consequential rates of growth in the demand for ecological services, we are in an era of novel co-evolution of ecological–economic systems. It is also a widespread perception that this has important consequences for both the research and the policy agendas.

Critical ecological thresholds are defined in terms of the level or density of ecosystem components. For example, thresholds in predator–prey systems are defined in terms of the relative density of each. If the relative density of one exceeds the critical threshold, the system will frequently experience discontinuous and unpredictable change. The perception that the dynamics of jointly-determined systems may be discontinuous around ecological thresholds is a characteristic feature of ecological economics. It differs from the Marshallian view that characterizes much research in economics (including environmental economics) though it is consistent with the growing literature in economics on non-linear system dynamics referred to earlier. There already exist numerous examples of discontinuous ecological change as a result of a gradual build-up of economic pressure. In many such cases large-scale modifications of ecosystems are the result of many local and apparently disconnected activities.

The connection is often very indirect indeed. Consider, for example, the link between migratory insectivorous bird populations and changes in insect (budworm) outbreaks in boreal regions of Canada. A set of thirty-five species of insectivorous birds is one of the controlling factors of the forest renewal patterns produced by budworm population cycles. Simulations based on long-term studies of budworm/forest systems dynamics indicate that if the bird populations were reduced by about 75 per cent the whole pattern of boreal forest renewal would be fundamentally altered, and the whole of the forest-based economy disrupted (Holling et al., 1995). A large proportion of these bird species spend the winter in Central America and parts of South America, where they are adversely affected by a range of incremental changes in land use (involving habitat destruction) and agricultural technology (involving the use of pesticides and herbicides). Radar images of flights of migratory birds across the Gulf of Mexico over a twenty-year period reveal that the frequency of trans-Gulf flights has already declined by almost 50 per cent, approaching the range of uncertainty in Holling's simulations. Hence, Canadian boreal forests and the economic activities based on those forests, appear to be threatened in a very non-incremental way by human population growth in Central and South America and the land-use pressures to which it has given rise.

One very general effect of human population and economic growth has been a general increase in the interconnectedness of ecological and economic systems in time and space (Costanza et al., 1993). The spatial span of ecological and economic connections has increased, inducing a rise in problems of transboundary externality. This is argued to have moved societies and natural ecosystems into such novel and unfamiliar territory that the future evolution of ecosystems has become much more unpredictable than it was for earlier generations. The image of ecosystem development that is informing ecological economics is much closer to the four box or life-cycle model developed by Holling, which identifies the point at which systems are most vulnerable to change to be precisely the climax state.

The third strand in the development of the approach follows directly, and concerns the nature and stability of equilibrium. It is this which explains the natural focus of ecological economics on sustainability (as distinct from Walrasian equilibrium). Recall that resilience is defined to mean the propensity of a system to retain its organizational structure following perturbation, and so refers to the stability of the structure rather than to the component populations of an ecological system (Holling, 1973, 1986; Common and Perrings, 1992). It is a measure of the sensitivity to disturbance of the 'integrity' or 'health' of the system. There is a natural link between sustainability and resilience. Sustainability, as a concept, has been given a bewildering variety of definitions which it is beyond the scope of this chapter to review. But as far as I am aware there is no definition of sustainability that does not imply maintenance of the productive potential of the asset base. System resilience is a measure of the robustness of that potential in the face of the stress induced by economic activity. If the resilience of the system can be protected, its sustainability can, at the same time, be assured.

The problem for economic policy lies in the fact that market prices do not indicate whether a system is approaching the limits of system resilience. This is due partly to the structure of property rights and other institutions, partly to our lack of understanding of ecosystem dynamics, and partly to the public good nature of many environmental resources. All of these factors contribute to the inefficiency of the current allocation of resources. Indeed, a great deal of environmental degradation can be shown to be inefficient: a consequence of the fact that individual resource users confront private costs that differ from the social costs of resource use. But it is important to note that while there is a very strong argument for improving the efficiency of resource allocation by addressing these factors, it turns out that efficiency in the allocation of resources is neither a necessary nor a sufficient condition for the sustainability of resource use (Common and Perrings, 1992). Indeed, historically, many ecological–economic systems that have been extremely long-lived have been grossly inefficient by conventional criteria.

4 THE PROBLEM OF BIODIVERSITY LOSS

To see how this combination of economics and ecology influences one's perception of the problem of environmental degradation, consider the case of biodiversity loss. Some years ago Paul Ehrlich warned that 'extrapolation of current trends in the reduction of (biological) diversity implies a denouement for civilization within the next 100 years comparable to a nuclear winter' (Ehrlich, 1988). Not all biologists share Ehrlich's apocalyptic view, but all agree that species depletion and habitat conversion both have an opportunity cost in terms of forgone ecological services, and that the potential exists for this loss to be 'catastrophic'.

The question I wish to pose in the light of my earlier remarks is what are the costs of biodiversity loss, and how should they be taken into account in the decision-making process? Biologists are generally suspicious of economic approaches to this issue, and the roots of their suspicion lie deep. More than twenty years ago, when the economics profession was confronted by the similarly apocalyptic vision of the Club of Rome report (*The Limits to Growth*) it had responded with ridicule, arguing that the world would never run out of resources for the very simple reason that as the prices of increasingly scarce resources would rise, users would switch to alternatives. Since then, those who made common cause with the Club of Rome have had to live with Wilfred Beckerman's (1974) ringing denunciation of their 'middle class obsession with ... the environment', while marking the deterioration in one indicator of environmental stress after another. Most now appreciate, as Beckerman pointed out, that the negative feedback effects of the price system may have a role to play in the conservation of biological resources, but few accept that prices are 'sufficient' indicators of the state of the environment.

How does an ecological–economics approach change our understanding of the problem of biodiversity loss? The first point to make is that the focus of analysis itself changes from species and habitats, and from charismatic species and habitats in particular, to ecosystems. From an ecological–economics perspective, the main ecological consequences of biodiversity loss, and so the main motivation for biodiversity conservation, turn out to be related less to the loss of genetic material than to the role of diversity in protecting the resilience of ecological systems (Perrings et al. (eds), 1994; Perrings et al. (eds), 1995).

Humanity benefits from a variety of ecological services (including life-support services) that are underwritten by a small number of key structuring processes. Each of these processes is mediated – for given environmental conditions – by some set of species. These are the drivers of the system. Many others play a passive role. They are passengers. However, if the environmental conditions change, the drivers often take a back seat and the passengers come to the fore. Biodiversity ensures that the system can continue to function as environmental conditions change. And since the major effect of continued economic growth is change in environmental conditions, this is an important consideration. The value of biodiversity does not lie so much in our willingness to preserve charismatic species or habitats; it lies in the insurance biodiversity provides against the loss of ecological services, including life-support services.

To see what this means for the economics of conservation, it is useful to distinguish between the value organisms have to individual users (their private value), and the value they have to society in general (their social value). Private value corresponds to the properties of organisms which make them of direct use in satisfying consumption or production needs. This is the value that informs the decisions of individual resource users. It is generally given by the market price of those resources and is reasonably well known. Social value corresponds to the direct and indirect services provided by organisms to all members of society. It includes all those effects which are external to the individual resource user's decisions, and is much less well known. The problem identified by the biologists, if only implicitly, is that the private value of resources is such that individuals have a positive incentive to exploit biological resources beyond the socially optimal level – the level that corresponds to the social value of those resources. *Either* resource users disregard the effect that their actions have on the wellbeing of others and are empowered to do so by, for example, the structure of laws, property rights, social conventions and so on, *or* resource users may be ignorant about the effect of their activities on others.

The biophysical basis of the direct value of organisms in consumption which makes them useful to individual consumers is much better understood than the biophysical basis of their indirect value which makes them useful to society at large. It is known that the indirect value of species varies. Some subgroups, the 'keystone species', have stronger feeding interactions with each other than with the larger food web (Paine, 1980). Others, the 'critical-link species' often found among decomposer micro-organisms, play a particularly important role in ecosystem functions (Westman, 1990). But it is still not yet clear how the mix of organisms influences ecosystem function (compare Solbrig, 1991). What is known is that since ecological systems are not globally stable, their perturbation beyond some ill-defined limit may induce change in the basic self-organization of the system. In terms of the biodiversity problem, deletion of one species may be 'catastrophic' in the effect it has on the organization of the ecological system.

The economic problem derives from the fact that the ecological component of the system is not observable through the price mechanism, and so is not controllable through that mechanism either (Perrings et al., 1992). The social value of the use of environmental resources is not knowable, even in a probabilistic sense, and so cannot guide environmental policy. Best practice, in these circumstances, is to 'stabilize' the ecological component of the system (Perrings, 1991). A stabilized system might still experience complex periodic or quasi-periodic motion, but its fundamental structure – its self-organization – would remain intact. It will not be surprising that stabilization and protection of ecosystem resilience are one and the same.

Ecological stabilization implies that the allocation of economic resources is physically bounded. Indeed, this turns out to be a major implication of an ecological–economics approach. In the case of biodiversity loss, since prices are imperfect observers of the ecological system for reasons already outlined, the depletion of species or ecosystem types will not necessarily be reflected by a rise in their prices. The price mechanism may not be conservative. Nor is there any reason to believe that the social opportunity cost of biodiversity loss will be knowable, *ex ante*. There is, therefore, no reason to believe that governments will be able to align prices with the social opportunity cost of resource use through the use of the tax system, and so no reason to believe that the economic overexploitation of biological resources can be corrected in this way. Ecological stabilization requires a different approach.

5   BIODIVERSITY CONSERVATION: THE POLICY IMPLICATIONS

The first point to make is that 'biodiversity conservation' is not the same as 'biodiversity preservation'. There is little advantage in trying to stop an evolutionary system in its tracks, and none at all in assuming that the existing mix of species is optimal. Many gains in productivity have historically been the result of specialization in production which is diversity reducing, and there is no reason to believe that this will cease to be the case in the future. At the same time, we need to be sensitive to the potential loss in future opportunities that is associated with species depletion or extinction. Biodiversity conservation implies the maintenance of that mix of organisms, communities, species and ecosystems which will underpin the resilience of the ecological–economic system.

While there is some scope for centralized (public sector) conservation or restoration projects, it is clear that conservation will be a lost cause unless individual resource users see it to be in their interests. The immediate causes of excessive biodiversity loss are *either* direct depletion through harvesting, hunting and fishing *or* habitat conversion – land-use change. The underlying causes are to be found in the structure of incentives which ensure that excessive biodiversity loss is privately profitable. Policies to redress the problem need to deal with the underlying causes. These include policies to remove the range of explicit or implicit subsidies that currently exist on the use of biological resources, of which producer subsidies in agriculture and resource subsidies underwritten by the structure of property rights (open access common property) are the most obvious (McNeely, 1988; Munasinghe, 1993; Perrings et al. (eds), 1994).

It is, however, important to emphasize that biodiversity conservation and restoration requires much more than just 'getting the prices right'. To be sure, there are potential gains in efficiency to be had in correcting obvious distortions in the price system and in allocating property rights – including intellectual property rights – in biological resources that are currently subject to unregulated access. But the allocation of property rights and the liberalization of markets are not panaceas. Both may improve the efficiency with which biological resources are allocated, but neither can ensure the alignment of private and social costs.

Indeed, the fact that biodiversity loss imposes costs on future generations that are unknown and unknowable is what puts the problem beyond the reach of conventional decision theory. To protect the interests of future generations requires maintenance of the resilience of the system, which means keeping it within the threshold of resilience. This is the region within which the system is most predictable, and so most controllable. But to keep within the threshold of resilience it is necessary to bound economic activity, and if the bounds are not to be unduly conservative (and so to impose unduly high costs on society) they should be sensitive to changes in both economic and ecological systems. What is needed, in other words, is a set of ecologically and economically sensitive 'safe minimum standards' (Bishop, 1993). Harvesting limits or seasons are well-established examples of species-specific standards, but if such standards are to regulate change in the mix of organisms then they need to apply either to all species having direct value in some habitat, or to the habitat itself.

It should be clear that, in one sense at least, an ecological–economics approach to the conservation and restoration of biological resources is no different to a standard economic approach. It is still concerned with standard issues of efficiency and equity in the allocation of resources; it is still reliant on prices as the main allocative mechanism; and it still addresses the problems raised by open access common property resources, and public goods. But in the face of the fundamental uncertainty associated with complex and discontinuous system dynamics, an ecological–economics approach leads us to fix the boundaries of human behaviour in a way that is anathema to many. If our understanding of ecosystem dynamics tells us that a particular pattern of economic growth is propelling the system towards a threshold that has never before been crossed, then an ecological–economics approach suggests that we hold back unless the act can be conducted in an experimental way, that is, unless its consequences can be bounded. It supports – indeed it justifies – application of the precautionary principle. We do not know if Ehrlich is right that current trends in the loss of biological diversity are propelling us towards a threshold that marks a denouement for civilization, but it would be foolhardy to find out the hard way.

6   CONCLUDING REMARKS

To conclude, let me come back to my starting point, Kenneth Boulding and his doggerel. I have argued that the main motivation for the ecological–economics approach has been the realization that economic and ecological systems are inextricably linked, that the joint system is fundamentally non-linear – indeed that it is riddled with threshold effects, and that the greater the demands made by the economic system on the ecological system, the greater the likelihood that we will encounter threshold effects of consequence. These are not, I believe, wildly improbable statements. Nor is the approach a wildly improbable approach. Herman Daly once observed that when it gets to the point when everything of consequence is external to one's model of the world, one had better change the model. It has taken people who are idiosyncratic – such as Daly and Boulding – to set us out in a new direction, but others much closer to the mainstream of economics and ecology are now raising the same questions. They might still not agree with Boulding that 'mere economics is stuff for the comics', but they are now addressing the very real problems he was asking us to consider.

REFERENCES

Anderson, P., Arrow K. and Pines D. (1988), *The Economy as an Evolving Complex System*, Santa Fe Institute Studies in the Sciences of Complexity V, Addison-Wesley, Redwood City, CA.

Arthur, B. (1992), *On Learning and Adaptation in the Economy*, Food Research Institute, Stanford University, Stanford.

Ayres, R.U. (1972), 'A materials–process product model', in A.V. Kneese and B.T. Bower (eds), *Environmental Quality Analysis*, Johns Hopkins University Press, Baltimore: 35–67.

Ayres, R.U. (1978), *Resources, Environment and Economics: Applications of the Materials/Energy Balance Principle*, John Wiley, New York.

Ayres, R.U. and Nair, I. (1984), 'Thermodynamics and economics', *Physics Today* **37**: 62–71.

Beckerman, W. (1974), *In Defence of Economic Growth*, Jonathan Cape, London.

Benhabib, J. (ed.) (1992), *Cycles and Chaos in Economic Equilibrium*, Princeton University Press, Princeton, NJ.

Bishop, R.C. (1993), 'Economic efficiency, sustainability and biodiversity', *Ambio* **22** (2–3): 69–73.

Boulding, K.E. (1966), 'The economics of the coming spaceship earth', in H. Jarrett (ed.), *Environmental Quality in a Growing Economy*, RFF/Johns Hopkins University Press, Baltimore: 3–14.

Brock, W.A. (1992), 'Pathways to randomness in the economy: emergent nonlinearity and chaos in economics and finance', SSRI Working Paper, University of Wisconsin–Madison.

Brock, W.A. and Malliaris, A.G. (1989), *Differential Equations, Stability and Chaos in Dynamic Economics*, North-Holland, Amsterdam.

Common, M. and Perrings, C. (1992), 'Towards an ecological economics of sustainability', *Ecological Economics* **6**: 7–34.

Costanza, R. (1989), 'What is ecological economics?', *Ecological Economics* **1**: 1–12.

Costanza, R., Kemp, W.M. and Boynton, W.R. (1993), 'Predictability, scale, and biodiversity, in coastal and estuarine ecosystems: implications for management', *Ambio* **22**: 88–96.

Cumberland, J.H. (1966), 'A regional inter-industry model for analysis of development objectives', *Regional Science Association Papers* **17**: 65–94.

Daly, H.E. (1968), 'On economics as a life science', *Journal of Political Economy* **76**: 392–406.

Daly, H.E. (1973), 'The steady state economy: toward a political economy of biophysical equilibrium and moral growth', in H.E. Daly (ed.), *Toward a Steady State Economy*, W.H. Freeman, San Francisco: 149–74.

Daly, H.E. (1991), 'Ecological economics and sustainable development: from concept to policy', Environment Department Divisional Working Paper No. 24, World Bank Environment Department, Washington, DC.

Ehrlich, P.R. (1988), 'The loss of diversity: causes and consequences', in E.O. Wilson (ed.), *Biodiversity*, National Academy Press, Washington, DC: 21–7.

Ehrlich, P.R. (1992), 'Ecological economics and the carrying capacity of earth', in A.M. Jansson, C. Folke, R. Costanza and M. Hammer (eds.), *Investing in Natural Capital, The Ecological Economic Approach to Sustainability*, Island Press, Washington, DC: 38–56.

Ehrlich, P.R. and Ehrlich, A.H. (1992), 'The value of biodiversity', *Ambio* **21**: 219–26.

Ehrlich, P.R. and Mooney, H.A. (1983), 'Extinction, substitution, and ecosystem services', *BioScience* **33**: 248–54.

Georgescu-Roegen, N. (1971), *The Entropy Law and the Economic Process*, Harvard University Press, Cambridge, MA.

Georgescu-Roegen, N. (1973), 'The entropy law and the economic problem', in H. Daly (ed.), *Toward A Steady State Economy*, W.H. Freeman, San Francisco: 37–49.

Goodwin, R.M. (1990), *Chaotic Economic Dynamics*, Clarendon, Oxford.

Granger, C. and Terasvirta, T. (1992), *Modeling Dynamic Nonlinear Relationships*, Oxford University Press, Oxford.

Holling, C.S. (1973), 'Resilience and stability of ecological systems', *Annual Review of Ecological Systems* **4**: 1–24.

Holling, C.S. (1986), 'The resilience of terrestrial ecosystems: local surprise and global change', in W.C. Clark and R.E. Munn (eds), *Sustainable Development of the Biosphere*, Cambridge University Press, Cambridge: 292–317.

Holling, C.S. (1987), 'Simplifying the complex: the paradigms of ecological function and structure', *European Journal of Operational Research* **30**: 139–46.

Holling, C.S., Schindler, D.W., Walker, B.W. and Roughgarden, J. (1995), 'Biodiversity in the functioning of ecosystems', in Perrings et al. (eds): 44–83.

Hommes, C. (1991), *Chaotic Dynamics in Economic Models: Some Simple Case Studies*, Wolters-Noordhoff, Groningen.

Jones, D.D. (1975), 'The applications of catastrophe theory to ecological systems', in G.S. Innes (ed.), *New directions in the analysis of ecological systems*, Simulation Councils, La Jolla, CA.

Kauffman, S.A. and Johnsen, S. (1991), 'Coevolution to the edge of chaos: coupled fitness landscapes, poised states, and coevolutionary avalanches', *Journal of Theoretical Biology* **149**: 467–505.

McNeely, J. (1988), *The Economics of Biological Diversity*, IUCN, Gland.

Munasinghe, M. (1993), 'Environmental economics and biodiversity management in developing countries', *Ambio* **22** (2–3): 126–35.

Odum, H.T. (1971), *Environment, Power and Society*, Wiley, New York.

Paine R.T. (1980), 'Food webs: linkage interaction strength and community infrastructure', *Journal of Animal Ecology* **49**: 667–85.

Perrings, C. (1987), *Economy and Environment: A Theoretical Essay on the Interdependence of Economic and Environmental Systems*, Cambridge University Press, Cambridge.

Perrings, C. (1991), 'Ecological sustainability and environmental control', *Structural Change and Economic Dynamics* **2** (2): 275–95.

Perrings, C., Folke, C. and Mäler, K.-G. (1992), 'The ecology and economics of biodiversity loss: the research agenda', *Ambio* **30**: 201–11.

Perrings, C. and Walker, B. (1995), 'Biodiversity and the economics of discontinuous change in semi-arid rangelands', in Perrings et al. (eds), *Biological Diversity: Economic and Ecological Issues*, Cambridge University Press, New York.

Perrings, C., Mäler, K.-G., Folke, C., Holling, C.S. and Jansson, B.O. (eds) (1994), *Biodiversity Conservation: Problems and Policies*, Kluwer Academic Press, Dordrecht.

Perrings, C., Mäler, K.-G., Folke, C., Holling, C.S. and Jansson, B.O. (eds) (1995), *Biodiversity Loss: Ecological and Economic Issues*, Cambridge University Press, Cambridge.

Puu, T. (1989), *Non-Linear Economic Dynamics*, Springer-Verlag, Berlin.

Scheinkman, J. and LeBaron, B. (1989), 'Nonlinear Dynamics and Stock Returns', *Journal of Business* **62**: 311–37.

Solbrig, O.T. (1991), 'The origin and function of biodiversity', *Environment* **33**: 10–23.

Vitousek, P., Ehrlich, P., Ehrlich, A. and Matson, P.A. (1986), 'Human appropriation of the products of photosynthesis', *Bioscience* **36**: 368–73.

Walker, B.H. (1988), 'Autecology, synecology, climate and livestock as agents of rangelands dynamics', *Australian Range Journal* **10**: 69–75

Walker, B.H. and Noy-Meir, I. (1982), 'Aspects of the stability and resilience of savanna ecosystems', in B.J. Huntley and B.H. Walker (eds), *Ecology of Tropical Savannas*, Springer, Berlin: 577–90.

Westman, W.E. (1990), 'Managing for biodiversity: unresolved science and policy questions', *BioScience* **40**: 26–33.

Westoby, M., Walker, B. and Noy-Meir, I. (1989), 'Opportunistic management for rangelands not at equilibrium', *Journal of Range Management* **42** (4): 266–74.

Index